Published to mark the 50th Anniversary
of the reopening of the Sadler's Wells Theatre
– which has welcomed many distinguished dance
companies from all over the world.

It is pleasing to find that the publication of 'The History of Dance' should coincide with the 50th birthday of the rebuilding of the famous Sadler's Wells Theatre on the heights of Islington. It was from here, after the Second World War, that the Sadler's Wells Ballet made its adventurous landslide – down to the Covent Garden Opera House, but leaving behind another branch of the company known today as The Sadler's Wells Royal Ballet.

Kaleidoscopic seems the word on first perusal of this fascinating book; picture after picture seems to recall those magic lantern slides that, in our childhood, were watched with so much excitement. The store of knowledge within this book is easily digested; each era has writings and illustrations that make everything – both for the student and the balletomane – a journey that never bores the traveller.

There are, for some of us, certain chapters of particular significance, dealing as they do with the very foundation of the life of today's ballet. So close are these chapters to each other that they seem to form a bridge between the past and the future. The chapters concerned are: European Folk Dance, Social Dance, Ballet de Cour, History of Ballet (in the seventeenth and eighteenth centuries). They are of great importance to the evolution of the nineteenth and twentieth centuries; to read them is to understand all that has gone before; efforts that submitted themselves to a selfless form of grinding, and, as the mills of God, they did 'grind exceeding small' – with the consequence that we have accepted it all as our birthright, remaining blissfully ignorant of the original birthpangs. As we study one elegant print after the other, with the accompanying captions that are apt and lively, there is eventually an encounter on page 138 with a picture of the famous Vestris standing on one leg – highlighted by the inclusion of the following lines:

'Every Goose Can'
A stranger at Sparta
Standing long on one Leg,
Said to a Lacedaemonian,
'I do believe you do as much';
'True (said he) but every Goose can.'

And so the goosey-gander world of the ballet can, as Vestris, continue to make one leg challenge the other – with an occasional outburst of a dazzling partnership; and technology will continue to capture and harness together bright pages of fleeting time, turning it all into a wonderful pirouette.

Dame Ninette de Valois
Founder of the Royal Ballet

THE HISTORY OF
DANCE

MARY CLARKE & CLEMENT CRISP

ORBIS PUBLISHING · LONDON

WE DEDICATE this book to the memory of our critic ancestors, the old men on the Island of Gaua in the New Hebrides who, according to Curt Sachs, used to stand by with bows and arrows and shoot at every dancer who made a mistake.

The subject of dance is so vast that in the space of one book it is impossible to treat every aspect. We have endeavoured to provide an outline guide for the general reader from which to move to more detailed study and we hope that our bibliography may indicate some of the important sources which we have used and to which the reader is referred. There are inevitable gaps but it is our hope that within the limitations of a single volume we may have conveyed something of the immense variety and beauty of dance.

We owe many debts of gratitude, our most immediate and important being to our editor, Marie-Jaqueline Lancaster, who made order out of chaos. We are very grateful also to Caroline Schuck who did much preparatory work on the manuscript. Clarissa Johnson, the designer, faced with hundreds of illustrations, has presented them most attractively; Sarah Coombe was a tireless picture editor, and we also had much help in picture research from Susan Bolsom. In checking certain areas in which they are specialists we have turned gratefully to Phyllis Haylor and Robert Harrold: any errors which remain in the sections they checked, are, however, entirely our responsibility.

The book would have been impossible without the resources of the library of the Royal Academy of Dancing.

M.C. C.C. June 1980

Previous page: Dancers of the Ballet Rambert led by Lucy Burge in Smiling Immortal, which was choreographed by Norman Morrice, and was first performed in 1977 at the Round House, London.
This page: Isadora Duncan dancing, from a series (1906) by Gordon Craig, one of her great loves and the father of her child, Deirdre. (Victoria and Albert Museum, London)

© 1981 Orbis Publishing Limited

First published in Great Britain by Orbis Publishing Limited, London 1981

Printed in Italy by New Interlitho, Milan
ISBN 0 85613 270 5

CONTENTS

INTRODUCTION

All nature in one ball, we find;
The water *dances* to the wind;
The sea itself, at night and noon,
Rises and *capers* to the moon;
The moon around the earth does *tread*
A Cheshire round in buxom red;
The earth and planets round the sun
Dance; nor will their *dance* be done
Till Nature in one mass is blended;
Then may we say, *the ball is ended.*

THUS ENDS a poem which serves as epilogue to an early nineteenth-century guide to the social dances of the period. Written 'by the late Judge Burnet', it enshrines one of the great truths about dance and about man's relationship to the oldest of the arts. Truly, 'all nature *is* one ball', in the sense that ordered movement lies at the heart of our universe, as it lies at the heart of the atom. It is this permanent and all-pervasive state of motion, from the pulse of our blood to the circling of the planets, which places man as a dancing figure in a dancing universe.

Dance is one of the most fundamental of human activities. It is an idea both reasonable and acceptable that, when primitive man had satisfied his basic needs for food and shelter, he should express his emotions through movement, through rudimentary dance, through the most natural and immediate channel of expression – his body. Dance, even in this lowly form, became the earliest of the arts, the germ from which other arts evolved. To guide his movement man must have marked out rhythms, and with the first chants and music he then embroidered that rhythmic base. With costume and mask, he then decorated the dance, and the first seeds of the arts had been sown. Were it not for the fact that a few animals may be said to 'dance', in that they perform repeated rhythmic actions for display or to mark out territory, or, as in the case of bees, to indicate

sources of food, man might well be identified as 'an animal who dances'. For in the creations of shapes and patterns of movement, both spatial and temporal, man can be seen to define himself, as well as his dancing.

In dancing, the ordering of movement, gesture, rhythm are the means whereby feeling is exteriorized, messages conveyed, today as in the very earliest times. In an imitative or emulative manner, dance seeks to link or identify the dancer with another being, real or supernatural; in corporate movement with a group or with one other person, dance stresses a belonging; in every case the dance is fundamental to the human psyche, a means of saying something that cannot be expressed in any other way.

As will be seen later in this book, the function of dance in primitive communities was, and remains, all embracing. It is a strong, binding influence in tribal life, a means of defining the

The Hindu god Krishna dances the rasa mandala, *a popular round dance in India, with his favourite cowgirl, Radha. He multiplies himself so as to be able to dance with all the other cowgirls as well. This detail from an eighteenth-century painting on cloth from Rajasthan is of the style used as a kerchief during the dance itself. Whatever its form, the Indian dance is a means of understanding the world and man's awareness of the divine.*

social identity of a group through the acceptance of rituals which mark the progress of the individual from cradle to grave. Birth, puberty, marriage, death, the cycle of crops as well as the cycle of life have their appropriate dances. And the spiritual as well as the physical image of the group is no less well-marked by danced appeals to gods, and propitiations of the spirits of the dead. In health and sickness, joy and fear, the dance is central to tribal life. Religious experience is strengthened by its function as a communal dance experience. Dance rites celebrate the nature of the tribal divinity; they invoke the divine presence; they partake of sympathetic magic in seeking protection for crops, requesting sun or rain; and they define the area of belief. These rites attend the initiation of the young into the full life of the group, and they can also be either maleficent or curative.

A major difference exists between dance in the East and in the West. It has to do with the original impulse behind so much dancing throughout the world, its inspirational spring in the religious life and faith of its practitioners. In what may acceptably be defined as 'high' cultures, in Classic Greece, in Ancient Egypt, the act of worship was initially accompanied by dance. From this there evolved danced and mimetic representations

which transferred the corporate ritual into a more remote form, in which the priest or the adept became the participant as 'representative' of the people, a professional performing for the assembled believers. Thus, instead of being a form of group magic, dance came to be concerned with creating effects upon the people, though those effects might still be said to be magical. In the East, the religious consciousness of the people was not diminished by this change: the spirit of the gods was perceptibly present in the newly emergent dance form. The dance of the Orient, of India, thus remained – and in many cases remains – in direct contact with the spiritual life of the people: it is still 'inspired' dancing.

In the West, the dance has lost this contact. In neither folk nor theatrical dance can such a profound unity with the spiritual existence of a people be seen. Folk dance survives as nostalgia, or in some Eastern European countries as a conscious attempt to retain a folkloric quaintness which is entirely out of keeping with present reality. Theatrical dance, both ballet and free or modern, reflects an urbanized and conscious tradition of performance for an audience. The dance in the West finds its richest sources not in man's relationship to God or to the natural world, but in man's concern with his own psyche. Dance in the theatre today, apart from its ephemerally amusing aspects, has a dual identity: it can be seen as the exploration of the inner landscape of man's feelings, or as a non-representational art concerned with its own spatial and temporal existence as movement, as in the masterpieces of George Balanchine.

If dance can be considered to have functions – ritual, social or artistic: dance in its earliest and most natural state as expression of feeling; dance as social communication and identification; dance as an art form, governed by aesthetic rules and considerations – it yet retains in all three forms a prime concern as a language of action, intention and aspiration. It is a language through which people define themselves, indicating national and racial characteristics as well as revealing more fundamental aspects of their nature.

A basic response to emotional stimulus – jumping for joy – is heightened, sharpened into dance. In primitive communities the dance may transcend everyday action merely by force of repetition (as work dances reproduce the stamp and shuffle of daily labour). It becomes a release of feeling either through participation or, as with dance audiences, through observation. In today's urban society the dance offers a means of releasing tension: witness the testimony of the film *Saturday Night Fever* (1977). It is this need to rid the body of its pent-up physical and muscular poisons which can be seen in sport (and also in football hooliganism) and in the enthusiasm for disco dancing which burgeoned at the end of the 1970s. The virtuosity displayed in clubs frequented by the young in many Western cities far surpasses that seen in most public dance halls. An increasing appreciation of dancing, encouraged by exposure to television and films, and by the greater availability of dance in the theatre, has encouraged

A group of local women perform a timeless round dance in regional costume on the quay of a Yugoslav seaport.

young people to emulate the skills of professional dancers.

Even in the field of education dance can serve to exorcize destructive tensions which might otherwise be turned against the schools themselves. A student from London's Royal Academy of Dancing opted, as part of her training as a teacher, to experiment with encouraging dancing among 'difficult' teenage girls in a large school in a tough area of London. The most illuminating comment upon the success of the student's work came from the Headmistress of the school, who declared after six weeks of dance classes (which the student astutely geared to reggae and hard rock music) that the girls were vastly improved in matters of discipline and physical appearance, and that the internal discipline of the school was also appreciably better after the experiment.

Among the young in every community, dance remains a means of sexual display. The age-old cry of licentiousness, of the dangers of lewdness in bodily contact, have been a recurrent theme in the comminations of the divines in most branches

The image of the round dance persists even today in the routines of the famous precision dance team – the Rockettes – at Radio City Music Hall in New York.

of the Christian – and other – faiths. In May 1979 a newspaper reported from Teheran that 'a revolutionary ballet created by the leader of the National Iranian Ballet company to celebrate the fall of the Shah has been banned by the Ministry of Arts and Culture. The newspaper *Bamdad* said that the Ministry had insisted that men and women dance separately'.[1] Yet the overt sexuality of some forms of country dancing, or of jitter-bugging in the 1940s, must be contrasted with the extreme stylization of another popular form: ballroom dancing, and especially exhibition dancing. Here, the role-playing implicit in the dance turns the dancers into stereotypes, and the complexity of their dress shows them as fantasy figures, both remote and improbable. These dancers therefore become as stylistically refined and unlikely as the sylphides, swan princesses and bemused princely heroes of nineteenth-century ballet.

Yet dance in the ballroom or the disco con-stitutes a basic activity for its practitioners (who may rehearse ten hours a week for their appear-ances). The undisciplined, natural dances of the people, such as the hokey-kokey and the 'knees-up', give an immediate release of feeling no different in essence from any social dance of the past ages. The emergence of dance as 'art' into the theatre is the history of man's alienation from dance, which started with the change in traditions of worship in ancient times. Aesthetic dance implies a system of movement dependent upon rules and disciplines, which radically alters the relationship between mankind and the dance. When dancers became professionals, dance entered upon an entirely new career – as display – only remotely referring to the life of the people, because it no longer involved them directly, although it served to communicate with them. The history of this relationship is the history of Western ballet, as it is of the Japanese theatre. In the West, it has meant the development of exceptional physical skills, the offering of an ideal of beauty which results from the refining of the human body through arduous training to create an expressive instrument. To hold the public's attention, ballet has had to turn to greater and more complex spectacles, increasing virtuo-sity in performance and presentation. The dancer and the dance thus became further and further removed from any possibility of close identifica-tion with the followers of the dance. An instru-ment has been forged to explore human relation-ships (or political ideals, or aesthetic theories) as spectacle rather than as experience. Ballet has become a spectator art, where dance was once a communal one; to counteract this curious situa-tion, the entire apparatus of the theatre is designed to help the audience to 'feel' with the performer, and thus to recapture, vicariously, what was once its own feeling. That the audience does so, that the ballet and all forms of dance are now popular as never before, is some indication of the theatre's success, and of man's continuing need for dance.

Roland Petit turned to Jean Anouilh, the French playwright, for the scenario of his ballet Le Loup, a tragic tale of a girl's love for a 'wolf man'. Here the couple are encircled and menaced by leaping men who finally hunt them to death.
The ballet was first produced in Paris in 1953 and remains one of Petit's most enduring successes, not least for its superlative design by Jean Carzou.

CHAPTER ONE

PRIMITIVE & ANCIENT DANCE

Ghost dance. Women of the Arapaho tribe sing and dance in this cult dance which evolved as a reaction against persecution by the whites. The bird symbol painted on the back of the seated man (at left) represents the eagle, which is also sacred to the ghost dance of the Sioux Indians. From a photograph taken by James Mooney in the early 1890s. (Smithsonian Institution, Washington DC)

Brazilian flute dance (right). These tribesmen of the Kamiura tribe on the Xingu River perform their ceremonial flute dance. The head-dresses are symbolic of the sun, from which these men believe they derive their fertility. In the sound of the wooden flutes the dancers 'hear' the voices of tribal deities.

DANCE EVOLVED as an expression of emotion, of joy or of grief, of terror or of wonder, in the face of the incomprehensible and the sublime. Cave paintings suggest rituals attendant upon hunting; the most primitive tribes dance to express their feelings. The importance of dance is perhaps nowhere more precisely revealed than in the greeting between Bantus, when a man from one tribe, meeting a Bantu from a different group, asks 'What do you dance?' Even in some countries in the West you can still identify people's class, their social milieu, by knowing what they dance.

The earliest records of the civilization which grew up round the Mediterranean show dance at its heart – as celebration or act of worship. The god could be perceived through dance, his presence invoked and evoked, his exploits recounted by movement that passed beyond daily gesture into the more stylized expression of dance. Priests and worshippers believed that they came nearer to the divine in understanding and feeling through dance. American Indians, Bantu tribesmen, the worshippers of Shiva, the heavenly dancer, and the Fathers of the early Christian Church, are all united in this common belief. But once the original religious impulse behind the dance has faded, as primitive inspiration gives place to formalized rite, the dance loses its first purpose and acquires a secondary though sometimes no less significant function as display. This is, in essence, how theatre developed from the Dionysiac festivities of Ancient Greece. The dancer ceased to be priest or celebrant and became performer: ritual evolved into art, and while basic attitudes were retained, they were masked with later accretions which hid the prime cause. The 'ring' dance – an invocatory round, primarily an act of worship – became a game or an unthinking ritual in which form survived when inspiration and meaning had died. The systematizing of gesture in Indian *mudras* suggests how the symbols

of faith have passed into a stylized language. The richness of much primitive tribal dancing depends upon the use to which the dance is put – its occasions; even the way it is clothed – rather than in any actual extent or intricacy of physical language.

The chief of a tribe of Brazilian Indians once said to an ethnologist 'We dance. But our dance is serious.' This gives a vital clue to the attitude that governs and has governed the dance of many primitive communities – dance not as entertainment or pleasure but as a means of expressing feelings, fears and aspirations. In Brazil, the tribal ceremonies are honoured and great care is taken in decorating the participants.

Stilt dancers of the Tchokwe tribe in Zaire. The African dance requires no special location; these Tchokwe dancers are performing in a clearing and wear costumes whose ritual significance is intimately allied to the ceremonial of the dance.

African tribal and regional dances have been, and still are, performed at almost every moment in the life of the race. The existence of the tribe from birth to death, its mundane routines and its spiritual aspirations and fears are all reflected in dance, which celebrates birth, puberty, initiation, fertility, courtship, marriage, death and burial. Dance rhythms are used to alleviate the tedium of work, and some movements reflect daily routines.

Painted, decorated, ritually mutilated or tribally marked, the bodies of African and Indian men and women are prepared for the dance. Confronted with Western civilization, the dances

survive – sometimes preserved as a means of retaining tribal identity; sometimes studied and protected in a conscious effort at securing a national heritage. For pre-historic man and man today in primitive and untouched communities, dance had and has profound significance. It is neither entertainment nor pastime, but absolutely central to his existence. The social structure of the primitive community can be said to gain much of its cohesion from the group activity of dancing. An anthropological survey would indicate the extraordinary range of dance forms and occasions for dancing among communities con-

Two Dogon dancers from Mali, West Africa, demonstrating the typical vigour and bravura of an African dance. Note the extreme complexity and artistic merit of the masks, which indicate to the tribespeople the function and nature of the dance.

sidered both 'civilized' and 'primitive'. At every point in man's life there is evidence somewhere of a dance which illustrates or celebrates the entire cycle of human existence and human emotion.

At its most important, the dance became the means of trying to understand the gods, of placating them, of appealing to them, or of entering into some communication with them. In certain communities the very understanding of the world and the cosmos was expressed through dance, as evidenced by the astronomical dances of ancient Egypt. The celebration of a cult and the recounting of its mysteries were traditionally set in

dance form. This ineradicable tradition of movement reflects man's basic physical response to his world: if bees dance to indicate to the rest of the hive the presence of pollen, how much more revealing are the movements of primitive man at the high points of his life.

It is necessary to stress the functional nature of all primitive dance. It was in no sense 'aesthetic'. It served a purpose – though as in certain religious rituals this purpose might become obscured and the dance itself become formalized – and that purpose was maintained so long as the community itself kept its identity. The perpetuation

Dancers of the Watussi tribe from Rwanda, East Africa. Tribal dancing can be drilled to give a remarkable unity of step, and the men of this exceptionally tall tribe use anklet bells to mark the rhythm of the dance.

of ancient dance rituals as unthinking survivals into the 'civilized' Europe of the Middle Ages may be a case in point. The ring dance, so popular in medieval times and surviving today in folk dance, is an echo faint but true of those dances which celebrated the early mysteries of faith round a tree or an altar at the dawn of Western civilization.

The gradual death of the worship of old gods and the spread of Christianity meant that many old dance rituals in Europe were to lose their prime significance. They ceased to be rite and continued instead as exhibitions of skill, and patterns of dance. They become in a sense 'art'. But their performance persists since the folkloric tradition itself persists, and in a few ancient dances today you can still perceive the ghostly imprint of pre-Christian worship.

An obvious example is the English *morris* dance. The title is a corruption of the word 'Moorish' in medieval times but the dance itself looks back further than that. It is a seasonal activity associated with Whitsun in which the leaping and bounding of the 'morris man' was a means of purifying the community and at the same time, by a form of sympathetic magic, of encouraging the crops to grow. Of the magical property of the dance itself which must once have been linked with the fortunes of a community, nothing now remains except the idea that *morris* dancing is 'lucky'. Nevertheless, even towards the end of the twentieth century there still exist in certain parts of the world communities wherein

Egungen masquerade dancers in Nigeria. Total masking under straw is not uncommon in West African dances. The frightening, and sometimes comic, effects obtained by these whirling, 'thatched' figures have occasionally been seen in the offerings of dance troupes which have visited the West.

dance retains a central place in the life of the people. In simple African villages, among the aborigines of Australasia, in the islands of South East Asia, and even among the surviving American Indians, dance is something more than a diversion or an entertainment.

AFRICAN DANCE

Music and dance are an essential part of the life of Black Africa, reflecting more strongly than in an urbanized Western civilization a direct response of the people to the life they lead, the emotions they feel, the seasonal passage of the year, and the inevitable progress of life itself. 'Dancing in the streets' may be seen as an expression of a nation's or a city's relief at some victory, as in London in 1945 when crowds danced in Trafalgar Square in celebration first of 'V.E. Day' and then of victory in the Far East. And in April 1979 people in the West were able to watch on television the reaction of the inhabitants of Jinja, Uganda who had just been freed by Tanzanian troops from the Amin regime. The cameras recorded the people of the town dancing in procession through the streets, singing 'we are free, we are free' and waving bougainvillaea blossoms. Spontaneous emotion, spontaneous dancing; this seems the key to many of the ancient traditions of African dance throughout that vast continent, and to its expression today.

In the predominantly village communities of Africa, dance and music – which are interdependent – elaborate costume and masking, are the outward signs of the people's spirit. It is important to note that in no part of Black Africa is there a community, a culture, a tribe, in which dancing is not an integral part of life; that dance is not to be divided into the various categories adopted by Western civilization, but is a single fact which embraces every facet of tribal life, uniting social and religious ideas, sacred and profane aspects; that all the elements of music, mask and dance, form a united whole and depend one upon the other, and cannot be properly understood except on these terms. It is also important to realize that the dances, ancient or modern, contain references or symbols that are alive and relevant to the life of the dancers; they are not 'museum' activities, or rites degenerated into unthinking repetition which have become 'performance' rather than 'truth'.

Dances take place at certain fixed dates in the year. The period of time between them can be as much as a decade; others depend upon imponderables – births and deaths. The dance ceremonial has a clear purpose in the life of a tribe but it is not the only ingredient; other components are costumes, music (choral or instrumental) and narrative. The locale for the dance is not usually a special place as in the West or a sacred area or hallowed spot used for rite and worship as in antique times. Africans for the most part dance in their villages, though occasionally the forest or a specially sacred location is used. Festivals also mean feasting; food and drink are specially gathered in, stored and accumulated. The rite is a moment perhaps for excess, but also for the exhausting of supplies as well as of bodies – here it bears traces of 'sacrifice'. You enter also upon a curious area of 'possession', in which the dancer lays himself open to being taken over by a spirit. He may not know which spirit, and the preparatory hysteric dancing and movement is sometimes intended to exhaust him so that he becomes the empty vessel into which the possessing spirit can be poured, or more correctly, pour itself. But the manifestation of spiritual possession also takes the form of a set ritual of movement, and in order to be prepared, the dancer must have at his command an understanding of several different vocabularies of movement which are the different languages of the different spirits. The performer may not know which spirit will take over; he has thus to be armed beforehand with his different languages, one of which the spirit will use. There is here an element of theatricalization or preparation which is highly complex, and the ultimate presence of the spirit is, in a sense, expressed in theatrical terms. There is further, in mask–culture dances, the idea of the dancer assuming the role of a character associated with the mask he wears: he becomes its body.

The dance gives unity to the community, a unity coming from shared experience that passes beyond work into matters of faith and is a kind of spiritual union. It thus defines the tribe, guides and shapes its world physically and spiritually. In initiation rites, the subject is identified as a young man or young woman within the tribe's terms, and the dance may be seen to express the knowledge of the world that the tribe accepts.

The dance-and-music ceremonies explain the nature of the life of the tribe and exist as a direct correspondence between the participants and their universe.

> 'Africans dance. They dance for joy, and they dance for grief; they dance for love and they dance for hate; they dance to bring prosperity and they dance to avert calamity; they dance for religion and they dance to pass the time. Far more exotic than their skin and their features is this characteristic of dancing; the West African Negro is not so much a blackish man or the cannibal man or the primitive man as he is the man who expresses every emotion with rhythmical bodily movement.'[1]

Colonial administrators and white missionaries with their inhibiting influences were, in their time, responsible for the stamping out of this essential feature of African life in larger communities.

The richness and range of African dance is very hard for the European to comprehend, used as he is to the idea of folk dance in his own continent as an interesting survival, occasionally carefully preserved, more often arbitrarily revived by enthusiasts interested in quaint social manners. The Westerner has to appreciate that in the vastness of Africa, with its extreme variety of cultures, one of the unifying elements is the people's dependence upon dance as a fact of living. In the sub-Saharan communities the tremendous force of African dance can also be sensed in all its vivacity and dignity and physical bravura, as well as in its religious and ritualistic fervour. Masked, on stilts, singly or in long processional lines, the dancers are totally absorbed in what they do. Their costuming can be extravagantly beautiful, with figures clothed in leaves; or simple, the dancers garbed in anklets and skirts; or mysterious, haunting, and truly awe-inspiring with huge masks and triumphs of painting and ritual tatooing on their bodies. It can be seen here, as in the offerings of dance troupes come to the West from Africa, that the dance is a way of life, a way through life, and a means of comprehending and organizing the world as the people perceive it.[2]

Basic to the dance, part of it, are the drum rhythms which do far more than delineate time: they mark the character of the dance itself. To African ears the drums inspire a response in movement more complex and diverse than in the most subtle Western choreography. Linked to this is the costume, which may in some cases be merely decorative (though specially conceived for dancing, and quite as remote from daily wear as the outfits worn in Western ballroom competition dancing) but which, in the case of mask dancers and fetish dancing, is sacred, ritualistic and even, in some instances, a dominant feature in the dance. Certain parts of the costume, anklets of shells or bells that rattle and help mark the rhythm of stamping steps, are common in much of Africa. Others, notably the masks and the more elaborate dresses that can cover the body and disguise the performer totally, have specific regional, tribal limits. Some masks, particularly in West Africa, are not allowed to be seen by sections of the community; women are shut up in huts, their heads swathed in cloth, so that they should not see one special burial ritual mask.

The mask probably typifies the most sophisticated aspects of the dance. It is pre-eminently sacred; not of itself, but because it is identified with the spirit of a god. It is filled with the presence of the god, and when the dancer puts on the mask he assumes the identity of the fetish (the spirit of some aspect of the divine as it is comprehended by a tribe). The wearer is thus transformed from his everyday self into a vessel of the fetish. The masks vary in size, from small coverings that sit on the forehead and hide part of the face, to enormous metre-high constructions in which a complex theology can be read by the members of the community. These can combine several identities of animal spirits, attributes of the gods, even entire concepts of a way of life. One mask was described thus: '. . . super-imposed on a very roughly human face are the horns of an antelope, the boar, the hippopotamus, the elephant; the mouth is that of a crocodile; on the forehead is a small toucan pecking a large chameleon.'[3]

Associated with the sacred mask dances is further costuming, dependent from the mask and joined to it, which covers the entire body of the masker with raffia and animal skins. On the Ivory Coast an initiation ceremony for men is conducted by a priest entirely swathed in a body-fitting outfit of cloth and raffia, the head hidden in a bag-like mask, who leads novices to an amazing structure of cloth over a wooden frame, supported by two men, representing a sacred ox.

No less extraordinary are the ritual mask dances in Mali following the death of a village notable. These rituals, which can last over a period of a week, re-establish order after the death, guide the spirit of the dead man to a resting-place, thus preventing the evil that might otherwise follow from having an unpacified spirit wandering through the community. Masks, song, dance and feasting are all part of the ceremony. The maskers wear long raffia skirts, but the masks are the most remarkable element. Blade-shaped, they can sometimes reach a height of five metres (sixteen feet), and during the dance the performer bends his torso so that the mask sweeps the ground.

On the Guinea Coast the mask dance acquires yet a further elaboration by being performed on stilts. Balanced on stilts sometimes two metres (six to seven feet) high, the body of the performer is totally covered, head and face are masked, and the trousers cover part of the stilts. The complex dance steps involve leaps and turns of extreme acrobatic skill.

Acrobatics of a different kind are found on the Ivory Coast where the supple bodies of girls who have not reached puberty are entwined round strong male dancers, and are thrown and caught and literally juggled in a ritual dance that is associated with a snake cult. Further south in equatorial Africa there are the same traditions, the same richness and extravagance of imagination in response to life.

In the Gabon there are white-faced stilt dancers; initiation cults for men in which they dance and leap round a fire in a hut especially reserved for the men of the tribe. In Zaire, warriors in huge feathered head-dresses jump in a war dance that reflects their service to their chief and their role as guardians of tribal safety. In Rwanda, a warrior dance recalls the safe return of a one-time king's élite troops from battle. Also in Zaire, huge pin-headed puppets, draped in sacking, are manipulated to remind a tribe of former rivalries as a dance takes place. Among tribes of the Central African Republic the ritual circumcision of young people is attended by dances, and superbly grotesque maskers lead the boys and girls in dances that mark the success of the operation and their readmittance into the tribe. Here, as in other regions of Africa, the women's dances sometimes take the form of a serpentine line of shimmying, shuffling figures notable for its precision and rhythmic power, as well as for the characteristic accompaniment of shrilling cries made by the women.

PRIMITIVE ABORIGINAL DANCE

Any discussion of primitive dance must take into account the fact of a living tradition among the aboriginal Australians, of a primitive way of life in which the dance is of central importance. It is the living proof of the closeness of dance to the very heart of a primitive society. In Central and Northern Australia the aborigines live in proximity to white people but still manage to retain their primitive and tribal identity. The aboriginal dance is most generally associated with the corroboree, a nocturnal dance celebration which takes place round a huge fire. The dance can be pure spectacle or it may illuminate a story related by the 'song man', a narrator who tells the tale, hums and beats time. The variety of aboriginal dance steps is considerable, with stamping and turning steps for the men, whose bodies are painted and whose dancing partakes of something 'inspirational' as a result of the close community of the tribal group round the fire. The aborigines love dancing. In dance, they reveal their happiness; women may form a circle and dance, clapping their hands, their shuffling steps and white daubed bodies affording a strong contrast to the more boisterous movement of the men. The various tribes among the aborigines have their own dances, but there is an interesting commerce among the peoples, who will 'sell' or exchange dances which then become the property of the purchaser and are no longer performed by the original owner. All over Northern and Central Australia, the aboriginal dance is influenced by the terrain upon which it is performed, either hard-packed earth or the softer sand of the dancing ground which has been cleared in the bush. Though not sophisticated, the dance reveals the bodies as being supple and well co-ordinated. For obvious physical reasons the mature women avoid the high, jumping steps performed by the men; the men stamp, their feet digging hard into the earth whereas the women glide. The man's style reflects the aborigine's feeling for the earth itself. With his feet exploring the earth's surface, with dust and sand eddying and swirling round him, he savours his own kinship with the ground.

But the aboriginal dance is neither merely social nor exhibitionistic. Through dance, the wandering tribes can express their myths about the creation of the world they know, about the spirits and ideas associated with every aspect of the natural and the unseen world. There are dances which only women may perform and watch and whose dancing area is also sacred to women. They have to do with the cycle of a woman's life from love-making to child-bearing. There are animal dances for women which are like potions to make a lover return, aspects of a society in which the idea of magic is very strong

Detail from an aborigine silhouette painting made with the tip of a feather. The vividness with which the artist has captured the movement of the dancing men compares very interestingly with the photograph below. (Haddon Collection, Cambridge University Museum of Archaeology and Ethnology)

Group of Australian aborigines performing at a corroboree (below). The fighting men of the tribe are armed with spears and arrows in a dance which in this case celebrates the initiation into the tribe of a young man after puberty.

and in which the magic itself is – to more civilized eyes – uncannily effective.

In these *djarada* dances the women glide, sway and turn, but they perform them only when the men are away. More secret still are certain initiation dances which take place in locations dedicated to the totemic spirit of a cult heroine, an ancestress who is also identified with a special tree, and the dancers paint the design of the fruit of this tree upon their bodies before dancing.

The male dance covers every aspect of the man's identity in the tribe. There are dances about the daily routine of fishing and hunting, dances about fighting, and animal dances in which the aborigine's observation of and identification with animals is marvellously manifest. Very mysterious is the relationship of dreams to the aboriginal culture, dreams in which guidance, warning and learning are all received from another world. Some dances are said to be 'found' in dreams; in others, the action of devils and the spirits of the dead are recreated. There are also some humorous dances in which the aborigine's lively comic sense is given full rein. Most sacred and most secret are the initiation ceremonies in which dance plays a crucial part. It is through these that youths become full members of their tribe, achieving the tribal identity which will be theirs for the rest of their lives. The kangaroo cult, although an initiation ceremony, is in effect a dance-drama in which a tribe's legends and beliefs are presented to the novice so that he may learn them and understand the tribe's history.[4]

MAORI DANCE

It is geography rather than any cultural link that now suggests a note about the Maori dance of New Zealand.

Maori dancing bears traces of the great colonizing adventure which brought the ancestral peoples of the Maori southwards from India via Samoa and Tahiti to New Zealand. In certain movements of the arms and hips you can still see evidence of a religious dance style from India but it has, inevitably, been much altered during the passage of centuries. For the Maoris, dances were a method of preserving the legends and themes of their historic past through mimetic performance: a canoe dance, performed by squatting women, tells of the migration across the Pacific; a war dance for the men is, in its ferocity of expression, a powerful reminder of the Maoris' great traditions in battle. Most spectacular is the *haka*, a dance used to convey anger or grief, but which now serves as a welcome for important guests – as when Queen Elizabeth visited New Zealand in 1977 and was greeted by a prodigious *haka* display. The best known and most beguiling dance of the Maoris is the women's *poi*. Each girl holds a pair of small reed-balls attached to strings, and these are twirled and swung, tapping against arms and legs, as the dancers move through the intricacies of this graceful dance.

In many of these Maori rituals there are references to the ancient sun worship which was the original faith of the people.

AMERICAN INDIAN DANCE

It is a commonplace that in many of the unspoiled cultures, worship of the sun can attain a primacy in the religious belief of the people and thus also dominates its expression in dance. Among the Plains Indians of North America, for example, the clockwise progression in a circle by the tribal dancers charts the journey of the sun through the sky. This essential response to one of the great mysteries of their religion is a first indication of the vital importance of dance in American Indian culture throughout the continent.

From their very first landings the explorers of the New World provided notes and anecdotes about the dancing of the American Indians. A water-colour painting by John White dating from *c.* 1585 shows an Indian dance in North Carolina. Over the next three centuries the iconography and travellers' accounts of Indian dance cover the whole of the North American continent from Quebec to Mexico.

The essential importance of the dance in the American Indian culture across the continent would be hard to overestimate. The tragedy is that contact and conflict with white civilization has corrupted and destroyed most of the Indian way of life, and has brought upon dancing the kind of ban which in earlier days was imposed

Corroboree dancers (far left). The corroboree takes place at night and the lighting from the fire throws into vivid relief the ritual painting of the body which is so essentially part of the preparation for this dance rite.
The dance of the aborigines is characterized by the stamping with which the dancer maintains his spiritual and physical contact with the earth.

American Indian shamans (far right) on Vancouver Island in a medicine mask dance, invoking the spirits which will cure disease. (Royal Ontario Museum)

American Indian Mandan dancers (below) with symbolic body painting. The motifs represent night and day, and the dance is a recapitulation of the tribe's myth which interpreted the birth of the world as that moment when light replaced darkness. From O-Kee-pa (1867) by the American artist and author, George Catlin, who specialized in American Indian tribal scenes.

upon the dance in Europe by the Church. As recently as 1904 the United States Government Regulations of the Indian Office forbade dancing and the repeal of this was not effected until 1934.[5]

The ban related inevitably to the idea of the Indian war dance – the most celebrated and probably the most misunderstood of the Indian dances. But the fact that the ban was considered necessary also gives an insight into the significance of dance in the Indian culture. In 1898, for example, a ghost dance cult emerged and found much favour among the Sioux. It was a reaction against the persecution of the Indians by the whites, and it was initiated by a Nevada Piaute who declared that an Indian Messiah would arise to bring back the Indian dead and the long-since-vanished buffalo. The white man would be driven out and the Indians would once more rule the land. The cult and its dance spread quickly, and the United States government, fearing renewed hostilities, was at pains to disarm the followers of the ghost dance and suppress it. In December 1890 a misunderstanding between the Sioux and the United States army at Wounded Knee Creek, South Dakota, resulted in the massacre of more than two hundred men, women and children.

Yet Ernest Thompson Seton, the artist-naturalist, could record an Indian tribesman of the South West declaring when the news came that the government wished to put a stop to Indian ceremonies:

'The Government may send its troops to shoot us down, but we will not cease our dancing.'

By virtue of the great expanse of land originally covered by the culture of the American Indians, there is an extreme variety of dances. There are certain unifying factors: that dance and song are intimately and inextricably linked in the performance of Indian dance; that the drum is very like the heartbeat of the ceremonial; and that, as in every other unspoiled community, the entire cycle of life and the relationship with the gods is exemplified in the dance. In Southern California, especially, there are records of a tradition in which the medicine-men, the shamans, were at the centre of creation and of animal myths that contained the essential beliefs of a very mystical people. Best known of the Indian mystical dances is the sun dance, a lengthy ritual held in summer which involved physical suffering as an offering to the gods. The participants would sometimes attach themselves with thongs through the loose flesh on their breasts to a central pole; others would partially flay themselves, all in the service of the deity whom they sought to placate. Among the Indians there tended also to be cult societies associated with animals and with dreams. In these the warriors could identify themselves with an animal or with a particular activity. Bear dancers in the North West danced and juggled with live coals; the initiates of the Kwakiutl cannibal society were starved in forest seclusion

until, ravenous and hysterical, they re-entered the tribal area for a frantic dance. They were then lured into the 'house' of the society by a naked woman dancing before them holding in her arms a simulated corpse. The ritual ended with a feast of dog meat as a substitute for human flesh.

In dances associated with animals there seems to be a double function. Some, like the buffalo dance, and the bull society dance among the Mandan Indians of North Dakota, were intended to lure the buffalo herds nearer to the village. Others, like the eagle dance, were a tribute to the bird as an object of special veneration. Among the Indians of the Pueblo, in an arid region, the eagle is the thunderbird, and the songs and ceremonies associated with the bird are still prayers for rain. Usually performed by two men, one representing the male the other the female bird, their dance movements copy the steps, hops and soaring of the eagle. Their naked bodies and legs are realistically painted; their headgear can terminate in a beak; and they wear feathered wings attached to their arms.

In these dances you can understand how the Indian extends his dance vocabulary by watching animals and transforming their actions into movement. With the buffalo dance, particularly, there is a form of sympathetic magic and also the idea of a tribute to the animal, a creature central to their economy.

Among the Yaqui Indians of the South West the celebrated deer dances are no less powerful; by dancing to honour an animal which is associated with rain, the performers are meant to acquire the deer's spirit and ensure good hunting.

Much of the Indian dance is overlaid with magical connotations. Among the Thompson Indians of British Columbia, the women performed dances carrying symbolic weapons during a time when their menfolk were at war, believing that they could thus ensure a successful outcome to the expedition. Among the Yuki tribe in California,[6] the women danced for days without sleep when their husbands were away at war, believing that their ring dance maintained their husbands' continuing strength in battle. In certain Indian tribes there were dream cults in which the members were united by the kinds of dreams and visions which they experienced or induced, and these they expressed in danced rituals. In the North West, along the Pacific coast, there were spirit dances which stressed the power of the shaman, the medicine-man, to cast spells, to curse and also to cure.

In the South West among the Hopi Indians there is a snake dance which expresses the tribe's belief that snakes can carry messages to the underworld and, more especially, to the rain-makers who lived beneath the earth, and in this the Hopi danced with rattlesnakes and various other poisonous snakes.

In some cases the beliefs of the Indians have been clothed in Christian garb. Among the Pueblo Indians the dance of the *matachins* is a ceremonial which seems to combine relics of European religious beliefs with earlier Aztec memories. The Indians first go to Mass, then dance *matachins*, involving the ritual slaughter in the open of a bull by a man with a knife.

Today the Indian dance must inevitably seem a poor shadow of its former glorious tradition. That it survives at all is due to the advocacy of certain enthusiasts, and the determination among the older Indians to preserve the very core of their cultural life. At a time when the identity of the American Indian is increasingly respected there seems some hope that their dance traditions will be rescued, preserved and honoured.

MEXICAN DANCE

The traditions of Mexican dance are traceable back to the Aztec culture in which there were 'houses of song and dance' attached to the temples and dedicated to the god of music and dance. Dance in honour of the gods was part of Aztec worship and each religious observance and festival had its associate dance and music, as did such social occasions as wedding feasts, where entertainment was part of the festivities. A Spanish monk historian has recorded a favourite dance of the Azetcs performed in honour of the god of war. In this dance the goddess of love was found ensconced in a rosy arbour surrounded by dancers bedecked with flowers while nearby, in artificial trees, little boys impersonated brilliantly coloured birds and butterflies, hopping from branch to branch in imitative movement. Warriors emerging from the temple pretended to kill the birds and the goddess led them to her arbour, paying them due respect as gods.[7]

The Spanish conquest of Mexico and the imposition of Catholicism upon a pagan faith reproduces – albeit much speeded up – the effect that Christianity had during the centuries of its expansion across Europe. The monks who came to Mexico were impressed by the natives' skill in dancing. They encouraged the dance as a mimetic form through which the teachings of the Church might be displayed to the people. The resultant dances (now no more than unthinking survivals of earlier dramatic narrations) also incorporated in disguised form some of the pagan beliefs from the older faith.

As with the American Indians, in the various regions of Mexico there are dances which serve as reminders of hunting rites and religious beliefs, such as the Yaqui deer dance and the *matachins*, these latter being ecclesiastical dances performed at funerals and on special church feast days. Among the surviving religious dances is that of the Concheros, who dance at fiestas, and in their performance the sacred impulse in the dance is evident; their dancing is still to be seen in church on some occasions. The Spanish *seguidillas* and *zapateado* were adopted and extended by the aboriginal inhabitants. The result was such dances as the *jarana* and the *jarabe* and the *huapango*. *Jarana* is the name of a small guitar, after which the dance is called; the *jarabe* is the most popular of Mexican dances and is both a polite social dance and a folk dance; while the *huapangos* are danced on wooden platforms to make the *zapateado* step more reverberant.

The *jarabe* has a long history in Mexico, and among the more intriguing comments upon it is a decree, dating from 1802, when performance of it was forbidden on pain of two years' imprisonment, while even to watch it could invite a couple of months in the cells. By the middle of the century, though, it had returned to popular favour and become widespread in its popularity, so much so that when in 1918 Anna Pavlova danced in Mexico City, she included a *jarabe* in her *Mexican Dances*. Today the *jarabe tapatio* (so called to identify it as coming from the Jalisco state where the people are known as Tapatios) is still a popular, spirited and joyous dance. Among the Mexican Indians there is a simpler version associated with wedding festivities and food.

Three other dances deserve mention: *los moros* (the Moors) is a relic of the Spanish occupation, a dance usually given by four men, whose leader is identified as St James. Performed on religious occasions, in some districts it begins in the atrium of the church, from thence the dancers process from house to house, repeating the same dance and the same steps at each stopping place. *Los viejetos* (the little old men) is danced by young men who disguise themselves with masks and lean on sticks. Their dance takes the form of a line which is always completed by the 'feeblest' dragging himself along. *Los Inditos* (the little Indians) is a maypole dance. The explanation of this European symbol is probably accounted for by its importation by the Spanish conquerors.

Aztec pottery figure of a dancer at a festival. Dances to honour the gods of war, music and dance formed part of Aztec worship. (Staatliche Museen Preussischer Kulturbesitz, Berlin)

The dance, performed in May, is presided over by the 'señor' (Our Lord) of Chalma, and offerings of eggs, necklaces, beads and flowers can be made to the saint after each dance. (There is a suggestion that this dance was encouraged by Catholic missionaries.)

The Conquistadores brought traces of Spanish dance ritual to the New World. In 1544 the first Archbishop of Mexico inveighed against the lack of reverence with which masked men dressed as women danced in front of the Sacrament. Even nuns as late as in the seventeenth century were recorded as dancing in the choir of their church 'contrary to modesty', while in Lima, Peru, dances figured in the processions for the feast of Corpus Christi.

The dance traditions, as indeed every other facet of life in the whole of South America, must be seen to reflect the influence of the Conquistadores. The conflict between the invaders and their faith and the existing order was to have its particular effect upon the dances of the native population. As had happened in Europe at the time of the spread of Christianity, the Church absorbed many aspects of the existing South American culture into its religious observances. The combination of Spanish and Portuguese cultural attitudes – notably those of music and of folk dances imported by the conquering troops – with an indigenous pattern of music and movement, produced an art that has been subject to many later influences as fresh cultural material has been absorbed. There is in Brazil a dance which can last from eight in the morning until nightfall which originated among the slaves imported by the Portuguese. Under cover of the dance the slaves, who were forbidden to fight with weapons, could kill each other. The dance now survives as a ritualistic fight and bears a strong resemblance to danced karate.

There is implicit in this cross-fertilization of cultures a liveliness which informs the dance traditions of the sub-continent. Among the more remote Indian tribes are dances which retain the same primitive force that can be seen in any aboriginal dance forms which have remained untouched by 'civilization'. Where the cultures have mingled, there result such exuberant displays as the Brazilian Carnival, in which an annual outburst of song, dance and the most preposterous costuming are combined with remarkable vitality. The revellers explode into long lines of *samba* dancing and indulge in virtuoso solo displays.

Easter dance, performed by Tarahumara Indians in Mexico. The combination of Christian dogma and ideas with the indigenous traditions of dance is hinted at here with the figure of Judas being carried on the shoulder of the dancer in the centre of the group. It is interesting to compare this raw material with the theatricalized version created by Martha Graham in her Primitive Mysteries.

CHAPTER TWO

RELIGIOUS DANCE

Acrobatic style in an Egyptian dance of the fifth dynasty (2440–2315 BC) is graphically depicted on this limestone relief from a tomb at Sakkara, Egypt.

WHILE DANCE was essential to primitive mysteries and cults, it also featured in more advanced faiths, including Christianity. In the ancient cultures of the Middle East, dance was a prime component of rites of worship and it would seem to have permeated the celebrations of the Jews as a reflection of the cultures which surrounded them. Thus, too, Christianity would absorb dance from the pagan mysteries, reshaping and re-identifying the attitudes therein expressed in church dance.

ANCIENT EGYPT

In the earliest records of the civilizations of the Near and Middle East, in the culture of Sumeria, Assyria and Babylon, you find clear indications of dance as part of religious rite. In the rich civilization of Ancient Egypt the annual cycle of life, dominated by the rise and fall of the waters of the Nile, seems to have its reflection in the worship of Osiris. The birth and death of the land, the soil's resurrection when the annual inundation came, are matched by the cyclic nature of the Osiris legend – his death, dismemberment and resurrection through the reconstitution of his severed body. The cult of the god was celebrated in rituals of dance and drama, partly to encourage worshippers and partly perhaps as a kind of sympathetic action to reflect the hope of continuation. This is an intriguing example of the kind of spectacle involving ritualistic and planned movement which will eventually result in mythological drama. Even in the second millennium, when King Thutmosis had his daughter recognized as his successor 'the nobles go forth rejoicing, dance and make merry, and all his subjects dance and leap.'[1] It is from early activities like this that you can perceive how dance became an essential in the religious observances of great cultures. What may seem initially a primitive form of dance is codified through ritual practice and placed at the service of a cult. Thence eventually emerges a spectacular form which will become 'theatricalized' in one way or another. As the years pass, this theatricalization may represent an abstract form of the initial religious image; eventually the form outlives the message and contact is lost with the first motivation of the dance.

Central to any attempt at understanding and envisaging the dance of Ancient Egypt is the vital importance to the Egyptians of the after-life. Indeed, much of our understanding of the civilization of the Nile lands depends upon the tombs, those staging posts on the journey to the next world. The progress of the corpse to its resting-place was attended by dances which were both an expression of grief and, it is presumed, a mimetic show which invoked gods and heroes to be propitiated for the benefit of the recently departed.

Furthermore, the Egyptian calendar of feast days, with its implicit relationship to various divinities, demanded celebrations of song and dance and ritualistic movement. Details of the nature of these celebrations are tenuous and, in the main, are to be inferred from paintings and reliefs. But, it is evident that there was a style of dance which made much of arm movement – poses, and processional lines in funerary dances suggest this – with leg movements that ranged from walking or stamping to the extreme acrobatic manner of the line of female dancers kicking their legs high in the air as they lean backwards (shown in a bas-relief from Sakkara). One well-known portrait of a female acrobat is in the pose known as 'the bridge', body curved in a semi-circle facing upwards. This pose is still seen in back-flips performed by acrobats today.

The importance of acrobatics in Ancient Egyptian dance (above) is nowhere more clearly seen than in this drawing of a female entertainer caught in the 'bridge' pose of the acrobatic somersaults during a ritual dance. A limestone fragment of the Ramesside period, 1305–1080 BC, from Deir el-Medina, Thebes. (Egyptian Museum, Turin)

A vivid portrayal of entertainers at a feast (below). A group of musicians and dancing girls from detail of a relief in a tomb at Thebes, c. 1500–1400 BC. (British Museum)

These are professional performers, the earliest of whom there is record. There emerged in Ancient Egypt a class of dancers who were employed to appear at funerary celebrations, and who were also entertainers; these were in addition to the dancers 'consecrated' as temple attendants to dance in religious services. (It is worth recording that dwarfs and midgets from the lands surrounding the Upper Nile were highly regarded as entertainers, acrobats and dancers. The existing traditions of dance in these areas may indicate something of what they were expected to perform then to amuse the court of the Pharaohs.)

The cult dance associated with Apis, the bull, celebrated the choosing, nurturing and sacrifice of this beast. The priests of Osiris performed funerary dances after the ritual killing of the animal, and the rediscovery of the new bull (who incarnated Apis after the sacrifice of his predecessor) was also attended by dancing, as was his entire brief life-span.

Egyptian priests also performed an astronomical dance round an altar which they identified as the sun itself, the fixed point of their cosmology.

Their own motions reflected the movement of the heavenly bodies in their course, and this dance is also to be traced in the worship of ancient Chaldea.

In Ancient Egypt peasants celebrated fertility rites – a commonplace of many primitive cultures – and a relief from a tomb at Giza dating from 2700 BC shows a round or choral dance of this nature. The aristocracy, though, had by then abandoned such early dance forms and there seemed to be no indication in the iconography of the period of any form of social dance.

Intriguing testimony to the Egyptian traditions of dance worship are found in two classical authors. Herodotus speaks of the annual festival of Artemis at Bubastis in which a barge procession containing dancers performed as the boats went down the Nile:

'On the way, some of the women keep up a continual clatter with castanets and some of the men play flutes, while the rest, both men and women, sing and clap their hands. Whenever they pass a town on the river bank, they bring the barge close in shore, some of the women continuing to act as I have said, while others shout abuse at the women of the place, or start dancing, or stand up and hitch up their skirts.'[2]

Apuleius in *The Golden Ass* talks of the priests of the Syrian goddess who:

'howl all out of tune and hurl themselves hither and thither as though they were mad. They made a thousand jests with their feet and their heads; they would bend down their necks and spin round so that their hair flew out in a circle; they would bite their own flesh; finally. everyone took his two edged weapon and wounded his arms in diverse places.'[3]

This form of ecstatic self mutilatory dance is to be found in several primitive cultures.

An Assyrian inscription from the Palace of Asshurbanipal shows a procession of harpers who are plainly performing a dance step and at Boghazkeui in Cappadocia there is a Hittite rock inscription of a company of gods and goddesses to whom processions approach with the male worshippers performing what seems a dance step, a record from 1200 BC.

GREECE

'But the things in which we take a perennial delight are the feast, the lyre, the dance, clean linen in plenty, a hot bath and our beds. So forward now, my champion dancers and show us your steps, so that when he gets home our guest may be able to tell his friends how far we leave all other folk behind in seamanship, in speed of foot, in dancing and in song.'[4]

From the very earliest moments of Greek civilization dancing was fundamental in the ritual of worship and in personal and social life. It was to remain basic to religious experience; it was to form part of military training, and in education, both intellectual and physical, dance was an integral factor. In dancing, the Greeks expressed both public and private feelings – though not in the direct physical contact of men and women dancing together as in the West in the last five hundred years. Dance was essentially linked in the Greek mind to music and poetry; there evolved a vocabulary of movement and gesture known as *cheironomia* which united dance, verse and music as aspects of the same single fact which was known as *mousike* (the art of the Muses). It is arguable, and most probable, that dance was introduced into Greece from Crete, where it was itself a vital part of Minoan culture. A Minoan vessel of the sixteenth century BC, known as the Harvester Vase, shows men on their way to the harvest led by a priest figure. The men sing as they perform a marching step and 'are interrupted by a stooping dancer, who breaks through the files and shouts at them'.[5] There are statuettes of dancing women which date from Minoan times or from the Mycenaean culture which inherited so many Cretan influences. A Minoan gold ring dating from 1500 BC, discovered near Knossos, shows a dance performed by four women in a meadow. The oldest Attic inscription on a wine vessel from the eighth century BC reads: 'Let him who dances best receive this'. On the island of Delos dancing was, from pre-historic times, central to the rites celebrated at the shrines of Artemis and Apollo: Theseus, returning from the slaying of the Minotaur, dedicated a statue of Aphrodite on the island and danced the *geranos* (crane dance)

The quality of movement in Greek dance is well demonstrated in this detail from a vase painting of a dancer at a festival to honour Apollo, c.410 BC. It was from paintings such as this that Isadora Duncan drew her first revolutionary inspiration to free dance from the vulgarity and constraints which corrupted it at the turn of the twentieth century. (National Archaeological Museum, Taranto, Puglia)

round Apollo's altar. Elsewhere in mainland Greece inscriptions from the earliest times tell of dance performances, competitions, the names of dancers and of their teachers.

According to an invaluable study on the Greek dances, the usually accepted divisions into *phora* (movement), *schema* (poses), and *deixis* (portrayal) are based on misconceptions. *Schemata* are patterns, brief and distinctive, that could be observed in a dance in passing: some recurred frequently, others were only to be seen momentarily. *Phora* implied carriage of the body, a way of movement and also of step. *Deixis* implied the assumption of a role or a characterization in a dance, not simply the pointing or gesture that is solely ascribed to it by some authorities, but a movement which clearly indicated an identity.[6]

The very first evidence of the Greek dance must be traced back to the magnificent civilization which flourished in Crete during the third and second millennia before Christ, but by the time of the Classic period in Greece itself – a thousand years later – that civilization had vanished. It was destroyed by conquering hordes and fire, and only legends and memories were left behind and borrowings which can be traced in other cultures. The excavation at Knossos revealed much that is instructive in the matter of Cretan dance. The civilization that Sir Arthur Evans unearthed had many points of contact

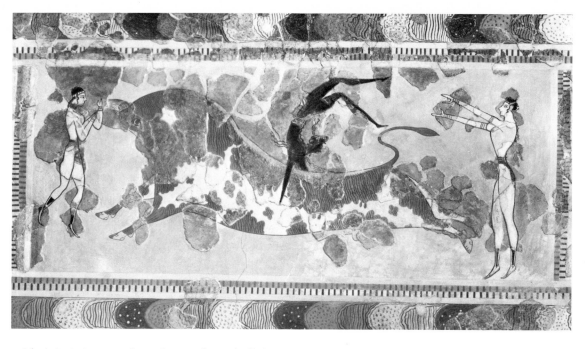

Bull dancers from the Palace at Knossos (destroyed c. 1400 BC). The acrobatic skill involved in bull dancing is evident in this detail of a celebrated wall painting. The ritual significance is now lost but the excitement of the spectacle is still communicated. (Archaeological Museum, Iráklion, Crete)

In Ancient Greece the Dionysiac cult, first seen in Crete, represented the wildest forms of physical excess, but gradually the rites became more ordered. In this Roman terracotta relief of the first century AD, a maenad and satyr dance gracefully with the infant Dionysos in a winnowing-basket. (British Museum)

with Asia Minor, such as the acrobatic bull dancing by youths and maidens and the use of music, dance and song in special ceremonies on feast days and celebrations. Dance was clearly an essential part of religious and ritualistic observances. The cult of Osiris, the resurrected god hero, was carried quite probably from Egypt through the Mediterranean to take root as the Dionysiac cult which eventually provided the origins of Greek tragedy. The Greeks believed that the oldest dance was connected with the birth of Zeus, in which a chorus of dancers impersonated the Curetes, the mythical saviours of the infant Zeus who preserved the child from being devoured by his father; they achieved this by the clash of their weapons and of cymbals. The origins of this dance would seem, in fact, to relate to a fertility ritual in which leaping men, shouting and beating weapons or staves together as they jumped, invoked prosperity for their crops and banished evil spirits by the noise they made. (This last is a tradition which can be observed in many primitive cultures, and it exists today in certain African tribal dances where evil spirits are inhibited by noise and leaping.)

Very early on there were also funerary dances, and by the eighth century BC there were representations on vases of dancers linked together, testimony to that fundamental activity which can be observed in medieval Europe as the *carole* and in social dances and children's dances today. This is the oldest formal pattern of communal dancing, the round, the closed circle of linked performers, which could, by breaking at one or two points, open out into a processional line or a serpentine figure. The fundamental impulse behind ring dances can sometimes be seen surviving today when, in a children's game, a central figure is surrounded by the ring of dancers. In its origins the ring dance was an invocatory round centred upon an altar or some other sacred object, perhaps even a tree, or a musician or priest figure. In some instances the ring dance might also be an invocation with the turning of the circle also accompanied by a turning of each individual (just as can be seen later on in time in the whirling dervishes). Intriguingly, it has been suggested that Cretan women sometimes broke the form of the ring to create a pattern or shape with their bodies which was maintained at the dance's end as an invocation or a tribute to a divinity; even the making of a lily pattern (that flower being sacred to the Cretan mother goddess) has been recorded.[7] In Crete there are also indications of animal maskings and animal impersonations in the dance. Some well-known Cretan figurines show priestesses handling snakes as part of a ritual to honour their chief goddess.

Garlands were carried in other rituals as emblems and frames for an image of the goddess of childbirth; the processional dance, as we have indicated, celebrated the harvest; and fertility rites and initiatory celebrations into secret cults were associated with frantic and ecstatic dance movement. The acrobatic element in bull leaping – the suggestion of skills rigorously trained – gives some indication of how serious and careful must have been the preparation for much of Cretan dance and ritualistic movement. In Greece the earliest civilization, that associated with and centred on Mycenae (whose great epics are the *Iliad* and the *Odyssey*), was to invade and conquer Crete. By 1100 BC Mycenae was itself to fall victim to other tribes on the mainland, and from this time come more and more records of dance and of dance myths, not least the Pyrrhic, the warriors' dance with its high leaping. (It has been suggested that its title relates not to Pyrrhus, son of Achilles, but to an etymological root *pyr* meaning fire, which indicates that it was a fire-leaping dance before becoming associated with martial activity. Fire-leaping is an activity to be found in many primitive communities.) The *Iliad* and the *Odyssey* make several references to the dance. In the first book of the *Odyssey*, the suitors, infesting Odysseus' palace 'when they had all finished and satisfied their hunger and thirst . . . turned their thoughts to other pleasures, to the music and dancing without which no banquet is complete.' And again 'from then till dusk they gave themselves up to the pleasures of dancing and the delights of song.'[8]

Most important of all Greek dances mentioned or implied in Greek mythology is the *geranos*. While this dance is usually identified as the crane dance, it is in fact a serpentine, winding dance performed at night, with maze-like twistings.[9] Also to be found are the earliest indications of that mysterious contagion of dance mania, a hysteria communicated among a group (which last surfaces in medieval Europe). In Ancient Greece the dance mania was seen to be the result of an offence against the gods; its more precise medical cause was an outbreak of some contamination, swiftly communicated, which impelled people into a muscular frenzy from which they were only released by an exhausted death. It was different from the wild flights of the maenads who were the abandoned followers of the Dionysiac cult. This cult was first to be observed in Crete and then emerged in Thrace and Phrygia. It is associated with the wildest forms of physical excess brought about by the intoxication of the god's presence, and in its most celebrated aspect the cult took the form of a hysterical race across the wintry countryside in a rout of exuberant and uncontrolled frenzy. Gradually the frenzy was tamed, though the Dionysiac rites continued, in a more organized form and much debased, into the second century of the Christian era. For men, there emerged the dithyramb, a combination of song and dance which celebrated vinous intoxication in spring in honour of Dionysos as god of fertility as well as of wine, with an especially tumultuous dance, the *tyrbasia*, associated with it.

Gradually the dithyramb became more ordered and more organized as spoken verse was introduced into it to replace the spontaneous effusion of high spirits. It became a hymn chanted in chorus and was accompanied by illustrative gesture and dance.

'We can accept, as a provisional formula, that a great many units of dance movement, which are also metrical units controlling the sung words, were traditional and that much of the art of the choral poet lay in finding new combinations of traditional units rather than in inventing new units.'[10]

Here the idea is presented of an essential unity between dance, poetic metre and song which was to haunt the poets and theorists of the Renaissance who sought the recreation of Ancient Greek tragedy. In this way the life of Dionysos was recounted, with episodes impersonated in mime and dance as verses hymned the god and recounted his actions. Elements of costuming made the representation livelier, and the performers joined in the ring dances around an altar. It has been suggested that so vivid and realistic were these celebrations that spectators could almost believe that they were reliving the action described.

Gradually, the leader of the dance became identified with a specific character in the song – he was the *hypokrates* (the answerer) who was soon to be known as the actor. Here is the origin of tragedy as a theatrical form. In 534 BC Peisistratos, dictator of Athens, established the city's great spring festival and a contest in 'goat song' (*tragoedia*) was won by Thespis and his chorus. 'Goat song', the literal meaning of tragedy, refers to the fact that the performers in the dithyramb impersonated satyrs and were called goats both on account of their appearance and also because of the sometimes licentious nature of their behaviour. The dithyramb, however, was also preserved as a dignified performance of choric song and dance and in 508 BC in Athens there was a contest in dithyrambic style, as distinct from the dramatic form of the tragedy. From this time date those annual contests held each year in the open-air theatre of Dionysos in which contending groups performed on the *orchestra* – the dancing space – and winners were awarded a prize. With the passing of the centuries the dithyrambic contests continued, becoming more elaborate and also more individually exhibitionistic, until in the second century

Terracotta figure from Tarentum in Italy, dating from the second century BC. It conveys something of the stance and the grace associated with the Greek dance in its later years. (British Museum)

of the Christian era they ended. Tragedy continued on its own path. Dance was essential, integral to it. Its characteristic dance was the *emmeleia*, dignified and entirely attuned to the theme of the tragedy. The male chorus, processing on to the *orchestra*, moved in a solid block; reacting to the drama, commenting, highlighting, they responded in song and dance to the action. At the same time comedy also emerged as a theatrical form. It had, like tragedy, evolved from the Attic festivals in honour of Dionysos. The spring celebrations had given birth to tragedy. It was in the winter festivals that a band of revellers, a *comus*, marched in procession carrying a phallus and chanting songs to Dionysos which were called phallic songs. Between the choruses the leader of the procession entertained the spectators with scurrilities and impromptu jokes and from this mixture of song and satire comedy evolved. After sacrifices and dances there came the ancient country sport of dancing upon greased wine skins and the festivities were concluded with general drinking and celebrations.

Eventually, the rough and ready jokes, the bawdiness, became sharpened into a literary and theatrical form. By the fifth century BC, at the time of Aristophanes, the chorus impersonated all kinds of beings, real and imaginary, costumed and masked with some complexity. The dance associated with them was the *kordax*, rich in vulgarities and lewdness. As comedy changed with the years, this dance element waned. The *kordax* became disassociated from its setting and

came to exist in its own right as a display of slapstick capers and physical vulgarities, continuing down to the time of the Roman Empire. But the theatre retained another coarse dance form with the invention in the sixth century BC of satyric plays in which stories from mythology were treated as grossly vulgar burlesques. The accompanying dance, the *sikinnis*, was like the *kordax* – a display of rudery, high spirits and acrobatic vulgarity. Like the *kordax* too it was to become very popular and survived into the Roman Empire, at which time it suffered the comminations and denunciations of the Fathers of the Church.

In addition to the rites associated with Dionysos there were many other cults linked with worship, all involving dancing in some form or other. Lucian, the second-century Greek satirist, observes 'not a single ancient mystery cult can be found that is without dances'.[11] And in Greece and in Asia Minor there is testimony to ecstatic and orgiastic dancing in the cult worship of Artemis, Hecate, Aphrodite, Pan, Demeter and Persephone, the latter being most importantly celebrated at Eleusis. The Eleusinian mysteries had to do with the return of Persephone to the earth, a symbol of rebirth and immortality, and it is thought that initiates into these mysteries were witnesses to some form of dance representation which explained the mystery to the observer and enlisted him in the rites. Orgiastic dancing was part of the Orphic rites, as also of many cults associated with imported deities, those gods whose worship had percolated into mainland Greece from further east. They included frenzied rites involving intoxication through the dance, self-mutilation and wild physical excess. Their justification was that they purged by excess – that they led the participant to achieve a consciousness of the divine through a systematic liberating of the body from its usual constraints, as can be observed even today in certain Voodoo dances in the West Indies, and in the traditions of the Turkish whirling dervishes.

The more 'open' worship at religious festivals also included dance. A processional dance, the *paean*, was a cadenced march to accompanying music. In Crete there was a dance which accompanied song known as *hyporchematic* dancing. For this the best boys were selected to perform an interpretative dance. There were dances for maidens (*partheneia*), and in Sparta, and later in Athens, the training of youths involved an adaptation of the ancient Pyrrhic dance which had by now developed into a martial display. It became a form of danced drill with armour and weapons, which in due time formed a competitive element in the great city festival in Athens, the Panathenaea. At this festival in honour of Athene, competitions for formations of Pyrrhic dancers were held, and by the fourth century professional female dancers were also to be seen in Pyrrhics, dressed as warriors and performing either seriously or as vulgar burlesque displays.

Roman period, effeminate youths and grotesques proliferated. By the first century AD the great festivals had become effete and gaudy. But it is at this time that there emerged the pantomimes ('pantomime' meaning one who imitates all things), those dramatic dancers whose prowess and example were to excite the popular imagination of the Greek and Roman world. Inspired particularly by the two most celebrated performers – Bathyllus of Alexandria and Pylades of Cilicia – in 22 BC the art of the pantomimes took hold of the public's mind and their performances supplanted many other theatrical forms. The pantomimes offered solo displays in which dramatic impersonations were given in dance and mime, the performers being gorgeously clothed, masked and accompanied by musical instruments. So great was public enthusiasm for

The dancing maenad (below), detail from a Greek vase painting, appears to be turning on her toes. The intoxication of her dance is conveyed by the movement of her costume. (Badisches Landesmuseum, Karlsruhe, W. Germany)

In Sparta, at the *gymnopaedia*, boys mimed boxing and wrestling in dance form. In this, as in other evidence of far-ranging folk and regional dance, you can see how close to the heart of the people's life was dance. Indeed it might be said that dance was the most essential expression both of the spiritual and emotional life of the Greeks:

'. . . a dance of boys and girls together who move in a row and truly resemble a string of beads. The boy precedes, doing the steps and postures of young manhood, and those which later he will use in war, while the maiden follows, showing how to do the women's dance with propriety; hence the string is beaded with modesty and with manliness.'[12]

Plato in his *Laws* stressed the importance of dance in education. To him the uneducated man is 'dance-less' and his teacher Socrates and his pupil Aristotle also stressed the importance of dance in shaping the whole man, mentally and physically.

Inevitably, in a culture in which dance was woven into the very fabric of life, there would emerge professionalism. In the earliest times there are records of teachers who were honoured as creators of certain dances for ritual performance. But they, like the performers, were still amateurs. It is in the third century BC that some kind of professionalism emerges. First, there was an association which united those artists – dancers, actors, poets, musicians and teachers – who were involved in the production of plays. These corporate members of the group of 'artists of Dionysos' were linked as servants of a divinity and a cult rather than as a trades union – their corporate entity was like that of monks of an order. Professional singers, muscians, dancers, acrobats and jugglers emerged later. Many were slaves specially trained; some were freed men; the women were courtesans who appeared at dinner parties as entertainers. With the debasement of the arts in later years, during the Graeco-

these performers that as Louis de Cahusac's early (1754), but detailed, history of dancing shows, riots often attended their performances. Their popularity was especially notable in Rome where they seem to have been alternately adored and abhorred by the Emperors – Domitian banished them from the city; his successor Trajan immediately reinstated them.

Pantomimes became great public heroes and their performance traditions lasted well into the final years of the Empire in the West, albeit the early Fathers of the Church had started inveighing against them. Many pantomimes also worked in the Empire of the East, finding in Constantinople a society entirely attuned to their art.

THE ETRUSCANS

Tribute must be paid here to the extraordinary culture of the Etruscans, sited on Italian soil but not part of its life until finally crushed and integrated into Italy by Roman power in the first century BC. The Etruscans, emigrants it is supposed from Asia Minor, constituted a sophisticated community populating twelve cities in what is now Tuscany. Their culture and language are lost, annihilated by Roman conquest, but there remains a vivid portrayal of something of their life and vitality, and of their dance, in the tomb paintings which survive in Tarquinia and Chiusi. In the boldly coloured frescoes which recorded aspects of the life that the dead had just left, paintings of the sixth and fifth centuries BC show dancing of exceptional variety and richness. There is a frieze of funerary chain dances, but more remarkable is the vivacious and brilliant portrayal of men and women prancing and twisting, caught in attitudes which suggest the most lively muscular display. These become oddly relevant when you consider some of the attitudes in Nijinsky's *L'Après-midi d'un faune* of 1912, with its hieratic walking steps. Beautifully costumed, the Etrurian figures argue a most sophisticated and highly-studied dance movement. Its implied joyousness, the fullness of life so magnificently preserved by the artists, the figures frozen in mid-action, the energy still undissipated in their bodies (like the frozen-motion photographs of Eadweard Muybridge) tell us that these dance scenes were intended to remind the dead of life and were no mere expression of the grief of mourners left behind. The style seems to owe little to Greek dance. It appears a language less consciously harmonious, less striving for a natural balance and rhythmic distinction or spiritual relevance than the Greek dance.

In the Etruscan tomb paintings of the early times – those of the sixth and fifth centuries BC – energy, the abundance of life's force seem all important. In later paintings there supervened a depression and a sadness in the face of death – the antithesis of the earlier joyous style.

One of many tomb paintings from Tarquinia, dating from the fifth to the first century BC. This example from the later period gives a most persuasive view of the dance manner of the Etruscans, and the inspiration from Greek dance is quite clear. The movement of the faun and the nymphs in Nijinsky's L'Après-midi d'un faune is highly reminiscent of this style.

ROME

In the earliest days of the Roman Republic, dancing was considered to be a necessary part of a young man's education, as it was in Greece. Quintilian observed that 'dancing was thought no disgrace to the ancient Romans' and Macrobius related that the children of patricians and senators attended dancing classes. The religious observances of Rome at this time also contained an element of dance. The best-known example was that of the Salii, the twelve dancer priests dedicated to the service of Mars. The college of Salian priests had been instituted by Numa Pompilius, second king of Rome, and in his *History of Rome* Livy noted how the priests processed through the streets, singing hymns and leaping and dancing armed with the *ancilia* (the sacred shield) and javelin.

In the various festivals associated with the gods there was some dancing. The Lupercalia was the occasion for half-naked youths to dance wildly in the streets, armed with whips; the Cerelia and the Agnolia also incorporated dance, and in the festival in honour of Pallas Athene, the *palilia* (the bonfire dance) was performed by shepherds in honour of the goddess to give thanks for the fruitfulness of their flocks.

At the period of the emergence of Rome as an empire, the decline of Greek civilization produced a shift in the cultural centre of the then civilized world, and a change of artistic style. For dance this meant a move away from those Greek traditions which had already become debased, and the establishment of a Roman theatrical form which was more dramatic and less danced. By the time of the birth of Christ, Roman taste in theatrical matters had become vulgar. Companies of strolling players roamed from city to city throughout Italy, seeking an audience for their travelling shows which combined dance and song, juggling and mime; even as early as the period of Terence (who died in 159 BC) the author could complain that the first performance of one of his plays had been ruined by the competition from a rope dancer and a boxer, and the prospect of a second performance by the rumour of a gladiatorial combat.

As already mentioned, by 22 BC the pantomimes became immensely popular entertainers. The most celebrated of them – men like the two notorious rivals Bathyllus and Pylades – achieved in Rome a following comparable with that of film stars today. With a supporting ensemble of musicians and chorus, the pantomime appealed to the populace by the skill with which he impersonated and evoked historical and mythological characters and also amused the public by comic or lewd antics. The style of the pantomimes was particularly impressive in its gestural power; the dance itself being less important than the revealing of character through imitative skill. Bathyllus was celebrated for his comedy; Pylades assumed a lofty manner and specialized in particularly heroic characterizations.

But with the empire, despite the fact that a ruler such as Caligula was an enthusiast for both song and dance, dancing had acquired a thoroughly reprehensible identity: Cicero had already declared 'no man ever dances, one might almost say, when sober, unless he is a madman'. Private persons of any social quality did not dance at all. 'Entertainers', both male and female, appeared in private homes, and dancing boys became favourites of senators and emperors. Their success, however, was more dependent upon their physical charm than their ability, for their dancing lacked any dignity or creative aspiration.

At its best the dancing partook of the nature of drama – there is a fascinating description of something very like a *ballet d'action* in Apuleius' *The Golden Ass*, in which the story of Paris and the golden apple is told in a form of dance-play. The action involved both pure dance and a kind of dramatic mime, but it is evident from Apuleius that the result was something very like a dance-drama in the ballet theatre of the eighteenth century. Some indication of the quality of the spectacle can be gained from these quotations from Adlington's translation of 1566:

'I saw, when the theatre gates were opened, how all things were finely prepared and set forth; for there I might see young boys and maidens in the flower of their youth, of excellent beauty and attired gorgeously, dancing and moving in comely order, according to the disposition of the Grecian Pyrrhic dance; for some time they would trip round together, sometime in length obliquely, sometime divide themselves into four parts, and sometime loose hands and group them on every side. But when the last sound of the trumpet gave warning that every man should retire to his place from those knots and circlings about, then was the curtain taken away and all the hangings rolled apart, and then began the triumph to appear.'[13]

There now follows a description of the setting and the entrance of the various characters in this

A Bacchanal with intoxicated revellers whirling round the central figure of the Greek god Dionysos (Bacchus). From a wall painting at the Villa Pamphili in Rome, dating from the first century AD.

Detail of a dancing gladiator, from a frieze of similar figures, performing a Pyrrhic dance. (Vatican Museum, Rome)

The decorative motif on this silver platter conjures up the liveliness and abandon of Dionysiac celebrations. Part of the Mildenhall Treasure, fourth century AD. *(British Museum)*

of all the people. She was accompanied by a great number of little boys, whereby you would have judged them to be all cupids, so plump and fair were they, and either to have flown from heaven or else from the river of the sea, for they had little wings and little arrows, and the residue of their habit according to each point, and they bare in their hands torches lighted, as though it had been the day and the feast of marriage of their lady. Then came in a great multitude of fair maidens: on the one side were the most comely Graces; on the other side the most beautiful Seasons, carrying garlands and loose flowers which they strewed before her; and they danced very nimbly therewith, making great honour to the goddess of pleasure with these flowers of the spring. . . . But the more pleasing Venus moved smoothly forwards more and more with slow and lingering steps, gently bending her body and moving her head, answering by her motions and delicate gesture to the sound of the instruments: for sometimes her eyes would wink gentle with soft motions to the music, sometimes threaten and look fiercely, and sometimes she seemed to dance only with her eyes. . . . After the judgement of Paris was ended, Juno and Pallas departed away sadly and angrily, shewing by their gesture that they were very wroth and would revenge themselves on Paris; but Venus that was right pleased and glad in her heart, danced about the theatre with much joy, together with all her train. This done, from the top of the hill through a privy spout ran a flood of wine coloured with saffron which fell upon the goats in a sweet-scented stream, and changed their white hair into a yellow more fair: and then with a sweet odour to all them of the theatre, by certain engines the ground opened and swallowed up the hill of wood.'[14]

The length and detail of Apuleius' description gives a more than fair idea of the Roman theatrical dance entertainments in the second century of the Empire. There is clear evidence of complex theatrical machinery and some indication of the quality of the dance itself which plainly aimed at advancing a narrative through mimetic and dynamic means. It is worth commenting also that the theme of the 'Judgement of Paris' was to be used both in Renaissance and Baroque spectacle, as for example in *Il Pomo d'oro* of 1667 performed in Vienna, in which a comparable style of presentation can be inferred, and also in a satiric version more recently, which was choreographed by Antony Tudor and shown in London in 1938.

But though there are continuing references in Roman literature, usually unfavourable, to people dancing, the dance itself did not seem rooted in the life of the people, and Roman theatrical taste dictated a much more mixed form of entertain-

mimetic version of the *Judgement of Paris*. After the appearance of the three goddesses:

'followed certain waiting servants; Castor and Pollux played by boys of the theatre went behind Juno, having on their heads round pointed helmets covered with stars; this virgin Juno in the Ionian manner sounded a flute which she bare in her hand, and moved herself quickly and with unaffected gait towards the shepherd Paris, shewing by honest signs and tokens and promising that he should be Lord of all Asia if he would judge her the fairest of the three, and give her the apple of gold. The other maiden, which seemed by her armour to be Minerva, was accompanied by two young men, armed and brandishing their naked swords in their hands, whereof one was named Terror, and the other Fear; and behind them approached one sounding his flute in the Dorian manner, now with shrill notes and now with deep tones to provoke and stir the dancers as the trumpet stirreth men to battle: this maiden began to dance and shake her head, throwing her fierce and terrible eyes upon Paris, and promising that if it pleased him to give her the victory of beauty, she would make him by her protection the most strong and victorious man alive. Then came Venus and presented herself, smiling very sweetly, in the middle of the theatre, with much favour

ment. In it dance was but one component, and not an important one. That dancing was associated with sexual licence and every form of vulgarity is learned both from the sterner Roman moralists and also from the comments of the Fathers of the Church.

From its greatest days in Ancient Greece dance had, like the civilization which had given it birth, declined; with Romanization it was to lose every impulse and attribute that had made it great.

JEWISH DANCE

A distinguished biblical scholar has suggested that, either explicitly or implicitly, the Old Testament provides evidence that many of the typical dances of antiquity can be found among the celebrations of the ancient Israelites. The form which these dances took may have varied but the intention of the dance, its devotional or spiritual object, was part of the great dance tradition of the ancient world.

'. . . a mere handful of men who offered the greatest example that the world had hitherto seen of what could be accomplished by subordinating will and personality to the guidance of the Divine Creator. . . . It was amongst these very prophets that the most interesting kind of sacred dance – the ecstatic dance – was in vogue with its wildness and extravagances; in this they, or at least the earliest of them, did not differ from certain classes of 'holy men' all the world over; where they did differ was in their development of the conception which underlay the purpose of the ecstatic dance, i.e. union with the deity; and it is just here that they stand in such bold relief from all others. The earliest prophets believed that this sacred dance was the means whereby the divine spirit came to them; this belief they share with others; but they rose to the higher belief that this means was not necessary for achieving the purpose for which it was used. It had served a useful purpose; but having served its purpose it was dropped. The prophets came to the realisation that there were more spiritual means whereby union with the deity was brought about; then the sacred dance found no further place among them. They had shed the husk but retained the kernel.'[15]

In those passages in the Old Testament in which dancing is recorded there is no hint of any disapproval or prohibition. It must therefore have been accepted as a usual aspect of worship and you may also infer that it formed an integral part of certain celebrations from the fact that dancing continued as an element in religious practice among the Jews of post-biblical times. Further, though mention of dance in the Old

Testament is rare, this does not mean that the dance itself was rare: there are five different Hebrew words for dance which are all used in connection with religious activities, save in one isolated instance.[16] Of the various types of dance, the best known (in the First Book of Chronicles) is probably that processional form used by King David and the people of Israel when they danced before the Ark. Here they were dancing in the presence of God since He was understood as being present in the Ark. The dance round the golden calf (in Exodus) seems to be a ring dance that may even be traced back to the Ancient Egyptian cult of Apis. Other references, such as the Psalm 'Let them praise His name in the dance' and 'Thus saith the Lord God: smite with thine hand and stamp with thy foot . . .' (Ezekiel) were both interpreted by the early Fathers of the Christian church as justification for using the dance in worship.[17]

Three dancing figures (left) are involved in the ritual for the feast of the Passover. From a fourteenth-century Hebrew manuscript detailing the history of the Exodus from Egypt and the preparation for the celebration of Passover. (British Library)

'And David danced before the Lord with all his might; and David was girded with a linen ephod. So David and all the house of Israel brought up the Ark of the Lord with shouting, and with the sound of the trumpet.' (II Samuel 6:14–15). This detail from a French miniature (below) from a bible moralisée of the thirteenth century depicts King David dancing before the Ark and at the window Saul's daughter, Michal, who 'despised him in her heart' for his dancing and playing. (Pierpont Morgan Library, New York)

It should be noted that the Phoenician god known as Baal was considered lord of dancing and the Assyrian word for 'to rejoice' also meant to dance. When (in the First Book of Kings) the priests of Baal leap around the altar while trying to make fire in the contest with Elijah, they are clearly performing an ecstatic ring dance. Another ring dance of the Jews is indicated in a Psalm with the text 'I will wash mine hands in innocency; so will I compass [circle round] thine altar O Lord.'[18] A similar ring dance was performed in post-biblical times at the Feast of Tabernacles where, after sacrifices had been offered, priests went in procession round the altar, singing psalms on each of the seven days that the feast lasted; a torch dance also took place in the Court of the Women in the Temple on the second day of the feast.[19]

There are in the Old Testament several descriptions of women dancing to welcome victorious warriors. The defeat of Pharaoh's hordes was celebrated (in Exodus) as: 'Miriam the prophetess, the sister of Aaron, took a timbrel in her hand; and all the women went out after her with timbrels and with dances./And Miriam answered them, Sing ye to the Lord for he hath triumphed gloriously; the horse and his rider hath he thrown into the sea.' Similarly (in Samuel) Jephthah returning from victory over the Ammonites is met by his daughter and her companions 'with timbrels and with dances.' When King David returned from slaying Goliath 'the women came out of all cities of Israel, singing and dancing, to meet King Saul, with tabrets, with joy and with instruments of music.'[20]

References such as these were seen as ample

justification in Christian times for the acceptance of dance as an integral part of early Christian worship.

CHRISTIAN DANCE

Very early on in Christian times the dance was equated with heavenly bliss – the angels and the blessed dance. Even more interesting is the Gnostic Hymn of Jesus attributed to St John in which dancing is seen as an attribute of divine grace: '. . . Divine grace is dancing. Dance ye all . . .' (Apocryphal Acts). The theologian Clement of Alexandria (AD 150–216) is cited as saying: 'Then shalt thou dance in a ring, together with the angels, round Him who is without beginning nor end, the only true God, and God's Word is part of our song.'[21] Here is a clear reference to ring dances as both a symbol of divine mystery and a means of earthly participation in those mysteries. By the third century there is evidence of dancing integrated into the ritual and worship of the Church. The spread of Christianity round the Mediterranean world involved the absorption of non-Christian rites into the Church – hence pagan survivals and celebrations were, like their participants, in a sense baptized, becoming part of the act of Christian worship. The obvious inference was that, by dancing, the worshipper emulated the angelic host. Thus, too, he sought to trample down vice and evil and acquire some perception of paradise. A survival of the angelic dance is to be noted in the fact that as late as the fifteenth century the *seises*, the choristers of

One of the best-known representations of angels dancing. Here they form a ring above the stable where the Christ child is being worshipped by shepherds. This detail is from the fifteenth-century painting The Mystic Nativity *by Botticelli. (National Gallery, London)*

Seville Cathedral, were dressed as angels. Their dance, which received the authorization of a Bull from Pope Eugenius IV in 1439, survives today but they are no longer dressed as angels (details of their present day costume are given later on in this chapter).

The concept of angelic dancing continued for many centuries. Some medieval dance hymns characterized this dance as being paradisal. From this there may also have evolved the Christian idea of the dance for the dead as exorcism of the power of the underworld. This also relates to the statement by St Ambrose that dancing by the faithful in imitation of the angels' round reflected the idea of the Resurrection and was part of a mystery revealed, since angelic dancing symbolized the trampling underfoot of the devil and his works. But it is to be inferred that by the fourth century the Church dance is in a state of deterioration. Women have joined in, dancing with men, and a licentiousness seems to have penetrated sacred festivities. Bishop Epiphanius sought to idealize the Church dance, seeing in dancing before the Lord an example of Faith and Good Works. Others of the Fathers, like St Augustine, railed against it, though without daring to ban it, since it had the sanction of Holy Writ. Augustine wryly observed 'He who would dance, may dance.' Yet in his *Epistle to Gregory*, St Basil says that the only occupation of the angels in Heaven is to dance, and he calls happy those who can imitate them on earth.[22]

The forms of Church dance as they evolved were both processional and, more specifically, concerned with expressing matters of faith. Some processional dances of the early Middle Ages have continued up to our own time and these not only reflect a belief in the dance as a therapeutic activity, even in the sense of casting out devils, but are also a survival of an even more ancient ritual to ensure good harvest. The dance for the dead and certain graveyard dances preserve an ancient tradition of dancing at the graves of the martyrs. Through dancing it was thought possible to express a belief in the Resurrection. It was believed that through this sympathetic imagery the dead would participate in the blessed and eternal dance of the angels. The graveside dance was also a reflection of the idea of treading down demons and protecting the dead from evil. The survival of these dances can be traced into the sixteenth and seventeenth centuries: in Languedoc in France the congregation danced in churches and cemeteries on certain feast days, and in Limoges in the seventeenth century dance rituals were held in the Church of St Leonard on the feast of St Martial. In Spain in the sixteenth century, at the time of St Thomas Villanueva, Bishop of Valencia, it was customary to dance before the Sacred Elements in churches in Toledo, Jerez, Valencia and Seville (although in AD 744 a Papal Bull from Pope Zacharias had forbidden all such processional dances – *danses balladoires* – because of their degeneracy).

In one of the earliest, and most influential, scholarly histories of dancing – that of Louis de Cahusac which was published in 1754 – there is well researched comment and some intriguing direct observation about the ecclesiastical dance. Cahusac cites, of course, the historical sanctions given by such Early Fathers as Gregory of Nazianzus (c.AD 330–390) in his letter to the Emperor Julian:

'. . . if you give yourself up to the dance; if your taste drags you into these feasts that you seem to love so furiously, dance; I consent to it. . . . But why revive the licentious dances of the barbarous Herodias, who spilt the blood of a Saint? Why do you not rather imitate those laudable dances that King David performed with so much zeal before the Ark of the Covenant? Those exercises of piety and peace are worthy of an emperor, and are the glory of a Christian.'[23]

More remarkably, he refers to the fact that:

'. . . in some Catholic countries, the dance still makes part of the ceremonies of the Church. In Portugal, in Spain, in Rousillon [France], solemn dances are performed in representation of our mysteries, and in honour of some saints. Cardinal Ximenes re-established in the cathedral of Toledo the ancient custom of the Mozarabic Masses, during which the people dance in the choir and the nave. Even in France in the middle of the last [seventeenth] century we still saw the people and the priests dance in a ring in the choir of the church of St Leonard. At the end of each psalm they substituted for the *Gloria Patri* this verse, which they sang with the liveliest transports of zeal and of joy: *San Marceau pregas per nous; et nous espingaren per bous.* Father Ménestrier, Jesuit (in the preface to his Treatise on Ballets, of 1682) said that he had seen in his time, in some churches, Canons and choir-boys who, on Easter Day, took one another frankly by the hand and danced while singing hymns rejoicing. . . . The dance of the Torches and that of St John's Day escaped the proscriptions (of the Fathers of the Church and Bishops). That of May 1 was revived, which was only a remnant of those stablished by idolatry. The first was performed by the light of several straw torches on the first Sunday in Lent; and the second around fires that were lit in the streets on the Eve of the Feast of St John.'[24]

There is a recurrent conflict to be observed throughout the Middle Ages and the early Renaissance between the traditions of ecclesiastical dancing and the moral reprobation of the Church itself. As early as AD 554 Childebert, King of the Franks, had proscribed the religious dance in all his lands. In the twelfth century Odo, Bishop of Paris, forbade church dancing with particular reference to funerary dances in grave-yards. Five centuries later, on 3 September 1667 the Parliament of Paris issued a decree proscribing all religious dances, citing those on 1 January, 1 May, the torch dances on the first Sunday in Lent and those held round bonfires on the eve of St John's feast day (23 June). Yet still the dance survived, and indeed became intimately linked with certain observances. In 1462 on the eve of *Corpus Christi* René, King of Provence, instituted a procession called Lou Gué which mingled Christian and pagan symbolism in a processional celebration which was interspersed with dancing. In Lisbon in 1610, on the occasion of the canonization of St Carlo Borromeo, his statue was taken in procession through the streets, with attendant dancing. And it is worth observing that the dance itself was patronized by the Jesuits.

The Society of Jesus – the Jesuits – made considerable use of the stage, and dance in particular, as a means of expressing religious, moral and didactic ideas. In France especially, the Jesuits favoured dance, and the scenic effects and stage facilities of their Collège Louis Le Grand in Paris were fully professional. The students appeared in ballets on pious or suitably religious themes. Père Ménestrier sj wrote the first detailed modern history of ballet in 1657.[25] He also provided scenarios, and descriptions of ballets performed, notably of *L'Autel de Lyon* and *Le Ballet des Destinées de Lyon* which were composed by him on the occasion of the visit of Louis XIV to the Jesuit College at Lyon in 1658. When the Jesuits were criticized for dabbling in the theatre, their response was a ballet (staged in 1726) with the provocative title of *L'Homme instruit par les spectacles*.

The Church's comminations against dance in church and in church precincts were propounded by bishops and synods alike. They were most usually directed against the licentiousness which became common at the end of the Middle Ages. The Church spoke against the inevitable lewdness which resulted from the participation of women, but also against the ideas of witchcraft and magic which became accretions on the religious dance itself. Nevertheless, religious dance had the unassailable sanction of Holy Writ, and of certain Fathers of the Church, and it is this which must account for the public's refusal to give up dancing, and the Church's desire to contain or at least control this form of dancing if it dared not eradicate it. Perhaps the most extraordinary aspect of the religious dance came in the outbreaks of dance mania and in the idea of the dance of death. Dance mania is a term which can be applied to recurrent outbursts of frenzied and uncontrollable movement which have occurred since the seventh century. It is suggested by some authorities that these epidemics were traceable to a poisoning caused by the consumption of diseased grain in rural communities. This form of ergotism can result in hallucinations, frantic and uncontrollable and

permanent physical shaking, not unlike that also associated with the nervous condition known today as St Vitus' dance (chorea).

As early as the year 1021 there is testimony to an outbreak of dance mania in the small Saxon town of Kolbigk. Chronicles published in the twelfth century tell of members of the congregation who suddenly broke into dancing in the churchyard on Christmas Eve, and whose disorderly behaviour brought about excommunication by the parish priest. The legend has it that the dancing continued for a year and only ceased when the ban of excommunication was raised. This pious record disguises, but does not totally conceal, the fact of an epidemic of nervous disorder which was to result in the death of several of the 'dancers'. In 1278 the town of Maastricht in the Low Countries was also recorded as being the scene of a similar epidemic. In this instance the dancers crossed a bridge which collapsed under their weight, throwing them into the river Moselle where they drowned.

These are just two examples from the several records which exist of medieval paroxysmic dancing. These all seem to be examples of hysteria communicated within a group and thereupon spreading furiously. The tarantism which first appeared in southern Italy in the fourteenth century was associated not only with a fear of the tarantula but also with the emergence of the *tarantella* as a dance.

Any further explanation of these extraordinary outbreaks is difficult. Both medical and pyschological evidence can be cited to suggest causes. The records of the events are unavoidably coloured by the naïvety or ignorance of the observers or chroniclers so that the events were subject to every kind of embroidery and exaggeration in the telling. Nevertheless, they offer some indication of the link which remained at this time between dance and faith. A more

Victims of the dance mania who were excommunicated for their abandoned dancing in the churchyard of St Magnus at Kolbigk, Saxony, on Christmas Eve in the year 1021. Detail from Hartmann Schedel's Liber Cronicarum, *printed in Nuremberg in 1493. (British Library)*

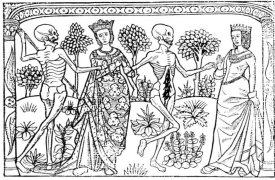

curious connection exists in the Dance of Death, which first emerged pictorially in church murals showing Death as a participant in dancing, leading away both the great and the humble. It was a concept which harked back to the idea of churchyard dances but it also conveyed the idea of a frenzied dance in which Death must inevitably claim the dancer. As with the dance mania, dancing was seen as representing yet another pestilence rather than a joy.

In the Middle Ages it must be recalled that there was a rich tradition of dance associated with Church feast days. Among the most extreme occasions was the Feast of Fools celebrated at the turn of the year, which included dancing, mumming and public festivities. Records of it at the end of the twelfth century suggest that it was often extreme and sometimes bawdy – the *Fête des fous* at Notre Dame in Paris was famous for its exuberance – and such undisciplined affairs were to fall under the interdict of the Church by the late Middle Ages. They were, however, widespread throughout Europe and the participation of the clergy often took the form of some kind of a ring dance.

It is not too far-fetched to say these sometimes orgiastic celebrations may be considered a survival of the Roman saturnalia. The Church was to put a pietistic gloss upon festivities marking the death of the year and on Holy Innocents' Day (28 December) a children's festival contained dancing as an essential part. An even more fascinating tradition related to the playing of ball games by the clergy and their deacons, whose most notable survival was the *pelota* game at Auxerre in France. The Dean led his canons in a dance, holding a large ball and tracing in his steps the labyrinthine pattern inlaid in the floor of the nave (which was destroyed *c.* 1690). During his dance he threw the ball first to one canon and then another after it had been thrown back to him, and this festival tradition persisted for centuries. The hymn which accompanied it sang of Christ's Resurrection; from pre-Christian mythology, the labyrinth came to symbolize an escape from the Underworld, and hence from death into resurrection. Thus the canons' dance at Auxerre was in essence a danced mystery embodying the hope of resurrection and its origins appear to pre-date the Christian faith which it ostensibly represented.

A comparable symbolic enactment of the Resurrection came in a *bergerette* danced as late as 1662 in Besançon. It was a line or ring dance performed by the priests on the first day of Easter. Such activities were in no way exceptional in the medieval Church. The Council of Avignon in the twelfth century forbade 'leaping, obscene movements and dances' in Church on the eves of saints' days, while Guillame Durand, Bishop of Mende in the thirteenth century, referred to dances as not unusual activities on the high days of the Church year: deacons dancing on Christmas Day; priests on St Stephen's Day; choirboys on Holy Innocents'; and subdeacons at Epiphany. Further, a liturgy used in Paris in the Middle Ages contains the rubric: 'The canon shall dance at the first psalm.'

Today, apart from certain worthy attempts to integrate dance into the religious life of the community, there remains but one authentic survival. This is the dance already mentioned of the *seises*, the choristers of Seville Cathedral who perform on each of the six days following the feast of Corpus Christi. Their costumes today are those dating from the beginning of the seventeenth century although their dance itself dates back perhaps another three hundred years (their earlier costume as angels was an obvious reference to the ecclesiastical belief in the angelic dance). Ten boys dance and play castanets for about fifteen minutes in an open space just below the high altar. The pattern of their dance has now lost any obvious significance but it has been argued that, like the midsummer rituals on Corpus Christi and the lighting of bonfires on St John's Eve, the rite is in fact a memory of far more ancient rituals of sun worship.

The dance in Spain has a curious mixed relationship with the Church. As was customary in Europe, attempts were made to stifle dancing as part of Church ritual; in 1780 a decree by

Charles III of Spain banned all dancing (save that of the *seises*) in churches and also religious processions. Yet dance survived and a tradition persisted in Spain of *romerias* in which people from a town went into the depths of the country for a day to some remote site, possibly the shrine of a saint, to dance and hold festivities in his honour. This again can perhaps be seen as a survival or a folk memory of some pre-Christian ritual.

In the 1920s there were still a few places in Spain where ritual dancing was performed as part of religious observances. One was the dance of *els cosiers* (the potters) performed in the village of Alaro on Mallorca on 29 July, the feast of St Roche, and again on 15 August, the Feast of the Assumption; and another at Felanitx, also in Mallorca, on St Augustine's Day, 28 August.

The dance of *els cosiers* was executed by six young men in medieval dress, with one other boy dressed in women's clothes. It involved turning circles of movement, and a whirling finale in which the performers spun round, each holding the end of another's handkerchief.

The dance in Felanitx was a solo performed by one man wearing a paper halo and carrying a wooden crucifix. By leaps and stamping, and apparently wild movements he processed down the aisle from the altar, dancing for the most part near the church door: the dance, known as San Juan Pelos (St John of the Dust), was exhortatory and traditional.[26]

The last example of popular dance which has survived on a religious basis is that of the pilgrims to Echternach in Luxembourg. Every year at Whitsuntide a procession of these pilgrims make their way to the shrine of St Willibrod (who died there in 739).

'Its origin is uncertain, but it dates at latest from the thirteenth century, and one account asserts that it was instituted during an outbreak of cholera; but perhaps it is much older – the survival of the spring dance of heathen races.

'The little town is now a place of pilgrimage for Germans, Belgians, and Luxemburgers, persons of different nationalities, but especially for epileptics and sufferers from St Vitus' Dance. . . . The younger people enjoy the dance, but there are many old and feeble persons who participate, and the exercise taxes their powers considerably. All pilgrims, however, must conform to the rules set forth, including the ascent of sixty-two steps to the shrine.'[27]

Regarding the survival of any religious dance in England, there are references to dancing by apprentices and servants in York Minster on Shrove Tuesday as late as the latter years of the seventeenth century; while on the Tuesday of Whitsun week, the tenants of the Prebend of Donington danced around the lectern in his church. At Salisbury, also at Whitsuntide, the

A detail from The Burial of the Sardine *by Goya, c. 1793. This popular masked festival to mark the beginning of Lent and the end of carnival time still takes place in some parts of Spain. (Academia de San Fernando, Madrid)*

parishioners of two country parishes near the city moved in a kind of processional dance to the door of the Cathedral to maintain their claim to certain privileges in a nearby forest. At Wells Cathedral there are references to liturgical dancing being held until the year 1339. (After the Restoration, the dance was transferred to Oak Apple Day – 29 May.)

A survey of social dance manners, published in 1829, provides an interesting comment on the religious dance and popular attitudes as the Georgian age waned:

'Our own country, at the present moment, possesses a sect of Jumpers, who, seeming to imagine that he who leaps highest must be nearest to heaven, solemnize their meetings by jumping like kangaroos, and justify themselves very conclusively from Scripture, because David danced before the Ark – the daughter of Shiloh danced in the yearly festival of the Lord – and the child John, the son of Elizabeth, leapt before it was born!

'The Methodists, on the other hand, maintain, in its full latitude, the doctrine of the ancient Waldenses and Albigenses, that as many paces as a man makes in dancing so many leaps he makes towards hell. Even the amiable Cowper, the poet, suffered his fine mind to be so darkened by bigotry, as to believe that a great proportion of the ladies and gentlemen whom he saw amusing themselves with dancing at Brightelmstone, must necessarily be damned; and, in a religious publication [Evangelical Magazine] now before me, I find it stated, that a sudden judgment overtook a person for indulging in this enormity; a large lump started up in his thigh while dancing; but upon his solemn promise not to repeat the offence, the Lord heard his prayer and removed his complaint.

Shaker meeting at Niskeyuna in New York State, 1873, showing one of the 'wheel-within-a-wheel' dances in action. These were religious exercises in which circles revolved in alternate directions within one another, with a chorus at the centre. Thus was symbolized the doctrinal basis of the Shaker faith; the outer ring was the circle of truth, the inner group of vocalists the perfection of God that lay at the heart of life. Detail from Leslie's Popular Monthly of 1885.

Whirling Dervishes today (above). The Turkish dance historian Metin And evokes the action at a Dervish ceremony: 'At the start their arms are crossed and pressed against their breasts with their hands grasping their shoulders and their heads inclined. Their bare feet are close together. At first they turn very slowly, their hands leaving their shoulders, and gradually the arms of the dancers are extended full length and held horizontally . . . As they gradually quicken their rotation, long white skirts become fully expanded like opened umbrellas . . .'

groups. The Shakers were first recorded in Lancashire in the 1740s. In New England their faith spread during the last decades of the eighteenth century and involved the building of Meeting Houses in which the ritual of their belief could be performed. Under the instruction of their then leader, Joseph Meacham, a dance, in emulation of the angelic dance, was ordained – the 'square order shuffle' – in which the congregation, dividing men from women, performed a dance having something militarily precise in its steps. There evolved splinter groups in the south and west of the United States who incorporated song and livelier dances. Lucy Wright, successor to Meacham as head of the sect, initiated ceremonies with skipping and ring dances, and until the middle of the last century the popularity and the fervour of these observances brought increasing elaboration and variety into Shaker ritual. Thereafter the cult declined.

The fact that these dances were in fact the outward release of tensions induced by a life of considerable austerity – humility, celibacy, meditation, hard manual labour and the submission of self to a communal way of life – suggests how intense they must have been as an expression of feeling in a highly-charged religious setting. This is one of the clearest examples of the use of dance as a sublimation and canalization of feeling through religious experience which might well otherwise have been expended in the round of everyday life.[29]

THE DERVISHES

The most spectacular form of religious dance is that of the Dervish order. Islam was inimical to dance, its austerity 'did much to discourage music and dancing and waged a relentless war against them'.[30] Yet despite this, traditional folk dance survived in Turkey, and the idea of using music and dance as part of a religious litany gained acceptance. This became part of the Sufi mystical tradition, whence sprung the idea of the Dervish orders of monks. Various groups of Dervishes became increasingly occupied with the idea of rotatory dance, with singing or crying out as part of their religious discipline, and the Mevlevi Dervishes especially became famous for this practice.

Founded in the ninth century by the Turkish poet and mystic Mevlana, their aim was the creation of a state of spiritual awareness reached by highly organized and continual whirling. By the seventeenth century the Mevlevi order was well known and their whirling, in white robes, with conical hats and arms outstretched, excited the comment of many travellers. Today the ritual still exists, and in their rotations and in their progress round the dance area the Dervishes symbolize the turning of the earth on its axis and the earth's revolution round the sun.

A writer in the same work, after denouncing those who admit dancing and other vain amusements into their schools, concludes with an alarming belief, "that this dancing propensity has, in some places, nearly danced the Bible out of the school!" '[28]

A late example of religious dance in the western hemisphere is that of the Shakers. It is not unique; at revivalist and primitive church meetings there is still testimony to ecstatic movement and dancing, as there is to snake-handling in certain areas. But the Shaker ritual is intriguing and well documented. The Shaking Quakers were discovered in Albany, New York; a group of immigrants from Manchester, their faith depended upon a belief in Divine Revelation, and their religious practice involved convulsive movement and dance. The tradition was by no means new; there were historical precedents for such 'inspired' movement among heretical and seceding sects of the Huguenots, and earlier Reformed

CHAPTER THREE

EUROPEAN FOLK DANCE

Peasants making merry (left), depicted with consummate skill by the scholarly German artist, Albrecht Dürer, from an engraving of 1514. (British Museum)

Two morris *dancers (below right) performing in acrobatic style. The figure on the right wears a Moorish turban. The name of this dance is a corruption of* morisco *(Moorish, moresque) acquired at the time of the Crusades. Similar carved figures can also be seen in Munich. (Goldene Dachel, Innsbruck, Austria)*

IN CONSIDERING folk dance in Europe you are faced with what may seem two conflicting facts: the spread of industrialization throughout Europe that inhibited and constrained folk dance as an aspect of the life of the people, and the attempts to preserve and encourage folk dance either as an act of nostalgia or as a conscious attempt to convey a national identity – the example of many Eastern European folk dance troupes illustrates this latter point.

The origins of 'folk' dance are naturally enough as old as the people who danced them. As has already been seen, dance is the earliest manifestation of human emotion, and the continued practice of dancing has inevitably developed a form of dance among the people which has been refined and sharpened in identity by the historical forces at work on any particular nation. You may thus see that a nation's folk dance can be understood as an extremely precise indication of its racial characteristics – an observation which is, of course, equally true of its folk songs and its legends.

But here the proviso must be made that although this is true of much European folk dance it does not apply to those less developed countries in which, as in Africa and parts of Asia, the dance continues as an expression of the religious life of the people.

It is not possible to detail here the vast corpus of folk dance found in Europe with any precision – it is a task that has occupied researchers and enthusiasts for many years and has produced an extensive body of works in which remote and half forgotten dances as well as continuingly popular folk routines have been recorded.

As some indication of the extreme wealth of folk dance in any one country, a more detailed description of Spanish dance is given later on in this chapter and this will serve to provide an insight into the range of dances possible in a single country. Similarly, it is worth noting that the programmes presented by such Eastern European folk troupes as those of Igor Moiseyev and Beriozka from the Soviet Union, of the Georgian State Dance Company, and of the Slask troupe from Poland, all convey something of the resources of folk dance which have been preserved and edited for stage performance without losing their essential nature.

A basic division must be made concerning the functions of folk dancing, between those dances which contain memories and references to religious or magical dances, and those which serve a purely social purpose. In the first there is an extraordinary persistence of ceremonies which antedate Christianity and enshrine attitudes of a far older religion, of a faith which goes back to the most primitive need for the dance in early

societies. In these, the matters of fertility, of worship of the seasonal gods, of tree cults and of curative dances can be seen. These dances, emerging as a vivid and direct expression of fundamental beliefs, gradually followed the natural process of most primitive dances and became a mimetic representation of those beliefs and then – losing even that dramatic origin – survived as a traditional dance incorporated into the social activities of a people. The dancing round a maypole, the leaping over a bonfire, the mimetic combat, all hark back to an original function as magic and worship which is now lost.

The social dance can be seen as a direct descendant of early celebratory dances and a development from such basic forms as the ring or round dance, which in its turn gave birth to the *carole* and which can still be variously seen throughout Europe as the *kolo* in Yugoslavia, the *hora* in Romania and the *khorovod* in Russia. It is a truism but, nevertheless, one which needs to be restated, that there are a number of recurrent themes in folk dance which can be traced across the whole of Europe and are also to be found elsewhere in the world. These involve such immemorial practices as the circling of a central

object representative of a divine force: a sacrificial stone, an altar, a tree. Others involve the representation of fertility symbols and the whole apparatus, common to so many societies, of rites and propitiatory actions involving the cycle of life itself from birth through procreation to death.

Of the ancient worship of the sun, there remain those undeniable traces in bonfire dances to be seen as far afield as Sweden and Spain. Celebratory fires were once lit all over Europe on certain festive days: Christmas, All Hallows Eve, May Day among them – and these are clear relics of a much earlier pagan tradition. The burning of a figure in effigy on the flames may even be a memory of actual sacrifice. In many primitive communities dances are performed round fires, and an extension of this comes with the processional dances in which flaming torches or brands are flourished – witness a one-time processional dance with torches in the Auvergne in France on the first Sunday in Lent.

In maypole dances, the totemistic nature of the pole itself involves both the idea of a symbol of divinity and of the fruitful and protective tree, the ribbons which habitually linked the dancers to the pole being understood as the vestigial branches of the tree and the direct links joining the celebrants to the pole as a source of fertility. The maypole as a focus for dancing stretches across Europe from north to south and its magic has been invoked by Finns and Swedes, by English and Spaniards (and is found in Mexico as a result of the Spanish conquest). Work, the daily round of labour, inspired dances; so too did courtship; and in comparatively recent times, the historical event of the Christian battle against the Saracens, manifested itself in the *morris* dance although this contains many elements from a much older tradition. The *morris* dance is arguably an ancient fertility ritual which acquired a new identity – without losing its earlier function – with the era of the Crusades. The stamping and leaping associated with the *morris* (in countries as far apart as Yugoslavia and England) refer back to rites of sympathetic magic to encourage high, that is fruitful, crops. The blacking of the face of one dancer, to identify him as the

Grenoside linked sword dance of South Yorkshire (above), a Boxing Day commemoration of earlier midwinter rituals. Six dancers with linked swords perform interweaving figures and clog steps, finally 'decapitating' their Captain to symbolize the sacrifice for the common good of the leader of the community – who then comes back to life.

Sword dance (left) in the Basque country: the leading dancer is supported by his men on the 'rose' made from their locked swords.

Moor ('morris' being a corruption of *morisco* – Moorish, moresque), was the continuation of a much earlier disguising; the use of horns, of a mock horse – the hobby-horse – and of a boy dressed up as a woman – *en travesti* – suggest ancient fertility traditions. Jack-in-the-Green, the spirit of green growth, of living, healthy vegetation, also features in some *morris* dancing. A dance in the Carpathians has been recorded in which:

'The Fool of the sword dances is completely covered in straw, like our own Jack-in-the-Green. On Shrove Tuesday he must dance with his hostess so that the year may be fertile, and then he jumps over the sword. As high as he jumps, so high will the corn grow.'[1]

Certain implicit older identities were conveniently disguised under the names of later folk heroes, such as Robin Hood and Maid Marian. A letter of 1575 refers to 'a lively Morris dance according to the ancient manner; six dancers, Maid Marian, and the Fool' and was most probably a memory of the rite associated with the death of the year, a symbolic killing of the old to encourage the appearance of new life, new crops with the new year.

The sword dances pertain to almost as antique a tradition, that of martial skill, simulated and sought, through dance display, through imitative use of weapons which prepared warriors for combat and also invoked success for them. Dances before battle can be found in Ancient Greece as in Bali. The clash of weapons, the ring of metal on metal, or the crack of wood on wood in contests with simulated weapons, recalls the noise that frightens away evil spirits. The Pyrrhic dance of Ancient Greece can be interpreted as an early stylization of this military tradition; the dance of the Curetes, with its attendant noises, as a fertility dance transformed into a warrior dance through the use of swords for noises.

But sword dances can also be seen as a reference to the battle between death and life and the rites attendant upon the end of the year and the hope of the new year at the winter solstice. In certain sword dances in northern England the adopted traditions from Scandinavian invaders can be appreciated. These involve the Fool as the sacrificial figure who ritually dies and is reborn, thus purging the community of its sins and returning with the promise of new life and a new year. The 'swords' in these dances recall the weapons of the invading Danes or Vikings; the linking of the simulated swords into a knot or 'lock' suggests a community among the participants or some secret uniting them. Various forms of sword dance have been listed in fifteen nations in Europe.[2] In Scotland, their familiar sword dance is radically different from that in northern England. Two swords are placed crossed on the ground marking out divisions in which the dancer must spring lightly and precisely, indication of a

Hoop dance performed by Basque dancers in northern Spain. Flower-decorated hoops are a commonplace of much of this type of dancing throughout Europe.

different tradition in which weapons aimed or pointed at the dancer's legs or feet were a stimulus to skill.

In the Basque regions the *ezpata danza* is a sword dance in which the male performers clash their swords and also use heavy sticks in simulated combat; at its end the dancers raise their leader above their heads in triumph. A link has been suggested between the *morris* dance and sword dances, indicating a common ancestry in the older rituals of the year's end. A tradition emerged in medieval Europe among the tradesmen's Guilds in the fifteenth and sixteenth centuries in Germany, Scandinavia and the Low Countries of skilled performance in the sword dance but the decline of the Guilds' power and ecclesiastical disfavour brought a decline in the dance's importance. As it survives today (and is taught for example in London's Royal Ballet School and delightfully displayed in that School's annual performances) the sword dance shows its participants winding in and out and interweaving in intricate patterns. The final locking of the swords in a 'rose' may also find the leader of the dance, who calls out the patterns to be followed, hoisted above his men – as in the Basque dance – as a symbol of resurrection. The sword may also be an alternative to the hoops used in some folk dances. 'In Ulm in 1551 boys danced the sword dance in the daytime and the garland dance at night. In the latter, each one had half a green hoop in his hand. And the figures were the same as the sword dance.'[3]

As for hoop dances (perpetuated for ballet-goers by the peasant dance preceding the appearance of Aurora in the first act of *The Sleeping Beauty*), they are found in Germany; there, too, the tradition of sword dances (from which hoop and garland dances seem to descend) can be traced back to the descriptions in Tacitus of a sword dance performed by the Germanic tribes-

A lively pairing of peasants from a series of French engravings, c. 1560, called Les Noces de village. *(British Museum)*

A joyous image of peasant jollification is conveyed in this detail from A Village Wedding *by Pieter Brueghel the Elder, the famous sixteenth-century artist nicknamed 'Peasant Brueghel' for his interest in village customs. The couple dance in the engraving above and the ring dance in this painting are vivid examples of the European folk dance of the time.*

men. Among the Basques there are also survivals of sword dances, short staves representing the one-time arms, which are performed in church at Corpus Christi, and the sword dance also inevitably featured in the mimic scenes which traced the conflict of Saracens and Christians in the *morescos* which were so widespread in the lands bordering the Mediterranean, in Spain, Italy and Provence.

The sword's traditional symbolic power to protect and ward off evil is seen in Turkish dances performed in front of a wedding procession to protect bride and groom from sorrow and evil. Sword dances even entered the social dance of the Renaissance. In his *Orchésographie* (1588), Arbeau describes and illustrates the dance called *matachins* which was an adaptation of an older sword dance called *bouffons* in which performers were armed with sword and shield and combined dance with pantomimic combat.

Most venerable of European folk dances and most widespread is the ring or round dance. Its origins have already been indicated; its occurrence can be found in the Balkan and Slav states and in Western Europe. A dance for both men and women, in its most primitive form it remains a linked circle, the dancers grasping each other by the hands, or as in the Yugoslav *kolo* holding arms, or shoulders, or waist belts. In some variations two circles revolve, one inside the other, and in these the sexes are sometimes separated. In others the dancers momentarily break the ring to perform individual turning movements before rejoining the circle. When the ring dance broke, it resulted in the chain dance of a single linked file like the *farandole* of Provence, or the chain dances of Norway. From the northern part of Europe there were also processional dances which in due time were adapted for court use as *entrées* (sections) for ceremonial occasions. Chains are a common factor in much Greek dancing, where the participants can sometimes be

seen linked by handkerchiefs, and this is also a characteristic of dances from Yugoslavia, from Bulgaria (the *horo*) and Romania (the *hora*).

In these the folk dance is seen in its simplest manifestation as the direct expression of happiness and the need to show joyous feeling. The round dance served, and less widely serves today, as a dance at every kind of happy occasion. The German *reigen*, the *farandole*, the Turkish women's *horan*, the *trata* performed on Easter Tuesday at Megara in Greece, the *hora* of Yemenite Jews, the old English *Sellenger's Round*, are all alike in their use of the circle and chain as the outline of the dance.

The couple dance, so usual in our society where men and women dance in each other's arms, is a relative late-comer in folk dance. Its origins, self-evidently, are found in dances of courtship, in display and imitation based on sexual attraction and sexual selection. It is possible to see the emergence of the dance for two from the line dance, itself a development from the ring or circle dance. When communities adopted the line dance there came an inevitable distinction concerning the direction of the dance – forwards and backwards rather than the repeated circling of the *carole* – and there evolved from this a matter of social distinction: who danced first, who led the dance, and from this also the idea of a couple emerging from the line to dance for the other participants. The *estampie* of Provence is the best indication of how the couple dance proceeded and with it came the implied idea of dancing towards a specific personage, the 'presence' to be honoured, the most socially important member of the group, and this was to be a central fact of Renaissance theatrical spectacle, which had as its focus a dedicatee to whom the entertainment was directed.

The couple dance, freed from the circle, assumed its identity as a dance of courtship, but it remains a relatively modern aspect of folk dance when contrasted with the antiquity of so many other dances in Europe. It would be unwise to date the couple dance's existence before the late Middle Ages and the emergence of courtly dancing in Provence. By emulation the peasantry adopted what had initially been an aristocratic form. Thus extended and enriched by new influences, the couple dance spread throughout Europe and acquired an identity as a courtship and wedding dance. The *lauterbach* of Switzerland, the Hungarian *czardas*, the Tyrolean *schuhplattler*, the Norwegian *halling*, the *jota* from Aragon, are all witness to the courtship style of dance and so, too, are the Italian *saltarello* and *tarantella* (despite this latter's attribution as a cure for the bite of the tarantula). In some couple dances, like the *bergamasco* from Bergamo, the pair emerged from a processional group to dance together before rejoining the enclosing circle of the dance. In a traditional Georgian couple dance, the *kartuli*, the chivalrous attitude of the men of Georgia towards their chosen bride

by the sixteenth century acquiring a discreditable aspect in the eyes of the Church. Lutheran principles were outraged: the *dreher* was condemned:

'scandalous, shameless swinging, throwing, turning and the allurements of the dance devils, so swiftly and at great height, just as the farmer swings his flail, that the skirts of the damsels, lasses and servant girls, sometimes fly over their girdles or even over their heads. Or they are both thrown on the floor together with many others who rush hastily and heedlessly after them, so that they all lie in a heap.'[4]

Responsible for much of the popularity of the folk dance, whether as couple dance or as group activity, was the cross-fertilization that occurred when in the seventeenth and eighteenth centuries the country dances of the English people were adapted and codified by dancing masters as *contredanses* or country dances and imported into France, whence they returned as a new dance fashion to England. It is in this way that folk dance has constantly fed the more formal social dances, irrespective of class. The examples of the Bohemian *polka* in the mid-nineteenth century and of 'square' dancing today – in which raw folk dance is translated to the city – are obvious.

Closed couple dance, sixteenth-century style, (above) is from the same village wedding series as the engraving on the opposite page; the present-day form of a czardas couple is shown (left) at a country wedding in Hungary.

is typified by elaborate rules: not even the hem of the man's coat may touch the girl.

From this initial inspiration there emerged more purely recreational dances for two. The *gavotte*, starting as a peasant dance of courtship in the Dauphiné, was elaborated as you will see later into a formal social dance for gentry and peasantry alike. The *ländler*, the Austrian peasant dance, and the similar German *dreher*, lie at the root of the *waltz* which was, by the end of the eighteenth century, to take Europe by storm. As regards the *dreher*, this couple dance was already

GREECE

Not surprisingly in a country to which everyone looks for the origins of drama in religious dance and ritual, you find a faint but persistent thread of continuity between the dances of today and those of ancient times. Everywhere throughout Greece there are local dances in villages and townships. In some regions, as in Thrace, for example, there are survivals of death and resurrection rites during carnival time. On the island

Greek folk dancers in national costume at Delphi, the scene of many festivals in ancient times. In 1951 a festival of dance and drama here included this classic example of what was originally an act of worship – the ring dance – and later a celebratory form of peasant festivity all over the world.

The 'chair' dance formed part of the celebrations at a circumcision ceremony. From an eighteenth-century Turkish miniature. (Topkapi Saray Museum, Istanbul)

of Skyros there are dances performed by a masked man in animal skins laden with sheep bells which must clash loudly as he leaps. There are, inevitably, closed ring dances: the *kleftikos* (mountain warriors' dance), the *hassapikos* (the butchers' dance), and the *syrtos*. Most popular is the *kalamatianos*, one dancer leading, waving a handkerchief and occasionally breaking away to improvise some more difficult steps. Very serious and noble are the *morolonghia*, funerary songs and dances.

These are, however, a mere handful from the extreme variety of Greek folk dance. The researches of Madame Dora Stratou into the dance of her country have resulted in performances which do much to preserve and encourage folk dance. In a programme note to a London season of her folk dance troupe there was an observation about the discovery in Crete of labyrinth dances. These were folk memories which might relate to Theseus' journey into the Cretan labyrinth and no fewer than fifteen such dances were eventually discovered, giving some indication of the possible continuity of Greek dance from Classic times.

TURKEY

Turkish dance, because of the geographical location of the Anatolian plateau, has been subject to many influences throughout history. Relics of various empires, invasions, and also the drift of Asian cultures have been absorbed into the fabric of Turkish life, sometimes through the wanderings of nomadic Turkish tribes. Yet another influence has been that of Islam, which inhibited dancing; the extent of the Turkish Empire from the fifteenth century onwards and the influence of Western industrial culture must also be taken into account. Dance in Turkey has been traced back to excavations at Catalhöyük, a site dating back to 6500–5650 BC, where wall paintings show men, probably priests, dancing to the accompaniment of drums.[5] Inevitably dance was to be associated with the religious life of Turkey; it was seen as a means of understanding the nature of the cosmos, and a fifteenth-century Turkish treatise analyses dance as a method of perceiving the divine. In a land so ancient and so central to the emergence of Western culture, there are many folk dances which embody ideas traceable to the worship of Dionysos, and the time of their performance in some cases indicates that the performers of today are aware that dances benefit the crops or the community by being 'lucky'.

Many of these dances indicate the remains of a shamanistic cult in which the priest-cum-intercessor leads a dance or impersonates an animal in masks that are relics of a more antique cult. Islam forbade men to dance with women and also decried the dance. Yet the Turkish peasantry have in some ways remained unaffected by this

influence and the folk dance of the past retained its liveliness and the mingling of the sexes. The isolation of some Turkish village life meant that many old songs and dances were kept alive, but latterly the increase of industrialization, radio, television and cinema, has weakened the hold of folk art on the people.

In the seventeenth to eighteenth centuries the Ottoman court encouraged public festivities to celebrate events, as did the European monarchies. The result was that accessions, marriages, any public event were attended by song, dance and amusements and displays of every kind, including Guild displays in which, as in Germany, dance was involved.

Two other urban dance traditions must be mentioned: that of the theatre in which the dance was at one time an essential element, and that of the dancing boys and girls. These were those thoroughly debased manifestations by 'entertainers', whose beauty was more marketable than their artistry. In the countryside, dances are to be found incorporated in the rustic rituals and farces which are still performed, and the great extent of Turkish folk dancing incorporates many traditional forms: chain dances, mimetic dances having to do with work, animals and combat – these last including sword dances. There are also dances like the celebrated *zeybek* in which the men perform in a kneeling position; others in which wooden spoons are used like castanets, and those remarkable *bar* dances in which a variety of walking, running and leaping steps are performed with light-footed grace.

ITALY

The regional dances in Italy conform to the same patterns as throughout the rest of Europe. There are sword dances at religious festivities: the

Dancing shamans or priests. These 'black' shamans wear loincloths and wave handkerchiefs which are symbolically coloured to represent the various claims of heaven and earth. From a late fourteenth- to early fifteenth-century manuscript. (Topkapi Saray Museum, Istanbul)

spadonari of Limone, or the dances at Giaglioni, Val di Susa, on St Vincent's Day. There are many such dances found throughout the length of the country, from the odd survival of a dance of flagellants in Calabria to a sword dance, the *taratata* 'one of the main features of the festival of the Invention of the Holy Cross' at Casteltermini in Sicily.[6] Both couple and courtship dances are well represented in Italy, from the *furlana* to the *trescone*, a wedding dance which is also an agricultural dance and can be traced back to the Middle Ages. Probably the best known in Italy are the *saltarello* and the *tarantella*, both courting dances, but there are also survivals of chain dances and sword dances which repeat the time-honoured ritual of hoisting a leading dancer upon the 'lock' made from the linked swords, and the simulated decapitation and resurrection of a Fool or victim. There are traces of *morescos* and of maypole dances – these last seeming to survive as an undercurrent to folk dance, their persistence a remarkable tribute to the power of folk memory even in our industrialized age.

France

The types of dance in France vary as much as do the people, from the Celtic traditions of Brittany (a region very rich in dance), to the *farandole* of Provence. In the Pays Basque the dance traditions ignore the barrier of the Pyrénées and this region

in particular has provided many steps which have been adopted and adapted by the classical academic dance. France's geographical situation means that in the east its dances will have links with those of its neighbours; in the south the spread of Mediterranean culture has inevitably meant influences from Italy as well as from the Moorish domination of Spain.

In France, too, you can find testimony to all the usual traditions of folk dance throughout the rest of Europe: maypole dances, bonfire dances, rounds, processional celebrations, and in the chapter on early religious dance there was evidence of extraordinary survivals. In *The Golden Bough* Frazer cites a dance which took place near Auxerre, where the last sheaf of the corn harvest was dressed as a puppet and formed the focus for a harvesting dance. At the end of the dance a pyre was made and girls stripped the puppet and placed it on the fire while dancing around it. He also notes how at one time in Bordeaux on the first of May the boys erected a maypole in a street and then adorned it with garlands and a great crown of foliage, and each evening for the rest of the month the young people danced and sang around the pole. In Brittany, in ring dances and chain dances, men perform with hands linked while the women dance with their hands on their hips, and as throughout much of France there are dances which involve particularly high stepping rather than leaps.

The most ebullient dancing, though, comes from the Basque country and here, in addition to the bravura of performance, there is still a very positive focusing of racial identity upon the dances. These are proudly preserved as an outward sign of Basque national feeling and there is a *casket* dance which has been performed in the Pays Basque on the Feast of St Peter without interruption for five hundred years. It is in this same region that, in a processional dance used in a pilgrimage, the leading dancer wears a facing-both-ways Janus mask.

AUSTRIA

Much of Austrian folk dance depends upon the insidious 3/4 rhythm of the *waltz* in its guise as the *ländler*. Generally supposed to have been a development from the medieval round, the *ländler* emerged as a couple dance, and in the Tyrol was developed to become the *schuhplattler*, in which the clapping of hands on knees and thighs, on shoes and lederhosen, and the emphatic accompanying foot stamps give it its well known character.

Development of the *ländler* into a 4/4 tempo occurred in Upper Austria, but it was the triple time of the original which resulted, as described elsewhere, in the infectious and undying *waltz*. Austria, as a great empire, experienced many outside influences upon its ballroom dances, the *schottische*, the *polka*, the *mazurka*, the *polonaise* all appearing both in public dances and in peasant gatherings. In the remoter regions of the Alps, folk traditions continued untouched, as in the New Catholic Dance of Salzburg, dating from post-Reformation times when the return to the older faith was celebrated with dances. Worth noting, too, are the sword and other ritual dances associated with carnival time and centred on the salt-mining areas: the men linked hilt-and-point as in so many European sword dances. In other sword dances the Fool – as in Italy – is decapitated upon the lock of linked swords, and there are attendant memories of pre-Christian rites with animal maskings. Garland dances were also celebrated in the late Middle Ages, either adopted and extended by the Guilds – the associations of tradesmen – of the time or preserved in a simpler form among the peasantry. There is also a tradition of carnival dances, the performers masked in grotesque fashion, and these Schemen processions incorporate dance and mumming and recall yet again the rituals of death and the renewal of a pagan era.

GERMANY

The extent of Germany's landmasses suggests how varied must be its folk dances, from those in the south, which repeat the dance forms of Austria to the more serious forms of the colder north. Most German folk dance is of comparatively recent date – not more than 200 years old – and relies a great deal upon variations of the *waltz* and *polka*. More ancient were the *reigen* (round) dances incorporated into Christian worship of earliest times, and these invited the eventual

The Tyrolean schuhplattler, *with its characteristic clapping of hands on knees, thighs, lederhosen and shoes, was a development of the* ländler, *whose triple time finally inspired the* waltz.

wrath of ecclesiastical authority which, as everywhere else in Europe, could not eradicate this ring dance. It is yet another example of the great trans-European chain dance, and by the time of the Minnesingers (the lyric poets of the twelfth and thirteenth centuries) the dance for the nobility had emerged as a stepped dance, while the peasants were to adopt a sprung dance form. In Germany of the Middle Ages the Guilds became influential in dance matters, adopting and extending popular forms. The coopers of Munich performed a *hoop* dance every seven years; the cutlers a *sword* dance; the drapers a *flag* dance – in each case the accoutrement of the dance was suited to the calling of the members of the Guild. The peasant dance remained simple, unaffected by the importation of foreign dances into other social milieux until the nineteenth-century craze for the *waltz* and *polka*, when these dances permeated to the lowest levels of society and the forms of dance known today became the traditional diversion of the simple peasantry. At the proper season the peasants moved round a maypole, or a Whitsun tree in the north; this tradition of dancing round trees persisted as a means of encouraging the fertility of fruit trees. On St John's Eve, as in other countries, dances with fiery brands took place round bonfires despite the Church's disapproval, and dances with work associations and animal links survived until very recently, witness a Rothenburg shepherds' dance in which the men came to town, feasted, and danced through complex patterns of movement.

BRITISH ISLES

Among the most intriguing points when considering folklore in dance is the widespread field of certain rites and dance forms. To account for the fact of the hobby-horse being found in England as well as in Greece, or of the same basic attitudes in the sword dances wherever they are performed, would be the matter for a very extensive ethnic study. In Britain, as throughout Europe, the last vestiges of the old religion persisted into the nineteenth-century folk song and dance until industrialization set about obliterating it with mills and mean streets.

It was the rescue work of Cecil Sharp at the beginning of this century which was to preserve and reconstruct many ancient English traditions in dance and song. The sword dance as part of a mumming was there, with the sacrifice of a victim and his subsequent resurrection; the *morris* dance (like the sword dance an exclusively male festivity) with its performers belled and beribboned; and the very odd Abbots Bromley horn dance, the performers wearing antlers and attended by quaintly dressed followers. In some villages the entire community seemed involved, as in the Helston furry dance; elsewhere the old round dances, maypole dances, and the country dances that had been exported and then reimported can be seen and have, like many other dances, been conserved and fostered by such organizations as the English Folk Dance and Song Society. Among the happiest preservations have been sword dances and clog dances of northern England, from Flamborough and Tyneside, and the universally popular sailor's hornpipe. The fascinating patternings which are a feature of these dances indicate a particular characteristic of the English folk dance – the variety of shapes which the dancers mark out on the floor.

(It was Dame Ninette de Valois who had the foresight to incorporate the teaching of folk dance in the curriculum of London's Royal Ballet School. For its enrichment of the Royal Ballet's repertory you need only refer to Ashton's *La Fille mal gardée*.)

For many observers, of course, the most fascinating dancing in the British Isles is to be found in Scotland and the most brilliant of this is to be found among the Highland clans. In their dances you see the polish that was to be brought to natural dance forms by a close contact with the royal court in Scotland (dating back to the time of the return of Mary Queen of Scots from France) and this is a style which was later jealously guarded and further developed by the determination of the Highlanders to preserve their social customs in the face of English law in the eighteenth century. Nowadays Highland dancing with its nimble footwork – best seen in the dances performed between the quarterings of crossed swords – is universally admired and presented world wide by communities of Scots who find in their dances a method of asserting a racial identity. This of course is an observation true of many immigrant groups: in the United States the dances of an 'old country' acquire a renewed lease of life when they are preserved among people who, though entirely American, retain emotional links with their land of origin.

In the more generally performed social dances of the Scottish people, reels and dances to strathspeys (slow dance tunes) are the favourite forms. They call for proud carriage as the dancers weave through the patternings of the sets. Though basically folk dances, reels, strathspeys and their like have retained an authentic life. They have never needed to be 'rescued' in a conscious act of preservation; like some dances in Spain, they remain an absolutely natural manifestation of the social life of the Scots at all levels of society.

In Ireland as in Scotland the performance of a dance calls upon great nimbleness. An Irish jig, as the word implies, demands high skill in footwork although the arms and trunk are held rigid. In Ireland there are traces of the ancient rites of fire worship in folk dances which survived into the eighteenth century, and these may even be identified in the *rince fada* (a longways dance) which is one of the forms of the Irish reel. In this, as in the jig, the continued vitality of this dance tradition can be noted in *ceilidhes* and dance gatherings of all kinds.

SPAIN

A more detailed study of folk dance in Spain is given here since there is arguably no other European country wherein the dance of the people retains such freshness and validity. It is not a conscious re-creation, a deliberate and slightly nostalgic attempt to return to a simpler way of life; nor is it, as with so much Eastern European dance, a politicized attempt to gloss over the harsher realities of twentieth-century living. In Spain, the dance retains its 'real' voice as an expression of popular feeling. Dance, at a village fiesta or as part of a family celebration, is still authentically an aspect of a people's temperament. And dance in Spain has ever been part of the life of the people.

During the period of the Roman Empire, Spain was celebrated in the Mediterranean world for the dancing of its people, and the dancing girls from Cadiz excited the greatest admiration among the Roman audiences. In the golden age of Spanish literature during the seventeenth century, dances were an integral part of dramatic performances, but it is the extreme richness of the folklore of Spain which must merit the consideration of anyone interested in dance. Regional dances are as different in manner and in accent as the dialects of Spain itself. They are distinct, and it is one of the tragedies of the theatre that so many audiences consider flamenco, the art of the Spanish gypsy, as the only acceptable manifestation. This is far from the truth. The range of Spanish dance encompasses the brilliant *jotas* of the north, the *seguidillas* from the centre and west, the *sardanas* of the east and the *fandangos* of Andalucia, the southernmost region, as well as the staccato footwork of the *zapateado*.

The *jota* is known by Spaniards as the 'father of Spanish dances'. It is most associated with Aragon and Navarre where its origins, however imprecise, are thought to lie, but something very like it is danced throughout the whole of Spain. It is a lively dance and the further north the more vivacious is its manner of performance. It was once thought, like the *tarantella* of Naples, to be possessed of curative properties and, like that Italian dance, it involves rapid and brilliant footwork. It also involves high, springing steps for the men which become slightly less airy for the women and it requires extreme flexibility of knees, ankles and thighs in order to perform its kneeling steps as well as its jumps.

The *seguidillas* is the chief and dominant dance in La Mancha and Estramadura, Old and New Castile. Like so many other Spanish dances it is performed with an accompaniment of guitar and castanets and like the *jota* it has permeated the entire peninsula. The best known of its variants is the *sevillanas* from Seville. Danced in heeled shoes (the *jota* is danced in rope-soled shoes), the *sevillanas* is distinguished by the beauty and elegance of the movements of arms, shoulders and trunk. Deeper into Andalucia the regional dance becomes the *fandango*. It is danced to the accompaniment of guitar and castanets and like the *seguidillas* it reflects the mood and the metre of an accompanying song. The *fandango* is fast, and can sometimes become furious with its percussive element of heel taps, known as *taconeo*, which combine with rhythm of the castanets. In the *fandango*, the movement can be seen to be more *à terre* when compared with the *jota*: just as the *jota* slows down the further south it goes, so does the dance itself retain a greater contact with the earth. Part of the charm and beauty of the *fandango* depends upon the use made by its female performers of their colourful skirts and the bending and swaying of torso and arms is sometimes stressed when the feet are still for a moment.

Very different, is the *sardana*, the most important dance of Catalonia. This coastal region of Spain was at one time under Greek occupation and relics of Attic culture remain in the dances which preserve the traditions of the ring dance. There are also survivals of older forms of dancing associated with the nobility, and the bows and salutations exchanged before a dance begins can be seen as traces of the historical relationship between this part of Spain and the courts of Provence.

The *sardana* has preserved a social identity which may be best seen when a group of dancers weave through the streets of a village, an expression of the collective spirit of the place. It has also a markedly individual accompaniment of pipes, drums and occasionally the cornemuse, a rustic bagpipe. In some cities the *sardana* is danced on festive occasions when, with the link-

ing of many people in the ring dance, it seems a fascinating survival of the medieval *branle* (described in detail in the chapter on Social Dance).

Another circle dance from the north, found in the province of the Asturias, is the *danza prima*, solemn, slow and ordered. Also from the Asturias is the ancient, serpentine *pericote de llanes*.

In the decade of the 1940s there was a conscious attempt to rescue and preserve folk dances of this kind which might otherwise have been forgotten or finally and utterly corrupted. The task was undertaken by an amateur organization, the Seccion Femina, which sought out, classified and encouraged folk dance in remote villages as in the main centres of dance. There resulted a tremendous harvest of dance and song, stimulated by competitions to invite local interest and even rivalry, with displays and national rallies which were extremely important amateur folklore festivals. From this enterprise there emerged a troupe which, in the early 1950s, showed much of the richness of true folkloric dance and music to a delighted public throughout Europe. The Coros y Danzas company were dedicated amateurs and their programmes showed such fascinating survivals as the Basque *suleitanas*, danced at carnival time, where men formed a circle and then advanced with a group of girls to fill a wine glass and then leap on the glass without spilling a drop. No less fascinating is a *bal de cavalet* from Catalonia performed by dancers on hobby-horses, carrying swords, recalling the Arab invasion of Spain. Most rewardingly the Coros y Danzas company stressed the double nature of Spanish dance: its regional manifestations covered both popular forms like the *jota* and *sevillana* and also dance rituals, primitive in form, which were intimately linked with the religious life of the people. These involved dances at shrines on festival days or on pilgrimages; dances in church after Mass; maypole dances; and strange survivals from a remoter religious past preserved in the further regions of Spain by the very isolation of the community who performed them. Primitivism of expression kept something authentically mystic about these dances and they also reflected the Spanish respect for the past. There is a very curious dance from the Asturias, the *corri corri*, which represented a king choosing his bride from a group of maidens who advance in single file upon this male dancer, beating their sides with olive branches to indicate their virginity, eyes downcast, and moving in a single repeated step, while the king sizes them up, and eventually makes his choice.

Even more antique is the *baile de Ibio* from the mountains of Old Castile, in which a group of warriors chose their leader. To the accompaniment of that most ancient of instruments, the conch shell, the men circle and form lines, bearing lances which they hold head-high and then lock into a wheel shape upon which the new leader is hoisted; this chain dance, a memory of a war dance, is an extraordinary survival.

In eastern Spain, the chief dance is the *jota* from Aragon, always identified with that region but known throughout most of the rest of Spain. It may be a derivation from the *fandango* of Andalucia, but it has, in Aragon, gained in speed and sheer bounce of execution and it allows considerable freedom of expression to its executants. It is still a dance of the people which is capable of development: its lively and stirring steps encourage performers even today to elaborate and embroider upon its form.

A ring dance for the unmarried, performed round an open fire in a courtyard at Santillana-del-mar in northern Spain.

*Antonio and Rosario
were the pre-eminent
ambassadors of the
Spanish dance. These
cousins made their debut
at the age of seven in
1928 – hence their
nickname 'The Kids from
Seville' – and for twenty-
five years danced together
superbly all over the
world. Antonio, who was
also a choreographer,
was acknowledged as the
supreme Spanish dancer
of his time.
This photograph, taken
in the countryside outside
Barcelona, shows them in
a flamenco dance in the
early 1950s before their
partnership broke up.
The taut pose of
Antonio's body and the
flare of Rosario's skirts
are typical of the passion
of the flamenco style.*

In the province of Catalonia there are dances in which the difference between the sexes is highlighted by the bold, leaping steps for the men and the simplicity and decorum of the women's dances, but throughout the province the dance style is in general more refined and delicate than elsewhere in Spain. Most important of all the dances of this region is the *sardana*, a chain dance. Even older is its companion the *contrapas*, an open chain dance which suggests religious antecedents. It is important, indeed, to stress the religious significance of Spanish dance. In some, the old traditions of pre-Christian worship have been submerged and glossed over as they have elsewhere in Europe. Yet, as elsewhere, certain physical attitudes serve as reminders of an older faith. Rain magic is hinted at in a dance in which church wardens throw jars of perfume onto the church roof where they break; fertility rituals are traceable in dances in which the men place ring-like cakes on the arms of young girls; a survival of bonfires dances, bell dances, and sword and stick dances are similar memories of the past. In the preservation of *moriscas* (*morescos*) the defeat of the Moorish infidels by Christian forces is still remembered.

In the North of Spain, in Galicia, the ancient dances are a reminder of Celtic ancestry and they even share some of the stylistic attitudes that can be seen in Scottish dances, but this is also the area in which the Basque dance is to be found. These Basque dances are celebrated for their virtuosity. They demand most brilliant footwork from men and women alike, and are characterized by high, leaping steps for the men and, of course, the *pas de basque* which remains in the academic ballet technique as a reminder of the debt which classic dancing owes to folk dance. In such virile displays as the *aurresku*, the element of showing off acquires great virtuosity as the bridegroom dances for his bride. Most famous of all in this region is the *zortziko* which, it is said, any true Basque can dance in his sleep. (It is a dance in 5/8 time intended as a ceremonial dance for men.) Most popular though of all the Basque dances is the *fandango*, a couple dance of both charm and brilliance.

Some indication of the range and variety of Spanish dance may be gained from the two lists published in 1950 of 'Occasions when dancing may be seen', with the postscript that: 'a church calendar is needed in Spain. Every saint's day is celebrated somewhere, every village has its own patronal saint with a fiesta on that day'.[7] An extraordinary variety of dance festivities are listed, from the men's sash dance outside the church at Malda, Catalonia on 2 January, right through the year until the festival of Nuestra Señora del Pilar in Zaragoza on 12 October. (Whatever the changes that have been brought by the intervening three decades, tradition still holds true and Spanish dance reveals something essential about the spiritual and temperamental life of Spain.)

Carmen Amaya (1913–1963) was the greatest Spanish gypsy dancer of her generation. An electrifying performer, she was the incarnation of the storming energy and the vast temperament of flamenco at its best. She made her debut at the age of four, dancing in waterfront bars in Barcelona. The company which she eventually founded was a family affair and in it Amaya blazed gloriously. Her greatness lay not only in her phenomenal bravura but also in the honesty and authenticity of her dancing.

It is, however, unfortunate that for many observers 'Spanish' dancing means predominantly that found in Andalucia, the southernmost region of Spain. The peninsula encompasses fascinating folk dance in the north and the centre of its mass, but it is nevertheless the dancing that reflects seven centuries of Moorish domination of the south that is the most thrilling and picturesque. The Moorish influence which permeated through the whole of Spain and reached into Provence, affected every aspect of the learning and the arts of the people as well as their political and social life. In dancing it brought a sinuosity of torso and a use of hands and fingers that suggest an almost oriental delicacy and subtlety; this sense is also conveyed by the rhythmic vitality of hand claps and heel taps and an expressive use of the eyes. These and the curves of arms and body all speak of a style far different from the usual run of folk dance throughout Europe. In the dance of Andalucia, too, the

dominance of the female performer is directly counter to that of most other European folk traditions. The stylized attitudes of the man, very drawn up, the body curved, an image taut and proud, offer a direct sexual contrast and complement to the flamboyant and brilliant display of the woman. The stylization of many of these Andalucian dances for theatrical performance, and the elaboration brought to them by the great Spanish dancers – Antonio and Rosario, Carmen Amaya and Pilar Lopez, as well as their illustrious precursors Argentina, Argentinita and Vincente Escudero – have accentuated and sharpened the image of Spanish dance without corrupting it.

The dance in Andalucia can be divided into three categories: flamenco, *classico españo*, and folk. Flamenco has its origins in the folk dance of the region around Cadiz. The arrival of gypsy tribes who made their way south through Catalonia, living a poor and nomadic life and eventually settling in the far south of the peninsula, meant that they absorbed the musical and rhythmic qualities of the native Andalucian tradition, embellishing them with their own gifts for vivid, physical and vocal expression. The result was the *cante flamenco* (flamenco in fact means 'Flemish' and refers to the Spanish conquest of the Netherlands in the sixteenth century when any foreigner was considered a Fleming).

Originally the gypsies preserved their dance and music very jealously in the caves and encampments of Andalucia, essentially grave and often sad. Gradually dance and music emerged from the tribal life of the gypsies into the towns, manifesting itself in cafés devoted solely to this form of music and dance during the late nineteenth and early twentieth centuries. It became recognized as a musical and dance form of extreme emotional intensity (musically it has two predominant forms: *cante chico*, flamenco proper, which is more cheerful than the *cante grande* or *cante hondo*, the deep and more tragic song). One of its strengths, an attribute which has kept it extraordinarily alive, is that within a given framework it relies upon improvisation. The flamenco troupe, the Cuadro Flamenco, comprises singers, dancers, guitarists and *jaleadores* who clap the rhythm. At its best it has an inspirational, self-intoxicating intensity; the performers are driven on by the commitment of their colleagues and their own deepening involvement with the feeling, the 'soul' of the dance or the music. Thus, within the stylistic framework of the form itself their temperament is freed, and the living quality of flamenco, which is not a set and arid form but a constantly evolving manner, is clearly to be enjoyed. In the best flamenco performances, despite a tendency to self-parody which results from public demand, it is possible to appreciate the historical components. These include the happy *alegrias* from Cadiz, the buoyant *fandango* from Huelva and, most popular of all, the *sevillanas* – all of which pre-date the gypsy involvement with Andalucian dance but which have been transformed by the gypsy temperament. At its worst, alas, flamenco has become a cheap tourist attraction in which vulgarity erases every other merit.

The classic Spanish style, *classico espaňo*, is a development and a stylization of elements of both folk and flamenco dancing codified in dance schools and destined for theatrical performance. The theatrical style has polished popular dance and it offers a contrast to the spontaneity and vitality of Spanish folk dancing.

It is most generally seen nowadays as part of the programmes offered by Spanish dance troupes. It is a style of dancing which approximates to the classical ballet in its lightness and elegance. Today it has a theatrical life in the offerings of major Spanish companies; historically it can be seen in the *boleros* and the dances of the gentry of the eighteenth century. Probably its most celebrated example remains the *cachucha*, which is so intimately associated with Fanny Elssler, but in many of the ballets of the Romantic age the great stars of the period like Marie-Guy Stéphan and Marie Taglioni were also attracted to this style of dancing, as is described in the chapter on the early history of ballet.

CENTRAL AND EASTERN EUROPE

It has been the policy of the Soviet Union to encourage the performance and the preservation of the folk song and dance of its varied peoples. With its hundred and eighty different national groups, boasting some three thousand dances, there have been immense opportunities for collectors and producers like Igor Moiseyev to find material suited to more than local performance. The various state folk dance troupes – of which the Moiseyev ensemble is the best known – have done much to explore the riches of folk art and preserve them, albeit it in a theatricalized form.

The vast extent of the Soviet Union, the no less vast difference between the folk dance of Estonia in the west and Azerbaijan and Uzbekistan in the south east, suggest two poles of extreme difference. From the Caucasus and from Dagestan in particular there are dances highly expressive of the men's virility: leaping dances to see which youth can jump the highest; acrobatic dances (from the village of Zovkra); serene, typically gliding dances for the women from the Kumik area; and, supremely, the *lezginka*. This is the

Ukrainian dancers in a gopak, showing one of the characteristically high leaps which are now part of the theatricalization of folk dance as presented by Soviet folk dance companies.

In this Polish ring dance (above), and the couple dance (right) you see the raw material that inspired the national dances so beloved of the nineteenth-century ballet masters. The delightful young people in these photographs could be transferred quite happily to a production of Coppélia.

most celebrated and most stylish dance of the region. At one time a war-like display, often performed by dancing between fixed daggers, it is nowadays better known in its theatrical form, appearing in the ballroom scene in Glinka's *Ivan Susanin (A Life for the Tsar)* and Khachaturian's *Gayane* and known to ballet-goers from performances by Nijinsky and Balanchine.

In Georgia the dances are the portrait of a proud and independent race. The people's history of struggle against invading Turks, Persians, Mongols is reflected in the war-like *khorumi* for the men and in the *parikaoba* duet for two men who challenge each other to single combat. This is the best known manifestation of the men's style, with its sharp, brilliant dances upon the very points of the toes, intermingled with fast rotating turns on the knee (padding of toes and knees is evident in theatrical performance but does not detract from the extreme skill of the men). With Georgian women the dance is often sinuously gliding and markedly oriental in influence. In the mainland mass of Russia itself the dance can emcompass the extremes of the Moldavian *hora* (a slow round for women) and the *jhok*, an impetuous dance for men and women; the *gopak* from the Ukraine, one of the most virtuosic show dances for men with its leaps, cobbler's steps and jumps over one leg; Uzbek *platter* dances in which the tradition of balancing an earthenware dish on the head after a meal is celebrated, and women's dances in which lilting steps are accompanied by the waving of handkerchiefs which also serve to link them in a chain. Mention has already been made of the *khorovod*, the circular dance usually associated with women in Russia. When the Bolshoy Ballet from Moscow first came to London, among its most enjoyable offerings was a group of dances from Glinka's *Ivan Susanin*. Here the *polonaise* and *krakoviak* were presented with such style and authority, such

grandeur of carriage, that their identity as nineteenth-century ballroom dances for the aristocracy was clearly evident (Gautier in his *Russian Journal* of 1866, records how court balls in St Petersburg always began with a *polonaise* in which the Tsar opened the dance by leading out a lady by the hand, with the other dancers gradually joining in behind him). It is odd, then, that these were in essence folk dances of a people subject to Russia's domination. They were, and remain, among the finest of Poland's dances.

But, like the *mazurka*, another of Poland's dances, they had been aggrandized for court and social, rather than folk, use and they had also entered the theatre. The *mazurka* was originally recorded as being danced in the sixteenth century. Thereafter its dignity, its heel clicks and its turning step (the *holubiek*) earned it a favoured place in the theatre and in the ballroom, where its melodic vivacity, the charm of its strong second beat, won it much favour during the second part of the nineteenth century. Its companion the *krakoviak* (Frenchified as the *cracovienne*), a dance in 2/4 time, and the *polonaise* (a processional dance in 3/4 time) were also found in the

Bulgarian dancers; a group of girls (below), skirts swirling, perform effectively in an open-air setting. As in so many Eastern European countries, the post-war years have seen a determined effort at preserving and perpetuating the dances of the people.

theatre. Fanny Elssler made a sensation dancing a *cracovienne* in *La Gipsy* in 1839, and Lucile Grahn and Jules Perrot were much admired in a *mazurka d'extase* in *Eoline* in 1845; these dances were inevitably to find their way into the nineteenth-century ballroom.

They remained, though, as popular dances among the Polish people, together with the *kujawiak* (a *waltz*-like dance having intriguing rhythmic changes), the vigorous *oberek* and a version of the *polka*. Other, less well-known dances, abound in Poland, a country in which the natural elegance and physical bravura of the dancers is reflected in the rich variety of the dance itself. Such regional dances as those from Zywiec in the south, and the mountain dances from the Tatra, are especially graceful to watch.

No less popular in the theatre, and no less well known is Hungary's great dance the *czardas*. Beloved of ballet audiences from its appearances in *Swan Lake* and *Coppélia* and the last act of *Raymonda* (which is in essence a Hungarian divertissement), the *czardas* like other Hungarian folk dances admits of much improvisation by its performers upon the basic 2/4 or 4/4

Bottle dance, as performed at Hungarian peasant weddings, when the cooks take pride of place with their carefully balanced bottles.

A group of Romanian men opening out into an active line dance, similar to many of those found throughout Eastern Europe.

rhythm and the fundamental steps. There is also in Hungary, as in other parts of Eastern Europe, a tradition of gypsy music and gypsy dancing in which indigenous folklore attitudes have been extended or altered by gypsy temperament.

During the sixteenth and seventeenth centuries a sword dance, the *hadjutanc*, was very popular in Hungary. Performers wheeled and intertwined and today it survives, as do so often sword dances, as a stick dance. Another stick dance, the *botolo*, was a couple dance suggesting man's power over a woman. In the eighteenth century there emerged a very curious dance, the *verbunkos*. It originated as a recruiting dance at a time when men were needed for the French wars. A recruiting commission would arrive in a village and the prospective soldiers were encouraged to dance in a circle around a corporal or a sergeant. Drinking and merrymaking would go on for several days until a sufficient number of men had been recruited. The dance became more stylized

in the 1830s, and a form emerged for the ball-room, and was also to be traceable in the music of the period. For peasant weddings an elaborate ritual was prescribed which led up to the wedding ceremony itself. Dance was an essential part of the events: a dance was held round the newly-weds' bed; bride and groom were conducted from their homes to the accompaniment of dancing. The manner will seem familiar to any-one who has seen Nijinska's *Les Noces*; in that great Russian ballet the life of a people and the ancient peasant traditions attendant upon mar-riage are as clearly present as they are in these Hungarian survivals.

In Hungary you can see many of the customary dance forms of Europe that have already been described: bonfire leaping on St John's Eve; maypole dances; minstrel performances at the time of the winter solstice; and work and celebratory dances associated with weaving, harvesting and the vintage.

In Romania you find dances such as the *hora*, the ring dance, and couple dances from Moldavia like the one named the 'oil cloth' which boasts great rhythmic vivacity, many leaping steps and claims an ancestry of over two thousand years back to Dacian and Thracian origins. It is in Romania that you can also find the presence of the hobby-horse in folk dancing. It is a reminder most probably of some ancient horse worship by nomadic tribesmen, or a piece of sympathetic magic having to do with the need for pasturing. Whatever the inspiration, the hobby-horse is to be found in folk dance and ritual in Romania as in Greece, in England, Spain, Poland and in Bulgaria; associated with good luck, it is sometimes, as in Cracow in Poland, a reminder of victory over an invading force by local cavaliers.

The pre-eminent Yugoslav dance is also a ring dance opening out into a line, the *kolo*, and it is performed throughout the country. Other dances

reflect the troubled history of invasions and occupations which have so marked the territory of what is now Yugoslavia. Near-eastern influences can be seen in a gypsy dance entitled *duj duj*, as also in the dances preserved in the small town of Vranje in the south of Serbia. In the north, wedding dances find unmarried men showing off in the Banat region by dancing around a knife stuck in the ground or with a bottle on their heads, or jumping over sticks

while the girls look on demurely. In Dalmatia there is a tradition of silent dances whose only accompaniment is the noise of the dancers' feet; such is the ring dance from Vrlika, and the *silent glamotch*. The historical basis of folk dance, the response of a people to some political cataclysm, or indeed to some great triumph, may also be seen in the *komitas* from Macedonia, a hill people's dance which is a reminder of their resistance to the Turkish domination of this area.

Romanian couple dance, with the women in national costume. The style of dancing has not changed much over the last four hundred years – as can be seen by comparing today's folk couple with the sixteenth-century French one shown on page 49.

CHAPTER FOUR

EASTERN DANCE

The classic, fundamental image of the Indian dance is that seen in this bronze from South India dating from the Chola period (888–1267). It shows Shiva in his manifestation as Nataraja, Lord of the Dance, dancing on the head of a demon.
The ancient legend has it that in this dance the world was shaken into chaos. Shiva represents Creation, Preservation and Destruction, and these three processes are implicit in his dance. His arms, which can number from four to eighteen, carry the symbols of the various attributes of his divinity, which are also to be read in the poses of arms and legs. Here he carries a small drum which represents the rhythm of creation, and a fire representing destruction. His right foot being raised suggests release, while his left foot is placed on the dwarf demon to symbolize evil overcome. The positions of his two free hands convey the ideas 'fear not' and 'for I am here'.

DESPITE THE Eastern influences during this century upon Western dancing in such differing styles as those of Martha Graham and Maurice Béjart, there is a world of difference between Eastern and Western dance. It is a difference which is not merely technical but more essentially spiritual. In many countries of the Orient the dance has retained those links with religious faith that were at one time the mainspring of Western dance, but which have now long since vanished. In the East the dance still reflects the spiritual attitudes of its cultures, and to understand Eastern dance you must forever remember this vitally important inspirational aspect: it speaks of the belief of millions as only the ritual of the Mass can do in the West. In many Eastern cultures – in that of Japan for example – the stage assumes a symbolic aspect; it represents the world, and it is an area upon which the dance may be used to invoke the beneficent influences of heaven. Thus, too, the performer will often acquire spiritual merit in certain Eastern countries because he becomes a vessel through which certain moral truths are communicated to the public. In some dances the performer seeks to suggest the idea of a divine being, hovering over the earth and expressing great love for it. (One authority has declared that 'The main idea of Oriental dance is found in the Japanese word *asobi* which means play, and comes from the idea of the play of the gods.')[1]

It is also necessary to the understanding of Oriental dance to see how the divine is an essential feature in the dance-dramas performed. From India eastwards the play of gods and demons found in the *Ramayana* and the *Mahabharata* forms the central core upon which many of the popular entertainments are based. In performance the audience will see dance actors impersonating gods and demons; in Javanese performances you sense more clearly than at any

other time the moral force and spiritual dignity which can inform the interpretations of certain dancers when they assume these divine roles. In the ultra-civilized art of the Japanese *Noh* it is impossible not to sense the elevation of spirit which breathes in every gesture and action of the Shite artist who has only attained roles of this stature after great intellectual and emotional searchings.

If the impulse behind much of the Oriental dance differs from that of the Occident – given that there is always a need to dance as an expression of feeling that transcends barriers of race or geography – then the technical form of the dance is also vastly different. At its highest, in ballet, Western dancing aims at the denial of gravity, at a refinement of the body's attitudes in an athletic style which seeks a purely aesthetic idealization of the human form, as you see in the insistence upon 'pointe' work for women or the elongation of the body in its linear outlines. The dance of the Orient asserts the importance of gravity. Feet may stamp or paw the ground, but contact with the earth is a constant of much Eastern dance. The stylized use of the torso and head and arms, the neck movements of Indian dance, the exquisite gesture of arms and fingers in Balinese dance, suggest a sophistication of style very different from that in the West. The exceptional subtleties of rhythm and movement found in the East must inevitably escape most Western observers but the virtuosity involved is, in its way, as great as that of any ballerina, and the emotional effects produced by the slightest movement can seem astounding within the context of a dance. (Take, for instance, a battle scene performed by Javanese court dancers in which the movement of a single finger by a female warrior is as thrilling and theatrically potent as Odile's thirty-two *fouettés* in *Swan Lake*.) At its most refined – in a Noh drama or a Kathakali dance play – the

aesthetic of the East becomes diametrically opposed to all the rules of ballet, yet its results are as beautiful and as theatrically powerful.

The setting in which Oriental dance takes place, the forces involved, are also totally different from those of Western dance: you have but to think of the numbers involved in a Western spectacle such as *Union Jack* or *Mayerling*, and compare them with the isolated performer of Noh, or the handful of characters needed to tell the vast drama of the *Ramayana*, to see how great the division, how different the aims, and how distinct the physical attitudes.

In this chapter some of the characteristics of dance in the Orient are described in an eastward progression from India, with its vivid dramatic dance traditions of the *Mahabharata* and the *Ramayana*, and the other dance styles of the sub-continent, along the road of their cultural expansion through Burma and Thailand and across Indonesia to reach Japan where a very different dance tradition exists.

INDIA

The classic theatrical dances of the Indian sub-continent form one whole. They are born out of the religious and spiritual experience of the people, and this they may be said to retain; the dance is an essential aspect and manifestation of the continuing vitality and richness of the people's religious life. Shiva, the central and most powerful figure in the Hindu trinity, is, as Nataraja, the Lord of the Dance. (A comparison can be made here with the Gnostic view of Jesus as the divine dancer and with the early Christian belief in the angelic dance.) Shiva is the incarnation of the

masculine dance – *tandava*; his consort Parvati is the representative of the feminine, lyric element – *lasya*. Legend has it that Shiva created heaven and earth when he performed his Dance of Creation.

The earliest Hindu religious book on dance, drama and music is variously dated between the second century BC and the third century AD, and it is to be understood as a sacred text for performers – the *Natya Shastra of Bharati*. There was no differentiation in it between the three performing arts; all were one in this original form of danced religious opera.

Indian classic dance contains three components: *natya*, *nritta* and *nritya*. *Natya* represents the dramatic quality; *nritta* is the rhythmic aspect of dance; *nritya* has to do with the expressive possibilities, the conveying of *rasa* (sentiment) and *bhava* (mood) through facial expression and bodily gesture. Although *nritta* may be seen as a 'pure' dance, *natya* and *nritya* are concerned with the exposition of ideas, feelings, themes, and to do this they use *abhinaya*, the 'carrying to the audience' – an idea of communication which uses four separate but interlinked and interdependent techniques in performances. These are *angik*, *vachik*, *aharya* and *satvik*. These four techniques have been categorized by their components: *angik* contains gestures of the body; *vachik* involves poetry, song, recitation, music and rhythm; *aharya* covers costume, make-up and jewellery, and *satvik* is the physical manifestation of mental and emotional states.[2]

In the *Natya Shastra* there is an analysis of gesture used in *angik abhinaya*. It includes thirteen gestures of the head, thirty-six glances, seven movements of the eyeballs, nine of the eyelids, seven for the eyebrows, six each for nose, cheeks, lower lip, seven for the chin, nine for the neck, sixty-seven hand gestures (*hastas*) – twenty-four for one hand, thirteen for both hands, and thirty *nritta hastas* (pure dance hand gestures). These last are only used in dancing while the others are used in drama. There are three movements for the belly, five each for the chest, waist, sides, calves, thighs and feet. There are also thirty-two *charis*, movements of one foot with calf and thigh. There are four ideal postures of the body which cover a distance from central balance. In all there are one hundred and eight *karanas*, units of movement including posture and gesture by hand and foot; all these may be seen carved on the four gateways of the great temple of Chidambaram in South India.

The other components of *abhinaya* are no less well detailed and considered: tempi in performance of various feelings; use and ritualistic ideas of costume; the command of the body's abilities to express feeling, to simulate, and actually produce, certain physical manifestations by control of mind over body.

Originally the teaching of dance was a sacred responsibility. Gurus (holy men) passed their lore on to pupils who, in their turn, became

Two female performers in a Kathak dance (left), detail from a Mogul painting of the late seventeenth or early eighteenth century. The elegance and refinement of this style during its greatest historical period are beautifully demonstrated here. (Victoria and Albert Museum, London)

Kathakali dancers (right). The one on the left is Shiva disguised as a huntsman. For this role – as a forest demon or aboriginal hunter – his beard and dress are black and he wears a special head-dress. The male dancer on the right is en travesti because Kathakali is thought to be unsuitable and too demanding for female performers.

Two dancing girls entertain Akbar the Great, the renowned Mogul Emperor who did so much to encourage Mogul culture. Detail from a late sixteenth-century Mogul painting of the Akbar school. (Victoria and Albert Museum, London)

theme unfolded through the rhythmic sequence of the music and the aid of *abhinaya* and the *mudras*, the symbolic hand gestures. At the base of Indian dance is also the *rasa* or mood of the dance, and nine *rasas* cover the emotional gamut of the Indian dance.

One of the great Indian dancers of this century, Ram Gopal, listed the nine moods as follows: *shringara*, the erotic; *rudra*, the furious; *veera*, the heroic; *vibhasa*, the disgusting; *hasya*, the comic; *karuna*, the pathetic; *adhuta*, the marvellous; *bhayanaka*, the terrible; *shanta*, the meditative.[3] There are five chief sub-divisions of the Indian dance: Dasi Attam (Bharata Natyam); Kuchipudi; Kathakali; Kathak and Manipuri.

Dasi Attam (Bharata Natyam)

This is the temple dance of South India. Deriving its name from the solo dances of the girls – Devadasis – who were dedicated to the service of the gods in the temples, it has latterly been known as Bharata Natyam (a dance following the principles of Bharata) in an attempt to get away from the moral stigma attaching to the Devadasis who combined temple dancing with sexual availability. It is a dance style demanding great virtuosity, its poses often evoking the sculptures of the temple in which it evolved; its practitioners (always women) are required to deploy a very open and beautifully linear manner. A Bharata Natyam recital or dance sequence includes dances which offer praise to various deities through the interpretation of poems (*padas*) which detail the performer's love for the god or the emotions inspired by human love. The dancer interprets the nature of such love in a slow exposition of the text of a *pada*, in which various attributes of the beloved and the varied feelings of the lover, are shown. In the *varnam*, expressive and 'abstract' dance are combined; there follows the joyous *tillana*, a brilliant and virtuoso dance, and the display ends with a calm postlude.

Kuchipudi

Dating from the seventeenth century when a prince was impressed by a village drama performance, Kuchipudi takes its name from the village of its origin and is a dance-drama recounting tales of the gods chosen from the Hindu epics of the *Ramayana* and the *Mahabharata*. Performed only at night by the light of flickering flares, Kuchipudi dance-dramas owe something to Kathakali but are performed by men of Brahmin or priestly caste.

Kathakali

A form of dance-drama indigenous to Malabar, where it originated in the sixteenth century, Kathakali marked a fusion of the ancient cultures associated with the Aryans and Dravidians,

teachers, and this might have led to some unity of dance forms throughout the entire subcontinent. But with the spread of dance lore and due to the vastness of the country, regional changes evolved which were encouraged by historical development. In South India, temple dancers were girls dedicated to the service of the gods, their style feminine and beguiling and suited to solo performance in temple and at court. In the south-west, dance became warrior-like and masculine. In the north, it was a cultivated and elegant art. In the north-east it emerged as something more delicate and gentle. By the end of the nineteenth century much Indian dancing had been thought dishonourable and vulgar, the province of prostitutes. Only through the advocacy of certain devotees and aesthetes has it been re-established in this century, seen not only as respectable, but highly honoured as an aspect of India's illustrious past.

Thus the essential nature of Hindu dance has been reasserted, an insight into its qualities being gained from a study of those antique South Indian statues representing Shiva in his Dance of Creation, Preservation and Destruction. In these statues the god is represented within an arch of fire, the *torana*, poised in hierarchic pose, the lines of his body, the dignity and beauty of his appearance and facial expression, indicating the sublime nature of his dance and its religious significance. This is the central image of Indian dance. 'The movement of Shiva's body is the world', but there are other divinities – Krishna the Blue God, Vishnu, Ganesha, Indra and Arjuna, and the goddesses Parvati, Kali, Sarasvati, Mohini, Lakshmi and Urvashi – no less identified with the divine dance. Indian dances all have a

and combines the *chakkyar* dance of the Aryans – a religious ritual illustrating a Sanskrit text – with martial dances of the Dravidian warrior caste and elements from other Dravidian rituals. Its title combines the two words for dance and play, and it developed under royal patronage. Its narratives are of gods and heroes, demons and warriors, who enact the great epics of South India in a manner at once simple in appearance and infinitely complex in style. Interpreted exclusively by men, Kathakali is intended to last all night and to be seen by torchlight. At the start drums, gongs and cymbals crash as two attendants hold up a vast, colourful silk curtain. Behind it is glimpsed a haloed head-dress and the stamp of belled feet is heard. Silver-clawed hands tear at the curtain and suddenly the Kathakali dance actors are revealed in all their glory. This preface is called the *thiranokku* – the curtain glance, which prepares you for the ensuing action. The characters appear, many of them wearing head-dresses combining mitres and vast haloes, the face beneath fringed with a rice paste frill and painted in a thick impasto of red and green and white. The colour used is an indication of the nature of the character; green or *paccha*, signifies a character refined and serene; green make-up broken by red stripes, fangs and white nose bobbles signifies demons; black faces, red beards and white moustaches show raging tempers. The body is clothed in a gold jacket and a crinoline of short skirts. The eyes flash blood-red. The belled feet beat out a simple step while the hands entwine and interweave in infinitely subtle movements. All this is the introduction which grips the attention and prepares the audience for the leisurely statement of long, complex dramas. In all Kathakali drama there is a vivid admixture of comic incident with passages of straight exposition and moments of bloodthirsty and terrifying menace. Pace is less important than richness of narrative or dramatic effect. The exchange of *mudras*, the flickering and exquisite language of hand gesture, demands a great deal of study from the performers (as does every aspect of their art, from make-up to vocal exercise) and from the audience as well. Kathakali drama is an amalgam of everything from low comedy to the noblest expression of man's relationship with the divine. Beneath the elaborate stylization of language and appearance you can appreciate powerful human emotion, and in this lies one of the secrets of a dance-drama which has preserved much of its historic immediacy; the situations exposed, the relationships implied, are still relevant to the faith of the people who watch and who perform. Two great epic sagas are favourites of the Kathakali drama, the religious narratives of the *Mahabharata* and the *Ramayana*. The telling of the tales is left to vocalists, who play gong and cymbals, while the accompanying drumming is crucial to the entire drama. The actor-dancers mime and dance their roles, with wicked characters sometimes screaming and yowling.

Kathak

This dance, based in North India and Pakistan, has an ancient style which originated with the itinerant bards – Kathaks – who imparted religious and moral instruction through their

Kathak dancers from the Punjab performing the chukras, *brilliant whipped turns – the best-known feature of the Kathak style, which combines Hindu and Muslim elements.*

story-telling. The addition of music and mimetic narrative and dance, account for the emergence of the form which is also unique in its combining of Hindu and Muslim elements. The style experienced a golden age in the sixteenth century at the time of Akbar the Great, its speed and grace and its embracing of non-religious themes bringing it to great prominence. At that time its refinement of manner was very considerable, but it later declined through its association with female performers of low morals. Fortunately the style received patronage from the princely courts in Lucknow and Jaipur, where the protection of the Rajah meant that Kathak dance was rescued from the opprobrium which had become attached to it. Today it is preserved as a notably subtle and virtuoso form of dance. In particular, its performers are trained and encouraged in the art of repeating a line of a poem and illustrating it at several reprises with embroideries and differences of emotional accent which serve to illustrate its meaning and further to expand that meaning.

Manipuri

In North East India, in the city of Manipur, the people – the Meities – have been somewhat isolated historically and geographically. Their art is central to their being, and their dance expresses something essential about the people. It is a style of floating, deliquescent grace for women, who are not supposed to indicate in their dance that their legs are moving. After a period during the eighteenth century when the dance flourished in Manipur, the arrival of British rule in the 1890s drove it into a few temples where it was preserved, still reflecting the people's religious faith in the worship of the god Vishnu. At the beginning of this century it was revived, due to the efforts of Rabindranath Tagore, who encouraged it as physical exercise for boys, and then for girls, at his cultural centre, Santiniketan, some distance from Calcutta. Today the style

is widely practised and its extreme fluidity of manner, the grace required to perform it, mark it as one of the most beautiful and harmonious of Indian dance forms.

Odissi

Lower down the east coast of India, in the region of Orissa, one of the oldest Indian styles is found, that of Odissi. The dance traditions there centred round the temples which date from the second century BC, and there is evidence to suggest that from the ninth century AD there has been a continuous tradition of temple dancing by girls and boys. Inevitably this style fell into disarray and disrepute as did so much other Indian dance. It has been carefully revived of latter years and now forms yet another strand in the rich fabric of the dance of the sub-continent. In origin, Odissi was often sensuous because of its relationship to the idea of love expressed in the poems addressed by the worshipper to Krishna, and even today Odissi dance is fundamentally an act of worship.

Bengal

Among the hill people of western Bengal a dance form has been preserved for over two hundred years, but not until the 1960s did it become known as anything other than a secret folk art. The Chhau dancers also turned for their themes to the *Ramayana* and the *Mahabharata*, but unlike the sophisticated Kathakali performers, these Bengali artists are urgent but simple in dance manner. There is none of the rich, facial decoration or complex *mudras* of Kathakali. Instead, the dancing of these warrior folk is made up of simple, leaping steps and percussive beating and stamping of the feet. But the characters in the drama wear superlatively decorated masks and

head-dresses – trembling creations of feathers and silver thread, like the crown of a Manchu empress. The costumes are no less sensational, glittering and splendid with gold and sequins. The masks serve to depersonalize the dancers and to dignify them, yet an innocence of manner shows through in the limited range of movement with its leaps and turns. A vocalist announces the scene, a rustic oboe plays, and five drummers sustain a rhythmic basis for the dance. The message of each scene is clear since the performers present the dramatic incidents with a noble simplicity exemplified by the masks and head-dresses and by the dignity or malevolence of their poses. Krishna appears, blue-faced and exquisite; a wear god rides a peacock and spreads a lustrous train of feathers; an evil demon enters, black-faced and hung about with death's heads. It is an art unspoiled, rich and beautiful.

BURMA

Burmese dance and music (below). Owing to the elaborate costumes in court performances, the dance tended towards stylized posture rather than lively movement, in contrast to the more vivacious courtly entertainments.
This detail from a Burmese manuscript of the nineteenth century provides a still apposite view. (Musée Guimet, Paris)

The Chinese poet Po Chu-i (AD 772–846) describes in a poem the visit of a group of Burmese dancers to the Chinese court:

At first blast of the jewelled shell their matted
    locks grew crisp
At one blow of the copper gong, their
    painted limbs leap
Pearl streams glitter as they twist, as though
    the stars are shaken in the sky
Flowery crowns nod and whirl with the
    motion of dragon or snake.

The Burmese dance, like that of so many countries close to the sub-continent, reflects the influence of India. But the natural aptitude of the Burmese people, their innate love of dance and music, meant that a lively national tradition already existed before this external influence was absorbed into their dance life around AD 300. As with so many nations, ritual dance was part of a cultural tradition already existing. What Indian dance gave was a codification of movement based upon the rules of the *Natya Shastra* which, subjected to the Burmese style and temperament, gradually evolved into a dance form entirely Burmese in identity. There are reportedly some two thousand physical components in the Burmese dance, based on thirteen movements of the head, twenty-eight eye movements, nine neck poses, twenty-four single hand positions, twenty-three movements of both hands, thirty-eight leg movements, five acrobatic poses, ten ways of walking and eight turning movements of the body. The absorption of external influences in dance and music appears to have been completed by the eleventh century AD, at which time the Burmese dance style is considered to have become truly national, with even the Hindu epics of the *Mahabharata* and the *Ramayana* acquiring an authentic national expression.

In court performances there was insistence upon both pure dance and upon dramatic recitation combining speech, song and dance to

Makuta dance. A group of graceful Burmese dancers (above) performs in front of a temple. This dance takes its name from the word for a golden and jewelled crown – makuta.

There exists a very close relationship between the music and movement of Burmese dance. The Burmese orchestra is a thing of glory. Percussionists are seated within golden pens, surrounded by a battery of gongs and drums whose visual beauty is no less ravishing than the sonorities they produce. The other instruments are woodwinds of various kinds. The placing of the dance within a musical phrase seems easily perceptible to Western ears and eyes, with the musicians taking their time and lead from the principal drummer, and passing melody and rhythm from one to another in a kind of 'jam session'. The dance manner today appears a mixture of styles culled from India and Thailand (Siam), its vocabulary having a neat, acrobatic charm. The appeal of the dance is immediate. The virtuosity of the artists is impressive, male dancers often providing intriguing parallels with the Western classical dance vocabulary. There are little jumps and turns, *pas de chat*, miniscule attitudes and poses which recall photographs of Nijinsky in his *Danse siamoise*. The whole atmosphere is happy; the dancers smile; their performance is devoted to the exposition of movement which affords them and their public aesthetic pleasure. In most Burmese dance the range of emotion is restricted to serene or joyous feelings. The costuming is extraordinarily pretty with much gold, silver and sequins for the men, and trailing skirts and delicate stuffs for the women.

In certain parts of Upper Burma in the Shan province, a tougher, more mountainous terrain has inspired dances concerned with fighting and with animals, and in parts of Burma there still exists a tradition of trance-dancing, and spirit dancing and exorcism rituals which are also used for divination.

THAILAND (SIAM)

Most interesting in the Siamese theatre is the dance-drama of *khon*. It is the oldest of the native forms of theatre and it contains many reminders of the once-strong connections which existed between Thailand and India, these being reflected in performance traditions similar to those of Kathakali. The performers are male; there is an accompanying narrative from an attendant vocalist; gestural language recalls the *mudras* of Indian dance; the tales all come from the *Mahabharata* and the *Ramayana*. But unlike Kathakali it is an art of the palace, of the aristocracy. The accompaniment is provided by an orchestra, and the costuming reflects a more eastward tradition of gold and silver fabrics, embroidery and paillettes, with curving epaulettes and gleaming mitre-like head-dresses.

There is also a theatrical dance form exclusively for women. This is *lakon*, whose libretti come from both legendary and historical sources. The

recount the dramas of Buddhist mythology and other heroic tales. From the court these dramatic presentations, called *zat*, moved into the countryside as simple entertainments for the people where, set in a circle on the ground ringed by bullock carts and lit by oil torches, they were known as *myay waing* (ground encircled). These possessed a liveliness and directness of expression very different from the stylized and ritualized court dance which, because of the elaborate beauty of the dancers' costuming, insisted upon posture rather than movement, on grace and distinction rather than vivacity or litheness.

Linked to the dance traditions of Burma is its unique theatrical form, the marionette theatre. Burmese marionettes are not toys, nor approximations of human figures, but idealizations and abstractions of characters, and by means of the most skilled manipulation their movements were informed with totally human quality. By inference, Burmese dancers were in turn set standards for movement by the marionettes which they had to try and emulate in performance. The movement of dances in the marionette style is still modelled upon the actions of the wooden figures worked by famous manipulators. By seeking to copy the marionette movement the dancers are set tasks requiring extreme physical skill and muscular discipline.

Thai male dancers in Bangkok (below) in resplendent costumes with ornate masks, decorated sashes and matched borders at knee and ankle.

Traditional Thai dance with a 'lotus room' setting (opposite, below). Note the extreme flexibility of the woman's arms and hands, emphasized by her masked partner's attitude.

style is feminine, slow, delicate, full of sinuosities, and again reflecting many of the traditions of Indian dance. The purer dance forms are those relating to exercises performed by warriors. Two preliminary dances have to be mastered before students can proceed further.[4] These comprise an 'alphabet dance' which is in essence a summation of the nineteen basic movements that students learn, and which are displayed in seamless flow of action: the other is a 'dance of fast and slow' which is thought to educate the body for polite social intercourse. From these preliminaries the dancers then move on to the solos which are the remains of a traditional art in

which there is much use of such accessories as fans and fabric in a slow-paced idiom.

KAMPUCHEA (CAMBODIA)

While there was still a monarchy in Cambodia, a troupe of palace dancers was maintained, comprising beautiful young girls who were trained at a school located in the royal palace. Because of their youth their bodies were still supple and it

Nine Apsarases, dancing divinities (left), on a bas-relief from a Bayon-style Cambodian temple frieze. The sinuous style, with its double-jointed hand gestures, depicted in this Khmer sculpture is true to Cambodian dance even today. (Musée Guimet, Paris)

was easier to achieve the extraordinary flexibility required in this curious palace art. The outline of the dance, its fluid and sinuous style, required hands, elbows and fingers to bend in unexpected and what must seem physically impossible angles, this last achieved by forcing fingers and elbows to become double-jointed. The style was somewhat effete, but its charm resided in the prettiness and delicacy of the performers. The themes were taken from the Hindu epics and the overriding influence came from Thailand. Costuming was, as always in the East, magnificent, with much use of real jewels and gold.

JAVA

The crown of the dance as it has survived in Java is in the troupe of court dancers attendant upon the Sultan of Jogjakarta. These, like the Gagaku of Japan, represent the most special artistry, one intimately linked with the *persona* of the monarch and with the identity of the monarchy. In Jogjakarta the dances partake of court ritual and one – a war dance dating from the eighteenth century (a *lawoeng*) and devised by an eighteenth-century Sultan – is so important that if the present Sultan is prevented from attending a reception, the dance itself becomes the embodiment of his presence, the dancers proceeding under the gold umbrella which is reserved exclusively for the royal personage.

The dances as performed by the royal troupe are of the most splendid dignity and beauty. Their nature as an apanage of the monarchy is illustrated by the fact that, on a visit to Britain, the troupe included three members of the royal family who appeared as performers. The role of a princess was taken by a princess – thus, in the twentieth century, art and life were united.

The traditions and dance language of the troupe owe something to the conquest of Java by Hindu princes in the seventh century. The Indian influence persists both in the use of Hindu epic religious themes – those of the *Mahabharata* and the *Ramayana*, for example – and in the adaptation of *mudras* into the texture of the dance. But these have been transformed by

national temperament and by the exigencies of court performance into an art of extreme formal beauty and integrity. The refinement of their expression owes something also to the fact that the training for certain roles can be lengthy – eighteen years – and the performers dedicate themselves to the interpretation of only one kind of role.

It is an art that may seem, on paper, to be remote and improbably refined. In performance it is not so. The accompaniment is provided by a gamelan orchestra, whose ravishing sonorities of bells and gongs sound from a platform behind the area reserved for the dancers. The range of the dances, even in the severely restricted excerpts that have been abstracted from much longer dance-dramas for Western consumption, is extraordinary. Extraordinary, too, are the nobility and grace of style of the women dancers. A group of nine girls, in a dance surviving from the seventeenth century, impersonate warriors, their movement indicating the special quality of feminine style: sinuous, very slow and with hand movements of enormous subtlety in which even a quivering of the fourth finger becomes exciting and vital within the texture of the dance. Impelled by the ringing of gongs and clatter of drums, the women draw daggers and fight in a combat infinitely deliberate in gesture, with slow thrusts and parries that have such implicit strength and ferocity that Western stage fights look positively demure by comparison. The male dance is much bigger and bolder in outline, but the sense of ritualistic power behind movement is ever present.

A fragment from the *Mahabharata* presents the Vishnu in battle with red- and blue-masked giants, whose hideous aspects do not prevent them from being roundly defeated. In this most rarefied art form, a great interpreter will, in the dance of the Orient, penetrate deep into both the character and the spiritual world which that character represents. Assaulted by capering giants (the conflict between comic and spiritually distinguished impersonations does not destroy any dramatic mood, rather it enhances it), the gesture and stance of Vishnu speak of divine serenity. The giants make assaults, trying to nip the god in the thigh; with elegant flicks of his robe, or by a hand raised in a gesture of enormous power to repel the giants, the dancer reveals how profound is his mastery of his art, achieved after years of study, both physical and psychic.

The themes of the dances speak of love and war; of a sultan awaiting his beloved and, elegantly comic, painting his face, then realizing the maquillage has gone far too far and consequently abandoning his projected meeting; two lovers giving powerful eroticism to their duet through deliberation, slowness and the exquisite appositeness of two curved hands meeting. In a battle between two girls who enter upon giant birds, dismount and fight, by the very slowness

of the tempo every cut and thrust is made infinitely dangerous.

The Javanese dancers who have visited the West do not give the impression that they are offering a stale re-creation, a nostalgic exercise, but rather a living and still relevant tradition. Beneath the gorgeous costumes, the continuing significance of the dance is felt by the performers and communicated to the audience. It is in this aspect, especially, that the Eastern dance and also the African dance can be seen as a true expression of a people's spiritual and social life. In the West the dance fever of disco, and other spontaneous explosions of social dance, are vital because they engage the active participation of part of a community. The *spectator* aspect of ballet and modern dance, even in the dutiful restoration of folk dance for performance, is an indication of an alienation between dancer and public that goes far deeper than the conventions of the Western theatre.

BALI

Dancing and music in Bali are as much part of native life as the air which is breathed and the food which is eaten. Towns and villages (and often every *banjar*, or ward, in them) will each support their own music club, gamelan orchestra and dancers in a spirit of lively rivalry. The performers are not professionals, nor are they paid for their services. They play or dance both for pleasure and because the community must have dancing and music – as it must have sowing and reaping and cooking.

'It is a living force, this dancing of Bali, which is capable of embracing new musical rhythms, new dance interpretations and, provided the basic rules of technique and form are kept, extemporary improvisations. It is a whole theatre of drama – heroic, romantic, farcical – and expresses, in artistic terms, the emotional range of an emotional people. In some forms it is a religious rite. At times of the periodic festivals, or when sickness or misfortune threaten, all the villagers go to the temple and evoke the forces of light against the forces of evil by means of the dance. Dancing in Bali is less a specialist art than a community activity, although the community treasures the special skill of its individual artists.'[5]

Of all the Balinese dances, the ravishingly costumed *legong* is probably the best known because it is the most visually enticing in its use of the child performer. It is thought to have developed from temple dancing, and like all the dances of Balinese women, it is richly feminine in manner with its flickering accents, its speed and its vivacity. Although it still retains some traces and overtones of drama, these have become

This Javanese dancer, performing for a prince, shows the clear influence of Indian dancing. Detail from one of the famous relief sculptures dating from the eighth century AD on the terrace walls of the great Buddhist temple at Borobudur, Java. These illustrate Buddhist texts and scenes from everyday life.

Balinese trance dance, the choral ketjak *(above), in which the men who are seated in circles within circles sway and call out, culminating in a mass frenzy.*

Barong dance of Bali (right), where a benign monster (barong), performed by two men joined by their costume, fights an evil female monster. It combines dance with prayer for the propitiation of evil spirits.

very much refined and abstracted and the stylization of this fundamental element has been increased by the extreme youth of the performers. With their bodies encased in brilliantly-coloured and gilded fabrics, their heads adorned with fan-shaped or mitred head-dresses, sometimes carrying fans, the little girls glide and step sideways; their necks and shoulders rippling, their hands flashing through gestures, their fans appearing like the wings of the birds and butterflies whom they impersonate in their dancing. Accompanying all the dances is the marvellous clangour of the Balinese gamelan orchestra, a combination of bells and metal xylophones whose sonorities have captivated Western ears.

The chief male dance in Bali is the *baris*, whose origin is uncertain but which is generally thought to have been a dance for warriors to raise their courage and concentrate their attention upon some forthcoming struggle. It is a ritualistic dance, not uncommon elsewhere in the East, but refined in Bali to an extreme degree, and its title refers to the files of soldiers on their way to battle. There are many different forms of *baris*: as a group dance its performers carry weapons, but it has also developed into a solo exhibition and it can incorporate certain elements taken from the battle narrations found in the *Ramayana* and the *Mahabharata*.

The *kebyar* gives some indication of the Balinese passion for dance. It is the invention of the foremost Balinese dancer of this century, Mario. It is a solo performed seated, the legs tucked under the body so that they provide a kind of springboard for the torso's movement. The dancer's body is bound in the habitual swathe of gold fabric, the performer is armed

with a fan, and the dance is in essence a further reflection of the extremely complex relationship existing between the Balinese dancer and the music of the gamelan. A piece of fabric hangs loose from the wrapping around the upper torso and this is manipulated as part of the dance. Movement can be fast, brilliant, inspired by the music to frenzy, or it can be calm. It forms a display of virtuosity in which the body, the arms, the fan, and the fabric express a variety of moods, highlighted by the play of gesture and facial expression.

That Balinese dance is rooted in the people's religious feeling, of which it is a natural and vivid expression, is seen in the *barong* which combines prayer and the exorcism of evil influences with the formal language of pure dance. The religious life of the Balinese is much concerned with his relationship with his ancestors, with his gods and with the spirits of his forebears; by admitting his fear in the face of the unknown he finds one of the chief inspirations for dance. The propitiation of the unknown, of evil spirits, the warding off of sickness and the avoiding of misfortune, informs the dance; in this way the fears are exteriorized and allayed. The *barong* is a benign monster, who fights the evil female monster, the *rangda*. To make the *barong*, two performers are joined under a fantastic costume to impersonate a particularly terrifying aspect of the beast.

From ritual dramas there develops a tradition of dramas, the characters variously and tremendously masked, with performances partaking more of religious drama than dance display.

The religious life is also manifest in the *wayang wong* whose themes come also from the Hindu epics. Unlike similar productions in Java, where it is a court dance performance, the Balinese *wayang wong* remains of the people, a simple and more direct village presentation owing much to that other famous form of theatre, the puppet play, wherein decorative leather puppets are manipulated as the protagonists of ancient religious drama.

A different form of dance-play is the *topeng* which recounts historical incident. It is again a masked art in which the historical dependence of Bali upon Java (of which it was once a province) remains a motive force for the action. Gloriously costumed and masked, the dancers' movements reflect as clearly as does their dress, the dramatic nature of the characters.

One of the most mysterious of the Balinese dances is the choral *ketjak*, a trance-dance for men. Seated in circles within circles, in the court of a temple, they sway, call out, and are gradually overtaken by a mass frenzy which, for all that it may be carefully planned, still retains spontaneity as the men react to themes chanted by a reciter or mime from the Hindu epics.

These descriptions give the merest outlines on which some Balinese dancing is based.[6] The extreme variety and wealth of the dance art of the Balinese people and its integration into their life at every level, explains why Bali is called 'an island of dancers'.

CHINA

In a culture as supremely civilized as that of ancient China, dance was considered part of the music and ritual of the court, and it was the moral aspect of these combined arts which concerned the earliest commentators. The *Lei Chi*, the classic Confucian book of rites, which deals with the minutiae of court behaviour, indicates that the music – dance and deportment included – had the nature of an expression through the body of moral law and its influence for good. It was 'to guard against men's tendencies to evil' and, as in certain Renaissance *ballets de cour*, movement to music was understood as a visible expression of an invisible law, as a method of attracting benign celestial influences and as a form of sympathetic worship. Of the nature of the dances themselves and their integration into court ritual, there are indications that they were slow, dignified and dependent upon pattern rather than step, as opposed to the livelier manner of regional folk dance which even in the fifth century BC was thought to be 'immoral' because the vivacity of movement could 'trouble the spirit' rather than soothe and order its actions. Politically the court dances were thus seen as a means of promoting the orderly ideals of good government (it is intriguing to note that under

Chairman Mao the ideas implicit in the performance of such ballets as *The Red Detachment of Women* or *The White Haired Girl* could also be thought to be political).

The continuation of court ritual, and with it court dance, from these ancient times is indicated in later records – both internal and of Western observers – but the Confucian ideals of order and inner tranquility must have become debased. There were in the China of the T'ang (AD 618–907) and Sung (AD 960–1279) dynasties professional performers, whose appearance can be traced in the poetry of the time. These dancing girls and court concubines were urged to emulate the orderly motions of court ritual, but their art was certainly less high in its aspirations as dance, and the prettiness of the girl dancers was an overriding criterion.

One of the rare indications about the earliest and uniquely Chinese dances has to do with the use of a long sleeve (known as the 'water sleeve') as a technical and expressive side to dance. In the period of the late Chou dynasty – the fourth century BC – a poem tells of rows of eight dancers, their sleeves:

> Rise like crossed bamboo stems,
> Then they bring
> Them shimmering downwards.

It appears that the use of sleeves was part of shamanistic worship, and it is possible to compare this use with dervish dancing of ten centuries later in Asia Minor, when the long sleeves of the dervish robes formed part of their ecstatic dance rituals. Sleeve dancing was widespread in China, and is recorded in a tomb painting in Korea dating from the fifth century AD. But the best-known evidence of sleeve dancing is in the figurines produced during the T'ang dynasty, showing female dancers tossing their sleeves in movement so graceful, for all that it is caught in a single pose.[7]

Classic Chinese texts suggest that young men of the Imperial families were all instructed in dancing as part of their education from the time of the Chou dynasty in 1000 BC, and commentaries dating from the sixteenth century AD give details of intriguingly similar ceremonial movement.

Yet despite the influence of Chinese ritual dance on the emergence of Gagaku in Japan (described later on in this chapter) it must be noted that China is not historically a nation in which dance was of any real importance. From the Sung dynasty onwards there are few records of dancing except for occasional references to folk performance which existed in the vastnesses of the empire. By the T'ang dynasty much dance had been proscribed as foreign to the ideal of Chinese womanhood – which was subservient, tottering, demure and anti-dance. In the view of the ministers and the intellectuals who made up the administration of Imperial China, dance was, apart from its peripheral influence upon court ritual, the merest entertainment, at best charming but minor, at worst vulgar and inflaming to the

The legong (opposite) is an essential image of the Balinese dance, with the young girl advancing, one hand holding out the gorgeous fabric of her costume while the other is extended in a fluttering gesture.

The sleeve dance formed part of shamanistic worship in China. This graceful figurine dates from the T'ang dynasty (AD 618–907). (British Museum)

Group of Chinese dancers rehearsing for The Red Detachment of Women, *a revolutionary work which was much performed during the years of the Cultural Revolution (1965–1969)*

Two artists appearing in The Monkey King, *one of the traditional Peking operas which are the staple of the Chinese classical theatre.*

passions. Further, the idea of binding the feet to produce those preposterous lotus-buds would inhibit any woman from dancing.

China's civilization was directed more towards theatre than to the dance. The nearest approach to dance in the traditional and beautiful Peking Opera is a refinement of gesture and the acrobatic feats, part of an acrobatic heritage which has for long existed in China. In the prodigious abilities of these acrobats you can even today note some traces of old folk rituals and dances.

The most radical and considerable development in the dance history of China must be seen to be the implanting of ballet in the artistic life of the country following the Communist Revolution in 1950. This was first encouraged by the friendship with the Soviet Union after the end of the Second World War, when Russian ballet training and the Russian repertory were introduced into the country. The decline in Sino-Soviet relations brought about the emergence of a more strongly nationalistic and politicized style of ballet typified by *The East is Red* of 1964.

'[This is] a portrayal of the long years of revolutionary struggle, and to accomplish its purpose three thousand performers took part. The opening scene set the tempo for the entire show. In it, about one hundred dancing girls garbed in sunny yellow costumes were arranged on the stage to form giant sunflowers. On the backdrop of the stage was a giant red sun, toward which the living sunflowers turned on the stage, forming a strikingly beautiful picture. The audience was not treated to a pure feast of the eyes, however, for the Chinese accompany their ballet with verses, if necessary or useful for teaching the desired lesson. Singers proclaim in their lyrics that "the sunflower seeks the rays of the sun; the people's hearts turn towards the Communist Party". In subsequent pageants that occupied many hours, scenes from the revolutionary past were depicted, where the . . . Long March and the perfidy of American aggressors were pictured with appropriate glory or opprobrium'.[8]

Since the fall from power of the Gang of Four in 1976, performances of more traditional ballet and the fostering of traditional dance training have been resumed. In most of the major cities of China, dance groups today preserve local traditions of folk dance.

KOREA

The dance in Korea reflects the historical and strategic importance of the country. The peninsula, in the heart of the Far East, forms a link, a bridge, between North Asia and the rest of the world; consequently the country has suffered invasions from north and south – often as a

passage between projected invasions of Japan and Japanese incursions into mainland Asia. This geographical vantage point has meant that over the centuries there has also been a mingling of cultures and the transmission through Korea itself of Chinese art and philosophy to Japan. (The adaptation of Chinese and Korean dance and music during the sixth and seventh centuries AD is responsible, as will be indicated, for the emergence of Gagaku in Japan.)

The earliest clear records of Korean dance can be dated back to the third century. Then, in a tribal society, dance was – as in so many other societies – an essential factor of religious worship and of the nature cult that surrounded the planting and harvesting of crops. Other strains which were absorbed into an emergent folk-dance language were from warrior dances, the aim of which was the instilling of martial frenzy before battle, and the ritual dancing associated with Buddhist worship or shaman cults. There later emerged a form of masked dance-drama, in which music, drama and dance were closely combined, and work dances which reflected the life of the peasantry. In the shamanistic or witch-doctor cults there were also dances associated with female shaman (or *mudang*) which reflected that priestess's identity as an intermediary between the people and their gods.

In the period of the Koryo dynasty (AD 936–1392) Buddhism, as the state religion, introduced masked dance forms that had originated in Central Asia. The influence of Confucianism was to be observed in the establishment of court dances of extreme dignity and elegance during this same period and in the succeeding Yi dynasty (1392–1910). Today there are dances recreated in the style of the mask dances of the fourteenth and fifteenth centuries which recall the satiric intent of such a style: farmers and tradesmen danced them then to mock the corruption and hypocrisy of the court and of the Buddhist priesthood.

Of recent years a conscious attempt has been made in both North and South Korea to preserve and revivify the ancient traditions of the country's dance. A point of departure was the survival of dances which were performed as entertainments at banquets and dinners among the nobility and wealthy merchant classes; these provided a basis for the folk dances which have been so carefully revived. Two elements are thereby protected: the ancient, traditional forms which include the surviving priestly dances, sometimes performed with a drum (which in some modern reconstructions stress the conflict between the monk or nun's awareness of Buddhist principles and the calls of the flesh), and folk dances which hark back in inspiration, if not in step, to the work dances of the peasants.

Among the other traditional forms, now revived, are those serene and graceful court dances which recall court entertainments of dynastic times. (It is worth noting that the name

Korean fan dance. The beguiling grace and charm of these dancers are typical of the appeal of the Korean troupes which tour the world.

by which Korea is known to its own people is *Choson* which means 'the land of the morning calm.') Mask dances survive and also a ring dance performed by women which, on one occasion in the sixteenth century, was given on the seashore so as to deceive an invading Japanese fleet into thinking that warriors were massing to repel the expected attack. (The subterfuge succeeded.) Today the tradition of female shamans and soothsayers has been prettified into fan dances of ingratiating charm and sweetness: their effects, as traditionally in Korean dance, depend upon the movement of the head and upper torso – the leg movements have always been less important, which can be attributed to the long skirts worn by the women of Korea.

JAPAN

The legend which is supposed to lie at the very source of the art provides an insight into an essential element of Japanese dancing. The tale tells of Ame No Uzume's dancing upon a wooden tub in front of a cave in which Amaterasu the sun goddess had taken refuge, and it is this concentration upon a limited space (suggested in the myth by the area of the wooden tub and found in actuality in the space of the *tatami* mat on which some liturgical dance still takes place) that indicates the exceptional focusing of effects which is central to Japanese dance.

In addition to the spiritual qualities implicit in Japanese dance – as in so much Oriental dance – there is the quality known as *okisa* which implies a strength or expansiveness, not of form or of physique or of the area covered by the dance,

but of the force acquired by the reduction of the dancer's efforts through concentration and restriction. (It is an idea which can also be sensed in the dramatic unities of Greek drama where passion and action are compressed within the narrow confines of prescribed time, space and theme.) *Okisa* conveys the need to plumb the depths of expression and it requires an elaborate and careful preparation on the part of the performer in his approach to gesture. Thus an audience is required to understand the value of the stillness which precedes a movement and also the length of time in performance given to gestural movement, so heightening its effect. The result is ideally a fluidity in movement which also brings great potency of image. All this can only be achieved by very considerable intellectual and spiritual awareness of the guiding idea which lies behind the aesthetic of the dance: as in so many Eastern cultures the dancer is ideally not merely an entertainer but someone whose performances are an exercise of spiritual as well as physical abilities.

But even though gesture is carefully prepared it does not exist as an isolated moment. It is the continuity of Japanese dance – its onward flow, rhythmic variety and physical and spiritual energy that is very important. This aspect is implicit in the Japanese word *ma*, which suggests the spatial and temporal links between one movement and the next – and this is not a void but a living concept. This can be understood in Western terms through Balanchine's realization of Stravinsky's scores. Both these masters of ballet make positive use of the space between the notes of a score, establishing the living and vital nature of an interval.

Any other comparisons between Western ballet and Japanese dance are those of extreme opposites. You can see in the work of Martha Graham and other pioneers of contemporary dance the awareness of gravity, of the earth itself, as a force of attraction. But Western ballet has ever sought the rejection of gravity and flight into the air. To achieve this it has called upon young and beautiful bodies, free-soaring, and the result has been that the Western dancer must ideally contemplate retirement by the age of forty. The Japanese dance adopts a stance which in effect stresses a close relationship with the ground. With gliding steps, and hips pressed downwards, it is a dance which reasserts man's identification with the earth from which he sprang and an acknowledgment, through this compression of imagery, of the pull of gravity.

Further, as in so many Oriental cultures, age enhances the dancer's abilities rather than constraining them. *Okina* – the old man's dance – is considered one of the most difficult and one of the most typical in its beauty of Japanese dances. The development of spiritual awareness among Japanese dancers reflects the progress of a man towards death, and the psychological training, the purification and deepening of mental attitudes

At a shrine at Nara, two female dancers (above) perform a traditional folk dance.

Japanese folk dance today (right): the vitality and rough energy implied in these performances is very different from the refinement of Japanese theatrical dance.

Detail from an eighteenth-century Japanese print (left) showing two female entertainers holding kotsuzumi – small hand drums. (Musée Guimet, Paris)

timing of gesture and movement comes as the fruit of long preparation. It can be equated with the idea of rubato in Western music, that rhythmic stretching within a given time space and musical phrase which yet maintains a forward pulse, and whose effects must be controlled through a wide appreciation of the rhythm of what is being performed.

Kabuki

There are two basic styles of dance in Japan. The first embraces religious and ritualistic dances, the court dance and the dances of the Noh drama. The second is concerned with Kabuki drama, deriving from rustic dances and the popular dances of folk and religious festivals. Kabuki refines these by adapting them for the stage, and as a more popular form (both in its appeal and in its emergence from a people's art) also adopts elements from Noh, from naturalistic gesture and from the popular dance. Those elements which have been taken over from the severely beautiful and ancient Noh plays are called *mai*. The popular style taken from folk art is called *odori*. The realistic mime movements and gestures which have been introduced from daily life are called *furi*.

are considered as important as any gaining of physical skill.

As was once true in the West, Japanese dance at its most intense, partakes of ritual and the performance of certain dances demands fasting and purification of the body in order to prepare the interpreter spiritually as well as physically.

In essence the Japanese dance requires that sublime simplicity which can only be attained after long years of experience and of soul-searching. It comments thus upon the tragedy of Western ballet where, as an artist ages and becomes wiser and better able to comprehend the art he or she serves, the body refuses to perform the sheerly mechanical aspects of technique. Because the Japanese dance is more spiritual than technical, the increased age of a performer can only bring increased greatness. Thus, as the years go by, the Japanese dancer becomes richer in understanding, more expressive, truer. There are great artists in the Japanese dance who are in their sixties and who by the grand simplicity of their movement, and by the exceptional concentration of their presence, convince totally and, indeed, achieve effects of spiritual communication with an audience unattainable by Western performers.

A great Kabuki actor said: 'There are no difficult theories in dance. One must simply create a pleasant atmosphere by moving gracefully with the rhythm of the music as the heart dictates. This is the essence of dance.'[9] This observation suggests also the vital importance of individual artistry and depth of spiritual perceptions. For the great Japanese dancer the appreciation of the

Kabuki developed from this more popular type of theatrical performance taking place at the Royal Palace in Kyoto. Detail from a screen dating from the later years of the Muromachi period (1336–1568)

As throughout most of the rest of the world, music is the fundamental element of the Japanese dance. Most Kabuki drama has an accompaniment from the *shamisen* (a three-stringed fiddle) and vocal music. Extra accompaniment is provided by a group of musicians placed behind the stage. The result is a musical style more brilliant and more appealing than the Noh's austere accompaniment of flute and percussion.

In contrast to the dance in the theatre, *shosagoto*, there is a *su odori*, a dance performed at a recital or a banquet by a performer not in costume but wearing a simple black kimono. In this style the dance may be merely celebratory, or it can be an adaptation of a stage dance. It is essential to remember that Kabuki is a living art and that its dance cannot be either hidebound or unwilling to develop, albeit it respects the past traditions of its style.

Ceremonial dances were first evolved by Shinto priests whose purpose, as throughout the whole spectrum of religious dance world-wide, was to indicate the divine presence, to suggest the divine nature, and to stimulate the feelings and ideas of the believers. The first dancers were called *miko*, and they were priestesses of the Shinto faith. It was felt that their dances could – as in so many civilizations – summon up the divine presence and bring peace to the souls of the dead. The dance also became a form of divine possession. These religious dances are called Kagura and they evolve from the idea of the mythic dance which beguiled the sun goddess from the cave where she was hiding and thus brought her back to illuminate the world. Herein is the basis of the Kagura style which lies at the root of all Japanese dance. The *miko* dances still performed today in the Imperial court and in temples, show the influence of Bugaku, those court dances which were imported from the Asian mainland in the seventh century. In some remote part of Japan, traces of shamanism remain in Kagura dance, but the originator of Kabuki was a wandering priestess called Okuni, who had at one time served at a shrine, and there is still a traceable link between Kabuki dance and the ancient forms of Kagura. The seasonal dances attendant upon the planting and harvesting of the rice crop were an even stronger influence: understandably, the success of this staple crop brought celebratory performances of dance and song, and from these there developed the popular dance elements to be found in Kabuki.

During the period between the eighth and eleventh centuries AD, Japan absorbed many foreign dance influences. These included dances from China, India and Korea, and also a masked Buddhist ritual called Gigaku. Further influences came from Bugaku, the court dance, and Sangaku, a combination of mime and acrobatics which was eventually to provide the basis for Noh drama. When certain foreign entertainments combined with, and were emulated by, a native tradition of song and dance they evolved into Gaguku, that ultra-refined music and dance of the Imperial household which is still preserved today.

In the Middle Ages a form of dance-drama, Ennen, emerged, which owed something to the influence of Bugaku, and there are still traces of it surviving in dances performed by specially trained priests and by young boys. There also came about a development from the ceremonial dances attendant upon rice planting and harvesting. These were brought into cities to create the style called Dengaku (field music) which was originally enacted by priests who formed themselves into performing troupes. This art became a favourite of the warrior class and the warriors even started to learn it. Today it survives in the Japanese provinces and it contributed to the development of Noh drama. Noh also owed something to the dramatic and acrobatic dance of Sangaku and to the patronage of shoguns (war lords), and to young warriors who had adopted a form of sung dance with a fan in which battle tales were recited in bardic fashion while the performers made simple movements and used a fan. It was given the title *kowaka mai*; when performed by women it was called *mai mai* or *kuse mai*; gradually there evolved a composite form which refined and adopted these and other elements to form Noh.

In Noh drama there is usually a comic interlude called Kyogen which separates the formal splendours of Noh and takes the form of dialogue-drama. The style of Kyogen is called *komai* and it,

like Kabuki dance, has its origins in the popular dance and song of the medieval period. Thereafter both went their separate ways. The popular songs and dances, called *furyu*, were often energetic in manner, with leaping steps. These in turn have had an influence upon Kabuki dance and account for its origins. For, in 1604, at a great festival in Kyoto where a considerable number of people had assembled to perform *furyu*, the priestess Okuni performed, and this marks the real origin of Kabuki.

Okuni's dancing was copied by other women, and a tradition of female performance of dance-dramas was established. But there also came abuses of the performance, and in 1629 women's Kabuki was proscribed by reason of its immorality and licentiousness. There ensued a quarter century of men's Kabuki which was in turn banned for very much the same reasons. Male performers were then required to shave their hair in manly style and to appear on stage as mature men. Finally in 1653 there appeared the first Onnagata,

Kabuki Gedatsu. First performed in 1744, the Gedatsu (meaning emancipation) portrays the freeing of the spirit from the trammels of earthly passion. The ghost Kagekiyo emerges from within the temple bell being held aloft by the actor.

the female impersonators, though this tradition had already existed in other branches of the Japanese theatre. This is the inception of the tradition of Onnagata performances in Kabuki and also the strict categorization of roles and performers.

Onnagata dance stressed beauty of costuming, the display of which was central to the codifying of this style. This in turn reflected the increasing beauty and lavishness of female costume at the beginning of the eighteenth century in Japan, and the respect for costume and the concern with its potential in the theatre helped fix the Onnagata dance itself and thereby helped increase the illusion of femininity of the performer. By contrast, there also emerged a dance style for the male performer – *tachiyaku* – and a development during the next century of a type of short Kabuki drama which insisted upon quick changes of mood and of costume, and thereby of dance style, thus impelling male performers to become more technically versatile as dancers. Furthermore the Kabuki drama acquired a fresh impulse when the Noh drama ceased to be the favourite and protected entertainment of the Shogunate government at the beginning of the Meiji era. Kabuki could now adapt the ideas of Noh dramas, and the Kyogen interludes between Noh plays were also introduced into Kabuki traditions. Up to the middle of the Meiji era the choreographic style of Kabuki dance had relied upon classic Japanese dance technique; now experiment and innovation were to infuse new life and new ideas into the Kabuki dance as well as into the drama itself. Thus, at the start of the twentieth century there evolved a new freedom of performance and this also brought about the emergence of a women's dance in which the actress dancer Fujikage Shizuki developed a dance for women which stimulated Kabuki actors

into giving rival recitals rather than theatrical performances. But Shizuki's endeavours revealed a basic fact about Japanese dance: away from the theatre it was the province of women. It had traditionally been the art of the geisha and the female 'entertainer' of the *demi-monde*: for them dance is another aspect of the femininity that their male clients wish to see.

Bugaku

Probably the most venerable and, to some eyes, the most beautiful dancing in the Eastern world is that associated with the Imperial Japanese household, which goes under the general title of Gagaku. The term Gagaku means elegant and refined music. It is a phrase traceable to the writings of Confucius (551–479 BC) and it was originally to be found in the Imperial Chinese court as music used for religious ceremonies. Nearly a thousand years after Confucius in the sixth century AD, Gagaku functioned in the Northern Wei dynasty of China and was already institutionalized and used on ceremonial occasions. By the beginning of the eighth century it had reached Japan at a time when many foreign (Korean and Chinese) musical and dance influences were being absorbed into the native strain of Japanese culture. At this time, in emulation of the T'ang Empire, an Office of Imperial Music was established to take charge of court music and dance. (There is evidence, though, that during the preceding three centuries musicians from Korea and China performed in Japan, and Japanese students went to the mainland in search of instruction in both music and dance. In 612 a Korean teacher opened an academy to give instruction in Gigaku to young boys, and this form of dance and its associated musical style was adopted in many Buddhist temples. It was a type of theatrical dancing using masks which fell into disuse in the Middle Ages: the masks exquisitely survive but the dance does not.)

Also in the eighth century the Office of Imperial Music (the branch called Gagaku-Ryo) took charge of all imported and alien musical and dance forms, and their range was varied, from orchestral music to the dance-drama of Gigaku and even the lively performances of conjuring and acrobatics.

Bugaku, whose literal translation is 'dance and music', was the form of movement adopted for performance to the accompaniment of Kangen (the actual music) which formed part of the overall concept of Gagaku. (When dance and music are performed together the form is called Bugaku; music alone in Gagaku is still called Kangen, which means 'wind and strings', and refers to the orchestral element of Gagaku.)

Although Bugaku contains traces of ancient native Japanese dance, its historical identity is chiefly concerned with the nationalization and preservation of imported forms from Korea, China, Manchuria and even India in the seventh to tenth centuries AD, and the native dances made

Ennosuke Ichikawa (above left) in the Kabuki drama The Mansion at Kawazura Hogen. *He is here seen as the white fox, but he also plays two other roles in this drama. His performance is an exceptionally dramatic one, requiring expert acrobatic skill and extremely quick costume changes.*

Two Bugaku dancers (above) in a Gagaku performance at Kasuga Shrine in Nara. Gagaku is considered to be one of the most beautiful forms of Eastern dance. It has long been associated with the Imperial Japanese household, having reached Japan from China early in the eighth century AD.

in imitation of these imported forms. What disappeared in their progress from their source to Japan was their original inspiration: formalized in the court of China, further refined in their adaptation to Japanese court life, they became exercises in elaborately beautiful stylishness. First intentions had long since disappeared. Bugaku featured in the grandest manner at court ceremonies and in the celebrations of Buddhist worship in temples in the Middle Ages.

In the eleventh and twelfth centuries the dances and music were performed by members of the court; with the rise of the Samurai class in the thirteenth century, and the transference of power from court to warlords, Bugaku lost both its popularity and for the most part the occasion for its performance. During the centuries of Samurai power Bugaku/Gagaku became restricted to the court and a few of the larger temples and shrines in and around Kyoto, the ancient capital of Japan. It was not until the late nineteenth century and the restoration of power to the Emperor, that Gagaku emerged from its seclusion. With the increased prestige of the Emperor Meiji, the Gagaku ensembles were brought to the Imperial palace in Tokyo and encouraged to perform. Today the Gagaku is part of the Music Department of the

Imperial Household; its performances are given in the Imperial Palace, a few shrines and temples.

The slowest tempi in Gagaku are those of the orchestral music, Kangen; Bugaku uses faster speeds, though even this is a comparative matter, and the effect of Bugaku dance is always of solemn, grave, ritualistically serene and noble movement. The inner changes of rhythm are very varied, but for the Western observer, untrained in the nuances of the style, such minutiae of structure must inevitably pass largely unnoticed. It is a dance form entirely stylized, long-elaborated, long-preserved, immutable, and immutably beautiful. The patterns for each movement and for each dance are venerable, and the idea of personal 'interpretation' by a performer is entirely alien to the style. What is called for from the great Bugaku performer, as from the great Noh actor, is the ability to penetrate to the very essence of the dance or drama, and reveal this in a performance which will show the style as still alive and emotionally moving to the connoisseur. Bugaku performance was traditionally an open-air celebration. Today, in presentation on the stage of the Imperial Household's Music Department in Tokyo, the open-air effect is obtained by use of a large skylight and the placing of gravel

Bugaku dancer in a samai *(left-hand dance) called* sanju *at Kasuga Shrine in Nara. Based on works from China, India and Indonesia, these gentle,* samai *dances demand great elegance of execution.*

around the stage. This stage is a raised platform, seven metres (twenty-three foot) square, one metre (three foot) high, its sides of black lacquer; a red-lacquered railing, six hundred millimetres (two foot) high surrounding it. In front is a narrow stair used by the dancers, leading to a square cypress wood stage five to six metres square, covered with a pale green damask carpet on which the artists must perform. The orchestra is on a platform just behind the stage.

The very precision of these arrangements, their hallowed traditionalism, indicates the essential refinement and prescribed, long-perfected language of the art itself. The repertory of Bugaku amounts to some sixty pieces, handed down from the very origins of the form, and they are divided into two groups, dependent upon their presumed countries of origin. *Samai* (left-hand dances) are works introduced or based on works from China, India and Indonesia, or subsequently composed in that style. Their performance manner is slow, gentle, and demands great elegance of execution; the performers wear chestnut-coloured robes. *Umai* (right-hand dances) are those imported from Korea or composed in emulation of Korean forms. Movement is more spirited, sharper, patterns more angular, the basic manner more humorous, the dancers' costumes of greenish shades. For the left-hand dance, the performers must enter the stage from behind a huge, flame-decorated drum on the left-hand side (stage right); those for the right-hand dance enter from the opposite side. The entry on stage, the leaving of the stage, with accompanying music, are part of the performance. Both left- and right-hand dances are sub-divided into three types – and contain a large number of court dances of ritualistic significance without programme. They stress the actual beauty of movement. A second group consists of military dances, their performers gorgeously costumed in warriors' robes, their movements simulating combat. The third group contains the 'running dances' and performers are masked. These recount such clearly programmatic ideas as a man hunting and eating a snake in the forest, or a dragon basking in the sunshine.

Costume is elegant and elaborate but not theatrical dress as in the Noh or Kabuki. For the most part the dancers wear a perpetuation of court dress of the Heian period (794–1192), and a mere visible edging of colour will be the sole indication of a magnificently complex and beautiful under-robe that is never seen save for this brief outline of colour. In many dances of courtly origin the outer sleeve of one robe is drawn back to reveal an under-sleeve of a different colour: in a dance in which the artists may perform a unison change of arm position, allowing the sleeve to fall forward, there will ensue a change of coloration which is an important feature of the dance itself. For military dances, the costume is simpler, as it is also in the running dances. For performance in religious surroundings the costuming will obey those ancient rules of the Shinto faith which call for purity – dress on these religious occasions is often white. In certain invocatory dances which we have seen, the tradition stretches back over one thousand years. And an example is in a fragment unknown to the public until recent years, from a long Shinto ceremony which lasts from dusk until dawn, in which a solo dancer in the white costuming of the Imperial Guard of the ninth century performs, holding a branch from the sacred *sakaki* tree which bears a representation of the holy Shinto mirror. The accompanying text sung by the chorus is translated as follows:

That pony
it asks me for grass
it asks me for water
I will give it grass
I will give it water.

For certain dances, masks are worn to stress or underline the ethos of the dance itself. Immobility of feature is an essential quality of the Bugaku dance. Feelings and ideas are expressed by bodily gesture; the masks which reflect Central Asian origins for some of the dances, serve in certain dances to reinforce the dramatic aspect of a character being impersonated when the dance itself may encompass very complex ideas. Even to the Western observer the Bugaku dance, the entire Gagaku performance, is one of timeless, hieratic beauty in which music and dance are inspired and informed by the same serene inevitability, by the same glorious weight of tradition and expressive dignity, by the same phenomenal power to communicate, even to the untutored eye of the West.

Intensely memorable are such moments as the dance by a prince so physically handsome that, to frighten his enemies in battle, he had to wear a grotesque mask; unforgettable are the expansive sweeps of huge sleeves which form a counterpoint to the stamping and pawing of the ground by feet emerging under fantastic robes; extraordinary, too, are the formal grace and implicit ferocity in warriors' dances where the combatants face each other in stylized movement, armed with sword or lance or shield. An ancient Bugaku guide to performance urges dancers to become like 'tinted leaves blown about on a mountain in a storm in autumn'. The impression of these noble performers is exactly that.

Noh

Not as ancient as Gagaku, but nevertheless representing seven centuries of performance, the Noh theatre is an art of illustrious traditions, piercing beauty and the greatest refinement in its dance element. This last is an integral part of the entire structure of the Noh drama and style. So important is it that the culmination of a Noh play is a dance in which the central, prime actor – the Shite – performs a dance in the venerable movement tradition of Noh. Identified under the general title of Noh-Mai, Noh dance might seem meaningless save in the context of the drama whose essence it is. It is an art which has been refined and stylized, subjected to all the subtleties and exquisite gradations of sensibility of which the Japanese aesthetic consciousness is capable. Noh, so pure, so dense, so entirely gripping to those prepared to understand it and accept its formal distinction, is an art in which experience is abstracted, purged, given its most intense expression, and its dance reflects these attitudes exactly. During his lengthy training the performer of Shite roles learns a vocabulary of mime/dance gesture and movement: these are called *kata* and they illustrate the words of the text, illuminating the inner sense of the play by movement that is a combination of acting and dancing. The *kata* are all long-established; the Shite's greatness depends upon his ability to transcend the form and thus show the audience the inner beauty and relevance of text and movement. The actual language of the dance may seem severely restricted; it is, in an odd way, typified by the snow-white foot covering worn by the Shite and by the apparently severely-circumscribed vocabulary of movement: simple liftings of the foot and leg; walking in which the heels are not lifted from the floor, but slid over the stage area; stamping movements; a rigid and unyielding carriage of the torso; occasional sideways turnings of the head; poses and gestures with the essential fan; the fact that the Shite is masked; progress that can seem no more than steps forward of backwards, or occasional shuffling circuits of the performing area. And yet, the subtleties are clear to see, and so is the exquisite beauty of expression. Rhythmically the performance is most complicated, depending upon a dense interaction of text, music and movement focused in the person of the Shite. In this can be traced some indication of the beauty – simplicity and directness eventually achieved through a most complicated procedure – that is a sign of Noh's enduring greatness.

As a final comment, the appearance of the celebrated Noh actor Manzaburo Umewaka in the play by Zeami (1363–1443), the founder of Noh drama, called *Sagi* (The Heron) deserves description. An Emperor sees a heron beside a pond and orders that his aides capture it. At their approach the bird flies into the air, but an aide shouts that the Emperor has ordered him to capture it. The bird settles on the ground, and the Emperor, deeply gratified, appoints the heron and the aide to court rank. The heron performs a dance of celebration. White-robed, Manzaburo Umewaka in the Shite role of the heron, seems the very personification of the bird in the supreme delicacy and stylishness of his interpretation, and never more essentially so than in his final dance, a masterpiece of performance which transcends every consideration of time, style and language. In another celebrated drama, *Sumidagawa* (The Sumida River) in which he impersonates – or more truly 'becomes' – a mad woman in quest of a son whom she discovers is murdered, this great artist is the incarnation of grief. The unity between text, movement and interpreter brings an awareness of the most admired quality of Noh – *yugen* – the beauty lying below the surface, a state achieved and then revealed to the spectator by the Shite.

A performer of Shite roles at Kofu Kuji in Nara. The prime actor in a Noh play – the Shite – ends the performance with a display of subtle movement in the Noh tradition of highly refined and stylized dance.

CHAPTER FIVE

SOCIAL DANCE

Engraving of 1616 (left) commemorating 'A Ball given in honour of the Queen [Anne of Austria] at the Louvre following a very magnificent banquet.' The setting of the ball, like that of a ballet de cour, shows the court ranged as spectators along the side of the hall with the royal party as the central 'presence'. There is an element of display in this dance which relates very clearly to court ballet. (Bibliothèque Nationale, Paris)

Practised partners (right) show how similar the style and positions of sixteenth-century couple dancing are to folk and 'country' dancing today. Hanging swords and daggers and voluminous skirts appear to pose no problem to this agile pair. By Virgil Solis the Elder (1514–1562) of Nuremberg, the acclaimed painter, engraver, etcher and woodcut artist. (British Museum)

URING THAT amorphous, and hard to define, period the 'Middle Ages', there was a considerable reference to dancing, though with no precise indication as to what it was like or how it was done. Illuminated manuscripts, the borders in books of hours and the chronicles of the period all reveal that people danced, and the contrast between gentry and peasantry is clear both in costume and in the physical poses of the bodies. Statements can be found about dancing as a postlude to medieval tournaments of the twelfth and thirteenth centuries, as when a floor collapsed under the weight of dancers after a tournament in North Wales in 1284. The *Bal des Ardents* of 1393 also indicates the importance of maskings and mummings in European high society, and the important contribution that was to be made by dancing.

To dance well was a necessary accomplishment for the nobility throughout the European courts. Both nobility and peasantry would still apparently perform round dances, especially the *carole* which was the perpetuation of that most ancient of dance forms and which involved song as well as simple dance steps. In its linked form it evolved into the *farandole* which presented its dancers in a single file with hands linked. In its circular form it became known as the *branle*. The major departure came from the South of France, where in the more 'civilized' Provençal courts there emerged a couple dance, a man and woman holding hands and moving forwards side by side, which was known as the *estampie*.

A social difference in the manner of performing became noticeable. For the court, the style inevitably reflected the emergence of refined social manners – the iconography of medieval manuscripts will show the nobleman and his lady dancing with their hands clasped. More boisterous are those illustrations which show the peasantry indulging in capers and high stepping movement.

For rare dances performed indoors in the early Middle Ages, the position of an open hearth in the centre of the hall of the Lord of the Manor or the castle meant that some dancing was performed round a fire – an intriguing reference back to bonfire dances. With the emergence of the chimney as a feature of architecture (as distinct from the central hole in the roof which allowed the smoke to escape) the fire was moved to a hearth at the side of the hall and a new area became available for the dance: the main body of the hall itself. Thus for the dance there opened up new possibilities of patterning. For exterior dances – those performed by the peasants as well as the gentry – these patterns of course already existed.

In the earlier part of the Hundred Years' War, England sustained the impact of French taste, as prisoners of war from France were received into English homes and their more refined manners

and the influence of their dance habits permeated English society.[1]

It must be understood, though, that the dance of the fourteenth and early fifteenth century was in a sense waiting for the emergence of the dance styles that were to come with the early Renaissance. It is the professional influence of the early Italian dancing masters and the social activity associated first with the Italian courts which impelled the social dance forward on its remarkable path for the next two centuries. The *basse danse,* that slow and noble dance, was to seem the last flowering of the medieval style.

The *basse danse* had been known since 1400 as 'the Queen of Dances' says Cornazano, the fifteenth-century dancing master. It was slow and stately, but also included light and tripping steps which combined a gliding movement with a rise on the toes. In the fifteenth century the *basse danse* did not have a regular arrangement of steps, but there seems to have been a richness and variety in its components. In his invaluable guide to the social dance of the sixteenth century, *Orchésographie* (1588) Thoinot Arbeau writes that 'the Basse Danse has been abandoned for forty or fifty years.' Its processional form reflected the old attitudes of chivalry, while the new dances devised by 'Domenico' and 'Guglielmo', the early fifteenth-century dancing masters, and their compatriots were to make the social dance of the nobility more beautiful and more varied. The work of these dancing masters is described in more detail in the chapter on the *Ballet de Cour.*

The *balli* were the particular creation of the Italian dancing masters of the Renaissance rather than any development from an existing step pattern. Devised for the highest levels in the society of its time, *balli* were dances of mixed measures specially choreographed in the sense that the dancing masters arranged accepted steps and also gave them a dramatic or mimetic nuance. Such titles as 'The Flirt' and 'The Constant Woman' suggest the themes of the dances and imply that the floor patterns – in which the originality of the piece lay – would feature dancers as individuals as well as in groups. These were figured dances, their form rather than their expressive nature being the criterion on which they were judged. They represented early examples of formal choreography in that they were completely stylized.

Antonio de Arena in his book on 'Bassas Dansas' *Ad suos companiones,* published in 1529, and written in macaronic Latin, makes reference to two dances of society, distinguishing between the *bassa danza* and the *brando.* The former was a couple dance, the latter a group one. The *brando* was the counterpart of the *branle* (described in detail later on). In Castiglione's treatise on manners, *The Courtier* (1528), he declares that the *brando* and the *moresco* were to be danced in private; if they were to be performed at any public occasion the courtier should be in some way disguised. The *moresco* (or *moresque*) has its basis in the Moorish conquest of Spain. In the fifteenth century it emerged as a solo dance, and also a double file dance, that is, a performance in which two lines of dancers faced each other. It also gave its name to the English *morris* dance, whose characteristic form from the fifteenth century seems to have involved six men with another as the Fool, plus a boy dressed up as a woman, and another man carrying the cut-out figure of a hobby-horse. Its performance was marked by virile stamping and thrusts of the leg, and by noise often contributed by bells worn on costume and legs and by the beating of sticks.

But as has been noted, the *basse danse* was soon to disappear. This reflected a desire for rationalization, and for the codification of all the arts which was to be so characteristic of the High Renaissance. In music, it can be seen in the separation of vocal and instrumental forms and even in the sharp division between religious and worldly music. In dancing, this implies a rejection of mixed forms which in effect the *basse danse* was. Its ancestor had been the *estampie,* a quiet gliding dance, and with the emergence of the *basse danse* with its grave measures there came a desire to follow it with a lighter and gayer dance – the *saltarello* – which was called by the Spaniards *alta danza* and by the French the *pas de brabant.* Eventually these two forms, contrasts of slow and quick, of serious and gay, had fused because they were so often linked in popular dancing.

As the different categories of social dance became more marked, the couple dance becomes simpler, graver, a stately processional dance for the court. But youth needed as always to be served, and the *galliard* emerged as a young people's dance forming the lively after-dance to the *pavane,* a slow peacocking dance of great dignity which,

The social dance of the Renaissance is depicted at its most relaxed in this detail of elegant couples dancing in a landscape from a beguiling painting by the Flemish artist Ambrosius Benson (1495–1550). (Utah Museum of Fine Arts, University of Utah; gift of Howard J. and Jennie Greer Stoddard in honour of John and Mary Preston)

contrary to some assertions, did not come from Padua. The *galliard* was to the *pavane* as the *saltarello* was to the *basse danse*. The importance of the *galliard* indicates the increasing popularity in society of lively dances. The popular chain dance emerges, the *branle*, a folk dance descendant from the medieval *carole,* which also becomes a court dance. (In the great festivities held at Bayonne in 1565, when Catherine de'Medici went to greet her daughter Elizabeth, the wife of Philip II of Spain, dancing played an important part, and each of the French provinces participating performed a social or folk dance appropriate to its region.) Among the other forms of dance in the sixteenth and seventeenth centuries the *courante* was especially popular. Its origins lie in a pantomimic dance suggesting courtship, and it was initially quite fast in tempo, but by the middle of the seventeenth century in France it had been codified in a much slower and graver form, and was celebrated as a favourite dance of the Sun King himself (Louis XIV).

The *sarabande* originated in Spain where, in the latter part of the sixteenth century, it combined songs and dances which were thought indecent and 'repulsive', because of their physical frankness, and unsuited to be performed by respectable people. It has been recorded that in 1583 anyone found dancing it in certain parts of Spain could be severely punished. It was nonetheless introduced into France and in the famous *ballet de cour* of *La Douarière de Billebahaut* of 1626 it was danced as the Spanish *entrée* (individual section of a ballet), by which time it had become a slow, elegant dance.

It is at this moment worth stressing that in an age where dancing itself was extremely popular, and where the dance was to be identified as a vital and often dominant element in court entertainments, there also came about a cross-fertilization between social dance and the forms used in the *ballet de cour*. The origins of this tradition can even be seen in the inventiveness of the fifteenth-century Italian ballet masters, whose dances were 'choreographed' in that they represented a personal arrangement of the social dance steps and,

as has been shown, their dances were often dependent upon a basic dramatic or emotional idea. There followed in the next century a relationship between court performance and social dance which was mutually advantageous.

In Arbeau's *Orchésographie* there is a very clear indication of the relationship between the *galliards*, the *allemandes*, and the *gavottes* which were used on social occasions, and the form which they took when they were included in a masquerade (*mascarade*). In relation to the *canaries*, whose final step he describes as similar to 'scraping the foot backwards along the ground as if one were treading down spittle or killing a spider', he also notes:

'Some say this dance is common in the Canary Isles. Others, whose opinion I should prefer to share, maintain that it derives from a ballet composed for a masquerade in which the dancers were dressed like kings and queens of Mauretania, or else like savages in feathers dyed to many a hue.'

Of the *pavane* he gives a vivid description of its use both in social and theatrical terms, that use reflecting very clearly a precisely similar function:

'On solemn feast days the pavane is employed by kings, princes and great noblemen to display themselves in their fine mantles and ceremonial robes... And it is the said pavanes, played by hautboys and sackbuts, that announce the grand ball and are arranged to last until the dancers have circled the hall two or three times, unless they prefer to dance it by advancing and retreating. Pavanes are also used in masquerades to herald the entrance of gods and goddesses in their triumphal chariots or emperors and kings in full majesty.'

It is interesting to note here that by the second quarter of the sixteenth century a great deal of music was published in connection with dancing. These collections of dance tunes, arranged for lute or instrumental ensemble, suggest the richness of source material available to anyone concerned in exploring the dance rhythms and musical forms relating to them.

Torch-bearers lead a dance to celebrate the alliance in 1612 of Elizabeth, daughter of James I of England (VI of Scotland) to Frederick V, Elector Palatine of the Rhine and later King of Bohemia. They were known as the 'Winter' King and Queen for their short-lived reign in Bohemia. It was their daughter Sophia's son, George I, who introduced the Hanoverian dynasty to the British throne some hundred years later. Detail from an engraving by J. T. Bry. (British Museum)

The title of the *branle* originated from the French verb *branler* (to sway from side to side) since this pendulum-like movement was an essential component of the dance. Arbeau records that the *branle de Malte* had been composed some forty years before he was writing, and he declares that it was a survival from a ballet danced by the Knights of Malta and in no way a borrowing from the social dance of the island. He gives another example of the *candlestick,* or *torched branle,* where the man selected a partner after taking a candlestick and walking round the room to seek out the girl with whom he was to dance; or that of Haut Barrois in eastern France which was danced in a masquerade by servants and sometimes by young members of the gentry 'disguised as peasants and shepherds, or for a lark amongst themselves at some private gathering.'

'Certain figures were common to all *Branles,* but within these figures a good deal of latitude was permitted and gradually a number of *Branles* became popular, some of them couple dances and others in chain form . . . The pantomimic themes (which gave individual flavour to these *Branles*) were greatly mixed in these various versions throughout France and it was in them that the form of the choral dance of the previous century is retained and developed. But though the French courts right from Henri III (1574–1589) to Louis XIV (1643–1715) favoured the *Branle* in its many forms, Italian society, at least in the first half of the sixteenth century, scorned it. Adopting the dance from the peasantry, French society danced it in groups, with three *Branles* at the beginning of a ball: a *Branle double,* sedate in nature, a *Branle simple* of a more lively character, and a *Branle gay,* extremely rapid in its movements. The dance consisted of running, gliding and even skipping movements, the unrestrained and boisterous steps of the country folk now being tempered by the more artificial behaviour of society.'[2]

Very different and very boisterous was *la volta,* another form of the *galliard.* It was unusual in that the couple dancing it moved and turned in a close embrace, with the man's arm around the woman's waist, and a high-leaping step in which the two bodies were pressed together. This was a unique distinction marking out *la volta* from all the other couple dances in which the man and woman moved either alongside each other or facing. *La volta* was considered bold, if not actually indecent, though we have evidence that it was a dance favoured by Elizabeth I, and in his *Henry V* Shakespeare makes reference to this dance's popularity in England with: 'They bid us to the English dancing school /And teach lavoltas high and swift corantos.'[3] By the beginning of the seventeenth century, however, it was disappearing from public favour.

With the age of Louis XIV as an absolute monarch it can be seen that the court ballet had rejected

the lewdness and coarseness often found in the ballet masquerades of Louis XIII. Similarly, in the social dance there came an increased desire for formal perfection and for elegance of manner – those qualities associated with the young Sun King's own appearances. This suggests the dominance of French taste. As with the other arts of the time there was the search for those ideals of classic balance and regularity which attempted to tame the arts and to provide them with rules and guidelines – a fact that is evident in the establishment of the King's Academies of Music and Dancing. Thus you also find in the period of Louis XIV the increased popularity of the *minuet.*

Characteristically, the *minuet*'s origins are as a rustic dance, probably from Poitou, where it was known as a lively dance in triple time. Its development into a dance for the gentry indicates that process of refinement whereby, yet again, folk art is transformed and eventually taken an almost unrecognizable distance from its origins.

Like the *courante* and the *gavotte,* the *minuet* became part of the usual suite of dances on social occasions at court; the popularity of these forms can also be traced in their abstract musical forms culminating in the keyboard and orchestral suites of J. S. Bach. In its later forms the small steps which were so essentially part of the *minuet* (as its linguistic origin *pas menu,* meaning little step, indicates) degenerated into a kind of mincing affectation, but in its great days as a court dance at Versailles it was elegant and very stylized. It was a dance which required considerable application and practice in order to polish it for public

The impressive presence of the monarch is well portrayed in this detail (above) from an engraving of a court ball celebrating the return of Louis XIV to Versailles. The King is dancing a minuet *and his pose has the clarity of an illustration to a dancing manual. (Bibliothèque Nationale, Paris). This graceful couple (right) also perform a* minuet, *complete with notation 'ground plan' of steps by Kellom Tomlinson, the eighteenth-century ballet master, composer and 'Writer of Dances and their Music for the Use and Entertainment of the Public'. (Royal Academy of Dancing Library, London)*

Detail (above right) from Nicolas Lancret's Pastoral Revels (1738). *Lancret, like his fellow artist, Boucher, was inspired by Watteau, and both specialized in painting* fêtes galantes. *(Wallace Collection, London)*

performance: designed for a couple, it encompassed considerable complexities of footwork, and failure to master these was considered to be an admission of social inadequacy. Its popularity and the need to be skilled in performance guaranteed its endurance, and it remained in vogue for well over a century. (Later nineteenth-century revivals were an attempt to recreate past glories in court circles, but by then the dance itself had become, as has already been suggested, entirely corrupt.)

Despite the supremacy of the *minuet*, another dance of peasant origin, the *gavotte*, remained popular in the higher ranks of society. Its origins lie in a peasant dance from the Dauphiné, but its introduction into court entertainments in the sixteenth century (where it consisted of a mixture of movements from *branles* and *galliards*) led to the establishing of a form that substituted dignity and stately grace for its original peasant vitality.

One other important and significant adaptation from the folk element appears with the emergence of the *contredanses*. These were in fact a linguistic adaptation of the English country dances and also a technical adaptation of them. French dancing masters imported from England the ruder and more vivid forms of jig and round dances, and elaborated them into group dances which formed

rounds and lines of dancing to make an elaborate choreographic shape through which the members of the court could tread – they may be seen even as an odd survival or echo of the *carole*.

The English country dance, transformed into the French *contredanse* and thence further transformed into dance figures grouped under the general title of *cotillon* (*cotillion* in English), was much in vogue in the eighteenth century. The latter's title derives from the French for 'petticoat' and it has been suggested that it was gained from the vivacious turning movements associated with one of its component dances. The *cotillon* returned across the Channel and entered the British ballrooms, where its form as a square dance for two couples was elaborated into a great number of patterns or figures with a further amplification when the performers used to give and receive forfeits (and sometimes kisses). From this it was in turn extended to cover the idea of a group of set dances, and in the latter part of the nineteenth century it was a more general term used to describe the final set of dances that concluded a ball. Its descendant was the *quadrille*, another square dance, which emerged during the Napoleonic years in France. It is best described in *The Quadrille and Cotillion Panorama* (1818) by a leading dancing master of the period in London, Thomas Wilson. His books on social dancing – instruction manuals, propaganda for his own classes and teaching – are the most valuable indication available of the dances and social manners of the period in London. It is an indication of the international interest in the subject that the *Quadrille* book was announced as published in London, Paris, New York and Philadelphia.

'This fashionable species of Dancing is entirely of French origin, and only differs from the well known dance, the Cotillon, by leaving out the changes; being much shorter, and frequently composed of Figures that require but four Persons to their performance; as may be seen from the first set of French Quadrilles that were publicly danced in this country, viz. Le Pantalon, L'Eté, La Poule, and La Trénise ... A set of Quadrilles generally consist of four, which are danced in succession ... these are usually danced before the company sit down or separate; to which is generally added one more, or what is generally termed a Finale.'

The names of the dances were those originally given in the very first set of *quadrilles* danced in London, and refer to the titles of the music – the final Trénise being a reminder of the name of the dancing master who originated it, M. Trénise.

Captain Gronow's gossipy *Reminiscences* indicate when the *quadrille* first appeared in the British ballroom. He declared that it was in 1815 at Almack's, the most socially prominent Assembly Rooms:

'... that Lady Jersey introduced from Paris the favourite Quadrille which has so long remained popular ... The 'mazy Waltz' was also brought to us about this time but there were comparatively few who at first ventured to whirl round the salons of Almack's ...'[4]

But for theatrical and social dancing it is the age of Louis XIV that marks a great divide. In ballet it represents the zenith of the *ballet de cour* in which the King starred as a young man. His decision to stop dancing meant that the impulse for the courtiers to emulate their master as a performer also ceased, and it is at this time that the professional theatrical performer comes into his own and 'ballet' leaves the court and moves into the theatre. But the age of Louis XIV was also an age when the arts were to find themselves subject to the rule of the Académie and to the implicit codification and rationalization of the art itself – the emergence of the Académie Royale de Musique and Académie Royale de Danse are testimony to this.

Theatrical dance received its vital codification with the acceptance of the five 'positions' as a basis for professional dance. 'Turn out', which is now regarded as one of the first prerequisites of the academic dance, is no more than an acceptance of a physical posture first established in the social manners – the walk and then the dance posture – of the court. The forms of social dance, the *gigue*, the *courante* and others were to be adapted and elaborated as theatrical forms. In these exceptional days of the seventeenth century the barriers between amateur and professional as performers, and between the actual forms of what the two classes performed, were not high. Nevertheless, there remained an essential distinction. It was a social accomplishment to dance well but it was kept within the framework of polite society. The noble amateur could view the most skilled professional with admiration, but it was unthinkable

Lady Jersey (second from left) introducing the first quadrille in a British ballroom at Almack's in 1815. This illustration from Captain Gronow's Reminiscences suggests the social importance of the Assembly Rooms and of the dance itself. According to Yates in his book A Glance at Almack's: 'The balls at Almack's are scarcely less crowded than the private parties and routs of our nobility. For want of space, the best dancers in the assembly have frequently to sustain the vexation of a sudden interruption ... there is no more dancing, and it is with difficulty they can even walk to their places.'

for social reasons that he should emulate the technical bravura of the paid performer.

It is worth citing as an exception, which yet proves the distinction between court and professionals, the occasion noted by Théodore de Lajarte in his catalogue of works staged at the Paris Opéra (Paris, 1878) of a performance of Lully's opera *Perseus* in June 1682 when as the *Mercure Galant* reported:

'On Sunday June 19 something was seen on the stage of the Théâtre Royal de l'Opéra which was an agreeable surprise to everyone present. The young Prince de Dietrichstein eldest son of the Prince of that name, Grand Master of His Majesty the Emperor, danced a ballet entrée by himself with wonderful grace. He appeared on the stage, magnificently masked as was the custom, and replaced one of the principal dancing masters whom M. de Lully employs. Monsieur [brother of Louis XIV] came to see him with an exceptional group of nobles. This young prince who has only been learning to dance for a year performed this entrée so exactly that he was universally admired.'

With the passing of Louis XIV in 1715 you are already present at the passing of an old dance order. The ultra-snobbish attitudes of Monsieur Jourdain's dancing master in Molière's *Le Bourgeois gentilhomme* of 1670 reflected an entire dependence upon the court for approval. By the beginning of the eighteenth century you enter upon a period when dancing is in a process of democratization. The proliferation of dance manuals, the remarkable work of the English dancing masters John Weaver and Kellom Tomlinson, the widespread influence of Pierre Rameau's *Le Maître à danser* in English and German translations, suggest how broad was the appeal of social dance at this time among the middle classes. With the progress of the eighteenth century you can note how French taste declined in influence, and how a more popular aspect of dancing was to be manifest among the middle classes.

Such a manual as Playford's *The Dancing Master*, whose eighteenth edition appeared in 1728 (the first was published in 1651), could list 718 'of the choicest Old and New Tunes now used at Court and other Publick Places'.

The 'public places' referred to were that extraordinary manifestation of dance enthusiasm in the eighteenth century, the public ball. These balls can be best studied in England, where there emerged a fashion for Assembly Rooms, the earliest of which were built at famous English spas. The social excuses for these buildings were several. Visitors came to the spas ostensibly to take the waters, and for the men there was the added attraction of the possibility of gambling; for everyone there was the social opportunity of meeting a wide variety of other visitors. The earliest Assembly Rooms in England were those associated with the medicinal properties of the waters at Bath, Tunbridge Wells, Epsom and Hampstead. The most celebrated of these spas was Bath where from 1705 Beau Nash ruled as supreme arbiter of taste and fashion. As part of the fashionable life of the spa, dancing took place in the evenings several times a week – in Bath, balls were held on Tuesdays and Wednesdays beginning at six in the evening and ending at eleven. Every attempt was made to preserve a spirit of decorum and respectability, and a form of despotism was evident in the behaviour of Nash towards his subjects, as there was later in other reigning figures of the Assembly Rooms such as Lady Jersey, who was the autocrat of Almack's, the most renowned of the later Assembly Rooms in London.

The pattern of dancing at Bath was strictly prescribed. The evening began with the *minuet*, danced by the two most socially important people present, and thereafter a sequence of *minuets* lasting for two hours was followed by a period of country dancing. At nine there came an interval for tea, and then country dancing was resumed until the ball ended on the stroke of eleven. By the middle of the century the Assembly Rooms were an accepted and vital feature of public entertainment.

The Assembly Rooms featured dancing, public concerts and masquerade balls, and the presence of an element of riff-raff and ladies of the town was an inevitable cause for scandal in some rooms. The Assembly Rooms run by Mrs Cornelys at Carlisle House, Soho Square, in London were famous for the masquerades held there, but also for a looseness of morals. Almack's, already mentioned, was the most celebrated of the London Assembly Rooms. It was opened in King Street, St James's in 1765 by a Scot, MacCall, known as William Almack. It was here that the most elegant and fashionable public could be found at concerts, masked balls and subscription dances. Although open-air places of entertainment also existed, notably at Vauxhall and Ranelagh, and public dancing was also held at these venues, it was the greater comfort, the better location and the exclusivity which guaranteed the success of Almack's, Mrs Cornelys' and the equally celebrated Pantheon in Oxford Street.

Attached to these Assembly Rooms, inevitably, were dancing masters who would advertise their services and also offer demonstrations by their pupils. Mr Yates, operating from Carlisle House in 1771, could advertise:

'After the Minuet, Cotillons and the Allemands are danced by his scholars there will be a Ball for the Company. There will be refreshments of Tea, Coffee, Lemonade, Orgeat, Biscuits, etc. and music in a different room for those who choose to make sets for Cotillons etc. before the scholars have finished.'

The pattern of these social occasions in London was echoed in the public balls held at the Opéra in Paris – a tradition which continued through the

nineteenth century. As a result of the success of masked balls given by members of the Royal family, de Cahusac notes that:

'By decree of 31 December 1715, public balls were allowed thrice weekly in the auditorium of the opera house. The directors had a machine built which raised the floor and orchestra pit to the level of the stage. The auditorium was decorated with chandeliers, with looking glasses at the far end, with two orchestras at either end and a refreshment table in the middle. The novelty of this spectacle, the convenience of enjoying all the pleasures of a ball without bother, or preparation or expense, gave this undertaking such a success that in an excess of good nature, which I have seen still obtains, people's enthusiasm went so far as to find the auditorium beautiful, suitable and entirely worthy . . . The Opera balls have put an end to private dances and we know that it is no longer fashionable to dance there. The two sides of the ballroom are occupied by a few lowly maskers, who follow the tunes that the orchestra plays. All the others push, mingle, jostle each other: it is the Roman saturnalia come again.'[5]

After the heyday of court activity following the Restoration in England, and the remarkable popularity of social dancing in the days of Mr Isaac (dancing teacher to Queen Anne and master to John Weaver), a change can be seen taking place in the nature of English social dance. The emergence of a new class of dancing masters, typified by John Weaver and by those other men who were subscribers to his work, indicates how the polite activity of dancing, once associated entirely with the court, was now spreading throughout the gentry. The influence of the court was to decline, despite the creation of the Royal Birthnight Ball. These annual balls were initiated at the turn of the seventeenth century and for them a new dance was specially composed by the official dancing master at the court. Thanks to the spread of choreographic notation in Feuillet's system, the dance could be published and circularized to various dancing masters, who thus were prepared to teach it to those people who hoped to attend the ball. (And indeed to those who would have it thought that they were attending the ball!) An exact parallel exists today, on a different social level, in the competitions for inventive dances organized by dance teacher associations. The winning dances are immediately written down and circulated to members.

The suggestion of a 'choreographed' dance supplanting the more usual forms is some indication of the extent to which social dancing was on the move. At this time the usual run of dances included the *gavotte* and the *sarabande,* the *rigaudon* and the *passe pied*, the *loure*, the *bourrée* and the *minuet.*

Supreme among these at the time was the *minuet,* but there is a remarkable comment upon its demise which is linked to the Royal Birthnight

Public balls were extremely popular in Paris at the end of the eighteenth century. This bal masqué *was given by the municipality of Paris to Louis* XVI *and Marie-Antoinette to celebrate the birth of the Dauphin in January 1782.*

Ball. A poem, published after the death of George III, lamented the ending of the Birthnight Ball and contained the following illuminating couplet:

> Through all the land the tragic news has spread
> And all the land has mourned the Minuet dead.[6]

In matters of dance fashion the eighteenth century was inevitably to look away from the court to the new social arbitration of the Assembly Room. Bath, under Beau Nash, was to impose different manners and a new mingling of society. At the Assembly Rooms in the provinces, and later in London, new and more even standards of social behaviour were required and were consequently spread by those returning from their stay at the fashionable spas. The increasing ease of transport meant an end to provincial and regional isolation and a greater interest in fashionable behaviour among a broader spectrum of upper middle class society – this was eventually of course to provide the material for Jane Austen's pen.

The popularity of public dancing was manifest in France where, by 1789, it was claimed that there were some seven hundred dance halls in Paris alone. Throughout Europe social dancing had by this time achieved an exceptional popularity, and it was to give birth to the great innovation in social dancing at this time. This was the arrival of the *waltz*.

> '. . . it witnessed the beginning of our modern ballroom dancing. It marks the great change from the "open couple" dance of the eighteenth century, as exemplified by the Minuet, and the coming of the modern "closed couple" dance.'[7]

The word *waltz* means to turn and it is generally accepted that the *waltz* derives from the turning dances so prevalent among the peasantry of Germany. The young Goethe provides intriguing testimony concerning the early days of this dance when he records how his father had taught him to dance the *minuet*, the *contredanse* (English country dances) and 'even the Waltz'. This last was thought difficult, though Goethe also declares that the country people were addicted to the 'Allemande, the Waltz and the Dreher: all the people had grown up with this national dance.'[8] The contrast in Goethe's dancing lessons between the venerable and courtly *minuet* and the 'popular' *waltz* was a contrast between two life-styles, between an aristocratic past and a middle class future. Soon the *waltz* was to sweep through Germany and Austria. Its vivacious steps, its turns, were a reminder of its true folkloric origins in the face to face, arms-embracing gyrations and leaps of the country folk's *ländler*. But it was being refined and modified in ballrooms by the end of the eighteenth century. These were not the ballrooms of the aristocracy but the public Assembly Rooms where the middle classes could disport themselves. The *waltz* is, in essence, a bourgeois

manifestation, and its greatest years in the nineteenth century are the great years of the middle classes. But its acceptance was to be slow: it was thought to be coarse and even lascivious because of a new freedom and a more intimate physical contact between its performers. It was also, through its whirling and through the intoxicating 3/4 time of its rhythm, a dance which evoked – subconsciously maybe – the ecstatic whirlings of far more ancient dances of auto-intoxication.

The *waltz* emerges as a musical and rhythmic form, and also as a dance form of urban life, in the 1780s. Known in Vienna first as *Deutscher tanz* and as *ländler*, it was featured in the public balls of that city, and soon swept Europe, making its identifiable stage appearance by 1800 in the ballet *La Dansomanie* by Pierre Gardel at the Paris Opéra.

There were, as the new century began, marked differences to be seen in the type of *waltz*. In Germany, the slower form of the *ländler* persisted. It is in Vienna and then in France that the more sophisticated, lighter, smoothly gliding and revolving '*valse*' emerges, intoxicating generations to come with its alluring pulse; an over-strong first beat followed by the weaker second and third beats in which there is also an implied rhythmic rubato. Not for nothing was it observed that instead of deliberating, the Congress of Vienna danced.

The punning joke '*Le Congrès ne marche pas: il danse*' was made by the Prince de Ligne to Chambonas as early as September 1814 before the Congress was formally opened. Parties of all kinds were unceasing and the Congress did dance. Edward Cooke wrote to Lord Liverpool in December: 'The Emperor danced polonaises with Lady Castlereagh, country dances with Lady Matilda. The Archduchess Catherine polonaised with Planta.'[9]

The fact that Congress danced is an indication of the extreme popularity of dancing with both the aristocracy and the middle classes throughout Europe. In her *Mémoires des autres* (1840) the society authoress Comtesse Dash talks of the beau monde, at the time of the Restoration of the Bourbons after the Napoleonic Wars, declaring:

> 'Every day during the season there were two or three balls. During that winter one could go dancing for 63 nights in succession, never returning home until five or six in the morning . . . The Galop, that famous Galop which has been so much danced since, made its appearance in the salons . . . and it became the favourite of the moment. The Mazurka was also launched at this time . . . It was danced by four couples and it was full of grace and energy. I remember how much difficulty there was in learning the famous "turning step" and the effect that it produced.'

The *galop* was possibly the simplest dance ever introduced into a ballroom. In 2/4 time a couple would dash down the room in a series of simple

steps, occasionally turning. Another dance of this period, the *mazurka* (originally a Polish round dance), conquered both the public balls and theatrical dance. In its socially refined form it depended upon a certain amount of improvisation by the dancers, which seems to have inhibited its popularity. In the theatre, however, it achieved immense success, making its first appearance in the ballets of the Romantic period and reaching its apotheosis in the Russian ballets of the late nineteenth century, where the presence of such well-known Polish-born dancers as the Kshessinski family gave it extraordinary vitality and brio in performance.

As the *waltz* crossed national boundaries and moved into France and England, it met with considerable opposition. In 1812 the London *Times* recorded:

'Monday morning a duel took place between General Thornton and Mr Theodore Hook. After exchanging one shot each the affair was amicably settled. It originated in a silly dispute on the subject of the dance called the Waltz, the General having praised it in high terms and the author having bitterly reprobated it as leading to the most licentious consequences.'[10]

Even by 1829 when the *waltz* had become universally accepted and universally performed, August Bournonville, the great Danish ballet master, only twenty-four years old and no prude, could remark about the waltz:

'One might overlook its violence, which causes the blood to race, and the disarray it causes in dress, yet I believe that as more cultured society, both in language, custom and dress as in all pleasures, differs from the lower classes, it also ought to make its dance a little less accessible to those whose mind and manners are lacking the requisite grace, because I consider that it is impossible to discern a degree of propriety in Waltzes . . . I do believe that it would not hurt to have a little less Waltzing at balls.'[11]

Even Lord Byron was against the waltz. He declared that the sight of his wife dancing with another man was like 'two cockchafers spitted on the same Bodekin'. But no amount of moral opprobrium could kill a dance which, as Captain Gronow records: 'turned the heads of society generally, descended to their feet, and the Waltz was practised in the morning in certain noble mansions in London with unparalleled assiduity.'

The *waltz* had arrived and the *waltz* did not go away. Other dances emerged and rivalled it for a time, but the fascination of its rhythm and the extraordinary emotional appeal of the dance itself have never really faded. Its greatest years were those associated with the Strauss dynasty in Vienna during the second half of the nineteenth century. With the emergence of operetta, the *waltz* inevitably became an integral part of the lyric

theatre. In ballets, operas, in symphonic music even, its insidious rhythms could not be resisted. Its attraction continued throughout the twentieth century, epitomizing a nostalgia for the unclouded society which people believed had given it birth. For Richard Strauss in *Rosenkavalier* it was the spirit of an age; for Ravel in *La Valse* it was the hectic dance of a doomed society. Even in the cinema and popular theatre of the 1930s *waltzes* were poignantly featured. We have but to remember René Clair's *Un Carnet de bal* or Noël Coward's *Bitter Sweet*; and the joyous Fred Astaire in *Swing Time* with Jerome Kern's 'Waltz in Swing Time'.

Even more remarkable is the fact that the *waltz* has never left the ballroom. At any dance function today, the *waltz* inevitably features. In the ballet theatre it is worth noting that the greatest box office hit that the New York City Ballet has had in recent years is George Balanchine's *Vienna Waltzes,* an apotheosis of triple time to the music of Johann Strauss, Franz Lehár and Richard Strauss.

The indefatigable Thomas Wilson decided to produce *The Correct Method of German and French Waltzing* in 1816, whose title goes on to declare that it contains 'Instructions for Performing all the Movements and Attitudes in that Truly Fashionable Species of Dancing, that, from the

The Original Mazurka (above), a detail from a mid-nineteenth century American lithographed music cover, indicates how the social dances of Europe were swiftly acclimatized to the New World. (Museum of the City of New York)

A cotillon (above right) in Edwardian times remained one of the central features of private parties. Usually a dance for an entire assembly, it contained complicated figures, and prizes were awarded for the best dancers. It was often led by the hostess and her partner and involved the distribution of 'favours' which served to break the ice at the beginning of a ball.

Frontispiece to Thomas Wilson's The Correct Method of German and French Waltzing of 1816 (right) illustrates the correct positions for the dance. (Royal Academy of Dancing Library, London).

Graceful Effect and Beauty of its Movements, has obtained an Esteemed Ascendancy over every other Department of that Polite Branch of Education.'

In it Wilson, who was writing in the years immediately following the end of the Napoleonic wars, declares:

'Waltzing since its origin, has ever been a particular favourite amusement in the higher circles of fashion; and from the recent influx of foreigners into this country, and the visits of the English to the Continent, where Waltzing, as well as every other species of dancing, are much more indulged in than in this country, it has now become much more fashionable with us.'

The argument of Wilson's introduction to his manual was to impress upon the public that the *waltz* was neither indecorous nor lewd, but elegant and graceful, and to be preferred to other forms of social dance.

As late as 1829, George Yates, in his survey *The Ball or A Glance at Almack's*, offers a commentary upon the social dance in the reign of George IV. Even in this age of the *waltz*, he can refer back to a dance which must have been merely a memory to the older performers of the day, when he reminds his readers of the late eighteenth-

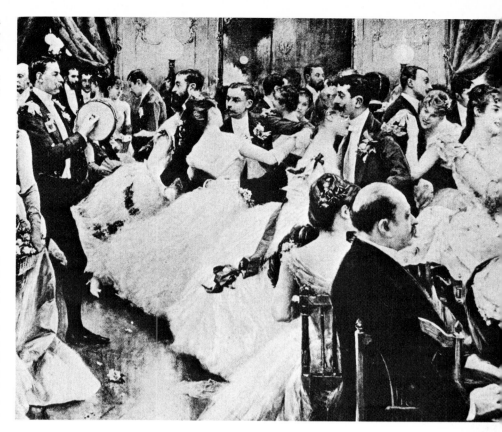

century ballet master John Gallini's advocacy of the *minuet*:

'Persons of every size and shape are susceptible of grace and improvement from the Minuet. The shoulders are drawn back, as it were, to retreat from sight or, as the French express it *bien effacés*, the knees turning well outward with a free play; the air, the shape, noble and unconstrained, the turns and movements easy; in short, to an actor, in all characters, it gives a graceful mien and presence. But in serious characters especially it suggests that striking portliness, that majestic tread of the stage, by which some actors from their very first appearance so happily dispose the public to a favourable reception; an influence of the first importance, which a good actor will hardly despise.' [Yates adds] 'Whilst an actor is in the exercise of his profession, he should, on no account, discontinue the practice of the Minuet.'

With the Victorian age, and the rapidly burgeoning wealth of the middle classes throughout Europe, you enter a heyday of both public and private social dancing. The literary testimony of the novels of the period, the extraordinary wealth of drawings to be seen in *Punch*, notably those by John Leech and later by George du Maurier, and the earlier caricature drawings of George Cruikshank, suggest how essential a part of life dancing was, not only with the aristocracy but also with the newly-rich middle classes as well.

As with the earlier *mazurka*, there was at this time a craze for adapting folk dances both for the theatre and the ballroom. A clear indication of this comes with the sheet music published during the period of the Romantic ballet. Lithographed covers by such artists as Brandard would show the stars of the ballet in a *redowa, varsovienne, polonaise, mazurka* or *polka* which they had danced in some celebrated ballet, while the music itself recorded the adaptation of this same dance to social demands.

The most important and the most lasting of these dances was the *polka*. Originally from Bohemia, it surfaced in Prague as a social dance of tremendous energy, and thence began a headlong career which was to bring it to Paris by the early 1840s and to London a few years later. By this time contemporary observers could say that it was a madness, a delirium, a frenzy, and polka-mania inflamed the private parties of the gentry and the public dances of the lesser orders. Polka-mania reigned. Its electric rhythm – one and *two*, one and *two* – galvanized the whole of Europe, it seems. An example of how the insatiable craze for *polka* disrupted the pattern of an evening's dancing comes from the report by the dancing master Coulon on a ball given by the Duke of Wellington at Apsley House, in honour of Queen Victoria's birthday in 1844:

'The Polka furore rose to such a pitch as to be danced, we are told, six times during the evening. Now this will not do. In our opinion the Polka, as an addition to the various amusements of a ball, stands certainly without parallel: still it ought by no means to detract from the usual amusements by superseding all other dances.'

(The enduring nature of the *polka* can be noted in the music hall song 'See Me Dance the Polka' which appeared in 1886, was made famous by George Grossmith, and still survives.)

In Paris, social dancing was no less important than in London, but here you also come face to face with the wilder excesses associated with public balls and masquerades so powerfully evoked in the drawings of Gavarni and celebrated also, later in the century, in the work of Toulouse-Lautrec. The forms of the dance in polite society were constantly being enriched and constantly being changed. *Contredanses* and *quadrilles* continued, *waltzing* of course was still supreme, *polkas, galops* and reels were all to be found. In addition there emerged such forms as the *schottische*, the *lancers* (a development from the *quadrille*) and several others which also survive in the 'Old Time' dances of today.

The tradition of public balls, exemplified in France in the eighteenth century by the Bals de l'Opéra, reaches a high point of exuberance and, indeed, of immorality in the pleasure gardens of Paris in the mid-nineteenth century. Most celebrated was the Bal Mabille in the Avenue Montaigne, opened in 1840 by Charles Mabille. From humble beginnings it developed into a haunt of pleasure of some luxury, and after having first attracted merely the servant class it became frequented by members of the Jockey Club and even of royalty. (The Prince of Wales visited it, crossing the Channel for a day to see the *cancan* which was by then flourishing, and catching a train back to London in the small hours.)

Soon the Bal Mabille became a magnet for all levels of Paris society, who went there not only to dance but also to watch the frenzied exhibitions given by young men and women who achieved an almost professional status in their execution of the increasingly acrobatic dances. A vivid contemporary description recalls the Bal Mabille scene:

'The mad, bad, merry music would strike up and a set formed, the . . . men chalking the soles of their shoes and planting their high silk hats on the back of their head, the ladies coyly examining the condition of their skirts. The foreigners and country visitors and *gobemouches* [bumpkins] would gather round, forming a wall six or seven feet, leaving a space of ten to fifteen feet for the dancers. Bang! And the dancers would commence their wild gyrations, the men slinging their limbs about as if they did not belong to them, the women frisking their draperies in time to the music, and posturing while revealing a liberal display of lower limbs. Faster and faster the pace would grow, the women more madly energetic, their postures more hideously indecorous, until the final bars of the tune would be wound up in a series of acrobatic movements that would call down the *vivas* of the excited and amused spectators.'[12]

The stars of these dances (the men were outshone by their female companions, who came from the lowest stratum of society but acquired extreme notoriety from the bravura of their manner)

The popularity of the polka – *and of George Grossmith's song of 1886 – was phenomenal, and all London sang:*

You should see me dance the Polka,
You should see me cover the ground;
You should see my coat tails flying
As I jump my partner round.

This music covers dates from 1889. (Raymond Mander and Joe Mitchenson Theatre Collection, London)

The cancan *at its most extravagant – in 1889 – was quite a contrast to the* polka. *The lady doing the splits is the notorious La Goulue (Greedy Guts). Her real name was Louise Weber and she rose from the gutter to riches, and then reverted to the gutter. The ladies on either side of her were known as La Sauterelle (The Grasshopper), Nini Pattes-en-l'air (Nini Paws in the Air), Môme Fromage (The Cheese Kid) and Grille d'Egout (Sewer-Grating). (Raymond Mander and Joe Mitchenson Theatre Collection, London)*

included such characters as Céleste Mogador, and the famous Rigolboche who became the absolute queen of the *cancan*. Their antics seem to capture something of the wildness of life during the period of the Second Empire. With the emergence of the Third Republic in 1870, Bal Mabille's great days seem to have gone, and this popular form of dancing was to become associated in the main with the theatrical form celebrated by Toulouse-Lautrec as he saw it at the Moulin Rouge. His portraits of Valentin-le-Désossé, and La Goulue fix the style most clearly.

In the Bal Mabille's heyday during the second Empire (1852–1870) *bals masqués* enjoyed comparable popularity. These public balls, which often marked the beginning of Lent or the period of carnival, were occasions of considerable sexual licence and illustrations such as Cham's and Gavarni's record the dancers' dubious moral attitudes.

SOCIAL DANCE IN AMERICA

In the nineteenth century America was to turn increasingly to the social dance as an expression of polite social ambition. This was at a time when the country itself was to move from an agricultural to an industrial identity. Naturally the forms of European social dance were adopted in America; the influx of immigrants was to bring some of the simpler and more earthy forms of popular dance to the United States, and in agricultural areas these more primitive forms and square dances were to remain consistently popular as long as

the ethnic identity of a group held true.

The social attitudes towards dancing in America by the middle of the nineteenth century were those common also to the European middle classes. Dancing was thought to be a perfectly acceptable form of relaxation when it did not provoke the tirades of the non-conformist church. In the better schools, social dancing was one of the subjects of instruction, and the mid-nineteenth century *Godey's Lady's Book* (edited by the headmistress of a girls' boarding school in Philadelphia) provided instructional articles on the correct way to dance. The *waltz*, inevitably, was at first greeted with some alarm, but by the 1830s it was accepted, if performed with a certain decent decorum. Other European dances, the *polka*, for example, were also to sweep America, but by the latter years of the century an authentic American dance emerged which was to cross the Atlantic to conquer the Old World.

This was the *military schottische* or *barn dance*. It owes its latter title to the fact that the *schottische* was first danced to a tune called 'Dancing in the Barn'. It was both simple and ebullient, with foot stamps, and slightly refined in manner it was to arrive in Europe and to sweep the ballrooms. A similar popularity was accorded to the *Boston two-step*, which owed a great deal to the fact that John Philip Sousa, King of the March, produced a vast body of popular marches headed by the 'Washington Post March', which lent itself particularly to the energy and bravura of the *two-step*. As a dance it was basically a marching step with interpolated skips, and its vivacity endeared itself to the younger generation in those carefree days of the early twentieth century.

But these are the years when ragtime is to open

up the vistas which lead towards jazz and the emergence of new dance forms to these new dance rhythms. An important forerunner was the *cake-walk*. It came into popularity in the last decade of the nineteenth century, when it was performed by Negro dancers in minstrel shows. It remained exclusively a dance for blacks, acquiring both a stylized costume – tall hat, tall collar and tails for the men, frothing, elaborate frocks for the women – and a stylized manner of high-stepping strutting. Elaborated and brilliantly performed, it acquired an almost theatrical flavour in its progress through the southern States to New York. From there it entered the ballrooms of society, but more importantly it crossed the footlights, and became a staple of vaudeville and of the musical comedy theatre. The *cake-walk* was to acquire musical respectability when Debussy included the 'Golly-wogs' Cake-walk' in the 'Children's Corner Suite' for piano which he dedicated to his daughter.

But the most popular of the dances which followed the *Boston two-step* was the *one-step*. Inspired by ragtime, it owed much of its attraction to the fact that, as Vernon Castle the exhibition ballroom dancer and teacher observed: 'it can be learned in a very little time by anyone, young or old, who is able to walk in time with the music – and, I might say, by many who cannot.'[13] With masterly simplicity the *one-step* required its performers to dance one step to a beat. This simplicity fitted it to a great deal of the ragtime music which dominated the period and as Vernon Castle added: 'when a good orchestra plays a rag one has simply *got* to move. The One Step is the dance for ragtime music.'

This comment is the key to radically different attitudes before and after 1910. Prior to that admittedly slightly arbitrary date, the main attraction of the dance lay in the steps and in the pleasure of movement. Thereafter the main impetus was from the rhythm of the music and the impulse it gave to the dance. The acceptance of a strong rhythmic thrust in dancing – owing everything to the music that was coming out of New Orleans – was to transform the new social dances of the wartime and post-war years.[14]

You can also see at this moment how the momentum behind the new dance forms and new dance crazes is to be found in the new music of the New World. Central to this new view of social dancing were the most celebrated exhibition dancers of the period, Vernon and Irene Castle.

The Castles had initially met in the theatre, and on their marriage in 1911 they continued to appear for a time dancing in revues, but by 1912 they were world famous for their extreme elegance and for the beauty and style of Irene's dress. In exhibitions, in appearances in clubs and plays, they did more than anyone else to popularize ballroom dancing. They were accepted and idolized by society on both sides of the Atlantic, and their advocacy was to make acceptable many dances which would otherwise have been socially dubious. Typical was the *tango*, which at this time created an extraordinary sensation.

The *tango*'s origins can be traced to a slave dance in Cuba, whence it percolated to the River Plate and by assimilation and adulteration emerged by the turn of the century as a popular dance of the Argentine. By no means respectable, it was introduced into Europe at the beginning of the twentieth century, and in France was transformed into a more polite form. But it was the Castles who elevated it to a dance accepted in any ballroom, by purifying it of its coarse associations and turning it into a thing of beauty. Its popularity thereafter was immense, so much so that in London (which also knew the *tango* thanks to a teacher, Gladys Crozier, whose book *The Tango and How to Dance It* was published in 1913) there emerged the craze for 'Tango Teas', held at the most fashionable hotels.

The tango *craze after the First World War, when it had become socially respectable. The women's backless dresses and the soft fabrics made the dance both more* risqué *and more enjoyable. The mood was exactly caught by Georges Barbier in this illustration for* La Guirlande des Mois, *Paris, 1920.*

The *tango* craze was to bring other dances of Latin American origin in its train, and of these the *maxixe* was to have the greatest appeal. It was a graceful dance much favoured by the Castles, who refined its more outrageous swooping movements. Its reign, however, was short and other attempts at novelty dances before the First World War which were no more successful included:

'. . . the *Furlana* from Northern Italy, and then came the *Lulufado* from Portugal, the *Roulli-Toulli* with its windmill-like action of the arms from goodness knows where, and the *Tao-Tao*, the biggest humbug of the lot, mere Chinese bunkum. All this came to nothing.'[15]

What did come was the *fox-trot*. Although the facts are not clear, it seems most likely that this dance was originated by a comedian, Harry Fox, who worked in the Ziegfeld Follies and as early as 1913 had introduced some quick trotting steps into a dance to ragtime music in his act. Here can be observed the continuing phenomenon – the influence of musical comedy, vaudeville, and music hall upon social dancing. Popular performers, dancers and singers, could by their advocacy impose a dance upon the general public which the fashionable dance teachers then quickly took up and profited by. (This holds true even today of disco dancing of the Travolta type – the 1977 film *Saturday Night Fever* started a craze which the dancing schools were soon to seize upon.)

Harry Fox's innovation was taken up by a dancing teacher in New York, who first organized a group of showgirls to demonstrate the *fox-trot* and then encouraged an audience to emulate them. Gradually a dance form emerged which, by 1914, was being shown and taught both in New York and London. The *fox-trot* was soon to replace the *one-step*, the Hesitation *waltz* (so enchantingly performed by the Castles), the *maxixe* and the *tango*. Its simplicity was part of its immediate appeal – especially at a time when, with the outbreak of war, men on leave were finding tremendous relaxation in public and private dances but had no time to learn complex new figures. An American teacher, defined the steps as: 'There are but two things to remember; first a slow walk, two counts to a step; second a trot or run, one count to each step.'[16]

THE JAZZ AGE

But the most vital impulse to social dancing in the twentieth century was to come with the emergence of jazz from New Orleans into metropolitan New York, and thence around the world. From the momentous day in 1913 when the Original Dixieland Jazz Band became established in New York, it took but a few years for jazz to dominate the field of popular music. The spread of recorded music through the popularity of the gramophone in the post-war years, and the emergence of widespread public broadcasting at the same time, helped propagate jazz rhythms and jazz attitudes as no music had been spread before, and in the exuberant, seemingly carefree days for young people after the end of the First World War, jazz became synonymous with freedom, good times, and an abandonment of many of the social attitudes and taboos of their parents' generation. From now on people dance what they want to dance; the cataclysm of the war broke down social barriers, and the advent of the *palais de danse* as a public dance hall – very different from the more exclusive assemblies and clubs of a previous age – helped free both dancers and dance.

One dance in particular seems to epitomize the freedom and the wildness of the 1920s. This was the *charleston*. Named after the town in Southern Carolina where it reportedly originated among

Note the precise angle of the male partner's hands on this 'Gossiping' fox-trot *music cover (above) of the 1920s which also records the encouragement – by way of high prize money – given to dancing by the* Daily Sketch, *one of the popular newspapers of the time. (Raymond Mander and Joe Mitchenson Theatre Collection, London)*

Vernon and Irene Castle dance the maxixe (left). *Their elegance transformed ballroom dancing into an art. About 1914 the* maxixe *was replaced in popularity by the simpler* fox-trot.

the black population, it was noted for sideways kicks and extreme speed of execution. Slightly adapted, but without losing any of its vivacity and speed, it emerged as a craze which seemed to infect the entire younger generation. Once again the stage was to launch the dance, in the *Follies* of 1923 at the New Amsterdam Theatre, New York, the first act finale introduced the *charleston*. From that moment it took over. The frantic kicking and side stepping associated with it were quickly to gain it a reputation as a dangerous dance. In London in July 1925 *The Dancing Times* magazine, then edited by the late Philip Richardson, organized a special Charleston Tea, at which the well-known exhibition dancers Annette Mills and Robert Sielle were asked to demonstrate this dance which they had lately learned in New York. Within a short time the *charleston* had swept into such ballrooms as the Hammersmith Palais, as well as fashionable houses (the then Prince of Wales was addicted to it – at the time of the famous song 'I danced with a man who danced with a girl who danced with the Prince of Wales'). So dangerous was the mania for the *charleston*, so frantic the kicking, that in dance halls throughout the country the letters PCQ (Please Charleston Quietly) were prominently displayed, and the newspapers indulged in fulminations, as furious as those once made by the Church about ring dances, against this orgiastic epidemic.

Some indication of its fantastic popularity comes with the Charleston Ball held by C. B. Cochran at London's Royal Albert Hall on 15 December 1926, when nearly ten thousand people watched competitions (among the participants Fred Astaire) and joined in the general dancing.

Other cult dances of the period also deserve some mention. Like the earlier *bunny hug* and *turkey trot* of the ragtime era – dances which made amusing references to animal behaviour – two dances of the 1920s found short-lived favour at the time of the *charleston*. These were the *black bottom* and the *shimmy* both are now remembered more through the popular songs of the era than for their actual steps, though the catchy line 'I wish I could shimmy like my sister Kate' seems to have passed into popular parlance.

A more distressing phenomenon of the jazz age and the depression in the USA was the dance marathon, marvellously portrayed in Horace McCoy's novel *They Shoot Horses Don't They?* These were spectacles as brutal in their way as any Roman circus. Hapless contestants were required to dance until, literally, they dropped, the ultimate survivors receiving a handsome cash prize which formed but a small portion of the gross receipts. As tests of endurance they were cruel, as dancing they were mere crass exercises in perpetual motion. At the end of two or three days all that the contestants could do was to drag themselves sleep-walking round the floor. By 1933 they were officially banned, their continuance to that moment being a terrible indictment of the

An Expressionist and satiric view of dancing in the 1920s (left). Detail from The Metropolis *triptych by the German realist painter Otto Dix (1891–1969). (Galerie der Stadt, Stuttgart)*

Bee Jackson (below left) as 1926 World Champion of the Charleston provides a characteristic and vivid image of the mid-1920s dance-mad girl.

Jitterbugging originated in the United States in the 1930s, and spread wider afield with the American Service forces in the Second World War. The 1950s style (right) demonstrates the athletic attributes required of both partners to complete a passable 'under-arm swing'.

plight of the unemployed who could find in them a promise of money not available on the labour market.

Throughout the 1920s and 1930s dance in the ballroom maintained its continuing identity as a polite art which transcended every social barrier. The basic technique of the 'standard four' dances – the *fox-trot*, the *waltz*, the *tango* and the *quick-step* – had been codified in England (codification is explained later on in this chapter) and the insidious rhythms of the so-called Latin American dances, above all the *rumba*, introduced a new form of sexual display typified by the gigolo image of the sultry Southern male. These dances, then as now, maintained their place as an acceptable social form; they featured in fashionable private parties as well as in such public affairs as hunt balls and dinner dances held at big hotels.

But, as always, a more popular and more spontaneous stream of dancing was emerging, dictated, all the time, by the kind of popular music that the dance bands were playing and which was becoming available through its instant dissemination by means of radio and gramophone records. If jazz had been the dominant rhythm of the 1920s it was soon to be superseded by swing or boogie-woogie and a dance style evolved in the 1930s in the United States called the *lindy*, or, more widely, *jitterbug*. Its origin is credited to a Harlem marathon champion, George 'Shorty' Snowden, who in the course of one marathon flung his partner away and began to 'improvise a few solo steps of his own'.

With the explosion of popularity of Benny Goodman's swing band in the mid-1930s, *jitterbug* became the dance of the young who responded frenetically to the new beat and also to the opportunities it allowed for improvisation, for the use of breakaway steps and for flinging a partner into the air.

Jitterbugging was an American pastime – at the New York World's Fair in 1939 there were some remarkable exhibitions of this athletic and frankly sexual dance – but with the entry of the United States into the war in 1941 it spread to every part of the world in which American service forces were to be found. This new and vital dance provided a release from wartime pressures and the entire aspect of popular dancing was thereafter to bear the imprint of this demanding and provocative display.

With the massive social and psychological upheavals which were to be felt among the young people of the post-war years, there emerged an even more strongly youth-orientated form of music and dance. This was exemplified by *rock 'n' roll*, introduced to delighted teenagers by the film *Rock Around the Clock*, made in 1956, which featured Bill Haley and his Comets. His music was a derivation from the blues and its pounding beat, simplicity of form, and the insistent, blatant sound of the newly-developed electric guitar began a new cult which was to find its greatest hero in Elvis Presley. Presley's numbers had a hypnotic force

over the young and they also typified the physical response to this music, with pelvic thrusts which gave such frank expression to the basic drive behind *rock 'n' roll*. The sexual impulse implied in the very words 'rock' and 'roll', which featured in the lyrics of so many of its songs, the rebellious extravagance of the movement, the basic emotion of the lyrics, were all examples of a specifically teenage culture. At a time when television and popular music had discovered how to communicate instantly, world-wide, with the young, *rock 'n' roll* became a fever which effectively isolated a teenage generation from the rest of society. It was the music of the young, it was their dance, and much of the rest of society felt both alienated and shocked by this uncontrolled hysterical manifestation.

Dancers of the late 1950s (left) caught in mid-lindy hop at a club with East-Ender Tommy Steele (first known as the Bermondsey Miracle) keeping the rhythm going in his early days 'doing the clubs'.

In *rock 'n' roll* as in *jitterbug* boys and girls were still dancing together, even if the dancing allowed them either to lose contact or indulge in such bizarre antics as the girl embracing the man's waist with her legs. But the next craze, the *twist*, went to the other extreme. For the first time in centuries dancers abandoned physical contact. Sparked off by the appearance of a singer called Chubby Checker, who sang and danced on an American television programme, the *twist* owed much of its appeal – and the appeal was to all age groups, all strata of society – to its very simplicity. It amounted to little more than pelvic gyrations 'as if drying your back with a towel' accompanying a foot movement that resembled the treading of a cigarette-end into the ground. It could be practised alone in front of a looking-glass; it could be danced alone in the most crowded locales; it isolated the man from the woman as never before in two hundred years of social dancing. It seemed, at the height of its popularity, to threaten the whole dance teaching establishment – until dance teachers quickly began to offer lessons in the *twist*, as they were to do later with disco dancing.

Succeeding musical fashions and succeeding dance fashions replaced the *twist*. In an age of instant news, of ultra-fast communication through television and radio, there came instant fashions in popular music and dance, thanks not least to television programmes which featured young people dancing to the pop groups of the day.

The dominance throughout the entire century of the Afro-American musical style was nowhere more apparent than in the popularity given to reggae music and soul music with the turn of the 1970s. It reflected the new social consciousness attendant upon all forms of black culture, and the most powerful influence of soul music in regard to dance has been in the emergence of a more brilliant and more taxing dance style. This is the dance that, in the 1970s, was to be found in clubs which catered specifically for the young. There is evidence of an unusual cross-fertilization between the demotic of social dance and theatrical dance, itself a tribute to the vastly increased popularity of theatrical dance among the young. Anyone visiting the clubs favoured by the young in the late 1970s could be amazed by the acrobatic skill and by the sometimes dazzling abilities of the performers, both black and white.

At a time when the younger generation was aware of an aimlessness in their own lives, and were convinced that society was often hostile to the urban teenager, dance became an exceptional form of release. At the Casino Club in Wigan, Lancashire, for example, the young danced the night away from Saturday night until eight o'clock on Sunday morning, their technical skill in producing what could rightly be called spontaneous choreography suggesting that in this dancing they found profound emotional and physical release. In December 1977 a British Independent Television programme took cameras into this Wigan club and provided a fascinating portrait of a way of life in which dancing was of crucial importance, forming the high point of the week. Young people from all over Northern England and a few even from London met for this weekly, cathartic ritual. The television programme showed teenagers dancing to soul music, and in the early hours of the morning plunging into the swimming pool, breakfasting, and making their way home – sometimes many miles across country.

Just as the mid-1950s film *Rock Around the*

December 1961 – the twist *demonstrated by its initiator Chubby Checker (below).*
The impact of the twist *was considerable as it allowed for anyone to dance alone – and to their own style – thus breaking up the traditional male-female partnership which had been prevalent for so long in social dancing.*

Clock was a watershed in the emergence of *rock 'n' roll*, so too did the gigantic success of *Saturday Night Fever* in 1977 mark the beginning of the disco craze. In this film John Travolta introduced to yet another generation of dancers a style with which they could identify. It was the age of the discothèque, with its darkness, noise and curious intimacy while, at the other extreme, the immense popularity of disco resulted in enormous, nation-wide competitions in Britain. In a way, the disco craze reflects the emergence of a new type of performer, of the social dancer as soloist and as choreographer. The identity of social dance is here called into question. It rejects the restraints of form, preferring instead extemporization and fantasy, or an individuality in evolving a choreo-graphed text which may almost be said to hark back to certain attitudes of Renaissance dance, as developed by itinerant dancing masters. Certainly disco dancing is arduous, often very exciting, and, essentially, fun. The image of the young dancer in the disco scene is a brilliant one. In a national 'Saturday Night Fever' Disco Dance Competition organized in Britain by the National Association of Youth Clubs, in December 1978, hundreds of young disco fans competed. It is significant that, as a Sunday colour supplement reported, 'Apart from actual dancing ability, teams are marked on visual impact and appearance, plus the way they interpret the music in dance.'[17] One of the young competitors summed it all up by saying 'The most important thing with disco dancing is to get behind the beat and just let yourself go with the music. We like to wear gym shoes because they're soft and comfortable and easy to move around in.'

But if this entire tradition of free expression and improvisation occupied the young, there remains a parallel tradition no less significant and no less popular. This is the world of ballroom dancing and ballroom dancing teachers. From the early 1920s until today Britain has been the dominant ballroom dancing country in the world.

In the early 1920s Philip Richardson, then editor of *The Dancing Times*, called a number of informal conferences of teachers of ballroom dancing in order to bring some kind of order into the ballroom world which, revolting against the autocracy of the Victorian dancing master and bedazzled by the new dances that had crossed the Atlantic, was in danger of developing into 'an artistic bolshevism'. The growing popularity of ballroom dancing competitions emphasized the need for a recognized codification of technique if judges were to have any standards from which to work on a common basis. Particularly, there was confusion about the two forms of *fox-trot* then being danced, slow and fast – the fast becoming the *quickstep*. This last was an amalgamation of the 'quick' *fox-trot* and elements from the *charleston* in 4/4 time, as 'slow, slow, quick, quick.' The most important step towards codification came in 1924 when the London-based Imperial Society of Teachers of Dancing set up its Ballroom Branch. This move 'had as great an influence on

ballroom as did the founding of the Académie Royale by Louis XIV of France on the ballet'.[18] The five teachers who formed the first com-mittee were Josephine Bradley, Eve Tynegate-Smith, Muriel Simmons, Mrs Lisle Humphreys and Victor Silvester – then a celebrated ballroom dancer but later to become the band leader whose name was synonymous with 'strict tempo' music for dancing.

Recognizing that the old technique based on ballet, with the feet turned out and the weight taken mainly on the toes (as in the *polka* and the old form of *waltz*), had totally been superseded, they established the new laws, based on natural movement and walking steps with the feet parallel, and worked out a syllabus for the teaching of the four standard dances: *waltz, fox-trot, tango* and *quickstep,* which was to be perfected as the 'English Style'. This was eventually to spread throughout the world and is today known as the 'International Style'. The supreme difference be-tween these dances and the popular craze dances was that in ballroom hold the man led the woman, in close embrace, moving forward as she moved backward and directing her progress across the ballroom floor. The formality of the style, there-fore, brought a well-mannered intimacy which appealed to adult couples; ballroom dancing as performed on purely social occasions had a romantic quality.

In the competition field, of course, the emphasis was to be entirely on technique, on musical response and a sense of performance on the ball-room floor that would attract both audiences and judges. To control the competition world, and especially to give any status to championship titles, the Official Board of Ballroom Dancing was set up in London in 1929; this grew out of the informal conferences. Its members included repre-sentatives of all the teaching organizations and also some independent members who played a prominent part in the world of ballroom. Philip Richardson was the first chairman and for over thirty years the Board functioned from the offices of *The Dancing Times* – until, by 1965, they had totally outgrown each other.

To the 'standard four' in due course were added the fast Viennese *waltz* and then the Latin Ameri-can dances, *rumba, samba, paso doble, jive* (a refinement of the *jitterbug*) and the *cha cha cha.* *Rumba*, with its mixed origins in African, Spanish and Caribbean rhythms, came essentially out of Cuba but was coloured also by the American jazz influence on Cuban dance halls in the 1920s.

'Basically the Rumba is the spirit and soul of Latin American music and dance: it has com-pletely fascinating rhythms and bodily ex-pressions which enable the lady dancer to express her grace and femininity and the man to show her off in this way while himself feeling the spell of the music and the sheer joy of being alive.'[19]

Rumba was comparatively late in arriving in

John Travolta in true disco stance, from the 1977 Paramount film Saturday Night Fever *which sparked off the disco craze.*

England. Until 1946 the version taught was basically the 'square' *rumba*, popular in the United States, with the couples dancing within the confine of a square. Later, however, and thanks almost entirely to the researches of Monsieur Pierre, a Basque living in London, and his partner Doris Lavelle, who visited Cuba many times, the Cuban *rumba*, danced on the second beat, became in 1955 the officially recognized version.

The *samba* is the dance of Brazil, taken there by African slaves but transformed into the national dance and exploding into the streets during carnival time in Rio de Janeiro. The Castles used it in their routines, Carmen Miranda exploited its thrilling rhythms in the movies and by the 1950s it had become world renowned and an essential ingredient in competitions as well as being greatly enjoyed by social dancers.

Paso doble, with its imitations of the bull fight, stems of course from Spain but was refined for the ballroom in the southern regions of France. It is a dance that lends itself wonderfully to the demands of 'exhibition' or 'demonstration' dancing – displays by professional ballroom dancers. The man represents the matador, the lady his cape and the opportunities for playfully embroidering upon the basic steps are boundless.

Unlike the other Latin dances, the *jive* is not a progressive dance and is, therefore, especially popular on the small or crowded dance floor. As we have said, it is a refinement of the *jitterbug* and it is a remarkable instance of intelligent dancing masters seeing in a popular craze the seeds of a more formal dance. Alex Moore, the foremost authority on ballroom technique and the first

Chairman of the International Council of Ballroom Dancing, said:

> 'An All England Jitterbug Championship . . . has just been held in London and I must confess that it was about the most disgusting degrading sight I have ever seen in a ballroom. Leap-frog, double somersaults, "kicking the ceiling", and peckin' were but a few of the "steps" used by the competitors in their efforts to gain applause. In spite of this I still think there is room for a mild Jitterbug dance in our ballrooms.'[20]

Cha cha cha is a descendant of the Cuban *mambo*, immensely popular because of the easy count of the rhythm and the very name which is chanted on the three quick steps which either precede or follow the two slow ones – 'step, step, cha cha cha!'

Two other forms of ballroom dancing must be mentioned. After the Second World War, in England there was a great revival of the old dances which had been so enjoyed earlier in the century, dances such as the *lancers*, the *military two-step* and the *veleta*. These appealed especially to the older generation and were danced in clubs throughout the country, mostly meeting in village halls but sometimes converging on the metropolis for such events as the national *veleta* contest held at the Royal Albert Hall. The appeal of this kind of dancing is essentially a communal one. Each couple on the floor is doing the same steps in sequence; usually the club leader, or the inventors of a new dance, start the proceedings and then all join in, moving round the floor in unison. The style was at first dubbed 'old time' or even, more ludicrously, 'olde tyme', but this gradually gave way to the more accurate 'sequence' as the modern and Latin ballroom dances were adapted to its form. There are now hundreds of these dances and competitions for the 'best inventive dance' are held throughout Britain, organized by the many teaching associations and blessed with Official Board approval.

Formation dancing, the 'ballet of the ballroom', was pioneered by Olive Ripman, a teacher skilled in all forms of dancing, and popularized especially on the television screen where the cameras could relish the complex patterns made by the teams of six or eight highly-trained couples in ballroom dance routines which were in fact choreographed very precisely. Britain pioneered the form but by the late 1970s had lost supremacy to Germany and the United States.

Today, as throughout its whole history, social dance continues to draw from many sources, being influenced always by the social climate of the time. The pattern remains the same; a dance springs from a people's response to a new rhythm or to a new treatment of an old rhythm and then is shaped and given rules so that it may aspire to a social accomplishment. It is not preposterous to speak of the art of ballroom dancing.

Some of the dedicated contestants (left and below) at the 1979 EMI World Disco Dancing Competition held in London. Disco dancing is totally personal. You may be performing solo, opposite a partner or be one of a crowd on the dance floor, but whichever way, what you do is your own choice – there are no rules, no conventions.

CHAPTER SIX

BALLET DE COUR

To distinguish them from the guests, the moresca dancers at the Vienna court of the Emperor Maximilian I wore almost uniform costumes of fashions dating from fifty to a hundred years earlier. Characteristic are their close-fitting masks of semi-opaque black netting, often worn by the women as well. This illustration of Maximilian leading a dance of the torch-bearers forms part of the Freydal Codex of unpublished water-colours inspired by the Emperor in 1502. (A facsimile in black and white was published in 1882.) The Emperor did much to encourage court mummeries and even knighted the famous dancing master Guglielmo Ebreo. (National-bibliothek, Vienna)

The elements of popular dance among the nobility (right) are well illustrated in this detail from a fifteenth-century manuscript. Note the 'one-man-band' musician playing his pipe and drum simultaneously. (Bodleian Library, Oxford – Ms. Douce 204, f. 15v, 1430-50 Catalonia, Roussillon)

DANCE IN the first millennium of the Christian era was to be found as a persistent ingredient of church festivities in Italy, France and England. Its popularity and a certain debasement of religious dance brought about interdicts from the Councils of the Church in the seventh century. Even so there is clear evidence of the continuation of dancing not only as a folk art, but as an entertainment associated with the courtly life.

In the popular music of the later Middle Ages there are many references to dance forms and there is also evidence of masquerades and dinner dances – the equivalent of fancy dress balls in today's terms – for the nobility. Among the most celebrated of these was the *Bal des Ardents* of 1393, in which the King of France, Charles VI, and four leading gentlemen of his court appeared as 'Wild Men of the Woods'. Their costumes were made of feathers stuck to their garments with tar and wax. The Duc d'Orléans, wishing to identify them, approached too closely with a torch in his hand and the highly inflammable costumes caught fire. The King was only saved from death by fire through the quick-witted response of the Duchesse du Berry, his aunt, who smothered the flames with the train of her gown.

Among the most constant of dance forms was the round dance, the *carole*, which was performed to a sung accompaniment. Examples of this dance can be traced back to antiquity, but it emerges clearly as a very popular dance song in Provence, and after initially being associated with May-time festivities it became one of the most widely known of dances. It developed into a processional dance combining steps with small hops and leaps and there is a record of it in Boccaccio's *Decameron* (1353):

'On the first day all the ladies and young men could dance and many of them could play and sing: so, when the tables were cleared, the queen called for musical instruments. At her command Dioneo took a lute and Fiammetta a viol, and began to play a dance tune. The queen sent the servants to their meal, and then with slow steps danced with the two young men and the other ladies. After that they began to sing gay and charming songs.'

There are further representations of the *carole* in Chaucer's version of *Le Roman de la rose*, and in paintings by Lorenzetti and Fra Angelico.

The chain-like round dance had as far back as it can be traced – which is some three thousand years – always been associated with another, linear form of dance with the participants holding hands in a chain. Sometimes linking up, sometimes broken into a single strand of movement, it followed the regular rhythms of the accompanying song or melody in the Middle Ages, when it was known as the *farandole*. At this time, too, it became associated with definite patterns in covering the ground, the dancers moving through formal shapes, passing under each other's arms, or coiling in a spiral and then unwinding. Arguably there evolved from this group dance an especially significant idea: *danse à deux*, the dance for two people (whose origins are explained above), but its importance lies in the implication of two people performing a dance as a focus for the attentions of a group. Further, the movement of the dance implied its having a 'forward' and a 'backward' progression, very different from, and more purposeful than the circular motion and the linear weavings typical of the *farandole*. This was the *estampie*, which may have originated in Provence in the twelfth century, and would seem to indicate the vital breakaway from the '*carole* line' as two dancers reflected in their partnership the ideals of courtly love which were then so important.[1]

There is another social dance that should be mentioned at this time and that is the *branle*, the other form of *carole*, which differed from the *farandole* by nature of its rhythmic variety: the alternation of quick and slow steps in the same phrase or passage of dancing. It was a dance of great popularity, and it is to be found as the basis of most folk dances by the fifteenth and sixteenth centuries. Among the peasantry it was enriched, corrupted, extended; among the gentry, too, it became very popular. Even the Knights of Malta 'devised a ballet for a Court masquerade, in which an equal number of men and damsels, dressed in Turkish costume, danced a round *branle*, comprising certain gestures and twisting movements of the body, which they called a Maltese Branle. It was some forty years ago that this *branle* was first danced in France.'[2]

An important contribution to the shaping of dance forms in the Renaissance was the *moresque* (*moresco*). This originated in the festivals and dramatic representations in the Midi in which the ideas of the Crusades and the threatening figure of the Moor combined with those elements that passed into Provençal literature from the Moorish occupation of Spain. In some mystery and miracle plays, and associated dances the figure of the Moor or a Jester (*Mattaccino*) appeared. In mock combats the defeat of the Moor was shown, but gradually the war-like connotations disappeared, the scene became mere entertainment, and in a concluding dance the figure of *Mattaccino* was sometimes tossed high in the air by the other dancers. An expansion of these celebrations came with the itinerant theatres which gave performances of mystery plays and included in them danced interludes. By the early years of the Renaissance there emerged *sacre rappresentazioni*, which were adaptations of mystery plays and festivals in honour of a saint; they contained dances (sometimes *moresques* and perhaps even *basses danses*), and the princes of the period, notably Lorenzo the Magnificent (1449–1492) in Florence, developed these into *trionfi* (triumphs), which began to acquire political and social importance. In them, interludes of dance and song and declamation were interspersed as a means of welcoming important visitors or of celebrating events.

In the Middle Ages the populace went 'masking' at Christmas and feast days and celebrated in processions and round games with their faces masked or daubed with soot. These *momeries* (mummeries or mummings in English) were considered the invention of the devil but the Church

Court ladies and gentlemen dancing a lively carole *(left), the popular chain-like round dance to sung accompaniment. From a French manuscript of the* Romance of the Rose *dating from the last decade of the fifteenth century. (Bodleian Library, Oxford – Ms. Douce 195, f.7)*

Recorded for posterity is the dreadful incident of the Bal des Ardents in 1393 (above) in which King Charles VI of France and his courtiers – dressed as 'Wild Men of the Woods' – were nearly burned to death. From a fifteenth-century manuscript. (Bibliothèque Nationale, Paris)

could do nothing to prevent them, and a treatise against these maskings in 1608 noted that they were 'a heresy condemned by the fathers of the Church'. *Momeries* were not confined to the common people, for the nobility also indulged. (Just before Charles VI and his companions caught fire at the *Bal des Ardents* they had been dancing a *moresque*.)

It is from the fourteenth and fifteenth centuries that there is evidence of dinner entertainments. In these, at the sound of trumpets a group of mummers would come in, sometimes borne upon decorated floats, or cars, to dance a *moresque* in costume for the delectation of the dinner guests. By the fifteenth century the *moresque* was the theatrical dance *par excellence*; to perform it the dancer had to be disguised and masked, and in court festivities as well as in mystery plays it was performed by gorgeously clothed characters. Its steps were not formalized and might be thought free and capricious with skips and heel beats – unlike the Italian *brando*.

In the court of Burgundy in the mid-fifteenth century the *moresque* was also being presented

The basse danse *for two dancers was slow and stately and developed from the earlier* estampie, *itself a breakaway from the circular* carole *type. Mid-sixteenth-century engraving by the Nuremberg artist, Virgil Solis the Elder. (British Museum)*

within the framework of a setting and in this it may be seen to foreshadow the *ballet de cour*. In 1457 when Hungarian ambassadors came to visit Charles VII of France they were entertained by *moresques* and mummings after dinner and by a mystery play. This featured wild children who leapt from a very well designed rock and it was accompanied by singers, trumpets and other musical instruments. At the court of Burgundy the entertainments were very extravagant; they included mummings, morality and mystery plays, dances and song. In Lille a huge spectacle was held in 1454, which included dancing, to celebrate the meeting of the Duke of Burgundy and the Duke of Cleves who had hoped to start yet another Crusade. In 1468 for the marriage of the Duke of Burgundy in Bruges, 'a huge whale was brought in, guarded by two giants, which had in its belly two mermaids and twelve or thirteen men strangely clothed, which mermaids and men came out of the whale and sang, danced, and leapt about.' The whole apparatus of French and Burgundian court entertainments in the mid-fifteenth century, with their masked characters, *moresques,* mimes, musicians, quite complicated machines, floats, decorative structures, all suggest something of the court ballet of the next century. What is lacking in these is a coherent theme, such as that which unified the court ballet at the time of the High Renaissance.

The difference between these and the contemporaneous Italian entertainments, and the cause for the Italian supremacy in this field was that in Italy these traditional displays were now to be refined by the inclusion of antique themes taken from Greek and Roman mythology.

In Italy two forms derive also from *momeries: canti* (celebratory songs) and *trionfi*. Lorenzo the Magnificent was a declared enemy of the traditional religious festivals in Florence and he sought deliberately to replace them with festivities in the antique style, and these provided an impulse towards the splendour of Italian Renaissance display and the *mascherata* (masquerade) in which music, dance and poetry were joined to form a theatrical idea. During carnival time in Rome in 1521 a remarkable entertainment was staged in the courtyard of the Castel Sant' Angelo in which a silk pavilion was placed on one side of the courtyard and fifty servants with torches illuminated the area. As Pope Leo X and his court watched from a balcony, eight ladies in Sienese dress appeared and danced a *moresque*. One then asked Venus to give her a lover worthy of her beauty. Eight men, disguised as monks, now appeared and danced a second *moresque* to the sound of a drum. From the pavilion emerged Cupid, and the monks and maidens pursued him. Just as Cupid was about to be caught he called upon his mother, Venus, and she appeared and offered the monks a magic philtre and gave Cupid his bow and arrows. He fired at the monks and they ran around in despair; they next approached the girl and addressed sweet words to her. She

answered by asking them to prove their worth. The monks threw off their habits and appeared dressed in magnificent silks and satins. They fought furiously among themselves and the survivor led the girl away in triumph.

Even more important was the influence of the intermezzo, a danced and sung scene serving as an interlude in a drama. The Italians had always ascribed an important role in their religious performances to dance and song, unlike the French who gave little stress to dance in their mysteries. In the *sacre rappresentazioni* the spectacular element was to become almost disproportionately important; in one of these, *Santa Uliva,* four *Mattaccini* danced with bells on their feet while brandishing naked swords. But, with the dawn of the Renaissance, the religious festivities of the Middle Ages seemed outdated and 'Gothic'. With inspiration drawn from the antique drama, intermezzi were introduced into plays and in the later years of the fifteenth century they were to become very popular. Intermezzi were to be found in pastorales – dramatic entertainments with pastoral and lyric themes. In 1502 in Ferrara five comedies by Plautus (the second-century BC comic playwright) were presented with interpolated intermezzi which contained *moresques* and *brandi*: warriors costumed in antique style appeared miming a battle to music, and Moors, brandishing torches, made a sensational entry. It was then that the words *balli* and its diminutive *balletti* were used. They have no specific balletic meaning but there are two elements of theatrical dance now manifest: a figured dance which was executed by characters in costume following a planned schedule of steps, and a pantomime to music.

Although the intermezzi that were interpolated between the acts of a play originally had some relevance to that play, or were conceived as having some symbolic reference to an event in court life, they soon acquired a relative independence. Their qualities as entertainment were to lead them in time to become the foundations of opera itself. Isabella d'Este, the beautiful patron of the arts and politics, is reported as saying that she found the play which was staged at Lucrezia Borgia's wedding in 1502 rather boring, and she only contrived to sit through it because of the entertaining intermezzi.

THEATRE–COURT SPECTACLE

The popular and courtly dance of the Middle Ages, the rounds and *caroles*, were fixed, repetitive arrangements of steps based upon the same rhythmic measure from start to finish. Even when introduced into the more theatrical setting of a Florentine mystery or the *sacre rappresentazioni* (those half-religious, half-pagan spectacles) they served only as interludes. Dance attained a conscious purpose and understood what it itself was doing only with the late fourteenth and fifteenth centuries. With the Renaissance, men started to create dance rhythms and from this time dance became an art in Europe. Prior to this it had always been a pastime, a pleasure, an expression of joy, a homage to the gods, even a spectacle – but it was not an art. Its rules had been few. Mimes and actors had danced and learned to dance by watching others. The relationship between dance and its music was arbitrary; the dance was traditional, handed down from generation to generation.

The emergence of dancing as an art is linked to the song and music of the early Renaissance. Instructional treatises of the fourteenth century indicate how structural and formal rules, those essential qualities of Renaissance philosophy, were being applied to dance. In Italy in the fifteenth century came an age in music of 'airs of dancing'; in Northern Italy particularly songs accompanied dancing. These songs were called *canzoni a ballo* and were common both to the ordinary people and to the aristocracy. In the district of Venetia the *villotta* was a choral dance containing a dialogue between a singer and a group of dancers. The *pavane*, the *galliard*, the *bergamasco*, the *saltarello*, the *piva rustica*, and the *romanesca*, were popular dances accompanied by songs, and on the basis of the song other dance rhythms could be invented and developed.

The dance of the Middle Ages was, like everything else, to be reshaped and rethought by the Renaissance. Both folk dance and courtly dance were redefined and given a new identity. In this

art as in every other, men were responding to the inspiration offered by an emergent understanding of the antique past. Later, in the France of Charles IX (1560–1574), the poet de Baïf and his associates wished to recreate the antique *melopoeia,* that euphonious verse which had to conform to a strict metrical scheme; from this there developed the idea of a dance no less strictly linked to metre. But for the early dancing masters of the fifteenth century the developing of dance forms and the codification of movement was more especially symptomatic of the desire to cultivate and rationalize the raw material of dance and of the human body itself. It is typical of the Renaissance that dance should become much more individualistic because of the emergence of professional dancing masters who served not only as instructors but as choreographers. These dancing masters were not like common players or mummers, but men respected, and sometimes the intimates and trusted confidants of royalty.

Earliest of the dancing masters of whom there is record is Domenico da Piacenza (or da Ferrara known as 'Domenico') who flourished in the early fifteenth century. His treatise on the art of dancing *De Arte saltandi et choreas ducendi* deals with two subjects in particular, the movement of the body and the steps. Domenico identified six qualities as being essential for the dance: measure, *maniera* (or manner), memory, the division of the dance floor, *aiere* (or elevation), and bodily movement. All these qualities suggest a most serious feeling for the abilities of the dancer and his attitude to the dance. A later dancing master and pupil of Domenico, Guglielmo Ebreo (known as 'Guglielmo'), gave more information as to what

Exemplary exponents of the dance, portrayed on the frontispiece to Guglielmo Ebreo's celebrated treatise on the dance, De Pratica seu arte tripudii *of 1463. (Bibliothèque Nationale, Paris)*

was required under these headings. Measure indicated the dancer's ability to keep time with the music; memory was the ability to remember the steps; division of the floor was also self-explanatory – the dancer's ability to accommodate himself to the area in which he was performing; *aiere* implied a lightness and rise and fall in movement; and manner was identified by Guglielmo as 'when one performs a single or a double step he should turn his body, so long as the movement lasts, toward the same side as the foot which performs the step, and the act should be adorned and shaded with the movement called Maniera.'[3]

These details suggest the importance already associated with style and polish in dancing. No less so do the details which Domenico gives of the types of dance. These begin with the *basse danse* (*bassa danza*) already mentioned, which was the slowest and most noble and was itself a development from the medieval *estampie*, a quiet and grave dance. In time the *basse danse* with its

A very recognizable carole *(above) accompanied by drum and bagpipes, with alternating ladies and gentlemen joining fingertips in the approved style. From an early fourteenth-century French manuscript. (British Library – Ms. N. Roy, 20 AXVII, f.9)*

stately, gracious attributes will be considered as entirely separate from the other dances proposed by the Renaissance masters. Domenico next introduced the *quadernaria* which was played one-sixth faster than the *basse danse*; there followed the *saltarello* which was two-sixths faster than the *basse danse*; and finally comes the *piva*, the humblest of the forms, identified in its name as a dance accompanied by bagpipes and to be found among the common people. Domenico also detailed the movements, the steps and positions of his system. Nine are called 'natural' and three are 'accidental'. This would indicate a codification of step, while among the 'accidentals' was the quality called *frappamento* which related to the way a dress or costume was worn or used in dancing and the way a lady might manage her train. Domenico also pointed out the difference between the *basse danse* with its less fantastic style and *balli* with their more sophisticated inventiveness. In *balli* and *balletti* – the *haute danse* – there

was more ingenuity, more vivacity and speed and more development by dancing masters. The *basse danse* was probably accompanied by *instruments bas* (musical instruments having a lower register and producing lower and softer sounds). The dances were performed in general by one man and one woman but a variety of combinations were possible, as for example in *la mercantia* (the coquette) which was intended for one woman and three men.

Furthermore, Domenico listed basic steps, and their combination in dances is clearly identified as being of his own invention: he thus became a choreographer. This view of dancing is enhanced by the later work of Ambrosio da Pesaro who, in his second treatise, gave fifteen varieties of dances, while Guglielmo (whose treatise is dated roughly as 1463) provided a most detailed and illuminating guide to the dance forms being shaped by these early choreographers and the qualities required of the performer.

Detail from The City of Good Government *by Ambrogio Lorenzetti (fl. 1319–47) in which the interweaving of the dance pattern in a* carole *indicates how variety was brought into the original ring-dance form. Lorenzetti painted this allegorical fresco – and its companion piece concerning Bad Government – in the Town Hall of Siena between 1337 and 1379. (Palazzo Pubblico, Siena)*

Here is Guglielmo's description of the *basse danse* for a man and a woman called the *piatosa*:

'First, two simple steps and a double, commencing with the left foot; then they make a *ripresa* on the right foot, and the man makes two *continenze*. During the time of the *continenze* the lady goes from the under hand of the man with two simple steps, beginning with the left foot. Then they take hands and make two *riprese*, one on the left foot, the other on the right, and then make two *continenze*. And all that has been said is done a second time, until the man returns to his place. Then they make a curtsey on the left foot and then two bars of *salterello*, beginning with the left foot and the man curtseys on the left foot. During the time of this curtsey the lady makes a half turn, then they go contrariwise, one to the other, with two double steps, beginning with the left foot.'[4]

(This description crosses time; exactly the same care in identifying steps and poses can be found in the codification of modern ballroom dancing which took place in England in the 1920s, as can be seen in the volumes of *The Dancing Times* of the period.)

At the end of his treatise, Guglielmo gave interesting details of his career. He had been working for thirty years and he listed the courts at which he had taught and composed as a dancing master for festivities, celebrations and marriages. These included occasions such as the Sforzas welcoming the Duke of Cleves in Milan; the Pope arriving at Mantua; and when the Emperor

Maximilian I knighted him at Venice. In 1475 at his native Pesaro, he worked in collaboration with Domenico, at the marriage of Constanzo Sforza and Camilla of Aragon. He details the festivities he devised on this last occasion: mythological figures served the meal and wine; a model of an elephant, bearing the Queen of Sheba, entered with two other elephants behind carrying towers filled with young ladies while young men danced around them. Then, after further allegorical and symbolic incidents, one hundred and twenty young men and women danced to the sound of fifes and other instruments, marking out geometrical patterns. Guglielmo also composed *moresques*, not simple dances but mimed and danced scenes with spectacular effects.

A couple of years after Guglielmo's treatise was published, Antonio Cornazano, an aristocrat and writer (remembered both for his works of piety and of obscenity), wrote a code of dancing in 1465, *Il libro dell'arte del danzare*, in which he noted how technique and new steps were constantly developing. The refining and stylizing of dance and its codification suggest how much was being contributed by the dancing masters in deliberately shaping the art. Both Guglielmo and Cornazano make a clear distinction between the dignity of the *basse danse* and the livelier and more springing rhythms and steps of the other forms which were generally classified as *balli*.

Cornazano declared 'Balletti, much in vogue in Italy for some time now, are compositions of different measures which can contain all the movements of the dance ordered on a suitable base'. These dances were not embellished with mime or mimicry: the dance itself was self-sufficient as expression and the dancers were expected to be noble, dignified, skilled and responsive to the dance itself. There were also professional dancers admired for their skill and agility. The nobleman (according to Castiglione in *The Courtier*, 1528) had to maintain a certain dignity of manner. In private he might dance *moresques* where he would have to be costumed, but these were not suited to him in public.

The emergent Italian dance technique was to influence the development and the nature of court spectacle, for outstanding painters and poets collaborated in these displays. In Bologna in 1492, for the marriage of Annibale Bentivoglio with Lucrezia d'Este, Diana's nymphs were attacked by savages and fled dancing to seek refuge with Venus. She reconciled the two groups and they danced together to end the action. At Urbino the Dukes of Montefeltro staged pastoral dances and *moresques* during the period of carnival. In 1488 the artist Raphael's father organized a performance there with dances by Lorenzo Lavagnolo, a famous dancing master in Milan, Mantua and Ferrara. In 1496, for the Paradise festivity organized by Lodovico il Moro, on the occasion of the marriage of Gian Galeazzo Sforza to Isabella, Duchess of Milan, Leonardo da Vinci devised costumes for the dancers and invented machines.

Lively dancers at a ball at the court of the Duke of Alençon (younger son of Catherine de'Medici and later the Duke of Anjou). He was an unsuccessful but persistent suitor of Elizabeth I of England this time. Detail from an anonymous painting, c. 1581.

One of the finest of the High Renaissance dance manuals is Il Ballarino, *first published in Venice in 1581, written by Fabritio Caroso and dedicated to Bianca Cappello, the second wife of Francesco de'Medici, Grand Duke of Tuscany. The book contains details of steps and deportment as well as different figured dances noted down by Caroso, and musical examples. It has superb plates by Francho, such as the illustration (left). (Royal Academy of Dancing Library)*

There were four masked couples who performed Neapolitan, Spanish, Polish, Turkish and French dances and then made a final general ball. The celebrated festivities at Tortona in 1489 organized by Bergonzo di Botta included a dinner in which each course was accompanied by music, song and pantomime, though it can be assumed that the dance element was slight. Theatrically speaking, the *sacre rappresentazioni* were elaborated after Lorenzo the Magnificent encouraged their linking to the idea of pagan *trionfi* in which dance became a part of the spectacle.

By the early sixteenth century there came a parallel development in the making of musical instruments to accompany dancing which meant that composers were writing dance music for the lute in particular. This music was called sometimes *balli* or *balletti* as well as being known by the actual names of the dances (for example *pavanes* and *galliards*). Thus the English composer Thomas Morley (c. 1558–1603) could write 'ballets and madrigals for five voices'. By the time of the dancers and dancing masters Fabritio Caroso and Cesare Negri at the turn of the seventeenth century, Milan had become the choreographic centre of Europe. In his treatise *Nuove inventioni di balli* of 1604, Negri cites forty of his pupils who were famous and working throughout Europe. In Negri's writings and in Caroso's *Il Ballarino* of 1581 a statement is clearly made about the theory behind each dance step.[5] Caroso also gives details of dances he has composed made up of five, seven or even ten parts and devised for one, two or three couples. These are called *balli figurati* or *balli compositi*. In his *Le Gratie d'amore* of 1602, written when he was seventy, Negri gives

details of his technique and of his dances, which must have made considerable demands upon the men of the time (he includes illustrations showing the courtier kicking at a hanging knot in order to practise jumps). By this time an elaborate technique and vocabulary has already evolved. Negri asked for well-stretched legs and feet, grace to avoid dryness of manner, and even something resembling 'turn out' (*i piedi in fuora*).

Thus, the birth of ballet as it is known today is due to the penetration of dance into all forms of Renaissance spectacle, into the comedies and tragedies in antique style – in which dance was essentially the intermezzo – and also into the revival of the pastorale. It was no longer a question of dances presented during court festivities, or of a final *moresco* at the end of a spectacle. As soon as theatrical representation begins – profane rather than sacred – dance is found: for example in the *Orfeo* of Politian (Mantua, 1471), an embryonic pastorale with music, a danced chorus of sixteen dryads was found in Act II, and the fifth act began with a dance of Bacchantes.

Dance was used for intermezzi between the acts of plays in many cities; dancers appeared in allegorical or mythological narratives with costumes and settings. In 1486 in Ferrara there were dances by nymphs and fauns in the pastoral *The Fable of Cephalus*. Nine muses danced in the suite of Apollo in the intermezzi which interspersed the acts of Plautus' *Menechmes*. In 1499 also in Ferrara, in an intermezzo in *The Eunuch* by Terence, the second-century BC Roman comic poet, one hundred and forty-four dancers appeared as peasants, miming work upon the land with gesture and movement regulated to the

The dancing master Cesare Negri, nicknamed Il Trombone, *performed on a warship before the admirals of the victorious fleet after the defeat of the Turks at the battle of Lepanto. His* Nuove inventioni di balli *was published in Milan in 1604 when Negri was in his sixties. It is an important treatise on dancing, with fifty-eight illustrations showing the correct method of performing court dance. His courtier (left) is practising leaping kicks at a bell-rope – an indication of the agility needed in the male dance of the Renaissance.*

music. Castiglione gives details of danced inter-mezzi in *La Calandra*, a comedy by Cardinal Dovizio Bibbiena shown in Urbino in 1513:

> 'We saw first Jason's moresco. The hero appeared on stage armed in antique style and dancing. He defeated the dragon, sowed the monster's teeth and men appeared from below the platform. With them, Jason took the Golden Fleece, dancing most excellently.'[6]

Soon plays were thought to be insupportable with-out intermezzi. Further choreographic develop-ments were suggested by the increasing vogue for horse ballets in which, especially at the court of the Medicis, a mythological or knightly tale was unfolded by *quadrilles* of horsemen enhanced by the intervention of singers, dancers and other players. (In Parma in 1628 Monteverdi provided the music for the horse ballet *Mercury and Mars*.) Among the most influential forces was the group of poets, musicians and writers in Florence who surrounded Count Bardi de Vernio in the late sixteenth, and early seventeenth, century and formed an *avant-garde* of the time. Advanced in their musical ideas, they were also eager for the revival of Greek tragedy, and among them the poet Ottavio Rinuccini played a notable role in the emergence of a musical theatre both in Florence and Paris, where he was under the pro-tection of Queen Marie de'Medici. The inter-mezzi inserted into the play *La Pellegrina* in Florence in 1589 are celebrated for their brilliant theatrical ideas in decoration and for the amazing feats of staging which they contained, and in these Rinuccini had participated.

By this time Italy had developed *dramma per musica*, a forerunner of opera, and by the start of the seventeenth century opera itself took the stage, usually containing dance scenes as a decoration to the action. Parallel with this runs the tradition of the pastorale, the mixed dramatic form based upon the theories of Greek satyric plays with their pastoral humours and adventures. In it were mingled recitative, processions, dance and chorus; the dance illustrated and lightened sung incidents. It was a genre which speedily went into decline after its emergence in the mid-sixteenth century, but one piece, Tasso's *Aminta* (1573) typifies it at its best. So successful was *Aminta* that it was performed throughout Italy, acquiring choruses, extra dances and additional music.

The popularity of danced, sung and dramatized entertainments in Italy inevitably meant that they would pass into France, and two in particular were to put down roots. These were the *mascar-ades* (masquerades) with their entries of maskers both serious and grotesque, their floats bearing allegorical figures and pagan divinities, which replaced the ancient *momeries*; and the intermezzi with their sung recitatives and their dances, either mime or figured pastoral scenes, which included gods and satyrs, nymphs and shepherds. Both these elements were to help shape the emergent French *ballet de cour*.

Italy had had an influence upon successive French kings and their courts: Charles VIII (1470–1498), Louis XII (1462–1515) and François I (1494–1547) had responded to the luxury, the festivities and the opulence of display. The monarch and the court were also impressed by the elements of fantasy and the brilliance of the balls and masquerades which they saw in Italy and which were very different from the dull fare of the *basses danses* which they knew in France. One of the earliest examples of this is the delight manifested by Charles VIII when he crossed into Italy in 1494 as claimant to the throne of Naples. In Milan and elsewhere the Frenchmen were dazzled by the magnificence of the festivities, as at the dinner ballet which took place in Tortona in 1489 to celebrate the marriage of the Duke of Milan. Each course of the banquet was introduced by an *entrée* of allegorical figures relating to the food being served. Thus, for instance, the fish was brought in attended by dancers representing Neptune and a troupe of sea sprites.

François I was an enthusiast for all things Italian and he summoned an army of artists from Italy (painters, sculptors, musicians) to work for him. His palace at Fontainebleau was decorated by the Italian architect, painter and sculptor Primaticcio and his compatriot artist, Rosso, and it was the setting for many Italian-style masquerades. In 1534, Niccolo da Modena was entrusted with making the costumes for the King and five courtiers for the marriage of the Comte de Saint-Paul. Under Henri II, the next king, there developed a more spectacular masquerade which sometimes took the form of a long procession of floats with courtiers in costume portraying allegorical or classical mythological scenes. They filed slowly past stands on which sat the monarch and the court. Sometimes verses were sung in honour of the prince and his chief guests by the masqueraders, or long speeches were made. (This tradition of rhetorical spectacle and tableaux vivants was to be found across Europe. In 1577, when William of Orange entered Ghent and the Archduke Matthew entered Brussels, they were greeted with interminable disquisitions by the worthy burghers of the respective cities in this same fashion.) At the court of Henri II the court poet devised verses to comment upon these allegories, which were printed and given out to the ladies of the court and were sometimes declaimed as the floats went past – a precursor of the libretti and texts of the later *ballet de cour*. In his *Le Gratie d'amore*, Cesare Negri gives a fine description of one of these masquerades: *Audacity* rode a lion; *Unease*, naked, sat on a thornbush; *Perseverance* clung to a rock amid restless waves; musicians disguised as shepherds accompanied this scene. Finally four kings and four queens in antique costume walked hand in hand carrying symbols of the elements: pearls for water, a rose for the earth, an arrow for the air, and a torch for fire. Four dwarfs were pages to the queens while four wild men carrying bludgeons held the reins of the kings' horses. The procession stopped, the kings and queens descended from their horses and danced a *brando*, then the savages fought, the dwarfs capered, and all the eighty-two characters in the masquerade danced another massive *brando*.

By the mid-1550s spectacular processions and tableaux all showed the influence of Italy. It is also interesting to note how the entertainments differed according to whether they were performed out of doors or indoors. In the open air the extravagance of the spectacle was all important. In celebration of entries into towns, official visits or the peregrinations of the whole court from one palace to another, maximum effect had to be achieved.

The masquerades staged inside the palaces were to become of greater artistic importance with the contribution of a poetic text during the latter years of the sixteenth century. An impulse to the dance itself came with the arrival of Italian, and more specifically Milanese, dancing masters. In 1554 the Maréchal de Brissac had imported Pompeo Diabono (whose pupil was Negri) from Milan, and as successive French monarchs revealed their love of dancing – François II, Charles IX and Henri III all patronized and protected Diabono – further Italian dancing masters arrived. They included Bracesco, Palvello, Gallino, Giera, Ernandes, and Tetoni. These men brought with them all the Italian figured dances like the *brando* and the *balletto* which, unlike the *coranto* and *galliard* (the best-known social dances of the time) were not subject to any fixed form and the ballet master-choreographer – who not only taught step and style but also developed the form of the dance – was free to invent. The *brando*, like the *moresque*, was a theatrical rather than a social dance. The *balli* and *balletti*, like the *quadrilles* and *contredanses* of later years, were danced by the court in general and had a recognized vocabulary. But by the middle of the sixteenth century all these various names and distinctions had been confused by the French and the general title ascribed to them was 'ballet'.

The dominant political figure of this time in France was Catherine de'Medici. Her formative years in the court at Florence had given her a taste for dancing and throughout her life she encouraged it, seeing in it both an attractive diversion in court life and also a potent political instrument. (Her maids of honour were expected to be good dancers and were often participants in the 'ballets' of her time.)

Under Catherine's influence the French court turned more and more to displays which would serve not merely to entertain but also to illustrate a political point. A masquerade (immortalized in the Valois Tapestries) was staged in 1565 at Bayonne with words by de Baïf on the occasion of Catherine's meeting with her daughter Elizabeth who had married Philip II of Spain. Models of rocks and trees were placed on decorated floats and inside each nymphs and knights were imprisoned. At a word from the King of France, Charles IX, these prisoners were liberated and

they danced together. Even more significant was the masquerade given in Paris, on 18 August 1572 in the Grande Salle du Louvre to celebrate the marriage of Catherine's daughter Marguerite de Valois to Henri of Navarre (later Henri IV). This was part of a series of festivities, and seven floats dressed with sea shells entered the hall with thrones at their summit upon which sat courtiers dressed as sea gods. An eighth float topped by a huge gold sea-horse bore Charles IX dressed as Neptune. Thereafter the gentlemen in the other floats joined the ladies of the court in a dance to end the masquerade. More politically significant was the masquerade joust some two days later, called the *Defence of Paradise*, which had been 'long-time prepared'. In the huge Salle de Bourbon a 'Paradise' was erected on the right-hand side. This was reached through a triumphal arch to reveal the Elysian Fields and above it was a wheel to suggest the heavens with planets, stars and signs of the zodiac simulated by lamps and torches. This wheel turned, as also did the Elysian Fields with its flowers and nymphs. On the left was built a 'Hell', a huge hell-mouth with devils and demons, and a large shining wheel within. Between these was the River Styx with Charon and his boat. Although this decoration was complex and dispersed, the action was simple. A group of wandering and misguided knights made assaults on Paradise and tried to seize the nymphs. The

King and his brothers defended the nymphs, repulsed the attackers and drove them to Hell, where they were seized by the devils. It is no coincidence that the wandering knights were Henri of Navarre and his Huguenot companions. However, the knights were then led from Hell to the Elysian Fields by court ladies – an allusion to Marguerite de Valois as the bride of Henri of Navarre. Then Mercury (in the person of Etienne de Roy, a celebrated castrato of the time) attended by cupids came down from the sky on a cockerel to make declamation and sing, and then ascended once more into the Heavens. Thereafter nymphs from the Elysian Fields danced and the enterprise ended with fireworks. At a time of acute religious and political unease there were messages here for all to read.

A prime example of the form of ballet at this time was the *Ballet des Polonais* of 1573. It was staged in the Palace of the Tuileries to celebrate the arrival of the Polish ambassadors to the court of the Valois where they were to elect Henri d'Anjou, Catherine's third son, as King of Poland. One of the rooms in the palace was converted into a temporary theatre, and tiered stands were placed along three sides of the hall from which the courtiers could look down upon the entertainment. This was directed to the 'presence' – that group of persons for whose benefit the entertainment was being staged. Thus, Catherine and her

Eight tapestries were woven in Brussels, c. 1580, to celebrate certain of the grandest spectacles of the Valois court under its presiding genius, Queen Catherine de'Medici. In 1573 the Ballet des Polonais was a propaganda entertainment in honour of the election of the Queen's third son, Henri d'Anjou, to the throne of Poland. For the tapestry scene detail illustrated here – 'The Reception of the Polish Ambassadors' – the event was transferred to the open air and the courtiers are seen in the final grand ballet, with the black-robed, widowed Queen as a central figure in the composition. (Uffizi Gallery, Florence)

At the court of Savoy, despite its relative unimportance, there was a tradition of elaborate entertainments which for more than sixty years were dominated by the d'Aglié family. Count Filippo d'Aglié (1604–1667) was producer, master of design and machines, poet and musician. Between the years 1606 and 1657 thirty-six ballets as well as many other entertainments were staged. These contemporary manuscripts from Turin convey something of their lively fantasy.

son Charles IX, and the newly elected King of Poland and the Polish ambassadors were seated on a raised dais towards which the entertainment was focused. The *Ballet des Polonais* was described by Brantôme, the contemporary chronicler:

'After having offered the Polish ambassadors a superb banquet the Queen had staged for them, in a huge room especially prepared and surrounded by an infinity of torches, the finest ballet that had ever been staged, made up of sixteen of the most beautiful and best dressed of the ladies of her household who appeared on a huge silvered rock, each one seated in a niche which was in the form of a cloud. These sixteen ladies represented the sixteen provinces of France, attended by the most delightful music that could be imagined. After having been paraded round the room on this rock and after having allowed everyone to admire them they came down from their rock and assumed a grouping cunningly devised. Nearly thirty violinists struck up a very attractive military air to which they walked and without losing the pattern of their ensemble they approached Their Majesties and halted. And then after having danced a "ballet", so ingeniously invented with so many convolutions, intertwinings and interlinkings, but in which nevertheless none of the ladies failed to maintain her correct position, at the end of an hour, the ladies came and presented to the King and Queen and to the other members of the royal family a golden plaque beautifully enamelled and worked on which was engraved the fruits and specialities of each province.'

Nevertheless, although the *Ballet des Polonais* may be seen as a danced display it is not yet in a proper sense a *ballet de cour*. Catherine de'Medici's favourite dancing master, Balthazar de Beaujoyeulx (the Italian Baldassarino di Belgiojoso), had choreographed the work but nothing in it as yet suggested the idea of a dramatic theme which was to characterize the true *ballet de cour*. The *Ballet des Polonais* in fact can be seen as the apotheosis of the figured dance.

This type of political spectacle without true dramatic theme was to continue, and a notable example came with the reception of the English Knights of the Garter by the French Knights of the Saint Esprit in Paris on 23 February 1585. The political occasion was a union implicit between France and England in the face of Spain as a common threat. After a service in the Church of the Augustins there was a banquet, a ball and a masque. In this latter the King of France, Henri III, led a group of twenty-four knights gorgeously attired, culminating in the moment when the maskers led by the King 'did express by the variety of casting themselves all the letters both in the King and Queen's name: a matter wondered at of all beholders for the good decorum kept at all handes in so strange a manner of dancing'. This spelling out in figures of the words Henri and Elizabeth made clear to everyone the importance which the French court attached to this new alliance with England.

The intellectual world in which the court ballet was evolving was one much affected by the humanistic concepts of the Pléiade and the Académie de Poésie et de Musique. This last had been founded in 1571 by the learned poet Jean Antoine de Baïf under the patronage of King Charles IX. It stood for musical and poetic reform according to the rules of Greek and Latin metre and prosody. It sought that ideal union of poetry and music (*melopoeia*) that Renaissance poets and humanists supposed was known to the ancients, and de Baïf himself had conceived an idea of choric dancing in which step and note were of equal duration. The result was the idea of a *danse mesurée* which would complement the *musique mesurée* which de Baïf and his followers hoped to achieve from the linking of musical rhythm to poetic metre. (The Académie's aim of reviving the metric verse style of the ancients was to prove sterile, but nevertheless there is a note in Caroso's *Il Ballarino* concerning his *Ballo del Fiore* in which he mentions 'a contre pas elaborated with true mathematics on verses of Ovid'.) Poets like Jodelle and Ronsard who, with de Baïf, formed the group of poets known as the Pléiade, were concerned with the preparation of court entertainments, and their theories concerning the relationship between the various parts in an overall unity were to find an expression in the *ballet de cour*.

These ideas were to reach their culmination in the *Ballet Comique de la Reine Louise* which was staged in 1581 in the Salle de Bourbon of the Louvre in Paris. It combined the various elements of the Italian intermezzi, of singing, pantomime, and figured dancing, with the ideas of de Baïf's Académie. This was the first true dramatic court ballet. (The word 'comique' was an indication that the entertainment was a dramatic one.) The occasion for the work was an important political marriage, that of King Henri III's favourite, Anne, Duc de Joyeuse to Marguerite de Vaudémont, sister of the Queen (Louise). For two weeks in the autumn of 1581 one of the greatest series of court festivities was presented in honour of an alliance expressly designed to suggest the King's dedication to the cause of the Catholics at a time when France was being torn by religious strife. The culminating event was the *Ballet Comique* which was master-minded by Balthazar de Beaujoyeulx. Like other Italian dancing masters, he had been imported by the Maréchal de Brissac in 1555 together with a band of Italian violinists. He first gained royal patronage as a violinist and as an agreeable man of the world, becoming successively *valet de chambre* to Catherine de'Medici, Marie Stuart (later Mary Queen of Scots), Charles IX and to Henri III. So important were the preparations for the Joyeuse festivities thought to be, that Beaujoyeulx was sent away from the distractions of court to plan this final display. On his return he

was given the finest collaborators among court musicians, poets and decorators and no expense was spared by the King in the creation of a work intended to astound by its opulence (it cost the then amazing sum of 400,000 écus). As finally staged on 15 October 1581, the work lasted from ten at night until half past three the following morning. Its theme was the freeing of man from the enchantments of Circe – its political and religious implications being those of the liberation of the nation from error by the royal power.

Catherine de'Medici was its presiding genius, and many of the court ladies appeared in it: gorgeously dressed and borne in on a float decorated to represent a fountain, there appeared Queen Louise, the Princess of Lorraine, and the Duchesses de Guise, de Nevers, de Joyeuse, de Mercoeur, d'Aumale, and other noblewomen. At the end these ladies presented emblems to the King and noblemen, each emblem bearing some apposite Latin quotation, and the work finished with a *grand ballet* in which the courtiers joined in the general dance. The significance of the *Ballet Comique* lies in the fact that every element in this spectacle – music, dance, speech, song – related to a single theme and developed a consecutive action. Here was the novelty and the innovation; this was indeed the first true *ballet de cour*.

Unfortunately, religious wars at the end of the sixteenth century were to inhibit the staging of any further ballets of this style though there are records of smaller works continuing this advance.

At the same time the idea was to spread across the Channel and in masques of Jacobean times the English practitioners, Ben Jonson and Inigo Jones, were to develop a specifically English form of versified comedy and danced interludes enriched with decorations after the Italian style by Inigo Jones. This was ultimately to differ from the French ideal, the main difference lying in the dominance of a poetic text initiated by Jonson.

With the new era in France under Henri IV the masquerade returned; this was in no small part due to the economies in court expenditure insisted upon by Henri's great finance minister Sully. The extravagance of the Valois court was gone, to be replaced by simpler entertainments of courtiers in costume, without elaborate decorative aids.

Several of these works were notorious for their obscenity. They also lacked the dramatic coherence of the *Ballet Comique*. The masquerades at the court of Henri IV took the form of a series of *entrées* (sections) which were court rather than theatrical entertainments. (A by-product of the French *ballet de cour* was the fact that it was taken into Italy by the librettist Rinuccini and the musician Caccini, and in Mantua in 1608 the *Mascherata dell'Ingrate* showed how the *ballet de cour* became adapted to a form of musical recitative.) In the meantime in France, under Louis XIII, a form of melodramatic court ballet emerged telling an action in pantomime and recitative with a succession of *entrées* both serious and comic leading up to a final *grand ballet*. Such was the famous *Ballet de la Délivrance de Renaud* of 1617 and also the *Ballet des Fées des forêts de St Germain* of 1625.

It is important to stress the popularity of court ballet as an entertainment (from 1583 to 1610 there are records of more than eight hundred ballets being presented in France). The style of these entertainments had also now become split into two; the dance element in the balletic *entrées* performed by the aristocracy and by professional dancers was often very carefully devised and elaborated in manner to suit the theme of the piece; the final *grand ballet* made use of the unadorned social dance of the period. In turn, Henri III, Louis XIII and Louis XIV gave royal patronage and royal participation to the genre, and the ballets in which they performed, or which they delighted in, were still linked to the outstanding political and social events of their reigns. The form of the *ballet de cour* was by then complex, sometimes rather discursive and lacking in the thematic strength of the *Ballet Comique*, but still dominated by the dance. With an interspersing of sung recitative there was a succession of mime scenes, dances first in noble style then in more grotesque comic fashion, and sometimes even acrobatic displays. The numerous *entrées* depended upon a single theme without developing it; the final *grand ballet* in which other members of the court might join was nothing more than a celebration of social dance. Devised to be seen from above by spectators who would be placed in stands around three sides of an area marked out by torch-bearers, the floor patterns were all important. Sometimes they were designed, as in the *Ballet d'Alcine* of 1610, to form ideograms which suggested the power of love or the delights of fame. Under the influence of the Duc de Luynes, who was Louis XIII's favourite, mythology and fable were replaced by images of knightly chivalry, as in the *Délivrance de Renaud*. During the later years of Louis XIII's reign elements of burlesque and buffoonery were to be found in the ballet masquerades which became popular. These were without dramatic interest, simply providing a series of contrasting *entrées* which juxtaposed noble with comic, exotic and grotesque elements.

A Monsieur de Saint Hubert, in a fascinating manual published at this time, noted that the most important thing was to find a suitable and relevant subject on which to hang the succession of *entrées* – he observed that a *ballet royal* had thirty *entrées*; a fine ballet had at least twenty, and a small ballet ten or twelve. He further pointed out that the subject should be well developed and each successive entry contrasted in style. What he failed to point out was that although the incidentals might be different, the treatment of these ballets was always the same and that court ballet, lacking in any true dramatic interest, was now a mere entertainment.

This decline during the years of Louis XIII's reign reflected the developments in the dramatic theatre itself. With the emergence of classical tragedy and comedy and the imposition of rules in the theatre (the unities), ballet was to find itself a peripheral art of the theatre because of the change in intellectual tastes. Nevertheless, the ballet was still popular both at court and with a more general public. In 1632, Horace Morel, who was famous for his skill in producing firework effects in court entertainments, was granted a royal warrant to present ballets before a paying public in the tennis court of the Petit Louvre, though this lasted for only a couple of years. More important for the Paris public was the fact that they were allowed to attend court performances – if they could get in.

Attendance at these court ballets was in many instances similar to the crush attendant upon ballet performances today. Their popularity and the public's desire to see the monarch was sufficient to guarantee a fearful mêlée. The nobility and members of the court earned their place at the performances by right, but for the wealthy bourgeoisie desirous of watching a court ballet there was some palaver involved. The usual locale was the Salle du Petit Bourbon, a large hall inside the Hôtel de Bourbon – today the site of the colonnades of the Louvre. The general public had to bribe or bluster a way through well-guarded rooms and corridors in the Palace to get to the hall. Tiered seats lined three sides of the hall, but

La Liberazione di Tirreno was a veglia *(an evening entertainment) staged in the Uffizi Palace in Florence in 1616 to celebrate the marriage of the Duke of Mantua to Caterina de'Medici, sister of the reigning Grand Duke Cosimo II of Tuscany. The second intermezzo shown here is a scene of Hell arming itself for the war of Circe against Tirreno. Engraving by Jacques Callot, the recorder of court entertainments, after Giulio Parigi, who was in charge of the decoration of Medician spectacles in the early seventeenth century.*

because these were always crowded the general public had to perch where it could. Inside the Louvre another slightly larger hall was used. At its doors the press of people was tremendous and fights would often break out. Sometimes the populace would queue all day in order to get in for the night's performance.

Such was the popularity of the *Ballet du Château de Bicêtre* that the court gentlemen performed it three times during the course of one night – at eight o'clock in the Louvre, at midnight at the Arsenal, and at four in the morning at the Hôtel de Ville. The performers did not finish until eight in the morning.

In 1636, Cardinal Richelieu completed the construction of his palace (Le Palais Cardinal) and in the Grande Salle des Comédies, ballets could also take place. They benefited from the machinery which was installed there to allow for considerably more decoration than was usual. It is worth noting also that at the Palais Cardinal, which was less well lit than the other locales, the public was given candles by which to read the libretti. The Palais Cardinal also made possible two innovations in the presentations of *ballets de cour*. First it provided greater opportunities for decorative effects, and in 1641 the *Ballet de la Prosperité des armes de France* excited great public interest because of its staging effects. However, these were relatively simple compared with the miracles being achieved at that time by Giacomo Torelli in the operatic stagings of the Teatro Novissimo in Venice. Secondly, the dancers in the court ballets no longer descended into the body of the hall; this created a ballet form more obviously theatrical in nature.

In the final *grand ballet* the dancers would sometimes form the letters of the royal name, and

it was customary that in the majority of *grands ballets*, particularly those known as a *ballet royal* in which the King or Prince appeared or was the ostensible patron, men alone performed. The ladies of the court appeared only in those ballets which took their name from a royal princess or an aristocratic lady; in these, court ladies danced alone or were joined by men. Mixed ballets had a certain vogue by the end of the sixteenth century, but there were none during the period of Louis XIII.

It was at this time also that professional dancers and acrobats took an increasingly important part. Originally only used in grotesque *entrées*, by 1625 professional dancers were to be found side by side with the nobility in all the *entrées*. It was only in the final *grand ballet*, that general social dance which had no theme and was purely geometric, that the nobility alone appeared. In all these court ballets in France the dancers were masked by the beginning of the seventeenth century. The masks ranged from simple dominoes (to cover the eyes) and false noses to entire false faces and heads for grotesque *entrées*. These enabled the performers to make the quick changes necessary for the many *entrées* that comprised the masquerade ballets of the time, and were particularly useful for establishing the preposterous characters of those who appeared in the grotesque *entrées*.

The extreme nature of some of these grotesque *entrées* is exemplified by the appearance of Henri de Savoie, Duc de Namours (1572–1632), who produced many ballets for Louis XIII and when old and crippled by gout still contrived to appear in a special *entrée* in which he was carried in a chair surrounded by dancers who in sympathy also affected the gout.

With Louis XIV the *ballet de cour* was to know both its apogee and its decline. It has been aptly noted that the festivities which were presented at Versailles during the reign of Louis XIV served not only the vulgar aims of flattery and extravagant display, but were also a means of governing. Louis XIV was a child of five when he acceded to the throne in 1643. With the regency of his mother, Anne of Austria, and the prime ministership of Cardinal Mazarin there came a growing taste for Italian opera, and because of the arrival of the great Italian stage designers Torelli and the Vigarani family, opulent display became more and more the fashion. The young King was early exposed to court ballet, and in 1645 the staging of the opera *La Finta pazza* with Torelli's designs included danced *entrées* which were intended to appeal to the child monarch. By 1651 the young King had demonstrated his abiding love for dance and had appeared for the first time as a performer – in the *Ballet de Cassandre*. In the following year he was to appear again in the *Ballet des Fêtes de Bacchus* and the monarch's affection for dance was to encourage the *ballet de cour* in its final glorious years despite the counter-claims of opera.

But these were times also of great unrest associated with the Fronde (1648–1653), that civil up-

Costume for a dancer as a sea nymph (left), dating from the beginning of the seventeenth century, indicates the skilled detail by which characters were identified through decoration on their costume. Shells, seaweed, fish-scales, a branch of coral, are all incorporated. (Victoria and Albert Museum, London)

rising which threatened the very throne of France. Thus a recurrent theme to be observed in the many grandiose court ballets of this period was praise of the monarchy and insistence upon the power of the throne; this is noticeable in the *Ballet de la Nuit* of 1653, in which the King took the role of the Sun – and hence was confirmed in his title as 'Le Roi Soleil'.

Despite the political unease, the King danced – contemporary records show that he appeared in no fewer than seven masquerades and ballets during the first two months of 1656. In the tremendous decade between 1660 and 1670 when the King ceased to perform, the extravagance, ingenuity and beauty of court entertainments were remarkable: horse ballets like the celebrated Carrousel of 1662 which celebrated the birth of the Dauphin; the extraordinary series of festivities given in 1664 under the title of *Les Plaisirs de l'île enchantée* at Versailles; and the new dramatic form of the comédie–ballet in Molière's *Le Bourgeois gentilhomme* of 1670, all suggest the intense importance which was attached to the idea of festivities at court. These glorified the monarch, his power, his wealth. They involved the greatest artists of the day in providing dramatic frameworks, design and music. And they further encouraged an appreciation of the importance of dancing as an activity. In due time the King's dancing master Pierre Beauchamps was to become the choreographer for the emergent form of the French opera–ballet which was created by Lully, who

had provided the music for so many of these danced entertainments in which the entire court participated. When Lully set out to create French opera, as Prunières the French historian observed, 'he had only to take from court ballet the materials needed for the construction of the edifice he wanted to raise upon the foundations of the Italian melodrama.'

The professional dancing masters who were involved in these *ballets de cour,* the public insistence on glorious and ingenious display, Lully's musical taste, and the distinguished literary contributors who were librettists to the ballets, were the forces needed for the next stage in the development of both opera and ballet in France.

But it must not be supposed that the *ballet de cour* expired there and then. The tradition was to continue for many years into the eighteenth century, and dancing as a necessary manifestation of the royal presence and as an accomplishment for the courtier can be seen in many occasions until the last years of the *ancien régime*. In 1723 the young Louis XV appeared in the *Fêtes grecques et romaines* staged at the theatre in the Louvre, taking the role of Augustus; and in 1721 he had also danced in the *Ballet des Eléments* at the Palace of the Tuileries. Similarly in 1765 at the court of Vienna the marriage of the Emperor Joseph II was celebrated by a court ballet in which the young archdukes and archduchesses were joined by other aristocratic children in a danced divertissement.

The Italian stage designer Giacomo Torelli worked in Venice from 1640 onwards and became celebrated for the brilliance of his theatrical machinery. He was sent to France in 1645 and in his stagings for court entertainments such as the ballet Les Noces de Pelée et de Thétis *(above), first performed in 1654, he initiated a new splendour of stage presentation. Louis XIV appeared in four scenes in this ballet. Engraving by Aveline, after Torelli.*

L'HVMOR TERREO FLEMATICO

CHAPTER SEVEN

HISTORY OF BALLET
SEVENTEENTH TO NINETEENTH CENTURY

In the ballet Il Carnevale languente *of 1647, staged by Count Filippo d'Aglié for the Duchess of Savoy (sister of Louis XIII of France), the four 'humours' or temperaments of the body appeared. This illustration from a Turin manuscript shows the earthly phlegmatic character, which was performed by Count Giorgio di Mombasilio.*

THE WORD ballet has, to its practitioners, a very clear and specific meaning. Even today, when the dividing lines between the various forms of dance in the theatre are becoming increasingly imprecise, the purist will identify ballet as that form of classic academic dancing which is based on the accepted five positions of the feet and which uses vocabulary of movement (and a vocabulary of French terminology) which has been developed in schools and theatres since the seventeenth century.

Though such basic physical attitudes as 'turn out' and positions of the feet already existed in the court of Louis XIV, their development as the fundamental of theatrical dancing owes everything to the emergence of a professional dancing caste in the theatre towards the end of the seventeenth century. The impetus for dance to move into the theatre as the place where it was to flourish is attributable to the fact that Louis XIV abandoned his role as a performer. When the King ceased to dance in 1670 the first tentative moves towards 'professional' ballet had been made. In 1661 the King had initiated the Académie Royale de Danse whereby he had commanded thirteen of the most celebrated dancing masters of the time to meet and to concern themselves with the 're-establishing of the art of dancing in its true perfection'.

Ironically this Académie was to prove impotent. Its members chose to rendezvous in a tavern known as The Wooden Sword, to tipple – rather than to meet in the room in the Louvre that the King had set aside for them – and for the next hundred years their influence on the art of dancing was minimal and the Académie itself ceased to function in the 1780s. It was the second Académie, L'Académie d'Opéra (soon to become L'Académie Royale de Musique) conveniently known as the 'Opéra', which was to prove the true nursery of French ballet and dance technique. It was initiated in 1669 when the monarch had granted a *privilège* (a royal licence) for the performance of opera.

The supervisor of the King's Music, Jean-Baptiste Lully, had initially shown little interest in this enterprise but in 1671 the first work was staged by the Académie at a temporary theatre which had become its home for the production of opera. This was *Pomone,* with music by Cambert and danced interludes composed by Pierre Beauchamps, the King's dancing master. Although the performances of *Pomone* were well received, the management of this opera theatre was inept and Lully, realizing its potential, contrived to acquire the *privilège* and made himself the new and extremely powerful head of the Académie. With few scruples, Lully was now able to install the operatic performances in a new theatre, and he entered into a collaboration with Beauchamps, who was to provide the dance scenes which were so essentially a part of the form of opera-ballet initiated by Lully.

Lully's collaboration with such distinguished artists as Molière (their supreme achievement was *Le Bourgeois gentilhomme*) and Racine, as well as Beauchamps, was to aid him in the shaping of the form of the opera–ballet. These elaborate and formalized musical treatments of classic and mythological themes, with their interspersed danced *entrées*, were to remain the pattern for entertainments at the Opéra until the middle of the eighteenth century. The increasing popularity of dancing in these spectacles was to bring about the vitally important founding of a dancing school attached to the Paris Opéra in 1713, even though another important change had already taken place. This was the emergence of the professional female dancer. In 1681 four ladies took the stage in Lully's opera–ballet *Le Triomphe de l'amour.* Their leader was Mademoiselle Lafontaine; her companions were Mesdemoiselles Fanon, Le-peintre, and Roland. Despite the emergence of

women as theatrical dancers, their position on stage was to be inferior to that of the men; female technique was rudimentary, their costuming prohibiting any sort of agility, and male technique was, thanks to the professionalism of the dancer, developing in brilliance. Lully died in 1687 but the art form which he had imposed upon the public at the Académie was to be perpetuated for many years. The popularity of dancing meant that the dance interludes in the opera–ballets were to gain importance and a constantly extending technical range meant that a certain virtuosity was now possible.

An indication of the technical possibilities of theatrical dancing at this time is to be found in Raoul Feuillet's *Chorégraphie* (1700), a manual concerned with the writing down of dance entries for the benefit of dancing masters. Feuillet made use of a system of notation already established by Beauchamps, and the book was translated into German and English. Its English edition is particularly noteworthy since it was a version by John Weaver (1673–1760), one of the most remarkable and innovative figures of English dance history whose work provides early indications of an artistic theory which was to dominate the latter part of the eighteenth century. Weaver, an author and theorist about dancing, as well as a dancing master and producer of danced entertainments, was concerned early on with the emotional and mimetic qualities associated with dancing. In *The Loves of Mars and Venus* (London 1717) he produced danced scenes in which words were entirely suppressed; his cast, which included Le Grand Dupré (1697–1774), one of the greatest French dancers of his time, was called upon to convey emotion and dramatic action through gesture and dance. Present here are the early manifestations of the *ballet d'action*, that form of theatrical dancing which sought to tell a story entirely through movement. While the opera–ballet still proposed vocal music as the narrative means, with dance as an illustrative adjunct, a few theorists believed that movement could be more than a mere decorative illustration to an already existing operatic scene. It is interesting to record that in December 1714, as part of a series of entertainments, the Duchesse du Maine invited two celebrated dancers from the Paris Opéra, Jean Balon (1676–1739) and Françoise Prévost (1680–1741), to mime Act IV, Scene V from Corneille's *Les Horaces*, expressive gesture being considered adequate to replace words. The beginnings of expressive dance are to be seen here.

Two of Prévost's pupils represented the conflicting strains in theatrical dance at this time. Marie Anne de Cupis de Camargo (1710–1770) was the ballerina as virtuoso; Marie Sallé (1707–1756) the ballerina as dramatic artist. Camargo was adored for the brilliance and vivacity of her performances. With an exceptional technique for the time, she saw no reason to hide her skills under her skirts, and in order that the public might admire her ability to beat an *entrechat quatre* she

took the unprecedented liberty of shortening her skirts to just above the ankle. It was the beginning of the accommodation of costume to the performer, which was to become vital in the emergence of dance dress in the latter half of the nineteenth century when Italian ballerinas were unwilling to mask their hard-won virtuosity with yards of billowing tarlatans and the shortened tutu emerged as the accepted costume for the ballerina.

The alteration in costume associated with Sallé was an entirely personal one and was dictated by artistic rather than technical considerations. On two occasions in her career Sallé left the Paris Opéra, which was her home theatre, in order to appear in London in works of her own devising. Most importantly she appeared there in *Pygmalion* in 1734 at the Theatre Royal, Covent Garden, then being run by George Frideric Handel as an opera house. In this ballet scene she took the part of a Greek statue come to life, and instead of taking the stage in the traditional, formal dress and complex hair style, she sought greater fidelity to the antique ideal by wearing soft draperies instead of the usual heavily panniered skirt, her hair hanging loose and naturally dressed.

Both ballerinas suffered reverses of fortune. La Camargo's brilliance was outshone by the arrival of an Italian virtuoso Barbara Campanini (1721–1799), known as La Barbarina, who was able to perform more *entrechats* with more sparkle, and swiftly won public acclaim. She was also to win more private affection from such personages as Frederick the Great, King of Prussia, for whom she danced in Berlin (he admired her 'boyish' legs). Camargo retired to a happy domesticity surrounded by a variety of pet birds and animals, leaving behind her the memory of a 'danseuse who bounded like a fury, cutting entrechats to right and left and in all directions', as Casanova records.

Detail of Lancret's Mlle Camargo Dancing (left) conveys all of her charm. (Wallace Collection)

Marie Sallé lost the affection of her London public, who had adored her so much that purses of gold had been thrown on stage as she danced, when she appeared in Handel's *Alcine* in male attire. In 1735 she returned to the Paris Opéra where she was able to apply some of her dramatic power to the *Acte des Fleurs* in Rameau's opera–ballet *Les Indes galantes*. In this she mimed the fear of a rose threatened by a storm and eventually rescued by a summer breeze. During the next five years her example and her talent were to soften the rigid performing attitudes in dance of the time, and on her retirement she lived quietly, occasionally dancing at special performances. By the time of her death she had been completely forgotten by her former public.

La Barbarina is one of the many examples of an Italian's virtuosity in the history of ballet. As has been seen, the art of ballet was born in Italy but its education was in France. Paris, as the centre of European culture, dominated many of the arts during the sixteenth and seventeenth centuries and as the polite language of Europe, French was adopted as a *lingua franca* for dance – then, as now, dance instruction made use of French terms. Nevertheless, the Italian taste for dancing and Italian training, which insisted upon a greater brilliance of execution than the more formal style in France, meant that Italian-schooled dancers would always be associated with an exceptional physical skill. This was true in the seventeenth and eighteenth centuries and was to acquire supreme importance in the nineteenth century when the ballet school in Milan would

Bernardo Bellotto's engraving (below) shows the grand manner of Hilferding's scene 'Le Turc généreux' from Les Indes galantes, *Rameau's opera–ballet in Vienna (1758). (British Museum)*

furnish ballerinas and *premiers danseurs* for most of the important theatres of Europe – not least in Russia.

The opera–ballet was to survive into the mid-eighteenth century because of the work of the greatest French composer of the century, Jean Philippe Rameau (1683–1764). His opera–ballets and lyric tragedies were a magnificent final statement about this particular form, and it was not until Gluck (1714–1787) that the new and liberalized form of opera gained sway. Gluck's operas showed the same concern for dramatic truth and independence which was to be the concern of the choreographers of the mid-eighteenth century who were seeking to establish the *ballet d'action*.

The emergence of the *ballet d'action* is a gradual process, but it is associated in particular with three ballet masters: Franz Hilferding van Wewen (1710–1768), his pupil Gasparo Angiolini (1731–1803), and Jean-Georges Noverre (1727–1810). Hilferding was born in Vienna, creating stagings in Stuttgart and then in St Petersburg. His work shows a very real desire to free ballet from its already outmoded procedures, and he is recognized as having influenced Noverre, who succeeded him in Stuttgart as chief ballet master at the ducal court of Württemberg. Hilferding's pupil Angiolini succeeded his master in St Petersburg, and it is he who acted as a bitter polemicist in a quarrel with Noverre as to who was the originator of the *ballet d'action*. Noverre, however, was definitely the most outspoken advocate for reform in ballet.

At the age of twenty-seven Noverre had achieved his first success at the Opéra Comique in Paris by staging *Les Fêtes chinoises*, an elaborate dance display which capitalized on the vogue for all things Chinese. He was invited by David Garrick to bring his 'Chinese' ballet to London and it was the fact that Britain and France were on the verge of the Seven Years' War, rather than any failing in the entertainment, which occasioned a celebrated series of riots in London in which the Theatre Royal, Covent Garden, was all but destroyed.

A contemporary record in the *Journal Etranger* reads:

'On Saturday the 15th November 1755 the ballet was given for the fifth time. There was no Parliament that day but the Italian Opera, supported by the Nobility, were opening their season (at the King's Theatre) and had attracted all the My Lords. The Blackguards (that is to say the rag-tag and bobtail of London) triumphed and made a horrible row; they tore up the benches and threw them into the Pit on the opposing party; they broke all the mirrors, the chandeliers etc., and tried to climb on to the stage to massacre everybody; but, as there is a magnificent organization in this theatre, in three minutes all the decor had been removed, all the traps were ready to come into play to swallow up those who might venture up, all the wings were filled with men armed with sticks, swords, halberds, etc. and, behind the scenes, the great reservoir was ready to be opened to drown those who might fall on the stage itself. All the public called for Garrick who had very good reasons for not showing himself. His partners appeared and promised that the ballet would not be given again and the Blackguards retired well pleased. This scene lasted until midnight.'[1]

It is significant that Noverre and David Garrick should be friends and should respect each other.

In the acting style of Garrick, at that time the supreme dramatic artist of the English stage, there was the same concern for dramatic veracity which was inspiring Noverre (whom Garrick called the Shakespeare of the dance).

That so much is known about Noverre's ideals for the ballet of his time is due to his *Lettres sur la danse et les ballets* (1760) a most detailed series of disquisitions upon the art of dancing. In them he offers a scalding portrait of the absurdities of the theatre dance in the mid-eighteenth century – from the sterile performance manner to the ludicrous nature of the *tonnelet* (a short, wired

Illustration (right) from a theatrical survey produced in Amsterdam in 1775, showing Mercury descending into a military camp at a seaport in Dido's Death, *an opera with danced interludes. (Theatermuseum, Amsterdam)*

Auguste Vestris (far left) whom Noverre called 'the new Proteus of the dance' for his versatility as a demi-caractère *dancer. This engraving of 1781 (after Nathaniel Dance), with the title in ancient Greek of 'Every Goose Can', was inspired by Plutarch's apothegm:*

A Stranger at Sparta standing long upon one Leg,
Said to a Lacedaemonian, 'I do believe you do as much';
'True (said he) but every Goose can.'

(Victoria and Albert Museum, London)

Scene (left) from Lully's opera-ballet Armide et Renaud (1686). *It was Armide who kept Renaud away from the Crusades in her enchanted garden in Tasso's epic poem,* Jerusalem Delivered, *which has inspired several ballets. The air of lubricity is explained by the fact that it is the frontispiece to a book (c. 1785) by Restif de la Bretonne, the mordant chronicler of manners and morals of his time. (Victoria and Albert Museum, London)*

skirt) worn by male dancers – and propounds a powerful corrective by way of reform.

'A well composed ballet must be expressive in all its detail and speak to the soul through the eyes; if it be devoid of striking pictures, of strong situations, it becomes a cold and dreary spectacle ... Steps, the ease and brilliancy of their combination, equilibrium, stability, speed, lightness, precision, the opposition of the arms and the legs – these form what I term the mechanism of the dance. When all these movements are not directed by genius, and when feeling and expression do not contribute their powers sufficiently to affect and interest me, I admire the skill of the human machine, I render justice to its strength and ease of movement, but it leaves me unmoved ...'[2]

Here is evidence of that continued dichotomy in ballet between technical virtuosity and expressive power. At a time when entirely hollow brilliance was considered the norm, and when danced *entrées* were no more than displays of style and elegance, Noverre's quest for expression was also symptomatic of the great change in intellectual ideals which was sweeping Europe during the second half of the eighteenth century. At the moment when the *Letters* were first published, in 1760, Noverre had been appointed chief ballet master to one of the most exceptional courts in Europe – that of the theatre-loving Grand Duke of Württemberg in Stuttgart. For seven years Noverre attracted eminent dancers in Europe to appear in an exceptional sequence of ballets. *Medea and Jason, Orpheus and Eurydice, The Death of Lykomedes, Antony and Cleopatra,*

Alexander, are but some of the works he staged. Alas, nothing of these remains, but equally important was the fact that contact with Noverre was to inspire many other ballet masters with the desire to broaden ballet's horizons, and thus the message of the *ballet d'action* could spread throughout Europe.

After seven years Noverre moved to Vienna where he was able to continue his work and also be associated with Gluck. Describing a staging of *Alceste* in 1767 Noverre noted that he had suggested to Gluck that:

'... he should break up the choruses and conceal them in the wings so that the public would not see them and I promised to replace them by the élite of my corps de ballet who would perform the gestures appropriate to the song and so dovetail the action that the public would believe that the moving figures were in fact the singers. Gluck nearly smothered me in his excess of joy; he found my project excellent and its realisation created the most perfect illusion.'[3]

During his period of service in Vienna, he had acted as dancing teacher to the young Archduchess Marie-Antoinette. In due time she was to become the wife of the Dauphin (later Louis XVI), and then Queen of France, and it was this fact which was to enable Noverre to realize his dearest wish, that of being ballet master at the Paris Opéra. His appointment in 1776, though, was not welcome. It broke the tradition whereby the succession to this very important post always passed from one ballet master to his assistant; with the retirement of Gaetano Vestris as ballet master it had been assumed that his deputies, Maximilien

Fontainebleau 1785

established herself in the capital as a successful courtesan – and entered the Paris Opéra School for a period of study under Le Grand Dupré. Within three years he was appointed as a principal dancer in the *noble* style at the Opéra.

Until well into the nineteenth century, male dancers were categorized according to style and vocabulary of movement into three genres: the most distinguished was the *noble* (sometimes known as *sérieux*), a style of great distinction and elegance; more brilliant and admitting of greater virtuosity was the *demi-caractère*; finally, there was the vulgar and grotesque *comique*.

In Paris, Gaetano Vestris earned speedy acclaim by reason of his undoubted technical skill and his very considerable dramatic ability. A contemporary wrote of him: 'The particular virtues of Vestris are grace, elegance and delicacy. All his steps have a purity, a finish which can barely be imagined and it is not without some justification that his talent is compared with that of Racine.' Small wonder that he inherited from earlier great dancers the title of *Le Diou de la danse* (the mispronounciation of *Dieu* being a reminder of his Italianate French) but he was equally celebrated for his insufferable vanity. This dancer who said that Europe contained only three great men, Frederick the Great of Prussia, Voltaire and himself, could also turn on a lady who had trodden on his foot and, when she apologized, say 'Hurt me madam! Me! You have only put all Paris in mourning for a fortnight.' These considerations aside, he was, nevertheless, a superb dancer who travelled Europe demonstrating the finest traditions of French dancing, appearing with marked success in Noverre's Stuttgart ballets, and he was also the begetter of a no less brilliant son. Auguste Vestris, the product of Gaetano's liaison with the dancer Marie Allard, was born in 1760 and died in 1842; his life thus spans the entire transition of dance style from the heyday of the eighteenth-century manner to the 'Romantic' world of *Giselle*. His importance is not merely as the most brilliant performer of his time (he assumed his father's title as 'God of the Dance'), but also as an inspired teacher whose development of the eighteenth-century technique was to be one of the formative influences upon the emergent style of Romantic dance. Among his pupils were Jules Perrot and August Bournonville, the two greatest choreographers – and two of the finest dancers – of the Romantic era. Auguste Vestris' training was central to the work of Bournonville, and the Bournonville 'school' was an elaboration and a development of Vestris' teaching.

Auguste Vestris' style was, however, not the grand *noble* manner of his father, but *demi-caractère*. He was a more brilliant executant than his father, which the elder Vestris attributed to the fact that 'Auguste has certain benefits which nature denied me – Gaetano Vestris as his father.'

Gaetano's relationship with the Opéra was always stormy, no more so than when in 1776 Noverre was imposed as ballet master in succes-

Gardel and Jean Dauberval, would share the appointment. Noverre's appointment caused a great deal of jealousy which neither his talent nor his royal patronage could surmount. Four years later the machinations of the dancers and the intrigues of Gardel and Dauberval forced him to resign; they thus gained the post which they had always considered rightfully theirs. Noverre's later years were to be marked by sadness. His pension was not very large and with the outbreak of the Revolution he found life increasingly difficult. He continued to stage ballets until 1793 (these he was forced to mount in London, having fled there after the Revolution because of his association with Marie-Antoinette); thereafter he devoted himself to writing, and died in France at Saint-Germain-en-Laye in October 1810. By that time, thanks to his influence on the several important choreographers and dancers who had worked with him, many of the reforms which he had advocated and ideals of which he had dreamed were becoming an actuality throughout Europe.

Although the latter part of the eighteenth century can be seen as the time when the choreographer came into his own it was also a period dominated by star dancers. Chief of these, and one of the supreme performers of the eighteenth century, was Gaetano Vestris (1729–1808). Member of an itinerant family of Italian dancers and singers, he was born in Florence and made his first appearances as a dancer as the whole Vestris tribe wandered across Europe from Naples to Vienna. At the age of eighteen Gaetano arrived in Paris – following with his family the trail blazed by his beautiful sister Marie-Thérèse who had

Costume design by Louis-René Boquet (left) for the elder Vestris as Adonis. Plumed and draped, the danseur is seen in his final elaborate apotheosis before the Revolution swept away the artificialities of the ancien régime style of costume.

An amused comment on back stage at the Paris Opéra (right) immediately following the abdication of Napoleon in 1814. A group of British tourists on the left are inspecting the merchandise while Auguste Vestris, as a cupid, partners a dancer called Mademoiselle Virginie. On the right the choreographer Louis Milon, dressed as a devil, is in conversation with the elaborately hatted Emilie Bigottini, a ballerina of the period. The costume of the performers suggests the new freedom of dress which was to liberate technique. (Bibliothèque Nationale, Paris)

sion to Vestris. This breaking with tradition was to inspire the mass of intrigues which made Noverre's tenure of office so difficult and was to precipitate his departure in 1781. A chief figure in the resistance movement to Noverre was Madeleine Guimard (1743–1816), who excelled in a light and delicate style adorable in its prettiness but without massive technical feats. Her great merits as a dancer were often obscured by the magnificence of her liaisons. Though not a conventional beauty of the time (she was thought too thin, and her companions called her *la squelette des Graces*), Guimard attracted the undying affection of many wealthy men and used the spoils of the boudoir in charitable works as well as in wonderful parties given at her *hôtel particulier* which was known as the Temple of Terpsichore. Because of her important protectors Guimard was probably the most influential single figure at the Opéra – it was she who served as a focal point for the anti-Noverre lobby (despite the fact that Noverre had created several fine roles for her).

As has already been described, it was with the departure of Noverre in 1781 that the old order was re-established and Maximilien Gardel was appointed ballet master with Jean Dauberval as his assistant. Gardel (1741–1787) is remembered as the dancer who first refused to wear the customary mask which had for years been part of the costume of the *danseur noble* in certain roles. He rejected it to ensure that the public knew that it was he and not Gaetano Vestris who was dancing. In his period as ballet master he was helped by his close friendship with Guimard, and once in power, he was able to rid himself of Dauberval and install his younger brother Pierre

(1758–1840) as his assistant. The loss of Dauberval can, with hindsight, be seen as a great blow to the Opéra. Dauberval (1742–1806) with his ravishing wife, the ballerina Mademoiselle Théodore, betook himself to Bordeaux, and it is there that he produced the work for which he is remembered today, and one in which his association with Noverre bore fruit: *La Fille mal gardée*. In this influential ballet, staged in 1789, there was for the first time a danced action which concerned itself with a far more realistic view of country folk than had been attempted before.

Gardel also attempted to incorporate Noverrean ideals at the Opéra, and in simpler and lighter-weight *ballet–pantomimes* he made a transfer to the dance stage of the fashionable comic operas of the time. His career was cut short by a tragic accident; an injury to his toe was left unattended and gangrene set in. He died in 1787, and was succeeded as *maître de ballet* by his brother. The reign of Pierre Gardel effectively lasted until the 1820s. During times of Revolution, Terror, Republic, War, Consulate, Empire, Restoration and the emergence of the new bourgeois society of the nineteenth century, Gardel remained at his post guiding the destiny of the Opéra and preserving it during this period of unprecedented upheaval. For this alone he has earned posterity's gratitude; more especially, he also produced a solid repertory of ballets – works like *Télémaque* (1790), *Psyche* (1790), and *The Judgement of Paris* (1793) – which were to prove among the most popular works for a period of thirty years. (In many of these he featured his wife, Marie Miller Gardel, whose technical brilliance was matched by an elegance of execution.)

Pierre Gardel (above) succeeded his brother Maximilien as ballet master at the Paris Opéra in 1787, and produced many successful ballets – in which his wife Marie Miller Gardel often featured – until the 1820s. His attitude here personifies the noble style.

With the comparative stability of the Napoleonic age, Gardel could set the ballet at his theatre on a secure basis. Notable dancers abounded and although Gardel has been reproached for not inviting many outside choreographers he yet permitted the creation of ballets by Louis-Jacques Milon and also encouraged the work of Louis Duport and Louis Henry to be staged. In the creations of all these choreographers it is evident that dance itself was considered important. Although in the tradition of Noverre, mime and dramatic playing were still an integral part of the ballet's fabric, they did not decline to the vast mimetic spectacles which were now to become fashionable in Italy.

At La Scala, Milan, Salvatore Viganò (1769–1821) became an exponent of the theories of Noverre in respect of dramatic staging: he owed this to his own studies with Dauberval, Noverre's associate, and also to the fact that his mother had appeared under Noverre's direction in Vienna.

Stendhal equated Viganò as a genius of his time with Napoleon, Canova, and Rossini. Two years after Viganò's death Stendhal said of his ballets: 'it was a new art which died with this great man.' This was an opinion generally shared in Italy at that time: Viganò's greatest ballets – *Prometheus, Mirra, Daedalus, The Titans, Othello* – excited enthusiastic comment on their grandeur as well as on their allegorical importance.

Salvatore Viganò was born in Naples in 1769 of a dancing family. His father, Onorato, was a ballet master much admired at that time; his mother, a sister of Boccherini, was a ballerina. The young Salvatore was taught to dance, but he also demonstrated talent as a composer and a poet, and his later career showed his concern with a poetic relationship between gesture and musical rhythm. After debuts in Rome, he went to dance in Spain with his uncle Giovanni Viganò and there he met and married the ravishingly beautiful Maria Medina. Equally important to his career was the fact that he also met Dauberval and the elder choreographer took the young dancer under his wing and invited him to work in London where he could teach him the finer points of the French style of dance. By the end of the eighteenth century the French style was dominant in European ballet. It was a brilliant style and, as already mentioned, Noverre had sought to correct and revise its excess of technical virtuosity in a quest for greater emotional and dramatic truth. (To this end he had advocated the banishing of masks as well as the ridiculous panniers and *tonnelets*.) Dauberval, his disciple and pupil, implemented these theories in his work. He sought excellence in pantomime declaring that it 'explains with rapidity the movements of the soul; it is a universal language, common to all time, and better than words it expresses extreme sorrow and extreme joy . . . I do not want just to please the eyes, I must interest the heart.'

In his choreography Dauberval aimed at this expressive character, as evidenced by the successful *La Fille mal gardée* and also by the famous *pas de deux* in *Sylvie* in which a faun and a nymph mimed a whole amorous intrigue as they danced. In 1790 Viganò made a great success as a dancer in Venice, on the stage of the Teatro San Samuele of which his father was manager, demonstrating the exceptional elegance of the French style. His first choreography came in the following year and in 1792 he staged a version of Dauberval's *La Fille mal gardée*. But it was in 1793 when he danced with his wife in Vienna that Viganò knew his greatest success thus far. Maria Medina's beauty was very lightly clothed in dances in which her husband had been inspired by the poses of classic statuary. The Emperor Franz II fell under the spell of the voluptuous Maria and her dress became all the rage. Not only were hair styles and shoes qualified as 'à la Viganò', not only did Beethoven compose a minuet 'à la Viganò' but when Maria became pregnant the ladies of Vienna aped the delicate rotundities of her form by clever drapery of their dress. In Vienna, Salvatore staged his *Richard the Lionheart*, and during the period 1795–1798 the Viganòs travelled throughout middle Europe performing, returning to Italy and then settling in Vienna again until 1803 during which time Viganò collaborated with Beethoven on *The Creatures of Prometheus*.

Nothing up to this time had been truly original in Viganò's work. His ballets were the conven-

Maria Medina Viganò (left), the wife of Salvatore Viganò. This portrait conveys both the physical allure of this very beautiful dancer and the style of Neo-classical dance.

The grandeur of Neo-classical stage design at the Teatro alla Scala, Milan is typified by this setting (above) by Alessandro Sanquirico for the garden scene in Memphis in Viganò's ballet Psammis, King of Egypt. *Italian mastery in stage design and a brilliant use of perspective – a dominant feature of eighteenth-century stage decoration – is still clearly apparent. (Victoria and Albert Museum, London)*

tional allegorical and mythological exercises in the current French style, but with his return to Italy in 1804, and his choreographic debut at La Scala, Milan with *Coriolanus*, there came an innovation in style. Viganò sought to reveal the mimed dramatic action on a basis of danced steps rather than the habitual mime which was performed in isolation. It can be said that in *Coriolanus* dance was sacrificed to pantomime but the silent oration of *Coriolanus* was admired as being comprehensible to all spectators without recourse to the libretto, as was necessary with the works of Angiolini, Rossi and the other choreographers of the age. Over the next years Viganò produced ballets in Milan, Padua and Venice, this latter city seeing the production of *Gli Strelizzi* in which he made a breakthrough. Up to this time he had combined mime (that was so much to the Italian taste) with the French dance that he knew from Dauberval. Now, he recognized the fact that mime itself was often mere dumb show in the Italian theatre, a gesturing of what should be spoken. He evolved a more fluid and expressive gesticulation, rigorously based upon musical rhythms. He could not yet dispense entirely with dance, with the conventional pas de deux and *ballabile* (a group dance usually executed by the *corps de ballet*) but he reduced dance's importance and justified its

inclusion in the action only on the strictest terms. In the oath scene of *Gli Strelizzi*, he made supreme use of picturesque groupings and of what were considered 'novel evolutions'. From 1812 onwards Viganò settled in Milan and on the huge stage of La Scala, with grandiose designs by Alessandro Sanquirico, he produced the immense spectacles so admired by Stendhal.

In 1813 in *Prometheus* – a vastly ambitious and uneven work in six tableaux – Viganò realized on stage many of Noverre's ideas about naturalness of gesture probably more surely than they were seen in Noverre's own works, and all performed in his own form of cadenced mime. In two works inspired by drama – *Mirra* based on a play by Alfieri and *Othello* based on Shakespeare's drama – contemporaries considered that the ballets equalled the pathetic and tragic power of the originals. In *La Vestale* and *Daedalus*, the audience felt that he touched the sublime.

In 1821 Viganò died while at work on *Dido*; his style which he had developed over a period of nearly twenty years had arrived at a musical, cadenced mime, firmly rooted in the score, that must have been somewhere between the ordinary theatrical mime of his time and dance and danced gesture.

Music was fundamental to this nephew of Boccherini. In his ballets he used passages from Mozart, Rossini, Beethoven, Haydn (introducing part of *The Creation* into *Prometheus*). In Sanquirico he found an ideal decorative partner. But he found no worthy successor. Gaetano Gioja, almost his contemporary, continued in the Viganò vein and Louis Henry also attempted to perpetuate something of this style. But neither man could recapture the imaginative power that was so clearly perceived in the work of this great choreographer. He was at times reproached for rejecting the dance but, as can be appreciated, his alternative of expressive pantomime could be as profoundly stimulating to the public as any other choreography of the time. It is worth noting, however, that one of the principal dancers in Viganò's troupe at La Scala, Milan, was the twenty-one-year old Carlo Blasis who was to become one of the most important pedagogues and theoreticians in the training of dancers.

At the same time as Neo-classicism reached its apogee in the first decades of the nineteenth century, another artistic movement was also emerging. Like Neo-classicism, Romanticism has strong roots in the eighteenth century. But its emergence as a powerful artistic stimulus was really to be felt in the years immediately following the downfall of Napoleon in 1815. Although in music, painting and literature it was in full flood by the 1820s it was not in fact to appear on the ballet stage until 1832 with the staging of *La Sylphide*. Nevertheless, one choreographer, Charles Louis Didelot (1767–1837), is an important precursor.

Charles Louis Didelot was born in Stockholm into a French dancing family. In Paris as a young

boy and as an apprentice dancer he saw ballets by Noverre and was impressed by them – he was in fact to call Noverre 'the Corneille of the dance' – and his admiration must inevitably have been further stimulated by his studies with Dauberval, whom he adored. In 1787 he went to London to dance with Noverre's troupe, where Auguste Vestris was also appearing, and he remained in London until the following year. An abortive return to Paris showed him that there was no chance of a creative career at the Opéra, by now firmly under the control of Pierre Gardel, and Didelot returned again to London. He staged some ballets which found little public favour but it is some consolation to record that in this season the public was prone to rioting in the theatre! (A disrespectful audience was also to call Madeleine Guimard, appearing in London in her forty-sixth year, *La grand'mère des Graces*.)

After his London disappointments Didelot arrived in Bordeaux, a city in which ballet was honoured with a superb theatre, le Grand Théâtre, and with Dauberval as ballet master. Didelot and his wife Rose had great success there in the season 1789–90 but the extremely difficult political situation in France compelled them to return to London where they appeared in *Amphion and Thalia*. In 1791 Didelot danced again at the Paris Opéra at a time when the most important changes in dance costume were taking place. Gone was the need to appear in *tonnelets* or in theatricalized versions of social dress from wig to heeled shoes. Revolutionary political upheaval banished clothing associated with the *ancien régime*. The Committee of Public Safety had invited the sculptor David to design costumes for the people of a free nation and the theatre reflected the same liberalizing tendencies. In *Bacchus and Ariadne* Didelot wore flesh-coloured tights, a tiger skin over one shoulder and grape leaves in his hair; in *Corisande*, later

that year, Didelot as a sylph wore a light, gauzy tunic.

In the next couple of years the Didelots worked in Lyon, where Charles Louis created anacreontic ballets, works fashionable at the time for their delicate, artless intrigues featuring fauns, gods, satyrs and shepherdesses. By 1795 the Didelots had returned to London for a five-year engagement at the King's Theatre. Didelot was now more successful as a choreographer and in one work he made use of wires to allow cupids to fly through the air, but the major production of the period was his *Flore et Zéphire* in which the use of wires, allied to a narrative in which flight was an essential part, showed air as the domain of the dancer. But more amusing is the fact that the appearance of the French *danseuses* aroused the anger of the Bench of Bishops. The supposedly immodest costuming of the ladies was thought to be wildly corrupting and enough to unleash a flood of divorce cases. The Bishops' inspection of the ballerinas' gauzy inexpressibles was to provide rich material for the cartoonists in an age when nothing was sacred from the venom of popular prints.

In 1801 there came 'a landmark in the history of the Russian ballet'. Didelot was appointed to the Imperial Ballet and there ensued what has justifiably been called the epoch of Didelot in the history of Russian ballet. For ten years Didelot directed the company in St Petersburg, improved the training at the school and shaped a fine ensemble of dancers. Personal tragedy haunted him; Rose died in 1803 (though two years later he married another French dancer, Marie-Rose Colinette) and at the same time injury curtailed his own dancing. This impelled him further on the path of choreography and teaching. The emergence of fine Russian dancers is also noticeable, although the brightest and most promising of these, the young Marie Danilova, died following a stage accident at the age of seventeen. Didelot's greatest achievement of this first decade in Russia was his *Cupid and Psyche* in five acts first staged in 1809, a version of a work already treated by Noverre, Gardel and Dauberval.

In 1810 his contract expired and as a result of various disagreements with the directorate of the Imperial theatres Didelot left Russia with his wife to work in London and Paris until their return to St Petersburg in 1816. His great output of ballets in Russia and his eminence as a pedagogue were responsible for a golden age of dance there. Among the most notable of his works in the next years were two ballets inspired by the works of Pushkin. The poet had written *The Prisoner of the Caucasus* in 1821; within four months of its publication Didelot had transferred it triumphantly to the ballet stage. His version of *Ruslan and Ludmila* was also a response to Pushkin's writing. In these, as in many other of his works in this second Russian period, Didelot's concern with historic and national themes was evident and his mimetic style allowed for a vivid presentation of

A M☉NUTE REGULATION of the OPERA STEP or an EPISCOPAL EXAMINATION.

human emotions. But in the late 1820s there were again disagreements with the directorate of the Imperial theatres and in 1829 a final quarrel ended Didelot's association with the St Petersburg ballet. Eight years later he was to die, still a resident of the country to which he had contributed so much.

EMERGENCE OF THE ROMANTIC STYLE

Because the Paris Opéra was itself somewhat reactionary – a temple of academism presided over by Pierre Gardel whose roots and attitudes were firmly based in the eighteenth century – it was only late in the Romantic day that it felt the full impact of the Romantic movement. The first indication that ballet was to change radically came in 1827. It was then that the twenty-three year old dancer Marie Taglioni made a first appearance on the hallowed boards of the rue le Peletier, which

was at that time the home of the Opéra.

Taglioni (1804–1884), daughter of a Milanese dancing master–choreographer Filippo Taglioni and his Swedish wife, was a somewhat unlikely figure to change the course of dancing. But like two other dancers of the century, Virginia Zucchi and Isadora Duncan, her influence was immense and can be felt to this day.

Taglioni was unpromising material for the career to which she was inevitably destined, being skinny, rather sallow and without any obvious physical charm. But her father placed her with the finest teachers and he himself undertook to polish her gifts so that by the time she was eighteen she had been shaped into an exceptional performer. She was in no way like the conventional ballerinas of the period; she had none of the physical glamour nor bravado of style that reflected the all too available sexual charms of the *danseuses*. Instead, Taglioni offered grace, demure charm and an incomparable lightness. Her lack of obvious physical allure meant that she had a different attraction to offer the audience – something discreet, intangible, other-worldly. Her abilities enabled her to take to the air at a time when *à terre* brilliance was the norm. Her thin physique, long limbs, the downward-sloping curves of shoulders and her long neck encouraged poses of dulcet grace which were in marked contrast to the bold attractions of her predecessors (except perhaps for the ballerina Thérèse Héberlé, who was also noted for her extraordinary lightness). Marie made her debut in Vienna in 1822, and it was not until five years later that she eventually appeared at the Paris Opéra. There, in partnership with her brother Paul, she appeared in an interpolated *pas* in the ballet *Le Sicilien*. The effect was sensational. Her way of dancing was found to be totally new in its floating gentleness, its decorum and its rejection of every bold artifice of the dancers habitually seen at the Opéra.

The great Danish dancer and choreographer August Bournonville, then in Paris as a young soloist with the Opéra Ballet, wrote of Taglioni's 'expressive and modest dancing . . . The more one sees this dancer the more one discovers the charm of her dancing and the most rigorous connoisseur could not resist her lightness, her ease and this voluptuous abandon which is essentially the real dancing of a woman.' Another observer

Marie Taglioni as La Sylphide. *Chalon's lithograph captures the transparent grace and the modest beauty of this greatest of the 'Romantic' dancers. This pose may still be seen in the version of the ballet created by August Bournonville for the Royal Danish Ballet in 1836 and preserved ever since.*

noted that Taglioni's style was 'Romanticism applied to the dance'. For the next four years Taglioni appeared at the Opéra and toured Europe – it is a tribute to the novelty of her performance that a new verb *Taglioniser* (to dance like Taglioni) was coined to explain the efforts of her contemporaries to copy her style. Certainly the rigorous training and discipline with which she prepared herself for her art and the adorable modesty and delicacy of her performance style were very new. New, too, was the use she made of the tips of her toes. By the early years of the nineteenth century a few adventurous *danseuses* had hoisted themselves up on the very points of their feet without any of the support that is today to be found in the ballerina's stiffened toe shoe. The feat of toe dancing was given impetus by the brilliance of an Italian virtuoso, Amalia Brugnoli, but it was Taglioni who was to ennoble it by giving it artistic merit.

In 1831 there was a change of management at the Paris Opéra. It was to become a private enterprise with some state support, and the man placed in charge of it was Dr Louis Véron, a medical man and, more importantly, an accomplished publicist and journalist. Under Véron's guidance during the next five years the Opéra was to flourish as rarely before and Véron's own astuteness and ability to manipulate public opinion meant that he could retire from the directorship with the unique distinction of having made (rather than lost) a fortune. Among his first actions was the re-engagement of Taglioni as the supreme ballerina of the company at a massively increased salary, and she was to feature in one of the more important new opera stagings. This was Meyerbeer's *Robert le diable*, first produced on 21 November 1831. Taglioni was to appear in the ballet of the nuns, in which ghosts of lapsed nuns rose from their graves at midnight to dance a wild Bacchanal in the moonlight. Here was one of the most crucial moments in the emergence of Romanticism onto the ballet stage. The recently installed gas lighting enabled effects of moonlight to play on the scene; the vaporous draperies of the nuns and Taglioni's ethereal and aerial flights, all provided a central image of the Romantic dance. The scene itself was much admired but more importantly it inspired the tenor in the opera, Adolphe Nourrit, with the idea of a ballet which should feature Taglioni. He suggested a Scottish theme and after consultation with Filippo Taglioni the idea of *La Sylphide* was born.

In this tale a young Scots farmer, James, due to be married to his sweetheart Effie, is lured away from the path of duty by a childlike Sylphide. She has watched over him for years and declares her love for him on the eve of his wedding day. Unable to resist her, James flees with her to the forest, but he has incurred the enmity of Madge, a witch, and she engineers the death of the Sylphide. At the end of the ballet, James is alone; he has seen the Sylphide's body borne to some sylphide heaven and he has watched Effie going to church to marry another man. He is an outcast both from the real world and the dream world so beloved of Romantic man. For the audience of the time the ballet was an incarnation of all the dreams that were so prevalent in this heyday of Romanticism, but for Parisian audiences the special charm was the appearance of Taglioni. In her performance observers noted the death of the old style. Here was the ideal Romantic artist, a vision who seemed to respond to the most ardent imaginings of the public of the time.

But it is worth insisting that Taglioni's was a style dictated by a highly personal manner and by a physique absolutely unlike those of the other dancers of her age. Although the central figure of the Romantic movement as a performer, Taglioni was not typical of the Romantic ballerina. Far more did she seem an idealization of femininity and her special genius as a performer – never called in question by any contemporary observer – placed her above the average run of *danseuses* of the period.

It is unwise to assume that the Romantic style of dancing sprung entirely freshly onto the stage of the Paris Opéra with the first performance of *La Sylphide* in 1832. As with every artistic movement it germinated slowly. Taglioni's appearances may have crystallized a particular image, but the Romantic dance itself can be traced quite clearly to the eighteenth-century dance and more especially to the teaching of Auguste Vestris. Increasingly it seems that Vestris was a profound innovator in the developments which he brought about in the dance of the early years of the nineteenth century. Valuable testimony to this is the fact that the two greatest choreographers of the Romantic period, August Bournonville and Jules Perrot, were dancers entirely formed by Vestris, and in their teaching and in their choreography they reflected ideals propounded by their master. August Bournonville in particular provides vital evidence in his writings during the 1820s of the importance he attributed to Vestris' teaching and to the innovations in style made by Vestris. He even noted that Taglioni's style, so highly personal, did not satisfy the most rigorous academic canons of the period.

The breaking down of the rigid categories of eighteenth-century dance, which had persisted into the nineteenth century during the long reign of Pierre Gardel at the Opéra, plainly owes much to the influence of Vestris. Thus the French style of the eighteenth century was to adapt itself to the new demands of Romanticism and the French influence was also to be felt in Italy. Carlo Blasis (1797–1878) was both French and Italian trained and his career as a pedagogue began with the publication of his first manual *The Treatise on the Dance* of 1820 (published in Milan).

Blasis, a pupil of Viganò, Dauberval and Gardel, was also the inheritor of the French school exemplified by Dauberval and Vestris. A clear indication of his indebtedness to the French style is shown in a letter which he wrote to August

This plate from Carlo Blasis' Code of Terpsichore, published in London in 1828, testifies to the teaching method of one of the central pedagogic figures in nineteenth-century dance technique. The Code provides some of the best insights into the development of dance technique during the 'Romantic' age.

Bournonville. It reads in part 'I tried to maintain and propagate the *belle école*, the school in which you were also raised.[4]

Albeit Blasis' method of training (which reached its pinnacle of importance during the years in which he was director of the ballet school of La Scala, Milan, and also taught throughout Europe) developed dancers outstanding for their virtuosity, this brilliance was firmly rooted in the academic traditions of the eighteenth century. The ballerinas who were to flower during the Romantic period were pupils of Vestris and of Blasis. They may have seemed a new breed of dancer – a view encouraged by the new development of pointe work at this time – but they were logically the descendants of the dancers of the pre-Romantic age.

DANCERS OF THE ROMANTIC AGE

The really important division between the ballet of the beginning of the nineteenth century and that of the 'Romantic' age (which took the stage with Taglioni's performance in *La Sylphide*) was the acceptance of the ballerina as the central figure on the stage and the gradual banishing of the male dancer to the ignoble role of *porteur*. (In 1870 he was to be banished entirely from the stage when the hero Franz in *Coppélia* was played by the prettiest girl in the Paris Opéra Ballet.)

Further, the Romantic ballet which capitalized upon fantasy and upon exoticism was an escapist theatre in which the female became an idealized vision of womanhood. The twin poles of her stage identity are to be found in Gautier's celebrated dictum about Taglioni and Elssler – that Taglioni was a Christian dancer and Elssler was the pagan. Implicit in this is the idea of the conflict between

Fanny Elssler as Zoë in La Volière (1838), which was choreographed by her sister Thérèse. In his biography of Elssler, Ivor Guest details the lunatic action of the piece thus: 'Thérèse Elssler played the part of Thereza, who, deceived long before by her lover, is bringing up her younger sister Zoë (Fanny) in a remote corner of San Domingo in total ignorance of the existence of the male sex.' Lithograph by Gauci from a drawing by J. Deffett Francis.

the spiritual and the sensual. Taglioni's supremacy in the ballet of her time is unquestionable; until her retirement in 1847 at the age of forty-three she was acknowledged as the queen of the dance, no matter what brilliant challenges might be offered by younger dancers. Her chief rival, in a rivalry very astutely stage-managed by the publicists of the period, was the Viennese-born Fanny Elssler (1810–1884). Her early career found her in Vienna, Naples and London but it was in 1834 that Dr Véron invited her to appear in Paris. The warmth and dramatic intensity of this radiantly beautiful woman guaranteed a public following. The audience became divided between Taglionists and Elsslerites and when Taglioni set off for St Petersburg (where her appearances were accredited with reviving a flagging public interest in ballet), Elssler reigned supreme in Paris. She became associated in the public mind with the Spanish dance, the *cachucha*, which marked her

first huge success in *Le Diable boiteux* in 1836. In this her 'Spanish' temperament and the sensuality of her dancing excited the public.

Elssler appeared in a ballet *La Volière* (1838) choreographed by her sister Thérèse, who partnered Fanny as she had done before *en travesti* – there were no male dancers in the ballet at all. And the following year the greatest role made for her, *La Gipsy* (choreography by Mazilier), allowed her to astound the Paris public in a *cracovienne*. There followed a decision to go to America, an Eldorado for dancers, and during a two-year engagement which took her down as far as Cuba, Elssler was paid five hundred dollars a performance. On her return to Europe she found the Paris Opéra closed to her as a result of contractual troubles, and her career from then onwards was spent in London, Vienna, Berlin and most gloriously in Russia. In both St Petersburg and Moscow, Elssler knew unprecedented triumphs and it is in these years that she set her mark upon *Giselle*. In this she provided an interpretation of such dramatic intensity and beauty that its effects may be felt even today: the tradition of playing the mad scene as a passage of high dramatic tension rather than as the gentler dance scene that the first Giselle, Carlotta Grisi, had created is entirely due to Elssler's innovation. Elssler's final performances took place in Vienna in 1851, and the next thirty-three years of her life were spent in a quiet affluence.

The ballerina's domination of the Romantic dance was no more evident than in the *Pas de Quatre* which Jules Perrot staged at Her Majesty's Theatre in London in 1845. Female dancing had made considerable strides during the preceding decades. Pointe work had emerged as a permanent and essential extension of women's dancing, though it should be noted that the light slippers of satin and silk worn by the ballerinas (carefully darned, and wadded inside with silk or cotton) afforded only minimal support for the foot and the supposed prodigies performed on pointe are very open to question. (It is not until later in the century with the emergence of a stronger Italian blocked shoe that pointe work could attain any kind of real virtuosity.) Nevertheless, the iconography of the period shows how vitally important was the image of the ballerina as a figure poised weightless upon the ground, her feet exquisitely and improbably tapering. The most interesting testimony to the importance of the Romantic ballet is to be found in the vast output of lithographs, prints, and other ephemera which celebrated the female dancer from the 1830s onwards. Despite the naïvety which lies at the heart of these records – delicious femininity dressed in a variety of beguiling outfits – they do give a very fair view of what the Romantic audience and the Romantic artists believed that dancing was about.

Ballet was an art of escapist illusion, of fairy tales and fairy tale history, presided over by the adorable divinities who skimmed and spun over the stages of Europe and America. In certain cases,

In 1846 Jules Perrot created yet another of those divertissements for the reigning 'goddesses' of ballet, which Saint-Léon called 'steeple-chases'. The Judgement of Paris *contained the* pas des déesses *illustrated here, with Fanny Cerrito, Marie Taglioni, Lucile Grahn and Saint-Léon as Paris. Perrot also appeared in it, as Mercury.*

as in Elssler's, they could move audiences by dramatic genius. For the most part, however, it was the combination of feminine charms and physical daring which seems to have entranced the public, as for example Carlotta Grisi's celebrated leap in *La Péri*, at the Paris Opéra in 1843, in which the ballerina flung herself from a nearly two-metre (six-foot) high platform to land in the arms of Lucien Petipa. When one night the leap failed to come off Carlotta, at some peril to life and limb, had to repeat the jump several times before the public were satisfied and would allow the ballet to proceed.

Grisi (1819–1899) was one of the quartet in the *Pas de Quatre* (with Cerrito, Grahn and the supreme Taglioni as companions). She came from a distinguished family which numbered the great

singers Ernesta, Giulia and Giuditta Grisi among its members. Of medium height, enchantingly pretty, she had a vivacity and a delicacy which won all hearts. Her early fame she owed to Perrot and her career with him is described later on in this chapter.

In the last years of her career she went to Russia, where Jules Perrot was then ballet master in St Petersburg, and appeared in *Giselle* there at the Bolshoy Theatre in 1850. Three years later she left the stage and lived in retirement until her death in Geneva in 1899.

Fanny Cerrito (1817–1909) was born in Naples and her talent was sufficiently obvious for her to be dancing leading roles by the age of fifteen. A career in Italy inevitably resulted in stardom at La Scala, Milan, towards the end of the 1830s

Lucile Grahn in the tragic moment at the end of La Sylphide *when the sylph's wings drop off after James has placed a poisoned scarf around her shoulders. The pose, so vividly captured in E. Young's drawing, can be seen in performances of the ballet today.*

where a rivalry with Carlotta Grisi began. It was to continue when both dancers appeared in the *Pas de Quatre* but by this time Cerrito was the established darling of London. She had made her debut at Her Majesty's Theatre in 1840 and she was fortunate enough to be there as leading dancer during the years of Perrot's incumbency at that theatre. For her he created *Ondine*, a ballet in which she has become immortalized through the shadow dance. Inevitably she was compared with Taglioni; she also entered into a contest of popularity with Elssler, but London had taken her to its heart and until 1847 she was to be the undoubted darling both of the public and of society. Her marriage to Arthur Saint-Léon (whose career is covered later on) brought her a choreographic companion who was to devote himself to her during their years at the Paris Opéra, but their marriage was to end when Fanny fell in love with the Marqués de Bedmar, a Spanish nobleman of wealth and charm as well as youthful good looks, by whom she bore a daughter – Mathilde. After the birth of her daughter she returned to the stage, appearing in the 1850s in St Petersburg and Moscow, and going to London to make her farewell in the *minuet* in Mozart's *Don Giovanni* at the Lyceum Theatre. For another fifty-two years she lived in retirement in Paris, dying in 1909 at the moment when the Diaghilev troupe was rehearsing in the Théâtre du Châtelet – a sylphide who had drifted over the stage in 1840 left the world at the same time as a group of Russian dancers prepared to honour in *Les Sylphides* a

style and a period that seemed to them beautiful, but utterly remote.

Lucile Grahn (1819–1907), also one of the *Pas de Quatre* quartet, was born in Copenhagen. She was a product of Bournonville's first years as ballet master and choreographer in Copenhagen. Her gifts as a dancer impressed him, and more especially he found himself very attracted to this young beauty. For her he prepared his production of *La Sylphide*, seeing in this pretty, sixteen-year-old girl an artist whom he could shape after the fashion of Taglioni, his 'ideal dancer'. Grahn did not respond to Bournonville's affection, and in 1838, two years after her Copenhagen triumph in *La Sylphide*, she opted for the greater challenges and the greater rewards of Paris, despite the fact that she had starred in several of Bournonville's works. Her success there was no less considerable than that of the reigning stars – notably Elssler. She took to the international circuit, appearing in St Petersburg and in London, and she settled, following her marriage to an Austrian tenor, in Germany where she was later to provide the choreography for a number of Wagner operas in their initial Bayreuth production. She died in Munich in 1907 where there is a street named after her.

The Pas de Quatre (one of the Perrot ballets which Saint-Léon called 'steeplechases') was a significant piece without being in any way important. Two years earlier Perrot had concocted a duet for Elssler and Cerrito since Queen Victoria, a balletomane at that time, had expressed a wish to see these two stars together. It was Benjamin Lumley of Her Majesty's Theatre who conceived the idea of showing the four reigning goddesses in a *pas de quatre*. It amounted to no more than an opening ensemble and variations for each of the ladies, precisely judged by Perrot so that no ballerina should outshine another, concluding with a final burst of charm and vivacity to set the 'groundlings' of the audience (which included Queen Victoria on two occasions) in a roar. This quartet, more even than its successors, indicated how public taste craved for the sensationalism of this kind of display, which was totally divorced from the nobler aspects of ballet although it brought together four of the greatest stars of a starry period.

Ballet had become emasculated. The cult of the ballerina was now firmly established in the public mind and for the rest of the century in every ballet house (save that of Copenhagen, where Bournonville preserved the proper balance between male and female dancing) the ballerina was to be the *raison d'être* of the performance. As Romanticism itself went into decline as an artistic force, its debased inheritance saw the triumph of Italian virtuosi such as Rosati, Salvioni, Boschetti and Ferraris who were to dominate the stages in Paris and Russia where they were in turn succeeded by Zucchi, dell'Era, Legnani and Brianza. It was not until the time of the Diaghilev Ballet that the male dancer was, thanks to Bolm and Nijinsky, to recover the position that he had known in the days of Gaetano and Auguste Vestris.

In Denmark, as with every other European monarchy, dancing was a polite art adapted to court entertainment. There are records of a Danish court ballet in 1634 and performances thereafter were prized, particularly during the reign of Frederik III (from 1648 to 1670). In the eighteenth century, professional performances were staged at the Royal Theatre. Italian and French dancing masters and choreographers appeared in Copenhagen but the most important figure and a vital formative influence was Vincenzo Galeotti (1733–1816). Born in Florence, his career took him across Europe; both he and his wife had been much influenced by the ideals expressed by Noverre and Angiolini on the subject of the *ballet d'action*. In 1775 Galeotti arrived in Copenhagen to take over the ballet company at the Royal Theatre, a post he retained until his death some forty years later, his last dancing performance being in 1812. Galeotti acted as both teacher and choreographer, and his creations bear testimony to a lively dramatic tradition. One ballet, *The Whims of Cupid and the Ballet Master* (1786), a short comedy work, still survives in the repertory of the Royal Danish Ballet – for whom it was originally made. It is in essence a series of national dances strung upon the theme of a Cupid who mis-pairs loving couples who come to his temple for blessing. A unique survival, the ballet has a foundation of good choreographic sense which has kept it alive albeit revivals and re-dressings have destroyed some of its period quality.

In 1792 the French dancer Antoine Bournonville arrived in Copenhagen from Stockholm where he had been working with the Royal Opera. A pupil of Noverre, he decided to settle in Copenhagen at the age of thirty-two and his elegance as a dancer earned him a very considerable position. He was unfortunately no choreographer, and his appointment as director of the Royal Danish Ballet on the death of Galeotti in 1816 was to prove a stultifying influence. However, his son August was to be responsible in due course for the re-birth of the company, and he gave it an identity which it preserves to this day.

August Antoine Bournonville (1805–1879) was born of a Swedish mother, and he was trained as a dancer by his father. His gifts were sufficiently remarkable for him to be praised by Galeotti when he made his first appearance in 1813. His early training in the noble traditions of the French school was enhanced by a first study period in Paris in 1820 where he worked with several of the greatest teachers of the time, men who had been colleagues of his father. There he made first contact with the teaching of Auguste Vestris. That summer was to be vital in firing his imagination. Three years later his father was dismissed as director of the Danish ballet, and this impelled August to seek leave to return to Paris in 1824 for a two-year study period. He had first thought of working with Maze, a dancer whom he admired, but Pierre Gardel recommended that he work with Auguste Vestris, and for two vitally important years the young Bournonville was taught, his style confirmed and then polished, under this great inheritor of the traditions of French eighteenth-century dance. From this inspiring pedagogue, Bournonville absorbed both a system of work and an understanding of dance which are the foundations of everything he was to do later. At the end of his two years of study he realized that to return to Copenhagen would be to return to the desert, and his success in the Opéra examinations and the offer of an engagement in the ballet company in Paris made his course clear. He offended the authorities in Copenhagen by taking two years further leave; in performances in Paris and in London he demonstrated his exceptional talent. He continued studying – he was acutely aware of the stylistic differences among the great dancers of his time – and his view of female dancing was much affected when he partnered Marie Taglioni whom he declared to be his ideal dancer.

The 'Romantic' ballet made much use of garlands and scarves as aids to choreographic positions – a tradition which lasted until the end of the century, witness the Kingdom of Shades scene in La Bayadère *and the garland dance in* The Sleeping Beauty. *This frontispiece to Théleur's* Etrennes à Terpsichore (*published in London in 1832*) *shows the pretty poses so favoured by the 'Romantic' dance. (Royal Academy of Dancing Library)*

Despite his French success and the fact that he was half French, Bournonville remained wholly Danish and dedicated to the idea of the betterment of Danish ballet. He was a man proud of being a dancer – he called it the finest career in the world – and one concerned with the improving of the social identity of dancers. Eventually he persuaded the King's ministers to allow him to return to Copenhagen in the summer of 1829 where his performances astounded the Danish audience.

The hero had returned, and in the light of his talent all was forgiven. So much so that he was given a contract for the extraordinary period of eighteen years as principal dancer to the Royal Theatre, as choreographer and leader of the ballet, and also dancing master to the court. From then on Bournonville's achievement is that of bringing about the rebirth of the company, for which he shaped a repertory and trained dancers to create a style, an ensemble, and a wealth of ballets which one hundred years after his death remain rich and fruitful.

In the first years of his work in Copenhagen Bournonville's task in teaching dancers and building a repertory was to create a mutually beneficial relationship between repertory and school. Bournonville, sustained by his Vestris training and by his own identity as an exceptional *danseur,* was also to avoid the fatal flaw so apparent in the ballet of this time in Paris and London. The Romantic age was supremely the age of the ballerina; it is then that the ballerina emerged as star and sole justification for choreography. But Bournonville, by his concern for the importance of the male dancer – a role which he had to fulfil in Copenhagen – maintained that essential balance between the sexes. Indeed his work showed a fund of good sense, of almost bourgeois morality, which avoided the sexual excesses of Romanticism in which the female dancer was either 'péri' or 'houri'. For Bournonville, his own pride in masculine technique, and his consideration for female dancers as respectable figures, produced ballets in which the actual identity of women rather than a fantasized status was maintained. It is curious to note that his version of *La Sylphide,* often considered one of his most important ballets, is in fact entirely untypical. In his memoirs *My Theatre Life* Bournonville makes one extremely pertinent observation: 'The love portrayed in my works has remained in a pure and worthy form' and this is true in everything known of his own choreography – as distinct from the restaging of the Filippo Taglioni masterpiece.

He could produce occasional pieces required in celebration of some event as in *The Fatherland's Muses* and he turned to both mythology (*The Valkyries*) and history (*Cort Adeler in Venice*) for themes. An event of the times such as the Great Exhibition in London in 1851 could produce *Zulma or The Crystal Palace in London* and, more importantly, his travels were to provide constant fire for his imagination. Spain was his inspiration

for *La Ventana* and *The Toreadors*; he looked towards Russia for *From Siberia to Moscow*; and his six years in Paris were to find a wonderful reflection in the ballet *Konservatoriet* (*The Conservatory*), a work whose first scene is still preserved and offers a portrait of the ballet school at the Paris Opéra as Bournonville knew it. But most important was Italy, a country he loved and which he declared 'a soil on which the soul can at the same time find rest and work'.

In *Flower Festival in Genzano, Festival in Albano* and the historical romance *Raphael,* Bournonville paid tribute to this land he loved. But it is supremely in his *Napoli* of 1842 that you see his genius at full stretch; he had spent four summer months in Italy and with a simple and charming narrative concerning fishing folk and sea sprites Bournonville contrived an action which pin-points the bustle and vivacity of Neapolitan life. Characters such as a macaroni seller, a lemonade seller, a street singer and comic drum-

On 30 May 1874 the drama, opera and dance companies in Copenhagen bade farewell to their old theatre and moved to the present Royal Theatre. Bournonville staged the final entertainment for the occasion and the artists of the company are seen in front of a backcloth which featured the new theatre.
The motto over the proscenium Ei Blot Til Lyst means 'Not for Pleasure Alone'; it is also inscribed over the stage of the present one.

Ballet, this scene, its dancers and their performing style, are enduring testimony to a genius of nineteenth-century dance and to the ennobling disciplines of the classic academic dance as Bournonville inherited and transmitted it.

From 1830, except for a period of three years when he worked in Stockholm as a producer, and then a year which he wasted in Vienna, Bournonville's career was spent entirely in the service of the Royal Danish Ballet. The traditions he inherited and cherished from Vestris were the bedrock of the dance style he taught. He created more than fifty ballets which provided almost the entire repertory of the Royal Danish Ballet during his lifetime and for several years thereafter. The identity which he gave to the Danish dancers and the Danish ballet itself is one which, despite the vicissitudes of the years, remains true and beautiful today.

Bournonville retired from the theatre in 1877. Two years later he died, but just before his death he saw the debut of a young dancer, Hans Beck (1861–1952), who was to be instrumental in preserving some of Bournonville's work for posterity. Beck was also to be coach and teacher to Erik Bruhn (b. 1928) a *danseur* of incomparable nobility. Across the years the tradition of Danish dancing has been maintained by the excellent Danish male dancers who are still the envy of the world. Today, artists like Niels Kehlet, Peter Martins, Ib Andersen and Peter Schaufuss are the heirs of Bournonville; Martins, in particular, has been renowned through his association with the New York City Ballet.

The tradition of a Bournonville-trained dancer shining in another company dates back to the days of Per Christian Johansson (1817–1903), a Swedish dancer trained by Bournonville who went to Russia as Marie Taglioni's partner in 1841, and who remained there for the rest of his life. As *premier danseur* in St Petersburg and then as a teacher both of women and men, Johansson is an essential link with Bournonville and with Vestris. By the end of the nineteenth century, the development of male dancing in Russia and the shaping of a dance style for both men and women in St Petersburg owed a great deal to the preservation of the elegance and technical qualities of the French school.

Nikolai Legat (1869–1937), a great dancer and teacher of the St Petersburg school, recorded that for the male variations in the Petipa repertory at the end of the nineteenth century, Petipa would go himself and crib *enchaînements* from Johansson's class for boys or the dancers themselves would work on variations with Johansson. Notable among Johansson's pupils was Lev Ivanov (1834–1901) the choreographer of the lakeside scenes in *Swan Lake* and the first version of *Casse noisette (The Nutcracker)* and the Polovtsian Dances from *Prince Igor* in their original staging.[5]

It is highly significant that the second great choreographer of the Romantic period, Jules Perrot, should also have been a pupil of Auguste

mer are all drawn from life, and their interpretation has inspired in the Danish ballet a continuing tradition of realistic mime-playing. Today, as in Bournonville's day, these roles, small though they are, contribute enormously to the ballet's success. He deliberately inserted these mime passages as a form of recitative between the many arias of pure dance. The culmination of the ballet, and one of the most intoxicating examples of dancing in the entire history of ballet, is the final scene of wedding celebrations which becomes an apotheosis of the *tarantella*. This cascade of dances represents all that is greatest and best about Bournonville as choreographer and as initiator of a school of dancing. The alertness and charm of the girls, the quickness and grace of their steps, are matched by a virile brilliance for the men who soar and spin and beat with elegance and a kind of manly joy which Bournonville described as his own best quality. Across all the years and the many changes which have inevitably affected the Royal Danish

Carlotta Grisi and Jules Perrot in Perrot's ballet La Esmeralda, *first produced in London in 1844. This greatest of Perrot's works was based on Victor Hugo's* Notre Dame de Paris *and fragments of it still remain in the Leningrad repertory, a relic of Perrot's production in St Petersburg in 1848. (Victoria and Albert Museum, London)*

Vestris in Paris. Bournonville has said of Vestris that he picked out three of his pupils in particular: his own eldest son Armand, who died in Vienna in 1825, Jules Perrot and Bournonville himself. Perrot was the best-known choreographer of his day, working throughout Europe. His creations were internationally known and were to provide an essential foundation for the St Petersburg ballet. He was born in 1810 in Lyon, France, a member of a theatrical family with a father who was a

stage machinist. His first theatrical experiences were as a child performer. Apart from ballet training he made an early career in those eccentric and clownish dances which were part of the popular theatre of his time and which were best seen in the work of Mazurier, an immensely popular acrobatic dancer and comedian known throughout France. The young Perrot copied Mazurier's style and in a double sense aped him, since he chose to perform the role of the monkey often found in popular entertainments. In later life he admitted that as a youth he 'had been a polichinel [clown] for three years and a monkey for two'. And it has been claimed that this acrobatic training prepared his muscles for the style of dancing which Auguste Vestris was to evolve specifically for him.

As a dancer in grotesque roles in various Paris theatres of the boulevards, Perrot was a success. But he was determined to work with Vestris and to move on from the street theatre to the greatest stage of the time. On seeing him and working with him Vestris advised on the only way of disguising his slightly awkward modelling of trunk and his far from classical looks. 'Never stay still; jump about, turn, move around, but never give the public time to look at you closely.' The result was a dancer described as 'a Zephyr with wings of a bat . . . a restless being of indescribable lightness and suppleness, with an almost phosphorescent brilliance.'

Even in 1840 the poet and critic Théophile Gautier, a most valuable observer of the Romantic ballet, could say 'Perrot is not handsome; he is extremely ugly. From the waist upwards he has the proportions of a tenor, there is no need to say more; but, from the waist down, he is delightful.' Perrot made his official debut at the Paris Opéra in 1830 where his talents 'overcame the scorn – we would even say the repugnance – that was felt towards male dancing.' By August of that year he had become the partner of Marie Taglioni, and the sobriquet applied to him – Taglioni's dancing brother – pin-points the aerial similarity of their styles. It can be seen how the Romantic dance, passing on from Didelot's use of wire to achieve flight, had now acquired the technical strength to invade the air on its own account.

By 1835 Perrot's reputation in Paris was preeminent and even in this feminist age his dancing was admired not simply for its virtuosity but also for an expressive power. Yet the domination of Taglioni in the Paris Opéra and the decline into which male dancing even then had fallen forced him to leave the Opéra in search of richer opportunities and richer rewards as a dancer throughout Europe. In 1836 Perrot arrived in Naples where he saw a young soloist, not yet seventeen, whose promise and whose beauty both attracted him. This was Carlotta Grisi.

At this juncture Perrot entered into a relationship with Grisi both as teacher and 'husband' (there is no trace of an actual marriage ceremony). He undertook her training and he soon presented her in London, a city in which he had already danced each year since 1830 and which was in time to become the chief base for his choreography. Thereafter the Perrot couple toured throughout Europe in a routine of performances, and careful training: for Perrot had a long-term view of making his own return to the stage of the Paris Opéra with Carlotta, whose talent flourished under his tutelage. ('Jules stood on my hips like the Colossus of Rhodes while I was lying on the floor, face downwards. It was to strengthen my hips', Carlotta observed.)

By 1840 they had arrived in Paris where they appeared in an entertainment called *Le Zingaro* at the Théâtre de la Renaissance. At this moment the Opéra itself was to lose both its principal ballerinas, Taglioni and Elssler, who had touring commitments, and Carlotta's success was sufficient to arouse the interest of the directorate of the Opéra. Alas, Perrot was not included in the contract which was offered to Carlotta to appear at the Opéra, but he nevertheless charged himself with the choreography for her debut in 1841 which was a *pas* interpolated into the opera *La Favorita*. Carlotta's beauty, charm and technical brilliance ensured her success. More importantly, she now had Théophile Gautier entirely under her spell. He had fallen in love with her, and his patronage, and in due time his imaginative idea for a ballet, were to be of vast importance in Carlotta's career.

While reading a book of Heinrich Heine's about German legends Gautier came upon the story of the Wilis, those ghostly maidens who dance to death any man they find. He saw immediately that this was an ideal subject for a ballet and originally thought of combining it with elements from a poem by Victor Hugo. But his lack of experience in creating a ballet libretto led him to ask Vernoy de St Georges, a librettist and playwright of the time, to collaborate with him. The result was the story of *Giselle*. Perrot was enthusiastic at the idea, as was the composer, Adolphe Adam, to whom the score was entrusted. Plans for Carlotta's appearance in another ballet were changed and *Giselle* was put in production at the Opéra. Speed

The Beauties of the Opera *was published in London in 1845, following a Paris edition, and it contains the stories of favourite operas and ballets of the period. The engravings which illustrate it are touching testimony to the 'Romantic' theatre. Giselle is seen in this detail as a Wili (one of the spirits of dance-loving maidens who have died before their wedding day), floating through the night just out of reach of Albrecht.*

was of the essence and Adam worked so expeditiously that he had the score drafted within a few weeks. He later declared that the ballet was almost entirely written in the Perrots' drawing room and that 'Perrot had a large finger in the pie'. Nevertheless the choreography was entrusted to Jean Coralli, first ballet master at the Opéra. It was he who drafted the action and created the ensembles, though it is known that Perrot himself devised all the dances for Carlotta and Lucien Petipa as Giselle and Albrecht. The ballet was an immense success, but it brought no rewards to Perrot, and he therefore looked towards London where he had worked regularly during the previous decade. He made his re-entry there by devising a *pas de fascination* for Fanny Cerrito, the darling of London, in *Alma* at Her Majesty's Theatre. This was so much admired that Benjamin Lumley, manager of the theatre and impresario, invited Perrot to become ballet master there. In 1842 Perrot had also shared in the first London staging of *Giselle* with Deshayes, the ballet master at Her Majesty's Theatre. And so from 1843 Perrot was to reign supreme in London.

For a period of five years he staged a series of ballets and *divertissements* that are among the greatest achievements of the Romantic ballet. In the major creations: *Ondine* in 1845 for Cerrito; *La Esmeralda* in 1844 for Grisi; *Eoline* in 1845 for Lucille Grahn; in *Catarina* of 1846 for Grahn; and *Lalla Rookh* of 1846 for Cerrito, Perrot produced romantic *ballets d'action* of the greatest distinction. All were hailed for their variety of drama; they were noted for the humanity that was evident in them and for Perrot's mastery in deploying large forces of dancers in crowd scenes such as the *tarantella* in *Ondine* and the *cour des miracles* sequence in *La Esmeralda*. In all these major works, mime and dance – hitherto often separated in their contribution to ballets' effects – were united to provide a cohesive dramatic structure.

Perrot produced other pieces, such as *Le Délire d'un peintre* of 1843, and the famous *Pas de Quatre* with Taglioni, Cerrito, Grahn and Grisi. This last was a nine days' wonder and over the next three years inspired companion pieces. In 1846 *The Judgement of Paris* featured Taglioni, Cerrito and Grahn with Saint-Léon as Paris, and Perrot himself as Mercury; in 1847, a year when the London public started to demonstrate its fickleness and responded enthusiastically to the appearance of the great operatic soprano Jenny Lind, Perrot staged *The Elements*, one of his most brilliant and danceable exercises in this genre, which featured Cerrito, Grisi and Carolina Rosati. Finally, in 1848, at what must now seem to be the evening of the Romantic era in ballet, he put on *The Four Seasons* for Cerrito, Rosati, Grisi and Marie Paul Taglioni, niece of the greater Marie who had retired in the previous year. In this year he also worked in Milan, staging a remarkable *Faust* for Fanny Elssler. He then joined an exodus to St Petersburg whither Elssler had gone to dance and Pugni, the composer, had travelled to

take up an appointment as composer of music to the Imperial Ballet. Perrot worked briefly in St Petersburg, returning to Paris in 1849 to stage his first and only ballet at the Paris Opéra *La Filleule des fées* for Grisi. Thereafter he spent the next decade almost entirely in St Petersburg reviving his greatest works for the Bolshoy Theatre there and creating others: *Gazelda*, *La Guerre des femmes*, and *L'Ile des muets* and *Marco Bomba*. But more important is the fact that his restagings of his greatest London achievements were to provide a magnificent basis for the St Petersburg repertory. *La Esmeralda*, *Ondine*, *Giselle* remained in the repertory for many years (and even today you may find traces of the Perrot repertory are preserved in *pas de deux* in the repertory of the Kirov Ballet and the Leningrad School).

Perrot's ballets were performed by the last survivors of the galaxy of ballerinas of the Romantic age, but they also served to shape the talents of such Russian ballerinas as Andreyanova and Muravyeva. But Perrot grew tired of Russia and it has been suggested that his relationship with the directorate of the Imperial theatres was not happy. On his return to Europe he found ballet in decline and his gifts unwanted. After some desultory creations he retired, and the last view of him is that of the venerable figure in Degas' paintings and drawings shown teaching at the Paris Opéra; ironically he is instructing dancers whose style and aesthetics were inimical to everything that he had represented and achieved during his years as a choreographer of *ballets d'action*.

Like every ballet master of his epoch, Arthur Saint-Léon came of a theatrical family. Born in 1821 he showed an early talent both as a dancer and as a child prodigy on the violin and within a few months of his fourteenth birthday he had made his debut in both disciplines. He studied dancing under Albert, one of the last representatives of the noble *sérieux* style; but Saint-Léon's physique and temperament were more suited to a virtuoso manner in which feats of brilliance were brought off with a dazzling energy – qualities which also marked the violin playing which he maintained throughout his career. At the age of eighteen he had already danced in Brussels, Vienna and Milan, but his important years begin with his appearance in London at the King's Theatre in 1843. At a time when male dancing was falling into disrepute Saint-Léon's virtuosity could still earn him public acclaim. It is at this period that he fell in love with Fanny Cerrito. They had first met two years before but now they danced together – prints of the period show them in *Le Lac des fées* and the *Pas Styrien* – and in 1845 they married. As a couple they excited considerable public admiration, though Fanny was the more important performer and Saint-Léon was starting to create ballets in which she could star. In 1847, however, they moved to Paris, where Saint-Léon was engaged at the Opéra as choreographer.

Saint-Léon's works in this period included their

In all Degas' miraculous outpourings of drawings of dancers there is rarely a male figure; here Degas portrays the ageing Jules Perrot as a teacher at the Paris Opéra. This illustration is one of a series of working drawings of the old man resting on his cane. (Fitzwilliam Museum, Cambridge)

debut vehicle at the Opéra, *La Fille de marbre,* which was a reworking of Fanny's early success the *Alma* of 1842. In *Le Violin du diable* inevitably Saint-Léon choreographed, danced and played the violin. His dancing was still considered remarkable, with prodigious leaps and pirouettes in a very masculine and bravura style, though observers were forced to note that a malformation of the shoulder made him look slightly hunchbacked. In 1851 Cerrito and Saint-Léon parted company; she to continue her liaison with the Spanish aristocrat and he to leave the Opéra. He worked in other Paris theatres before setting out in 1854 for Lisbon. For two years he danced and choreographed at the San Carlos Theatre and then set out on a tour of Germany accompanied by the ballerina Louise Fleury. In 1859 his career reached its high point; he was named as ballet master to the Russian Imperial theatres and for eleven seasons between 1859 and 1870 he divided his time equally between St Petersburg (where the ballet season at the Bolshoy Theatre only occupied the six winter months) and the Paris Opéra

where he was engaged to provide fresh ballets nearly every year.

In St Petersburg he inherited from Jules Perrot a magnificent company and a fine repertory. Each season Saint-Léon had to produce a ballet new to the repertory which would feature the guest star, who was often imported to the Imperial theatres to enliven the company. In 1859 he had Carolina Rosati, for whom he made a version of *Jovita*; thereafter he created new ballets or provided totally fresh revisions of previous successes. During this decade his ballets pleased not only the public but, more importantly, the administration of Tsar Alexander II. His works were marked by brilliant numbers in which the dancers could shine; by exciting stage effects and a feeling for the *'le merveilleux'* (the marvellous); by classical inventions which set off the gifts of the principal artists and – very special to Saint-Léon – character dances which made use of folklore. Throughout his partnership with Cerrito the couple had been seen in balleticized folk numbers like *La Redowa polka*. Now, in St Petersburg he developed this further and a culminating statement was his *Koniok Gorbunok* (*The Little Humpbacked Horse*) a Russian fairy tale whose theme remains dear to audiences even today.

Saint-Léon's works were excellently tailored for his ballerinas, and two dancers in particular shone during his time in Russia. The first was Marfa Muravyeva (1838–1879), an enchanting artist whom he also encouraged to dance in Paris, where she appeared in his *Diavolina* and *Néméa*. The other was the German-born Adèle Grantzow (1845–1877). Grantzow was one of the most tragic figures in nineteenth-century ballet, beautiful, intelligent and brilliantly gifted. Saint-Léon found her his ideal interpreter and had sent her for training to Madame Dominique, a superb teacher in Paris; later he had supervised her debuts in Moscow and St Petersburg and in Paris. In Saint-Léon's *Fiammetta* and *Diavolina* in *La Fille mal gardée*, as Giselle in Paris, and in a role intended for her – that of Naïla in *La Source* – Grantzow excited universal admiration. Unfortunately, throughout her short career she was accident-prone; illness and injury constantly set her back and her untimely death came at the age of thirty-two, as the result of medical malpractice which led to the amputation of a leg.

At the end of the 1860s Saint-Léon set about preparing a new ballet for the Paris Opéra which would star Grantzow – *Coppélia*. Charles Nuitter, archivist at the Opéra, devised the scenario taken from E. T. A. Hoffmann, while the score was commissioned from Léo Delibes who had already produced the more melodious and charming half of Saint-Léon's earlier ballet *La Source*. The work had been set in motion in 1868; various delays ensued, not least Grantzow's illness, and it was not until the spring of 1870 that the ballet reached its final rehearsals. Its star was then to be another tragic figure in ballet's history – Giuseppina Bozzacchi, no more than a child in Madame Dominique's classes when she was chosen to replace Grantzow as the heroine, Swanilda. By the time of the first performance on 25 May 1870 she was still only sixteen but the charm and vivacity of her acting and her technical grace foreshadowed a glorious career. However, this was not to be. Soon after the ballet's *première* the Franco–Prussian War broke out and the Opéra was closed. Her health undermined by earlier privations and by the rigours of the siege, Giuseppina fell victim to smallpox and died on the morning of her seventeenth birthday. By then Saint-Léon was also dead; he had collapsed a couple of months earlier in a café and died at once, worn out by his labours as ballet master at the same time to two great theatres, one in Russia and the other in France. His death and the end of the Second Empire heralded the sunset of Romantic ballet.

Ballet itself had now become a declining art in France, where it had known such great days. There were no French ballerinas to inspire public enthusiasm. A grievous loss had been the death of the young Emma Livry. Born in 1842, and also a pupil of Madame Dominique, she had shown a wonderful charm and grace in her dancing, so much so that Marie Taglioni had been lured back from retirement to coach her and in 1860 to choreograph for her *Le Papillon* with its pretty score by Offenbach. Two years later Livry was watching a dress rehearsal of an opera when her dress caught fire and she was appallingly burned. After eight months of agonizing suffering she died, and with her the brightest hope for a French ballerina to rival the Italian virtuosi who now dominated the stages of western Europe. It is to these Italian virtuosi, products of the Blasis school in Milan, that you now have to look for a continuation of ballet's development – notably in Russia.

The entire development of ballet in Russia during the nineteenth century is due to the participation of foreign ballet masters. The first third of the century was the era of Charles-Louis Didelot. His successor, Antoine Titus, had been entirely undistinguished as a choreographer but he was responsible for the engagement of Marius Petipa as *premier danseur* in 1847. Over the next two decades the Imperial Ballet knew first Perrot, then Saint-Léon, as ballet masters but in the season of 1869–70 Petipa was nominated first ballet master, a post which he was to retain until 1903. Almost the entire span of nineteenth-century ballet in Russia may be seen to fall under the guidance of

Emma Livry in Le Papillon. *Photography still needed lengthy exposures, and the early dance photographs relied upon careful, static poses, rather than any attempt to suggest movement, to immortalize the artists of the mid-nineteenth century.*

Carlotta Grisi and Lucien Petipa in La Péri. This ballet, first produced in Paris in 1843, was a Persian extravaganza – hence the skirt worn by Petipa. Lucien (1815– 1898), the older brother of Marius Petipa, was the better-known figure in France, as principal dancer at the Paris Opéra and subsequently choreographer at that theatre. A handsome man and an outstanding dancer, he is remembered today as the first Albrecht in Giselle.

French choreographers; with the collaboration of Italian virtuoso dancers, you can see two of the elements which were to form the glories of Russian dancing and Russian ballet in both that century and the next.

Marius Petipa (1818–1910) was born in Marseille where his father, Jean Antoine Petipa, was at that time ballet master. While still a child he was taken with the family to Brussels where his father was to be ballet master. Marius started dancing lessons at the age of seven and made his stage debut at the age of nine, following in the footsteps of his older brother Lucien and his sister Victoria. Like every other dancing family, the Petipas wandered the earth. From Brussels they went to Antwerp and then Bordeaux and in his seventeenth year the young Marius was engaged in Nantes as a soloist. He rejoined his family for a trans-Atlantic excursion and they had a brief and financially unrewarding visit to New York, thanks chiefly to an absconding manager. On their return to Paris, where Lucien was now *premier danseur* and was to create the role of Albrecht in *Giselle*, Marius joined the class of Auguste Vestris and partnered Carlotta Grisi at a benefit performance. He was next engaged in Bordeaux as *premier danseur*, dancing in productions of *Giselle* and *La Fille mal gardée* and also staging four small

ballets. A year later he was engaged to dance at the Royal Theatre, Madrid. His sojourn there was successful; he danced and created several ballets but he was obliged to leave when challenged to a duel on a matter of honour – he believed discretion was the better part of valour.

In 1846 he returned to Paris but no engagements were forthcoming. By now Jean Petipa was working as a teacher in St Petersburg and it is not unreasonable to assume that it was he who suggested to Titus that Marius should be invited to succeed the retiring *premier danseur*, Emile Gredelu. Marius arrived in St Petersburg in 1847 and he found himself dancing with the leading Russian ballerina Yelena Andreyanova (who happened to be the mistress of the director of the Imperial theatres, Guedeonov). Petipa appeared in *Giselle, Paquita, La Péri* and *Satanella*. These last three he mounted for the company, but any hopes that he might continue as choreographer were to be dashed by the arrival of Jules Perrot. During the Perrot decade, Petipa danced leading roles but his only choreographic creations were brief dances which he staged to show off his first wife, Maria Surovshchikova. Even with Perrot's departure, Petipa was not to be given the chance he hoped for.

Arthur Saint-Léon was appointed to succeed Perrot. He was not prepared to give Petipa any chance to develop a career as a choreographer until the season 1862–63 and the arrival of Carolina Rosati as the guest ballerina for the winter. Saint-Léon was reluctant, it seems, to choreograph a

vehicle for this lady, an exceptional dramatic ballerina now past her prime. Thus it fell to Petipa at last to be entrusted with a full-length work, and he set about his task with meticulous care and an appreciation of the opportunity which was to mark his every creation thereafter. He turned to ancient Egypt for his theme – excavations in the desert were attracting public attention at that time – and he sketched a dramatic plan from Gautier's novel *Le Roman de la momie*. This narrative idea he then took to Paris so that it might be expertly carpentered into a scenario by Vernoy de St Georges (librettist of *Giselle*, and of *Le Papillon*, and also of two other subsequent ballets for Petipa, *La Camargo* and *Le Roi Candaule*, as well as of numerous operas and operettas). The result was a ludicrous plot, which Petipa now broke down into a more carefully planned sequence of dances and mime scenes. These details he then gave to Cesare Pugni, an experienced musician who occupied that remarkable post of 'composer to the Imperial Ballet' – a post in which he was to be succeeded by Ludwig Minkus. Armed with a score and detailed scenario, Petipa then set to work creating the three acts and seven scenes of *Pharaoh's Daughter* (as the opus was to be called) with considerable speed. First produced at the Bolshoy Theatre, St Petersburg in 1862, this extravaganza was the first of the long succession of ballets *à grand spectacle* with which Petipa was eventually to dominate the Imperial Russian Ballet and to prove himself the supreme choreographer of the century. *Pharaoh's Daughter* made his

Tableau from the second act of Don Quixote, *with Sophia Fedorova and Mikhail Mordkin (at right) in the version produced in 1900 by Alexander Gorsky for the Bolshoy Theatre in Moscow.*

reputation. In its exorbitant length and exuberant style can be traced those elements which were to reach their apogee in *The Sleeping Beauty*, his work which remains the supreme achievement of classical academic dancing and the greatest challenge alike to ballerinas, soloists and, indeed, to ballet companies even today.

Petipa's creations were the result of careful consideration of the work of those masters with whom he danced. From Perrot he learned the virtues of dramatic structure and of poetic dancing. It would seem that what is now lost from most productions of *The Sleeping Beauty* is its sense of dramatic progress, so clearly to be perceived in the detailed notes which Petipa prepared for himself and for Tchaikovsky and which have survived, ignored by most producers of the work today. From Saint-Léon he observed the way in which brilliant and effective numbers could be created to show off ballerinas as well as soloists, and how ensembles in folkloric numbers could be achieved. His own genius shaped and aggrandized these materials into the spectaculars which were to bring him acclaim. In them you can still observe the masterly control with which he balanced group dances against solos, processions with set displays, and the unerring sense of proportion with which he shaped a narrative and placed dance sequences.

With the success of *Pharaoh's Daughter*, Petipa was named second ballet master and on Saint-Léon's departure for Paris in 1870, Petipa at last found himself promoted to first ballet master.

His task was 'to put on a new ballet at the beginning of every season' and this command, effectively from the Tsar, he fulfilled. *Don Quixote, Trilby, La Camargo, Le Papillon, The Bandits, La Bayadère (Bayaderka), Zoraya, Roxana the Beauty of Montenegro, The Daughter of the Snows, Mlada* and other ballets occupied him during the decade of the 1870s. These works were produced to order and in each a huge company, for whose technical style he was also responsible, was shown off.

Petipa's career as first ballet master in St Petersburg was to be furthered by the appointment in 1881 of I. A. Vsevolozhsky as director of the Imperial theatres. A former diplomatist, playwright and talented amateur artist, Vsevolozhsky was a man of great charm and an inspired choice for the post. During the eighteen years of his office he did much to improve working conditions for the Imperial Ballet, and it is during his time (in 1886) that the Imperial Ballet transferred from the Bolshoy Theatre to the Maryinsky (now Kirov). He was an admirer and supporter of Petipa at a time when the ballet master's career had reached a low point – his St Petersburg audience were becoming bored with the lavish but meaningless spectacles he was dutifully producing.

It was the arrival of Virginia Zucchi (1847–1930), an Italian ballerina, which was to fire the imagination of the St Petersburg public with a renewed interest in ballet. Rejected by the school of La Scala, Milan, she nevertheless emerged from a varied dance training as a most accomplished performer. It was not simply her technical prowess which gained her Italian fame but her prodigious dramatic gift which burned through her every role; by 1883 she was starring at the Eden Theatre, a bizarre amusement house in Paris, in *Sieba*, a preposterous dance work by Manzotti which was much to Parisian taste at that time.

In 1885 came a contract to appear at a popular summer theatre outside St Petersburg. Part of a complex of amusement gardens, the Kin Grust Theatre was no temple of the muses yet Zucchi's appearances there electrified the public. Alexandre Benois devotes a whole chapter of his *Reminiscences of the Russian Ballet* to the artist whom he called 'the divine Zucchi'. In these reminiscences you sense the profound influence that this unique artist was to have upon the public in St Petersburg.

La Bayadère *of 1877 is one of Marius Petipa's finest achievements, a drama concerned with crime and its punishment and set in the India of fabled times. The heroine, Nikiya, is a temple dancer, a bayadère, loved by Solor, a young warrior. But Solor is obliged to marry Gamsatti, daughter of a Rajah. In order to dispose of her rival, Gamsatti causes Nikiya to be given a basket of flowers containing a poisonous snake which kills the bayadère. She dies, and in the most celebrated scene of the ballet, set in the Kingdom of Shades, Solor dreams of finding Nikiya again, surrounded by the ghosts of bayadères. In the final act the ghost of Nikiya appears at the wedding festivities of Gamsatti and Solor, whom the gods punish by destroying the temple in which the wedding is taking place. This photograph of Yekaterina Vazem as Nikiya, with the snake, indicates the opulence and the improbability of the costuming of the period.*

Inevitably Zucchi was invited to appear at the Imperial theatres and for two years in such works as *La Fille mal gardée* and *Pharaoh's Daughter*, in *La Esmeralda* and *Brahma*, Zucchi revitalized ballet in Russia. The magic of her presence, the extraordinary emotional power of her performances gripped the imagination of the public and also of other artists. Regrettably, she was forbidden the Imperial stages by the Tsar's command because of a liaison with an aristocrat and her later career brought her no comparable triumphs (although she did appear in the Venusberg scene in *Tannhäuser* in Bayreuth in 1891).

However, her impact on the Russian ballet had been decisive. So too was to be that of another Italian, Enrico Cecchetti (1850–1928). Born in a theatrical dressing room in Rome, a pupil of Lepri who was a pupil of Blasis, this tiny, bouncing virtuoso appeared in Russia first in 1887 and for twenty years he performed and then taught in St Petersburg and Warsaw, helping to polish and to strengthen the technique of generations of Russian dancers. Thus, through Johansson and now through Cecchetti, the two mainstreams of Euro-

pean classic dance training can be seen to combine on Russian bodies and Russian temperament to form a uniquely Russian style of classical dancing. The Italian invasion of Russia continued, bringing a series of virtuoso ballerinas as guests for each season in St Petersburg. Most important was Pierina Legnani (1863–1923) whose prodigious technical skill was not only an inspiration but also a challenge to the Russian dancers. Her ability to turn thirty-two *fouettés sur place* has been immortalized in the role of Odile in the Petipa/Ivanov *Swan Lake* but she also created the leading roles in Petipa's *Raymonda* and *Cinderella* (in which two years before *Swan Lake* she performed the thirty-two *fouettés*) and in *The Talisman* and *Bluebeard*.

Other Italian guest stars during these latter years of the century were Carlotta Brianza, who was the first Aurora in *The Sleeping Beauty* in 1890 and the heroine of Petipa's *Kalkabrino* of 1891, and Antonietta dell'Era who was to be the first Sugar Plum Fairy in Ivanov's *Casse noisette* (*The Nutcracker*).

It is to I. A. Vsevolozhsky that you must also

A group from the first St Petersburg production of Swan Lake *in 1895. The pose is one taken for a photograph in a studio rather than from the stage setting.*

look for a further enhancement of the ballet at this time. His patronage of Tchaikovsky had dated back to his early years as director of the Imperial theatres when he had assured production of Tchaikovsky's operas and had obtained a pension for the composer from the Tsar. In an attempt to improve the musical standards of the Imperial Ballet, Vsevolozhsky invited the composer to provide a score. Tchaikovsky's first attempt at ballet music had been the disastrous *Swan Lake* given in Moscow in 1877. After rejecting the idea of *Ondine*, Tchaikovsky responded eagerly to Vsevolozhsky's suggestion of *The Sleeping Beauty* and the glorious score which resulted from his collaboration with Petipa remains the crowning achievement of ballet music. In 1892, two years after the production of *The Sleeping Beauty*, Tchaikovsky again provided a score for the Imperial Ballet. This was *Casse noisette* which was staged as a double bill with Tchaikovsky's short opera *Iolanthe*. Despite the fatuity of its libretto, prepared by Petipa, *Casse noisette* inspired magnificent music from Tchaikovsky. Petipa's illness at the time of the production meant that the choreography was entrusted to the second ballet master, Lev Ivanov, who for some years had worked dutifully as Petipa's assistant. In *Casse noisette* his talent was somewhat confined by Petipa's detailed synopsis, yet he managed in the Snowflake sequence and in the *grand pas de deux* to produce choreography of exceptional beauty which has never been improved on.

Two years later, following Tchaikovsky's death, a memorial performance found the second act of *Swan Lake* being given its St Petersburg *première*. For Legnani as the Swan Queen and for the artists of the Imperial Ballet, Ivanov created the lyrical scene which can still be admired (as Act II of the complete work) today. Ivanov's temperament responded exactly to that of Tchaikovsky and when in 1895 Petipa undertook the production of the entire *Swan Lake* ballet, Ivanov was to produce the choreography for the fourth act, and he assisted Petipa in part of the staging of Acts I and III. Although Petipa was now in his seventies, his genius showed no signs of abating. In 1898 he produced *Raymonda,* where again he benefited from a superior musical score, composed by the young hopeful of Russian symphonic music A. K. Glazunov. Although the ballet's scenario, about Crusaders and Moors in Provence, was intractably stupid, the majesty of Glazunov's writing and the undimmed brilliance of Petipa's inventions have guaranteed it a continuing place in the repertory.

Two years later, with *Les Ruses d'amour* and *Les Saisons,* two one-act ballets staged at the smaller court theatres, Petipa and Glazunov collaborated yet again. By now, a magnificent new generation of young Russian dancers was emerging from the Imperial schools. Kshessinskaya (1872–1971) reigned supreme: she was the first Russian Aurora and the first Russian ballerina to

master the notorious thirty-two *fouettés*. The virtuoso Preobrazhenskaya, darling of the gallery, the noble Trefilova, Julia Sedova (or Siedova), Lubov Egorova and their juniors Anna Pavlova and Tamara Karsavina were part of an exceptional flowering of prodigiously gifted dancers produced by the Imperial schools. They were, however, trapped in a repertory which was bound by convention, and ultra-conservative even by ballet's conservative standards.

In 1903, Marius Petipa staged what was to be his last ballet. This was *The Magic Mirror*, a piece whose failure is in part attributable to the director of the Imperial theatres, Colonel Telyakovsky, who was intolerant of the artistic attitudes still propounded by the venerable Petipa. The ballet was a disaster and at the age of eighty-five Petipa was called upon to retire. His remaining years (he did not die until 1910) were spent in retirement, though it is significant that in 1905, at the time of the first, abortive revolution, the dancers of the Imperial Ballet who were by now without a positive artistic leader sought to have Petipa restored as first ballet master. In the fifty-six years of his service to the Imperial Ballet, Petipa had created a style, provided a repertory and despite all vicissitudes had brought the Imperial Ballet to a pinnacle of excellence unsurpassed by any ballet company.

Nikolai (Nicolas) Legat (1869–1937) was one of the greatest male dancers in the latter years of the Imperial Ballet. A pupil of Christian Johannson, he started teaching as a young man in Russia and numbered many of the most illustrious dancers among his pupils. He left Russia in 1923 and eventually settled in London.
This studio portrait shows him as the hero, Jean de Brienne, in Raymonda, *for which Marius Petipa was the choreographer.*

CHAPTER EIGHT

HISTORY OF BALLET
TWENTIETH CENTURY

Baron Adolphe de Meyer was one of the most distinguished photographers of this century, and his photographs of Vaslav Nijinsky are the liveliest and most evocative evidence of the dancer's genius. In 1912 he produced thirty-three photographs of Nijinsky's L'Après-midi d'un faune. These inspired pictures seem to have an erotic bloom which exactly catches the concentration and aura of Nijinsky's personality when immersed in the role.

DESPITE THE supremacy of the Imperial Russian Ballet in St Petersburg it was nevertheless the last flowering of an art in decline. Like the Empire which supported it, it had become stultified and inimical to all forms of change. It reflected precisely the aristocratic and hide-bound attitudes of the court audience which it entertained. In Moscow, however, a more adventurous and dramatically lively tradition had been initiated by the arrival there of Alexander Gorsky (1871–1924) in 1898 to stage a production of *The Sleeping Beauty* from his notation of the Petipa masterpiece. In September 1900 he became *régisseur* of the Moscow ballet company and for the rest of his life he was to remain in Moscow as ballet master of the Bolshoy Theatre. Under his guidance the relatively unimportant troupe gained new life and prestige. The Moscow audiences responded sympathetically to Gorsky's taste and his innovations. In his revisions of Petipa works–notably of *Don Quixote* – he brought a new dramatic veracity which reflected the same ideals as could be perceived in the work of the Moscow Arts Theatre. In his own stagings of such works as *Salammbô*, *Gudule's Daughter* and his revisions of *Swan Lake* these ideals were realized. It is to Gorsky you look for the first modern symphonic ballet: he staged a version of Glazunov's Fifth Symphony in 1916. 'He led the Moscow ballet out of a blind alley to the position of a mature artistic ensemble capable of seriously competing with the ballet in St Petersburg.'[1] Certainly Gorsky's creations were to be far more in tune with the new spirit of the twentieth century, which was even then making its impact upon Russia, than the marmoreal splendours of the Imperial Ballet. After the Revolution, Moscow was to become the capital city of the Soviet Union. Gorsky's identity as an important innovator in the ballet of a new society was thus confirmed.

The tragedy of the St Petersburg Ballet – if you can accept as tragedy the idea of the greatest company in the world without an artistic head or true artistic purpose – can be summed up in the title which Mikhail Fokine gave to the third chapter of his *Memoirs*: 'Beginning of Service, and Disappointment in the Ballet.' In this very remarkable passage Fokine becomes a powerful witness to much that was right and even more that was wrong with the Imperial Ballet when he joined it.

Mikhail Fokine (1880–1942) graduated from the Imperial School and was accepted into the Maryinsky Ballet by the time he was eighteen. A pupil of Johannson and the Legat brothers (Sergei and Nikolai), he was a dancer of exceptional gifts and remarkable good looks. His misfortune was to be both intelligent and intolerant of the stultifying atmosphere within the Maryinsky Theatre. An idealist, Fokine was full of hopes and aspirations for his art, but these were aims entirely foreign to most of his companions in the company. Beautiful pirouettes and a mindless acceptance of the by now ludicrous conventions of the old ballet, in which naturalistic costuming for the mime performers went side by side with the traditional tutus and tunics and pointe shoes of the dancing personnel, were all that were required.

It was against this that Fokine sought to rebel, at a time when revolution itself was in the air. The winter of 1905 had been a period of civil unrest which was to reach even within the secluded walls of the Imperial Ballet itself. The dancers demanded various liberalizing concessions, of which nothing came, and for Fokine the period was more remarkable for his first approaches to the directorate of the theatre to create ballets of a more free theatrical kind. In the winter of 1904 at a time when Fokine was concerned with the liberating of ballet from rigorous conventions, Isadora Duncan had made her first phenomenal appearances in St Petersburg. Though it is unwise to attribute any direct link between Duncan and Fokine, it must be seen that Duncan's genius, her simplicity and power over an audience, and her choice of music, were to have a great effect on the future of dance.

By 1907 Fokine had embarked upon a career as a choreographer. His earliest ballets, *The Vine* of 1906, the two-act *Eunice* of 1907, *Le Pavillon d'Armide* of 1907 and *Egyptian Nights* and *Chopiniana* of 1908 all gave evidence of a wonderful new talent which the ageing Petipa had recognized.

But it was Fokine's collaboration with the artist Alexandre Benois, the librettist and decorator for *Le Pavillon d'Armide*, that was to prove crucial for ballet's history. Alexandre Benois (1870–1960) was a member of a group of young St Petersburg intellectuals much concerned with the arts and with their role in the theatre and in the society of the new century. He was a member of a distinguished artistic family, of mixed Russian, French, German and Italian blood. He had first become really obsessed with ballet when Virginia Zucchi appeared in St Petersburg, and during the years of his education at the Mai Academy (an outstanding private school in St Petersburg) he had formed close friendships with young men all variously interested in the arts. The group, with Walter Nouvel, Dima Filosofov, and other like-minded enthusiasts – later to include the exceptionally gifted young Jewish artist Léon Bakst (1866–1924) – met nearly every day to read, and discuss artistic problems of the time.

It was in 1890 that they were joined by a young cousin of Filosofov's from the provinces, S. P. Diaghilev (1872–1929). Sent by his family from Perm to St Petersburg to study law, the eighteen-year-old Sergei Diaghilev joined the Benois–Filosofov circle in which his rough provincial edges were to be polished and his amazing energy, rather than any especial artistic gift, was to be remarked. Over the next years Diaghilev was educated by the members of this circle – they called themselves the Pickwick Club of the Neva – and his natural aptitude and great love of music obviously suggested a creative career. With Nouvel he was to explore the riches of Russian music of this time, but his interest in ballet was minimal: he had attended *The Sleeping Beauty* dutifully enough, Benois and Bakst in particular being enthusiastic about it, but his own taste for ballet was not to be fired until Petipa's *Raymonda* of 1898. An interview with Rimsky-Korsakov was to extinguish any hopes he might have harboured of a musical career and it was the unquestioned artistic drive which impelled Diaghilev that found an outlet in a closer association with Benois and Bakst and an involvement in the world of painting.

Both these men were establishing reputations as artists and by 1895 Diaghilev, who had in any case far greater ambitions and social pretensions than his companions, found himself a young man very much *dans le monde*. Crucial to his identity at this time was his first encounter with Savva Mamontov and his Muscovite circle. Mamontov, a million-

aire industrialist, had devoted himself to the furthering of the work of Russian painters and Russian composers. In 1885 he had been able to set up a private opera company – the Imperial theatres' monopoly prohibited public operatic performances outside their portals – and operas by Russian composers ignored by the official theatres were staged with designs by such exceptional artists as Vrubel, Korovin and Vasnetsov. This was in itself a profoundly original event. Diaghilev admired the work of Mamontov and his circle and saw in it a cause he might take up.

By 1897 Diaghilev, at the age of twenty-five, had set out on what proved to be an extraordinary career. He began by arranging small exhibitions of British and German water-colours in St Petersburg. This venture was followed by an exhibition of Scandinavian painting, and with his very considerable social contacts and the patronage of such committed figures as Savva Mamontov and Princess Tenishcheva (whose support of crafts at this time was no less remarkable than that of Mamontov), Diaghilev was to make a more positive effect upon the Russian art scene by the foundation of a magazine *Mir Isskustva* (*The World of Art*). It was a journal intended to reform the artistic taste of Russia and to liberate art. Between 1898 and 1904 the magazine and an artistic movement which became associated with it propounded a theory of art for art's sake: the magazine's motto was 'Art is free, life is paralysed.' Offering patronage and encouragement to such creators as Bakst, Benois, Somov, Serov, Korovin, Bilibin, Dobuzhinsky, Lanceray, *The World of*

Alexandre Benois: design for Le Pavillon d'Armide *(above). The set design is the 1909 version prepared for Paris. (Ella Gallop Sumner and Mary Catlin Sumner Collection, Wadsworth Atheneum, Hartford, Connecticut)*

The film director Sergei Eisenstein captures the elegant façade of Diaghilev as impresario in this caricature (above right) but he also indicates Diaghilev as the dominant figure in the foreground, with his dancers as a backdrop for his activities. The male dancer, lower right, is Nijinsky as the Golden Slave in Schéhérazade. *Jean Cocteau said of Diaghilev's downward-curving eyes that they looked like 'Portuguese oysters'.*

Nijinsky's costume as Armide's favourite slave (left) is for the first Maryinsky Theatre production of Le Pavillon d'Armide *in November 1907. (Victoria and Albert Museum, London)*

Art was to establish Diaghilev, and his reputation was further enhanced by the annual exhibitions which he organized and which were to reveal both Russian and Western European art to the St Petersburg public. It was inevitable that he should also become involved in some way with the Imperial theatres. In 1899 the delightful Prince Volkonsky became director of the Imperial theatres (albeit only for a year) and it was he who entrusted Diaghilev with editing their annual year-book. Hitherto a worthy but totally unexciting document, it was transformed by Diaghilev, with the assistance of Benois and Bakst, into a superb example of book production. It was also, and characteristically, vastly more expensive than had been budgeted, and the wrong size. But it was beautiful. At the same time Diaghilev was invited to take a position in the Imperial Theatre with special responsibility fot a new production of Delibes' ballet *Sylvia*.

The appearance of this new broom with a retinue of new decorative associates among the ultra-reactionaries of the Imperial Ballet was to arouse every form of mistrust and dislike. Diaghi-lev's private life was called into question – he was homosexual – and with great discomfiture he found himself jockeyed from his position, since the artistic cabal against him was too well en-trenched in positions of power at court. Five years later, at the time of the abortive revolution during the winter of 1905, Diaghilev attempted to support the artists of the ballet in their struggle for greater artistic freedom and proposed the founding of a Ministry responsible for the fine arts in Russia but this, too, was frustrated.

It was in this same year that Diaghilev was to achieve his greatest success in the field of exhibi-tions. After months of travel and research throughout Russia he had assembled a superb and unprecedented exhibition of Russian historical portraits. It was shown in the Tauride Palace where it offered a mysteriously apt summation of Russian art under the tsars. Diaghilev made a prophetic speech at a banquet which preceded the opening of the exhibition.

> '... We are doomed to die to pave the way for the birth of a new culture, which will take from us all that remains of our weary wis-dom ... We are witnesses of the greatest moment of summing up in history, in the name of a new and unknown culture, which will be created by us, but will also sweep us away. For that reason I raise my glass to the ruined walls of the beautiful palaces as well as to the commandments of a new aesthetic ...'[2]

In those phrases there seems to be both an extraordinary understanding of the future and also an idea of what Diaghilev's own role in that future might be as one of the creators of a new aesthetic. The Tauride exhibition was Diaghilev's final gesture towards Russia made *in Russia*. During the next years his task seemed to be the revelation of the arts of Russia to Western Europe which had so inexact a view of their greatness.

In 1906 he presented a Russian exhibition at the Grand Palais in Paris, with the cream of Russian arts and crafts shown in carefully considered settings which would enhance them. For the following year he presented a series of concerts of Russian music in Paris. These concerts involved but a small part of the galaxy of artists in Russia in works representing the exceptional riches of Russian composition at this time. Glazunov, Rakhmaninov and Scriabin played and conducted their own work; Arthur Nikisch and Blumenfelt conducted, and their success was immense. But outshining them all was the presence of Feodor Chaliapin who was presented in a fragment from *Prince Igor* and in a scene from *Boris Godunov*. Chaliapin's dramatic genius and his miraculous voice were to astound and ravish Paris. The success of this operatic fragment inspired the desire to bring a complete Russian operatic season to Paris the following year.

Chaliapin was obviously central to the enter-prise and *Boris Godunov* had to be prepared. It was unthinkable that it should be shown at the Grand Opéra, Paris, under anything but the best conditions and during the winter preceding this 1908 visit to Paris, Diaghilev and Benois, who was involved in the production, scoured 'the Tartar junk shops and other special places in the Alexandrovsky and Shchukin market where antique materials were sold, buying up silk and brocade shawls, embroidered collars, head-dresses and so on.[3]

The net result was that Paris was bowled over not only by the grandeur of musical performance and by Chaliapin's genius but also by the opulence and authenticity of the stage picture. For the first time Paris was to see Russian stage design which broke with all the fusty traditionalism which still existed in the opera houses and theatres of the West. Diaghilev had plainly learned his lesson from the Mamontov enterprise. The rebirth of design in the West under the inspiration of Russia had begun. This was to burst fully upon the West in 1909, for following on the success of the operatic season, Diaghilev and his Paris impresario Gabriel Astruc decided that the glories of the Russian ballet must also be seen.

The problem, though, in showing Russian dancers was the repertory then in use in St Petersburg. After the retirement of Marius Petipa in 1903, the Imperial Ballet had had no guiding choreographic identity. The Imperial schools were now producing a truly astounding generation of dancers but, as Fokine's *Memoirs* indicate so clearly, the repertory remained the elaborate and complex *ballets à grand spectacle* of Petipa. Fokine himself was establishing a reputation in Russia as a choreographer but his innovations were hardly encouraged – his first major piece for the Maryinsky Theatre, *Le Pavillon d'Armide* of 1907, had been given a grudging first performance at the end of an evening which had already contained the full-length *Swan Lake*. Thus, in discussion with his committee of friends – the group including Benois, Bakst and Nouvel – Diaghilev realized that in order to show off the dancers, a fresher repertory was essential. The dancers would be available for a Paris season during their lengthy holidays from the Imperial theatres and it was decided that a Paris season should take place in May 1909 with a repertory combining Fokine ballets, and operas. Financial backing was to come from members of the Imperial family and a repertory of operas and ballets was decided upon. Events were to deprive the enterprise of the expected financial support and the operatic contribution was reduced to *Ivan the Terrible* and an act each of *Ruslan and Ludmila* and *Prince Igor*. For the ballet it was unthinkable that the dated magnificence of the Petipa repertory should be shown. Benois' existing association with Fokine, and the Diaghilev group's admiration for the new choreographic style he was evolving, meant that Fokine was the inevitable choice to provide the new repertory.

The ballets chosen for Paris were not in fact new. *Le Pavillon d'Armide* was revived for Paris; the *Egyptian Nights* of 1908 was re-titled *Cléopâtre* and gloriously re-designed by Leon Bakst; his *Chopiniana* originally staged for his pupils in the Imperial school was renamed *Les Sylphides* by Diaghilev and re-designed by Benois; a final Divertissement under the title of *Le Festin* contained virtuoso numbers from the old repertory of the Imperial theatres. On 18 May 1909 at a *répétition générale*, and on the following day at its opening performance, the Saison Russe by artists from St Petersburg and Moscow marked the rebirth of ballet in the West. (It is ironic that the theatre chosen for this enterprise was not the Grand Opéra but a house dedicated to melodrama, the Théâtre du Châtelet. This, characteristically, Diaghilev had refurbished at considerable expense as a temporary home for his troupe.) The casts included the cream of the younger generation of dancers from both St Petersburg and Moscow as well as Chaliapin and some of the finest singers from the Imperial Opera.

But the season would not have made such a stupendous impact had it not been for the ballets of Fokine. These were innovative even by St Petersburg standards; for Paris, accustomed to the dismal, danced interludes in operas and the occasional undistinguished ballet performed by technically brilliant but artistically limited dan-

Mikhail Fokine and his wife Vera Fokina in his ballet Le Carnaval, *as Harlequin and Columbine. Le Carnaval (1910), set to Schumann's piano masterpiece, is a work of delicate, amorous intrigue which has proved almost impossible to revive. It would require the subtlest artistry and technical skill to bring its Biedermeier charms to life on the stage today.*

cers, they had the force of a revelation. Because Fokine had had the courage to break away from the stereotyped attitudes of the classical formula his dancers were revealed as far more expressive artists. Ballerinas like Anna Pavlova and Tamara Karsavina astounded not just by their technical excellence but by the emotional force of their interpretations. Among the men, inevitably Vaslav Nijinsky's prodigious physical gift took the audiences' breath away, as when making an exit in *Le Pavillon d'Armide* he leapt off stage and seemed to soar upwards out of sight; but it was probably Adolph Bolm at the head of the Polovtsian warriors in the *Prince Igor* scene who most effectively shattered the current image of the male dancer. Instead of the portly and effete figures who took male roles when they were not entrusted – as in *Les Deux pigeons* and *Coppélia* – to buxom ladies, there was the ferocity and unquestionable virility of Bolm and the whole of the male ensemble

Like Noverre, whom he so closely resembled in his ideals for dramatic and dynamic veracity, Fokine was concerned with the exact matching of dance language to theme. It is difficult today, when *Les Sylphides* has become part of the *lingua franca* of ballet, to appreciate how innovative was this rejection of arid virtuosity in favour of a softer, more aerial style. Fokine had looked back across the years and understood what Taglioni meant. Today, Taglioni and Fokine are seen in an historical perspective and their importance in blazing trails for later dancers and creators can be understood.

It was in *Prince Igor* that he gave to the male dancer a virility which had been denied him since the Romantic age. In *Le Pavillon d'Armide* an evocation of the eighteenth century was poetically brought about; in *Le Carnaval*, created in St Petersburg in 1908 and taken into the Diaghilev repertory two years later, figures of the *commedia dell'arte* were used to make a witty comment on the nature of love in a ballet which even today, mangled though it is in performance, retains a delicious nuance of lovers' caprices. In *Cléopâtre*, which also featured the phenomenal beauty of Ida Rubinstein (a private pupil of Fokine's who played the mime role of Cleopatra) a new exoticism reached the stage. This was in part due to the superlative design of Léon Bakst. In the following year Fokine and Bakst were to produce the ultimate statement in this exotic style with *Schéhérazade*. Today the whole world of *Schéhérazade* may seem preposterous, but Léon Bakst's setting is the greatest piece of stage design of this century by reason of the emotional effects produced by a masterly control of colour and decoration, and Fokine's narrative achieves a potent impression of the enclosed and perfumed air of the harem.

Supremely Fokine gave the Ballet Russe, in the first three years of its existence, its essentially Russian identity in the public mind. *Igor* had shown barbaric Russia; *The Firebird* of 1910 was to fix in the public's mind the magical and

hieratic beauty of the Holy Russia of legend; *Petrushka*, the single greatest work produced by the Diaghilev Ballet, remains the perfect evocation of a Russian historical scene. In it are mingled elements of folk art in the dances of the crowd – an historically accurate setting in Benois' designs – and a tragic theme expressed through dramatically vivid dance, combined in a ballet of unprecedented and unparalleled dramatic cohesion. *The Firebird* had brought Diaghilev's first commission to the young composer Igor Stravinsky; in *Petrushka*, with Stravinsky working in closest collaboration with Fokine and Benois, there resulted a ballet in which it is not possible to separate one element from another. Their interaction is total.

These Fokine ballets were to help establish the Ballet Russe in the public mind as the most exciting and most important artistic enterprise of the first decades of this century. With the Ballet Russe it was possible to see the finest dancers of the age in the best choreography of the age, set against the finest stage design of the age to the sound of some of the most brilliant theatre music of the age.

Tamara Karsavina as the Firebird, Mikhail Fokine as Tsarevich Ivan, in The Firebird (1910). These original costumes were by Léon Bakst, since those provided by the designer Golovin for the first staging were unsatisfactory.

In addition to these seminal works Fokine's long-time fascination with the antique world of Greece, which had marked his earliest choreographic efforts with *Eunice*, resulted in a couple of ballets on Greek themes: *Daphnis and Chloe* and *Narcisse*. It is significant that the score for *Daphnis* was commissioned by Diaghilev from Maurice Ravel during the Saison Russe of 1909. Ravel, a meticulous creator, did not complete the score until 1911 and the ballet was not finally produced until 1912. By this time important changes had come about in the nature of the Diaghilev enterprise. The seasons of 1909 and 1910 had been given by artists of the Imperial Ballet during their lengthy annual leave. The organization was in no sense permanent. The repertory which Diaghilev presented was the fruit of discussions with his committee of collaborators. In the first two ballet seasons the public had been accustomed to identify the Russian dancers with all that was new, so when Benois persuaded Diaghilev to present *Giselle* (revered in Russia) with Karsavina (1885–1978) and Nijinsky (1888–1950), it was not successful. Even the superb quality of the dancing could not persuade Paris of the merits of what was to them an old-fashioned ballet long since vanished from the French repertory.

Giselle was to be the cause of the radical change in the structure of Diaghilev's work. In the winter of 1910 Nijinsky had appeared in *Giselle* at the Maryinsky Theatre. He decided not to wear the theatre's own costume for Albrecht, preferring instead the Benois-designed costume he had used in Paris. The Dowager Empress Marie attended the performance and found the cut of Nijinsky's brief jerkin offensive; he also omitted to wear the customary *culotte* which ensured that no signs of masculinity could affront the most modest gaze. The directorate imposed a fine for this infringement of the theatre's rules; Nijinsky refused to pay (probably on the insistence of his friends); and he was promptly fired. Diaghilev, deeply involved with Nijinsky as lover and guide to his artistic development (which he had fostered in the roles devised for him in the repertory of the Ballet

Russe), had now to accept responsibility for his further career. Thus Diaghilev, who had not up to then shown that he considered the Saison Russe as a regular fixture, was forced into considering the establishment of a permanent ensemble. Works had already been initiated and commissioned for future Saisons Russes. Now, with some adjustment of the engagements of the Maryinsky artists with their home theatre, he had to consider creating a company which might tour, and would continue the work of revealing a new form of ballet to the world.

To this end he engaged Fokine as choreographer, Karsavina and Nijinsky and Bolm as principal artists (Anna Pavlova was a mere visiting luminary, who from the beginning saw her own destiny as a star as one unable to join in the corporate efforts of the Russian dancers), and Maestro Cecchetti as teacher. Dancers were recruited for a permanent *corps de ballet* and the vital and essential figure of S. L. Grigoriev was engaged to act as manager and *régisseur*. In 1911 the Ballet Russe came into existence as a company and Diaghilev assumed a far more positive role in its destiny than heretofore. Although Benois, his long-time adviser and mentor, was named as an artistic director, the Ballet Russe now became Diaghilev's company; in its every manifestation it reflected his taste. The autocratic side of Diaghilev's nature, always very strong, now matched his artistic control.

The company toured throughout Europe to immense acclaim. Without any permanent base (until a decade later when Monte Carlo offered it a haven), the Ballet Russe was a gypsy troupe, though rooted deeply in the Russian understanding of ballet as an art of the theatre. (It is ironic to record that the company never played in Russia; a proposed season at a new theatre in St Petersburg was frustrated when the building was burned down.) Nijinsky was inevitably the focus of much of the creativity and the following year his importance was to be further accentuated when Diaghilev encouraged him to make his first choreography. From his very beginnings Diaghilev had demonstrated a concern with the new in all the arts. Even within the three years that the Russian dancers had been in Western Europe, new choreography, new design, new music and a new way of dancing had been imposed upon the public consciousness. But for Diaghilev it was already time to move on. Fokine's ballets for the 1912 season – *Daphnis and Chloe*, *Thamar* and *Le Dieu bleu* – repeated a used formula and none of them was particularly successful. For Diaghilev there came the additional satisfaction of channelling his own very strong creative drive into the shaping of Nijinsky as a choreographer.

For his first ballet, Debussy's *Prélude à l'après-midi d'un faune* was to be the inspiration for a brief dance work that marked the emergence of an entirely new identity for choreography on the classical ballet stage. Nijinsky had been revealed in each work in the company repertory as a

Vaslav Nijinsky (below) in Danse siamoise *from* Les Orientales, *a divertissement staged by the Diaghilev Ballet in 1910. A short, rather static dance for Nijinsky, it was a souvenir of a visit by a troup of Siamese dancers to St Petersburg some years before.*
This photograph by Druet was used for a souvenir book of the Ballet Russe in Paris and also served as the basis for a celebrated portrait of Nijinsky in this pose by Léon Bakst.

Nijinsky's Le Sacre du printemps *(above) occasioned one of the most notorious riots in the French theatre at its first performance in 1913. The designer Roerich was a specialist in archaeological studies and his costumes suggest primitive Russia. The 'turned in' poses of the dancers' feet indicate something of Nijinsky's deliberate rejection of the grammar of classical ballet.*

The drawing (right) by Cocteau captures something of what then seemed the percussive 'angular' force of Stravinsky's score for Le Sacre du printemps. *The composer is seen at the piano.*

performer of genius; his roles were most often exotic or mysterious and once a costume and make-up had been put on, the quiet and uncommunicative young man (he was only twenty-three years old) was transformed into a new being totally credible and uniquely exciting. Nijinsky was to prove a genius no less amazing in choreography.

The creation of three ballets during the next two years marked the emergence of a profoundly novel form of theatrical dance. But it was to be an experience taxing both for Nijinsky and his interpreters. For the thirteen minutes of *L'Après-midi d'un faune* – a ballet made for himself as the faun and for only seven nymphs – no fewer than one hundred rehearsals were needed to impose upon classically trained bodies Nijinsky's conception of a flattened and hieratic dance in which the interpreters moved in a single plane in profile to the audience. This was in its essence a ballet which transformed walking steps into the most subtle form of dance. Bakst's set and costumes spoke of the artist's love for Greece and Nijinsky's own performance as the faun was precise in its evocation of the sensuality of a goat-like figure. The final gesture in which the faun sinks down upon a nymph's abandoned scarf was to scandalize the willingly scandalized Paris public. Diaghilev had the double satisfaction of having presented Nijinsky as a choreographer of the new, and also of having stirred up a scandal which could only result in tremendous publicity – involving as it did letters to the press from such masters as Odilon Redon and Auguste Rodin – and resultant box office activity.

In May of the following year, 1913, Nijinsky's next two ballets were presented within a fortnight of each other. With them the banner of modernism in the Ballet Russe was raised even higher. *Jeux* had a score specially commissioned from Debussy. It is the most mysterious of Nijinsky's four ballets (*Till Eulenspiegel* coming later); the setting was a garden at twilight, with Nijinsky, Karsavina and Schollar; the argument of the ballet was flirtation – but ambiguous, and arguably a comment upon homosexual intrigue that would have been inadmissible played straight on the stage. The dancers were supposed to be tennis players and one of the particular interests of the work is that for the first time in twentieth-century ballet contemporary dress was seen on stage.

Gone was the exoticism of *Petrushka* or the essentially Russian image of many of the other ballets in the repertory. Here was twentieth-century man on stage; indeed Diaghilev, asked about the ballet's period, said 'we date it 1930'.

Jeux was calmly accepted. *Le Sacre du printemps* which followed it on 29 May 1913 provoked one of the most astounding riots in the French theatre since the battle of Victor Hugo's *Hernani* in 1830. The spark which lit the tinder of protest and which also fired the work itself was Stravinsky's score. The most uncompromising of his compositions thus far, it celebrated the cracking of the earth at the end of the Russian winter as the fierce cold lost its hold on the land and a primitive ritual celebrated the rebirth of spring. A score of extreme rhythmic complexity was presented to Nijinsky; to enable him to start elucidating it, Diaghilev turned to the system of eurhythmics evolved by Emile Jaques-Dalcroze as a method of musical analysis and appreciation. Jaques-Dalcroze provided as assistant to Nijinsky a young Polish girl, one of his most brilliant pupils, Marie Rambert. It was Rambert (later to become a founding figure of British ballet) who was to aid Nijinsky in decoding the music's complexities. In costumes devised by the painter–archaeologist Nikolai Roerich, Nijinsky's dancers stamped and pounded in a dance language which carried modernity further even than *L'Après-midi d'un faune* and *Jeux*. The harsh, driving energies of the music, so abrasive to ears used to Massenet, and the general air of barbaric ritual all proved too much for an audience whose vociferous rejection of the ballet accounts for one of the most boisterous first nights in ballet's history.

In August 1913 the Diaghilev company set sail for a tour of South America. Diaghilev himself did not accompany the troupe as he detested sea travel, not least because he had been told that he would 'die on water' (in fact he was to die in Venice). On board ship, to the amazement and consternation of the entire company, Nijinsky announced that he was going to marry a young Hungarian who had joined the Diaghilev ensemble more as an admirer of his than as a performer. On arrival in Buenos Aires, the marriage of Vaslav Nijinsky and Romola de Pulsky took place. The tour proceeded, marked only by a curious incident in which Nijinsky refused to appear in *Le Carnaval* one evening. The company duly returned to Europe and Grigoriev, as stage director of the tour, presented himself to Diaghilev on his arrival in St Petersburg. Diaghilev showed Grigoriev a telegram he had received from Nijinsky inquiring about rehearsal details for *La Légende de Joseph* which was to be his next ballet. He then handed Grigoriev a telegram to be dispatched. It came ostensibly from Grigoriev and informed Nijinsky that because of his failure to appear in *Le Carnaval* without excuse he had broken his contract with the company and his services were no longer required. Thus Diaghilev, wounded in the deepest fibre of his being by the betrayal of his love for Nijinsky, ended a relationship which had revealed Nijinsky as both a dancer of genius and a choreographer profoundly far-seeing in his innovations.

Diaghilev's next move was characteristic. He persuaded Fokine, who was still nursing a grudge against him, to return as choreographer and principal dancer – on Fokine's conditions, which also included his reinstatement as *premier danseur*. But it was obvious that Fokine in his thirties could not impersonate the youthful Joseph which was to be the leading role in *La Légende de Joseph*, the

major presentation for 1914 with a score commissioned from Richard Strauss. Consequently Diaghilev had to look for a new young dancer and he found him in the person of Massine.

Léonide Massine (1895–1979) was a dancer with the Moscow Bolshoy Ballet who had also made successful appearances as an actor. In this beautiful young man Diaghilev was to find a new and malleable talent to shape and encourage. Between April and June 1914, the months prior to the First World War, Diaghilev presented three ballets by Fokine: *Les Papillons, La Légende de Joseph* and *Midas*, and two operas – *Le Coq d'or* and *Le Rossignol*. (Diaghilev continued to present operas and to be involved in operatic seasons during the entire existence of his company: in these pre-war seasons he was to present Chaliapin and others of the greatest Russian singers in important stagings.) None of Fokine's new works could be accounted a success during this season and the outbreak of war was to mark a complete creative break in the offerings and in the identity of the Ballet Russe. In the pre-war years the company had been sustained by the generosity of wealthy patrons; its creations, extraordinarily new though they were on the ballet stage, were yet essentially rooted in the cultural world of pre-Revolutionary Russia. Although Diaghilev's own background was Russian, now, with the outbreak of war he chose to remain in Italy, moving in 1915 to Switzerland. His company was entirely dispersed and he had, spiritually, opted for a European existence in what must seem a prophetic decision. It was also a moment when he appeared to gain a second wind. The 'old' Ballet Russe was dead; the links with the Imperial theatres were cut; so, too, was the bond with such influential figures as Alexandre Benois. Now in his forty-second year, Diaghilev had in effect to build a new company around Massine. He had Cecchetti as a teacher; thanks to Grigoriev, who had rejoined him in Switzerland, he was re-assembling a company; and he found a new and more adventurous group of advisers whom he might consult in Igor Stravinsky and two young modernist painters, Mikhail Larionov and Natalia Gontcharova. Most rewarding of all, he had in Léonide Massine a young artist whose creativity he could guide as completely as he had guided Nijinsky's. But existence for the 'new' Ballet Russe was precarious.

The society that had supported the Russian dancers before 1914 was gone. Tours had to be arranged wherever possible and these included two bizarre visits to America, for the second of which the American impresario Otto Kahn insisted upon the presence of Nijinsky. Nijinsky had been interned in Austria and it was the intervention of the King of Spain, Alfonso XIII, a great admirer of the Ballet Russe, which had secured his release. He rejoined the company in New York, but his dancing had suffered from enforced inaction, and he was already showing signs of the temperamental instability which was shortly to cut him off from the world. When Diaghilev and

Léonide Massine as the Miller in his own Le Tricorne. *This photograph, taken at the time of the ballet's first performance in London in 1919, evokes his youthful genius – he was only twenty-four years old at the time. Massine's pose here suggests the impressive power of his stage presence, a quality which was uniquely his throughout his long career as a dancer. (Picasso's design for this costume is shown in colour on page 179.)*

Massine returned to Europe in 1916 Nijinsky demanded, and received, control of the company for an American tour. This was to prove disastrous. Without Diaghilev's or Grigoriev's guidance the company was riven by factions and Nijinsky's *Till Eulenspiegel* took the stage only half-finished. The entire enterprise was fraught with disaster and America never saw the Ballet Russe at anything near its best.

In Europe, however, Diaghilev and Massine and a few selected members of the company were benefiting from a remarkable burst of artistic activity. Massine had already proved himself as a gifted creator in some small early ballets; now he was to produce and plan a series of fascinating works. The group's stay in Italy was to inspire *Les Femmes de bonne humeur*, and with *Parade* the modernist future of the company seems to have been proclaimed. *Parade* was a work devised by Jean Cocteau with a score by Erik Satie, and designs by Pablo Picasso – his first work for the theatre. It was intended as a translation of Cubist theory to the lyric stage, and in its view of reality, and in its décor (most notably with the constructed costumes for the two Managers) it showed the path which the company was to take during the next years.

It was in this same year that Diaghilev and Massine in company with Manuel de Falla made an extended tour of Spain, gathering material for a work which eventually was to become *Le Tricorne*. But financially Diaghilev was living from hand to mouth. In order to guarantee work for his company he sent his dancers, with Nijinsky again as their leading artist, on a tour of South America, a disastrous enterprise which brought nothing but trouble and which was to mark Nijinsky's final flight from reality. On the company's return to war-torn Europe, fit-up tours were all that could be achieved. Nijinsky took his family to Switzerland where he was to sink into the insanity from which death would at last release him in 1950. Diaghilev watched his dancers dispersing during 1917 and 1918 in order to earn their livings where they might; the idea of the Ballet Russe was saved only by a contract to appear at the London Coliseum opening on 5 September 1918 as part of a music hall programme. The end of the war found the Ballet Russe with a largely new ensemble save for its faithful principals. Lydia Lopokova, who had participated in the early seasons, rejoined them and the beginning of 1919 saw a wonderful upsurge in the company's fortunes. This was marked by the performances of two Massine works which remain today as masterpieces of their kind: *La Boutique fantasque* and *Le Tricorne*.

In these ballets you see the maturing of the talent which had been evident in Massine's very first work for Diaghilev, *Le Soleil de nuit* (1915). In the four years since then Massine had demonstrated an exceptional mastery of dance characterization. A product of the Moscow school and company, where Gorsky's dramatic style pre-

dominated, Massine showed in his early ballets a concern with forging a choreographic style which could deal with an extreme variety of characters and which specialized in the vivacious presentation of often grotesque personalities. The dances for the dolls in *La Boutique fantasque* and the eccentricities of the Shopkeeper and his assistant are matched by the preposterous and very amusing characterizations he created in *Les Femmes de bonne humeur*. For *Le Tricorne* – the *only* successful Spanish ballet – Massine and Diaghilev had been guided on their tour round Spain by Manuel de Falla and by a young gypsy dancer, Felix. The latter instructed Massine in the intricacies of Spanish dancing, but it was Massine's own genius which was able to transmute these into choreographic gold.

By 1921, however, Massine had also fled the hothouse atmosphere of the Diaghilev entourage. He married the English dancer Vera Savina and worked in the commercial theatre. Diaghilev was

Original photograph of the New York manager from Parade *(1917). The two 'constructed' figures of the Managers who present the entertainment in* Parade *are the most notable example of the Cubist theories in this ballet, devised by Cocteau, for which costumes and sets were designed by Picasso, with music by Erik Satie and choreography by Massine.*

now without a choreographer. Furthermore, the political, social and economic conditions in Europe, just recovering from war, were inimical to the Ballet Russe. Touring contracts were hard to come by, and in an attempt to give himself a breathing space and an opportunity to recoup some funds, Diaghilev decided upon an extraordinary plan. He had been very impressed by the fact that the musical comedy *Chu Chin Chow* had been playing in London for over a thousand performances and he hoped that a great fairy-tale classic ballet might have a similar appeal for the London audiences. To this end he decided upon a revival of *The Sleeping Beauty* as *The Sleeping Princess*, identifying the ballet thus because he declared that not all his ballerinas were beautiful. The choreography was prepared and staged by Nikolai Sergeyev who had been *régisseur* of the Maryinsky Theatre from 1904 to 1917 and had fled Russia at the time of the Revolution, bringing with him the theatre's production notebooks which contained Stepanov notation of the entire repertory. From these he prepared the ballet (as he was later to stage many productions of the Imperial Russian repertory in the West). For designer, Diaghilev turned to Léon Bakst. Bakst adored *The Sleeping Beauty*, and had been presented to the composer Tchaikovsky at the work's *répétition générale* in 1890. More importantly, he had designed an abridged production which Anna Pavlova had shown on Broadway in 1916. Although a sick man, Bakst was thus able to produce a mass of superlative designs within an astonishingly short period: his view of *The Sleeping Beauty* certainly represents one of the greatest feats of stage designing of this century.

In order to rehabilitate Tchaikovsky, a composer then viewed with an incomprehensible sniffiness by the intellectuals of the period (who were obsessed with the kind of Stravinskian modernism to which Diaghilev had introduced them), Stravinsky himself was asked to edit and amend the score. Further, Diaghilev assembled a galaxy of Maryinsky ballerinas to undertake the role of Aurora. Chief among these was Olga Spessivtseva (b. 1895), the supreme classical ballerina of this century, who had graduated from the Imperial School in 1913 and joined the disastrous American tour of the Ballet Russe in 1916. Diaghilev also secured the presence of Vera Trefilova (1875–1943), a ballerina of the noblest style, and of Lubov Egorova (1880–1972), both of whom had settled in Paris following the Revolution and were to teach there in later years. As Lilac Fairy, and later as Aurora, Diaghilev chose Lydia Lopokova and he endeavoured to secure the original Aurora, Carlotta Brianza, to make appearances. Brianza, who was now fifty-three years old, asked for six months to get herself into trim for the role. Diaghilev could not guarantee this and, instead, the first Aurora became the Carabosse of the production (though for one performance Maestro Cecchetti, still the company

ballet master, returned to this mime role which he had created). As Prince for this galaxy of Auroras Diaghilev enlisted two great *danseurs nobles*, Pierre Vladimirov and Anatol Vilzak. The cast list of the ballet in first soloist roles and even in attendants was a roll-call of the most distinguished dancers in the West.

Certain revisions were made to the choreography, such as the introduction of the Sugar Plum Fairy solo from *Casse noisette (Nutcracker)* and some new dances were arranged by Nijinsky's sister, Bronislava Nijinska (1891–1972), who had rejoined the company from Soviet Russia.

The staging opened at the old Alhambra Theatre in Leicester Square on 2 November 1921, but despite the production's appeal to such connoisseurs of classical dancing as Cyril Beaumont, Sacheverell Sitwell and Arnold Haskell, the general public in London had never before been exposed to the grandeur and fantasy of the Petipa style. The initial goodwill towards the production faded, and on 4 February 1922, after 105 performances, the ballet was taken off. Diaghilev left London before the end of the season, and Grigoriev wrote of his departure: 'To see the curtain descend for the last time on *The Sleeping Princess* was more than he could bear.'

Besides being a disillusioning experience the production proved a financial millstone. Diaghilev had been supported in this enterprise by the impresario Sir Oswald Stoll who was now faced with the financial debris of what had also been an economic disaster.

The Diaghilev company managed to rescue a last act divertissment, *Aurora's Wedding* which, ironically, was to prove extremely popular during the subsequent years of the company's life. However, the discovery of Nijinska's gifts as a choreographer gave Diaghilev new heart. As the company picked itself up from this catastrophe, Nijinska choreographed her first piece, *Le Renard*, in 1922 and in the following year she was entrusted with a major work. This was *Les Noces*, a cantata on which Stravinsky had been working for several years. Its theme was a Russian peasant wedding, and it was one which lay very close to the heart of Diaghilev who had wept when Stravinsky had first played him the music. He had waited to find a creator capable of treating its complexities and in Nijinska he found such an artist. Her realization, and Natalia Gontcharova's austere designs, were the perfect visualization of Stravinsky's view of the peasant heart of Holy Russia. It was also to prove the Ballet Russe's last backward glance at its homeland.

In 1922 the Diaghilev troupe received the inestimable benefit of a permanent home. The company was invited by Prince Louis of Monaco to take up residence in Monte Carlo for six months of the year, in order to participate in opera and ballet seasons. There is implicit in this fact a change of identity in the company. Cut off irrevocably from the Russia of the Soviets, the Ballet Russe now came much more under the

Lydia Sokolova and Anton Dolin, Bronislava Nijinska (Nijinsky's sister) and Leon Woizikoski, in Nijinska's Le Train bleu *(above). This 'danced operetta' (1924) took a light-hearted view of the smart set in the south of France, with Dolin creating a sensation as the acrobatic* beau gosse. *The clothes were by Chanel.*

Le Bal *(right) was choreographed by George Balanchine for the Diaghilev Ballet in 1929. Designs were by de Chirico, and the costumes repeated the architectural motifs of the set. Alexandra Danilova and Anton Dolin are seen here.*

influence of French musical and painterly taste. As an ensemble situated in the most fashionable pleasure resort in Europe, the company had also acquired a smart audience who were worldly and easily bored. It was a period in which Diaghilev's obsessive quest for the new was also to become a pursuit of ephemeral fashion. Whereas before 1914 he had made fashion and had been effortlessly in the *avant-garde,* he now seemed involved in a restless search for novelty with which to justify his identity.

By 1924 the influence of the Ecole de Paris can be clearly seen. This was the year in which Nijinska produced her other masterpiece for Diaghilev, the airily decadent *Les Biches* with its luminous designs by Marie Laurencin and a score by Poulenc. Youth was now to become an obsession with Diaghilev. His secretary and aide Boris Kochno joined him in 1923 at the age of twenty. A young dancer from Kiev and pupil of Nijinska's, Serge Lifar (b. 1905) joined him in this same year at the age of eighteen. In 1924 Diaghilev took the exceptional step of engaging a young English prodigy who had just celebrated her fourteenth birthday. This was Alicia Markova. In 1924 the gifts of another young English dancer, Anton Dolin (b. 1904), were also celebrated in *Le Train bleu,* an ephemeral piece which epitomized everything that was most chic and transitory about the Ballet

Russe. At this time Nijinska parted again from Diaghilev, and Massine returned to provide choreographies over the next few years for the Ballet Russe, notable more for their adventurous design (as in the ravishing *Ode* of Pavel Tchelitchev) than for any comparable choreographic innovations.

The most important event of this period was the recruiting of a group of four dancers who had left the Soviet Union while on a concert tour in the Baltic. All four were soloists with the ballet company in Leningrad (the former Imperial Ballet at the Maryinsky Theatre), artists of a high calibre who had already achieved a reputation in the Soviet Union. They were led by Georgy Balanchivadze (b. 1904); the other members were Alexandra Danilova, Tamara Gevergeyeva and Nicholas Efimov.

Diaghilev was eager to acquire artists of this standing and was more than happy to learn that Balanchivadze was capable of producing ballets for the operas which were such an important part of the Monte Carlo seasons. Here, he soon discovered, was a remarkably gifted young choreographer. Diaghilev changed this Georgian name to Balanchine, and for the remaining years of the Ballet Russe, Balanchine was to be its resident and principal choreographer.

These late 1920s were a period when Diaghilev, already suffering from bad health, appears to have shown some lack of interest in his company. The repertory seemed much flimsier than the core of master works which were preserved from the first years of the company. It would be idle to pretend that pieces like the surreal *Roméo et Juliette* of 1926 or the lightweight *Pastorale* of the same year could stand much comparison with *Les Sylphides, Petrushka* or *The Firebird.* Indeed, the decorative brilliance of the Ballet Russe now far outweighed its choreographic distinction in new creations. Balanchine was, however, to escape from the trap of amusing novelties in 1928 when he produced his first ballet to a Stravinsky score. This was *Apollo,* and in its formal distinction, in its loving reassessment of the classical academic dance, his own influential style emerged to shape a more modern identity for classical dancing in the West.

In the following year Balanchine was also to produce two other noteworthy pieces, *Le Bal* and *Le Fils prodigue.* In this season it seemed that some of the old power had returned to the Ballet Russe. The company was stronger than it had been for some years; Karsavina had returned in *Petrushka,* Spessivtseva was appearing in *Swan Lake,* Dolin had returned to the company after some years absence, Lifar (the first Apollo and the first Prodigal Son) was at the height of his powers, the young Markova was on the verge of ballerina status and such trusted and important artists as Lydia Sokolova, Léon Woizikowski, Lubov Tchernicheva, Alexandra Danilova, Felia Dubrovska, Vera Nemchinova were leading the company. It was a blaze of glory in dancing as well as choreography and it marked the end of the Diaghilev

This portrait of Ida Rubinstein, in her dressing room at the Theatre Sarah Bernhardt before her appearance in the drama Secrets of the Sphynx, *suggests something of her hieratic beauty. Never a great dancer, it was Rubinstein's physical allure which brought her to fame in the first Diaghilev ballet season (1909), in such roles as Cleopatra.*

Ballet Russe. In the summer of 1929, after the Paris and London seasons, Diaghilev bade farewell to his dancers (who then had a short season at Vichy) and went, as usual, to holiday in Venice. There he fell ill; his body exhausted by twenty years of endeavours for the Ballet Russe and by his reluctance to obey medical instructions for his diabetes, could stand no more. He died on 19 August 1929 and was buried on the island of San Michele – and with him the Ballet Russe.

As a postscript to Diaghilev's work in the 1920s the pre-war efforts of two wealthy individuals to establish enterprises designed to produce rivals to Diaghilev's productions must be noted. Ida Rubinstein (*c.* 1885–1960) had gained the attention of all Paris in 1909 when her exotic beauty was revealed under Bakst's veiling in *Cléopâtre*, but she was not a dancer, and her private lessons from Fokine served merely to polish her stage presence. As early as 1911 she had initiated a troupe which presented spectacles of which she was the central attraction: these included *Le Martyre de St Sébastien* (with music by Debussy, based on a text by D'Annunzio and choreography by Fokine), *Hélène de Sparte* and, in 1913, *La Pisanelle*; these were all designed by Bakst. In these her beauty and a certain dramatic ability were sufficiently powerful to provide a focal point for the important contributions of composer, designer, choreographer and librettist. After the First World War she made appearances as an actress and in 1928 started up a company which performed fitfully between then and her retirement in 1935. Known to its members as *la compagnie des répétitions de Madame Rubinstein* because of incessant rehearsals and few performances, it involved many of the most distinguished creators of the time. Stravinsky's *Baiser de la fée* and *Perséphone*, and Ravel's *La Valse* were staged for Rubinstein's company. Choreographers included Bronislava Nijinska, Kurt Jooss and Massine. The fatal flaw was Rubinstein's obsession with appearing as the star. As Frederick Ashton, a young dancer with her company noted, she insisted on featuring in a central role, and after the other dancers had built the production up towards her entrance it would 'sag right down' with the further disadvantage that Rubinstein's stage presence was timorous rather than commanding. Not all her distinguished collaborators – and they were among the finest – could bolster up this uncertain performer; Diaghilev was venomously amused when he went to see an early performance of the company. (It was the Paris Opéra which benefited after 1935 when it inherited works that Rubinstein had commissioned for future seasons.)

More considerable were the efforts of the Swedish millionaire Rolf de Maré (1898–1964). As a result of his friendship with Mikhail Fokine this amateur of the arts decided to initiate a company, Les Ballets Suédois, which despite its Swedish name was fundamentally a showcase for the painters and associates of the Ecole de Paris and the musical collaborators known as 'Les Six'. De Maré centred the company upon his friend Jean Börlin (1893–1930), who became choreographer for the entire repertory of twenty-four ballets created over a period of five years and was also the leading dancer. The repertory and its creators reflected de Maré's affection for Paris. Apart from a few works which made use of Swedish folklore the ballets in their decoration and music called upon many of the brightest talents in France. *Skating Rink* had a score by Honneger and décor by Léger; Léger also contributed the designs for *La Création du monde* with its score by Milhaud; *Relâche* was designed by Picabia with a Satie score. Blaise Cendrars, Claudel and Cocteau were among the librettists; Bonnard, de Chirico, Steinlen and Jean Hugo were among the artists who contributed to the set designs and costumes.

The American artist
Gerald Murphy provided
the designs for Within
the Quota, *a ballet about
American immigrants
staged by the Ballets
Suédois in Paris in 1923,
with a score by Cole
Porter.*

For a period of five years the Ballets Suédois toured Europe and the United States. But Jean Börlin did not have the creative strength to sustain an entire repertory, and gifted though the dancers were, the achievement of the Ballet Suédois was less than the sum of its distinguished parts. It ceased operating in 1925.

One other post-Diaghilev company merits attention Les Ballets 1933 was created in its title year by the wealthy English art lover Edward James, with the collaboration of George Balanchine and Boris Kochno. The company's purpose was to provide a frame for the delightful talent of the Austrian dancer Tilly Losch, James' wife. But the company also included other gifted artists, among them Tamara Toumanova and Natalie Leslie Krassovska, and its repertory was dominated by Balanchine's genius. After the only two short seasons it gave in Paris and London, the beauty of such works as *Errante, Songes* and *Mozartiana* and the satiric force of *The Seven Deadly Sins* are still remembered; in part due to the beautiful designs provided by Tchelitchev, Bérard and Derain. The failure of this company, lamentable as it may seem, did have one benefit for the future. It freed George Balanchine from any further commitment to Europe and he was able to

accept the invitation of Lincoln Kirstein to establish himself and the classic ballet in America.

With the dawn of the 1930s the political and social climate of the Western world underwent radical changes. The Wall Street Crash of 1929 and the subsequent Depression, the spectre of unemployment, and the emergence of Fascism and Communism as potent political movements, were all indicative of a world in which ballet would seem an unnecessary luxury. The decade of the 1930s was, however, to be an important time in the development of modern dance, both in Europe and America. These developments took place despite the fact that ballet had lost the two great names of the preceding twenty years – Diaghilev, who had died in 1929 (and with him died the impetus behind the Ballet Russe), and Pavlova, who had died of pneumonia in The Hague.

Anna Pavlova (1881–1931) had been among the first of the Russian Imperial stars to find success in tours outside her native land. As early as 1907 she had made guest appearances in Europe, and she participated in the early Diaghilev Russian seasons. She maintained her connection with the Imperial theatres until 1913 but in that year she settled permanently in the West with London as her base, forming a company with which she was

SHÉHÉRASADE

Léon Bakst design (left) for the Chief Eunuch in Schéhérazade (1910). The dance stage had not seen set designs and costumes of such brilliance in colour, and extravagance of effect, since the great days of the ballet de cour.

Léon Bakst design (right) for an ephebe in Fokine's Narcisse, first produced by the Diaghilev Ballet in Monte Carlo in 1911. The ballet was no success, but the design, as can be seen, benefited from Bakst's intense love and understanding of antique Greece.

Pablo Picasso: design (above) for Massine as the Miller in Tricorne *(1919). One of a numbered set of stencil reproductions from Picasso's original hand-coloured lithographs, published in Paris in 1920. The costume designs for* Tricorne *are a magnificent distillation of the styles of regional Spanish dress for the stage.*

thereafter to tour the world. Pavlova was the supreme example of the star ballerina. Her repertory included certain full-length ballets of the traditional repertory, such as *Giselle* and *Don Quixote* in which she could shine, but she is remembered more for the shorter dance numbers in which her gifts were appreciated by millions. In 1905 Fokine had given her the most famous of her solos, *The Dying Swan*. In such other morsels as *The Dragonfly, Christmas, Californian Poppy*, Pavlova was able to enchant and captivate a world-wide following. Her repertory was less seriously 'artistic' than that of Diaghilev; Pavlova was a traditional artist believing in the traditional virtues of the academic dance, and modernism had no place in her understanding. Her repertory had perforce to be 'middle of the road', geared to an unsophisticated and often totally innocent audience to whom Pavlova was the *only* dancer. It was also a repertory that could travel easily. Pavlova once declared 'I want to dance for the whole world'; no city seemed too remote, no conditions too arduous for this great apostle and missionary of the dance. Because of her ceaseless labours ballet reached an entirely new public, and her dancing inspired generations of people with a love for ballet. Even today the magic of her name is probably more evocative of the image of the ballerina than any other. Thus her mission to the world can be seen as the greatest achievement in popularizing an art, one comparable with the cinema and the gramophone in evoking a response to a new experience. The fruits of this can be seen most vividly in the inspiration she offered to young people who, because they had seen her dance, wanted to dance themselves. One such was Frederick Ashton, who has said that it was the sight of Pavlova dancing in South America, where he spent his childhood, that 'injected the poison' that made him one of the greatest figures in dance of this century.

Whatever the ardours of her career – and Pavlova never spared herself in her ceaseless touring – she remained to the very last, when she had worn herself out for her art, a great dancer.

It is possible to argue that the extinction of the Diaghilev and Pavlova companies was instrumental in preparing the way for the national endeavours in Britain, France and the United States which were to prove so fruitful for the future. During this time, though, when Marie Rambert and Ninette de Valois were labouring to create a truly national ballet in Britain and George Balanchine and Lincoln Kirstein were giving classical ballet its roots in America, public taste for the glamour of the international Ballet Russe was satisfied by the emergence of new, Russian-cosmopolitan companies. These were the Ballet Russe companies who were so influential and so popular during the 1930s but who were doomed, by their very lack of roots and a school, to extinction.

Characteristically, the rebirth of the Ballet Russe came from Monte Carlo. René Blum (1878–1942) had been appointed director of the Monte Carlo Opera House where he had already known Diaghilev in his capacity as director for plays and operetta. In 1931 he initiated the Ballet de L'Opéra de Monte Carlo. At the same time a Cossack officer V. G. Voskresensky (1888–1951), who assumed the name of Colonel W. de Basil, had joined forces with Prince Zeretelli in a Russian opera company based in Paris. Soon Blum and de Basil united and a ballet company emerged which picked up the fallen standard of the Diaghilev troupe. This was the Ballet Russe de Monte Carlo in which Blum was supposedly artistic adviser and de Basil business manager. Many of the former Diaghilev associates were recruited, notably S. L. Grigoriev as *régisseur*, and to the ranks of ex-Diaghilev dancers like Dubrovska, Woizikowski and Nemchinova were added three young girls in their early teens: Tatiana Riabouchinska, Tamara Toumanova and Irina Baronova, who achieved instant popular success (merited by their precocious technique as well as their artistry) and were known as 'the baby ballerinas'. George Balanchine was initially engaged as choreographer, and gave the company such delights as *La Concurrence* and *Le Cotillon*, but the feverish politicking in the company caused him to leave and in 1933 he was engaged by Edward James as director and choreographer of the short-lived but glorious Les Ballets 1933 Balanchine was succeeded in the new Ballet Russe by Léonide Massine who soon created a series of ballets which made him the best-known choreographer of the decade.

His claim to fame at this time was as the creator of two symphonic ballets – *Les Présages* to the Tchaikovsky Fifth Symphony (first produced in Monte Carlo in 1933) which told of man's conflict with his destiny, and *Choreartium* to Brahms' Fourth Symphony (first produced in London in 1933) – which were early successes of the Blum–de Basil company, but caused a furore among music critics. Plotless expressions of cosmic themes, they served to show off the very considerable resources of the Ballet Russe. It has been astutely observed that the scores were attractive to the canny de Basil since they were out of copyright, but in their rather generalized thunderings about life and destiny they suited the mood of the time. Massine was to continue exploiting this vein of symphonic music with the subsequent *Symphonie Fantastique* of Berlioz (1938) which caused less commotion because of the symphony's own dramatic content, Beethoven's *Seventh Symphony* (1938), *Rouge et Noir* to the Shostakovitch First Symphony (New York 1941) and Haydn's *Clock Symphony* (produced in London in 1948).

Parenthetically it must be noted that there is nothing new in this use of the classical repertoire: a version of Beethoven's *Pastoral Symphony* was presented in London in 1829; Isadora Duncan danced to entire symphonies; today such choreographers as Kenneth MacMillan, Maurice Béjart

Anna Pavlova in her solo The Dragonfly, *to Kreisler music. 'Over the matter-of-fact aspects of dancing – that is, dancing* per se *– I have attempted to throw a spiritual veil of poetry ...' wrote Pavlova, and even today the priceless testimony of brief film extracts reveals the artistry that has enshrined her name as the supreme symbol of ballet. This photograph, taken in New York in 1914, despite the curiously 'retouched' foot, speaks of an exquisite physique, and a nobility of style (still to be seen in the Leningrad Ballet) which redeemed even the most inconsiderable of Pavlova's solo numbers. The Dragonfly was based technically on a cascade of jumps; Nadia Nerina, who was taught this solo by the former Pavlova dancer Cleo Nordi, said: 'It never stops except for a few seconds when the Dragonfly alights on the ground and plays with its wings – you have only a couple of seconds to catch your breath before you are darting off again. It was the most tiring solo, apart from Firebird, which I ever danced, and it lasts only a minute and a half. Like other Pavlova solos, it looks deceptively easy.'*

and John Neumeier use the symphonic repertory and no protest is made. But in the 1930s Massine's experiments both delighted and scandalized. Although most of these works have now passed into the history book from the living repertory, they were markedly influential at a time when Massine himself was the most acclaimed choreographer in the West.

Massine's importance to both Ballet Russe was multiple. As active choreographer, as creator of much-loved existing repertory works, as dancer and as artistic arbiter he was a powerful force. At a time when Blum and de Basil had discovered how incompatible they were as associates, Massine became an important weight with which to tip the scales of good fortune for one company against another. By 1938, after a period of artistic in-fighting which centred round the devious de Basil, there resulted a tangled web of intrigue and a splitting of forces which produced various

changes of name and identity in the Ballet Russe and in its titular holding companies. De Basil inevitably found himself in a position of power, but Blum was able to initiate another company and quarrels and litigation ensued, which had to do with rights to repertory, dancers, choreography and to the vitally important Monte Carlo label. All this was carried out over the period of five years in which the Ballet Russe 'companies' toured both in Europe and North and South America, and in Australia with immense success.

By 1938 two enterprises emerged. One, the 'Original Ballet Russe' of Colonel de Basil, featured Riabouchinska and David Lichine, Baronova and Anton Dolin among its stars. The other, the Ballet Russe de Monte Carlo, was directed by Blum and was backed by American money with first Mikhail Fokine and then Léonide Massine as its choreographer-in-chief, and Danilova, Markova, Toumanova and Slavenska,

Eglevsky and Youskevitch on its list of stars.

It was the Ballet Russe de Monte Carlo which then made extensive American tours, alternating them with European seasons, and which was to go to America finally in 1939 under the direction of Sergei Denham and Massine. There it was to remain, touring from coast to coast, and existing with Danilova and Frederic Franklin as its leading stars until the 1950s, closing finally in 1962. The Original Ballet Russe company of de Basil went to Australia in 1938, and returned there in 1940. It eventually reached the United States and also performed in South America. This company returned to Europe at the war's end, but as Covent Garden audiences discovered in 1947, it was a pale ghost of itself. So far as London and Europe were concerned the legend of the Ballet Russe was

dead. It was to be revived only in 1956 when the authentic Russian ballet, the Bolshoy Ballet from Moscow, showed how totally different was the real thing.

SOVIET RUSSIA

On the night of 15 March 1917, when Tsar Nicholas II abdicated, *The Sleeping Beauty*, that grandest homage to the Imperial ideal, was performed by the Imperial Ballet at the Maryinsky Theatre in St Petersburg. At the end of the performance the Marseillaise was sung and greetings were addressed to members of the Provisional Government. The Revolution had come.

Léon Bakst: a design (above) for the décor of the Awakening scene in The Sleeping Princess *as presented by the Diaghilev Ballet in London in 1921. As* Sleeping Beauty, *the ballet was first performed in St Petersburg in 1890, and there have been many versions in Russia and in other countries since that period, but the production still maintained by the Leningrad Kirov Ballet is superior in dancing and in design to any other.*

In the midst of a disastrous war the whole fabric of Russian society was destroyed, and by October 1917 and the Bolshevik Revolution, the continued existence of ballet in Russia could be seen as being in peril. The function of this most refined and remote of arts was called into question in a people's republic. It is here that tribute must be paid to a great man who stands among the most profoundly influential forces upon the existence of ballet in this century. This was Anatoly V. Lunacharsky. A man of wide culture, a writer and critic, he was deeply interested in the arts, deeply committed to the Revolutionary cause, and a trusted aide and friend of Lenin. In the turbulent months that followed October 1917, when cold, hunger and political ferment marked each day, Lunarcharsky, appointed People's Commissar for Enlighten-

ment, was to prove the ideal man for the task. It was he who had to mediate between ardent revolutionaries, eager to do away with the ballet, and the artists of the ballet itself. By 1919, with the theatres nationalized, workers were pouring into performances, offering rapt attention to an utterly foreign art which until that time had been available only to the aristocracy, the wealthy bourgeoisie and the student intellectuals who crowded the upper reaches of the theatres.

In return for army rations, artists of the Imperial theatres gave concerts for the troops and special performances for the trades unions. Despite the appalling conditions, the performances were popular but the repertory contained nothing new. Obviously a new identity for the ballet would have to be forged, and it was at this time that

Lunacharsky began his massive efforts to preserve the ballet. The hard-line Marxists were convinced that ballet must be destroyed. Furthermore, they saw enemies within the ballet: bourgeois *avant-garde* creators who were eager for artistic freedom; didactic supporters of *proletkult* who wanted to give absolute artistic control of the arts to the workers so that art might organize the masses. The earliest years of the Revolution had freed the creative spirit of many Russians; the tragedy is that too soon this weight was replaced by the no less repressive hand of doctrinaire Marxism. The following crucial statement by Lunacharsky seems to sum up everything of his wisdom and everything of his battle.

'We must remember that the proletariat, having taken possession of the country, wants also a little enjoyment. He wants to admire beautiful performances. He wishes, and in this he is a thousand times correct, to live by the various aspects of his heart and soul . . . while I remain People's Commissar for Enlightenment this work of introducing the proletariat to the possession of all human culture shall remain my first task, and no kind of alphabetical primitive communism shall turn me away from this task personally.'[4]

Naturally ballet was subject not only to ideological attacks but also to various perversions by people seeking to make it more 'popular' or 'relevant'. The introduction of ideas from the circus and acrobatics was advocated. An extraordinary figure, Nikolai Foregger (1892-1939), proposed a kind of machine ballet. Foregger, an aristocrat, believed that the dance 'strengthens the basics for self discipline in the masses, provides practice for the learning and mastery of rhythm (mass dances), which is so necessary in all labour processes.' To this end he initiated dramatic productions and also dance revues in which groups of performers imitated machinery, gears, pistons, motors. His *The Dance of the Machines* of 1923 in Moscow is the most celebrated illustration of this new ideology of movement. But the aesthetic behind it smacked too strongly of *proletkult* and Foregger was eventually forced to abandon his work. His later years were spent in Kiev and Kharkov assisting in the production of Soviet operas and ballets.

In 1921 another extraordinary figure arrived in Russia. Isadora Duncan (1878–1927) had first appeared in St Petersburg in 1904; seventeen years later she was a different figure in every sense. From being the young woman who had danced barefoot for a chic audience, she had achieved world renown but had also known deepest tragedy with the drowning of her two small children. Despite her improvidence, and her failure to realize most of her great educational plans, she still burned with the belief that dance might alter the world for the good – and where more ideal than the new Russia of the Socialist revolution? She arrived in Moscow in 1921 and by dint of badgering the

commissars she was given a house in which to live (ironically it was the former *hôtel particulier* of the Moscow ballerina Alexandra Balashova). She was also given the opportunity to teach children, and her school raised the banner of modern dance in Soviet Russia (and stayed open until 1946). Duncan herself embarked on yet another amorous adventure which proved more disastrous than any previous ones. She married the gifted but boorish poet Sergei Esenin, and their antics inside Russia, and in the United States and Europe where they travelled, were a degrading trail of brawls and drunkenness. But Isadora's genius left its imprint in the Soviet Union. Her idealism for the young transcended all circumstances, and for a brief time she could be said to have set the children of this new society dancing. But the prospects for ballet were still gloomy. Lunacharsky had to battle against the trades unions, who sought to interfere with the ballet. The old classics of the repertory were still performed – as were versions of such ballets as *Petrushka, The Firebird, Renard, Pulcinella* – but they were now being altered to make them ideologically suitable, with princes turned into the more acceptable figures of shepherds. What was missing was a new Soviet choreography and a new identity, a new language in place of the old vocabulary of the classic dance.

In Feodor Lopukhov, Leningrad had an important choreographer for the new age. Appointed director of the former Maryinsky Theatre, he both extended the language of the classic dance with such acrobatic feats as the splits and backbends, and introduced elements from the demotic arts into stagings. Oddly enough, his new *Casse noisette* of 1928 was wildly unpopular because the worker audience thought that an old classic had been desecrated. In Moscow, Kasyan Goleizovsky was producing spectacles using a dance language of considerable freedom, offering a kind of 'plastique' that featured the body beautiful, which reached its apogee in *Joseph the Beautiful*. (In

The two sides of Soviet ballet creativity during the 1920s: the first scene of Joseph the Beautiful *by Kasyan Goleizovsky (below), was an exercise in 'plastique' and first seen in Moscow at the Experimental Theatre in 1925; the propagandist and ideologically acceptable* The Red Poppy *of 1927 (above right) took as its theme a revolt by oppressed workers in China who were helped by sympathetic Russian sailors.*

the early 1920s Goleizovsky exerted a considerable but passing influence on a very young dancer – George Balanchine – who was making his first choreographic essays in Leningrad.)

But still no acceptable 'official' identity for the ballet had emerged in this first decade after the Revolution. Lunacharsky, as spearhead of the conservationist movement, was still under attack. The staging in 1927 of *The Red Poppy*, with choreography by Lashchilin and Tikhomirnov, at the Bolshoy Theatre in Moscow, revealed a theme proper to Soviet society expressed in an acceptably heroic language. Dealing with a revolt by oppressed workers in China, and the aid offered to them by Russian sailors, the ballet 'initiated the heroic theme in Soviet ballet that became inseparably associated with its style and content.'[5] *The Red Poppy* marks the beginning of the emergence of an authentic Soviet style and subject matter for ballet. Heroism dictated the style, the aspirations of the workers were to give dramatic impetus to the themes.

Over the years that have elapsed since *The Red Poppy*, Soviet choreographers have mined this rich vein of the proletarian struggle against an oppressor. Typical and celebrated examples are *The Flames of Paris* (choreography by Vainonen and music by Asafiev, Leningrad 1932) which dealt with the French Revolution; *Laurencia* (choreography by Chabukiany, music by Krein, Leningrad 1939) based on Lope de Vega's drama *Fuente Ovejuna* about oppressed peasantry in Spain; and most recently, *Spartacus*, first produced by Leonid Jacobsen in Leningrad in 1956, subsequently restaged by Igor Moiseyev in Moscow in 1958 and given its definitive version by Yury Grigorovich in Moscow ten years later. Perhaps *Spartacus* more than any other ballet typifies today's adaptation of the theories implicit in *The Red Poppy*. To a cinematically effective score by Aram Khachaturian, Grigorovich has created a powerful if simplistic view of the Roman slaves' revolt. It has been given credibility by the total dedication to their roles of the foremost artists of the Bolshoy Ballet.

But even with the success of *The Red Poppy* the battle to preserve ballet was not fully won. Towards the end of the twenties, ballet's enemies could still declare 'classical ballet must be annihilated' and various demands for the introduction of a demotic style adapted from sport and the circus were made. A leading champion of classical ballet and one whose influence was as profound as that of Lunacharsky was A. Y. Vaganova (1879–1951). A one-time ballerina at the Maryinsky Theatre, Vaganova had become on her retirement a teacher in a private ballet school and then had moved to the erstwhile Maryinsky School. Her great gift to Soviet ballet was the development of a teaching system which is one of the finest in the history of dance. On the basis of the traditional and aristocratic language that had reached its peak in the Maryinsky Theatre, Vaganova expounded a method that produced a broader and more expansive physical image for the dancer, without any loss of refinement. The great prowess and distinction of Soviet dancing today owes everything to Vaganova's teachings which, by the time of her death, were in use throughout Russia in the new schools which had been established in each of the Republics of the Soviet Union. One of the crucial factors in tipping the balance finally in favour of classical ballet was the graduation of Marina Semyonova (b. 1908), one of Vaganova's first pupils, whose miraculous gifts seemed a triumphant assertion of the beauty and relevance

Maya Plisetskaya (right) as Kitri in the first act of Don Quixote (first performed 1869) with the Bolshoy Ballet in 1963. Unchallenged prima ballerina assoluta *of the Moscow Ballet, in this, as in every other role, the intensity and passion of her dancing mark her as one of the greatest dancers of our time. Natalia Bessmertnova and Mikhail Lavrovsky (far right) in the third act of* Swan Lake *with the Bolshoy Ballet in 1969. She is married to Yury Grigorovich, Bolshoy director and chief choreographer; he is the son of choreographer Leonid Lavrovsky, and noted for heroic roles.*

Galina Ulanova, born in St Petersburg in 1910, was a pupil of Vaganova. She was first the glory of the Kirov – having made her debut there in Chopiniana *in 1928 – and then of the Bolshoy in Moscow to which she transferred in 1944. Here she dances* Chopiniana *again, a year before retiring in 1962 to devote herself to coaching young dancers in her former great roles.*

to the new society of the academic dance. But, with victory in the struggle for survival there also came the imposition of the appalling and stultifying theory of socialist realism initiated by Stalin, which was to chain and imprison all the arts.

An officially imposed aesthetic was proposed – that art is 'in its very core a deliberate purposeful struggle for the victory of communism; an evaluation of life in the light of communist ideals'. To ignore it was to court disgrace and disaster and the ignominy of public recantation – as Shostakovich knew. It brought a return to the dullest sort of realism in décor and in painting; its only merit was that the classical ballet had shown itself able to submit to its rule and was thus safe. However, even the classics required some 'adjustment' and *Swan Lake*, notably, has been perverted by being given a 'positive' ending in which Odette and Siegfried, by reaffirming their love, can survive and destroy the force of evil represented by von Rothbart.

During the Stalin years, however, the Vaganova system was codified, and established those foundations for Soviet dance upon which today's excellence stands. For Soviet choreographers the task was clear though not easy. All the experimentation associated with Diaghilev had passed by his homeland. The very interesting experiments by such Soviet choreographers as Goleizovsky, Lopukhov and even Foregger had been stifled by the mid-1920s. The brilliantly promising young Balanchine had left Russia in 1924. By the 1930s a new generation of choreographers was to dominate Soviet ballet, using themes drawn from acceptable socialist ideas, but also and very rewardingly from world literature. Pushkin, inevitably, was to provide the inspiration for such ballets as *The Prisoner of the Caucasus, The Bronze Horseman,* and *The Fountain of Bakhchisarai.* Other Russian authors used included

Turgenev, Gogol, Lermontov and Leskov. Choreographers turned to Shakespeare to create versions of *Romeo and Juliet, The Merry Wives of Windsor,* and *Othello* among others. Another favourite and acceptable source were Russian folk tales, which could spark off such thrilling ballets as *Taras Bulba* and *The Heart of the Hills* in which inspiring use was made of folk dance elements from the extreme richness and variety of dance throughout the entire USSR.

During the 1930s the choreography of Rostislav Zakharov, Vakhtang Chabukiany, Leonid Lavrovsky, Leonid Jacobsen was to provide a solid basis of full length ballets for the new repertory. Their creations, which gave golden opportunities for dancers and inspired the Soviet audiences with an increasing love for ballet, can be seen as an intriguing development of the nineteenth-century *ballet à grand spectacle.* It took Western choreographers another twenty years to master the extremely difficult art of making full-length ballets which are today so much in demand by Western audiences.

Probably the most successful of all Soviet ballets was *Romeo and Juliet* as staged by Leonid Lavrovsky in Leningrad in 1940, with music by Prokofiev. Ulanova and Konstantin Sergeyev were the lovers. It was the last important work before Russia entered the war. The Leningrad Kirov Ballet was evacuated to the Urals, Ulanova and Lavrovsky were transferred to the Bolshoy Ballet in Moscow in 1944, and *Romeo and Juliet* entered the Moscow repertory in 1946.

By the end of the war, ballet policy inside the Soviet Union concentrated particularly upon the Moscow troupe. It emerged as the most massive of companies and today, under Yury Grigorovich – Lavrovsky's successor – it is a company of blockbusting power. Nevertheless, Leningrad continued to produce dancers of exquisite refinement

(the distance between Leningrad and Moscow can still be judged artistically as it was in the nineteenth century) and it is Leningrad that has provided the choreographic talent so necessary for ballet's survival – Yury Grigorovich, Igor Belsky and Oleg Vinogradov (now director of the Kirov Ballet) are all products of the Kirov Company.

In 1956 there came the Russian performances as influential for Western eyes as Diaghilev's 1909 Paris season. This was the first appearance by the Bolshoy Ballet from Moscow in the West. At the Royal Opera House, Covent Garden, the curtain rose on Ulanova in *Romeo and Juliet* and the West was conquered by the Russian ballet once again. The total involvement of the Russian dancers in their work, Ulanova's genius, the virility of the male dancing and the power of the older dancers in character roles revealed to a sophisticated Western audience a very different way of dancing. Choreographically the advantage was still with the

West; technically it was obvious that the Russians had developed even greater virtuosity and had found not only a grander way of moving but also a more adventurous identity for the partnership of men and women in ballet.

In 1961 the Kirov Ballet also came West, to Covent Garden. Less immediately spectacular, this was ballet which satisfied both the connoisseur and the general public. The heritage of a great classical tradition was obvious, lovingly preserved in the dancers' immaculate schooling. It was to prove interesting in the following years to compare the Kirov's flawless Kolpakova with the Bolshoy's flame-like Plisetskaya. With the younger generations of dancers there have come from Leningrad such artists as Alla Sizova, Yury Soloviev (1940–1977), Ludmila Semenyaka and a *corps de ballet* unrivalled in the world. From Moscow the acclaim has been shared by Ekaterina Maximova, Natalia Bessmertnova, Vladimir Vasiliev, Mikhail Lavrovsky among others.

Three Leningrad artists of the younger generation opted to dance in the West. Rudolf Nureyev was the first, leaving the Kirov in 1961; later Natalia Makarova and then Mikhail Baryshnikov followed. All three sought the challenge of the free artistic climate of Western ballet. All three have brought further renown and honour to their parent theatre, by their artistry.

Irina Kolpakova, leading ballerina of the Leningrad Kirov Ballet, as Aurora (below left) in The Sleeping Beauty *in 1961. Kolpakova was the last ballerina to be formed by Vaganova. A flawless classical stylist, she is an artist who justifies the nineteenth-century classical repertory by a wonderful combination of aristocratic style and delicacy of manner.*

Vladimir Vasiliev as Spartacus (left). Khachaturian's score for Spartacus *went through several choreographic incarnations (the original performance was in 1956) before Yury Grigorovich created the definitive version for the Moscow Bolshoy Ballet in 1968. Based on the revolt by slaves in ancient Rome,* Spartacus *epitomized the politically orientated aesthetic of Soviet ballet and, in Grigorovich's version, the heroic energy of style which so suits the Bolshoy troupe. Vasiliev gave extraordinary humanity as well as prodigious technical ardour to his portrait of the doomed slave leader.*

BRITISH BALLET AND OFFSHOOTS

In Britain there has always been a tradition of fine dancing. But despite this natural impulse towards dance it was never fostered or codified by patronage or pedagogues until the twentieth century. In the eighteenth century, English dancing masters were both influential and adventurous. John Weaver stands at the crossroads of the theatrical dance as an important innovator and theorist of the *ballet d'action*, yet he was not an isolated figure. Men like Mr Isaac who had been dancing master to Queen Anne, John Essex who translated Pierre Rameau's *Le Maître à danser*, Josias Priest who choreographed the dance scenes in Purcell's operas, and the dancing master Sir John Gallini later in the century, are all representatives of a lively and sincere concern with both social and theatrical dance. The great tragedy was that there was never any attempt at establishing an academy, nor were the Hanoverian monarchs (unlike the Stuarts who made possible the court masques) prepared to give the kind of patronage which supported ballet in every other European centre.

Thus dancing for the English meant the visits by 'the French dancers' or those Italian virtuosi whose appearances excited such admiration, or on occasion such scandal.

It is almost fortuitous that London became an important balletic centre during the heyday of the Romantic movement. Because Benjamin Lumley, manager of Her Majesty's Theatre, engaged Jules Perrot as ballet master for a period of six years (1843–1848), London benefited from the creative outpourings of this master choreographer. All the great stars made their seasonal visits and London took them to its heart, notably in the case of Fanny Cerrito. But despite Queen Victoria's affection for ballet, her concern went no deeper than that of an admiring spectator. A few English dancers attained some kind of fame – James Sullivan Frenchified his name to James Silvain and partnered Fanny Elssler, Carlotta Grisi and Lucile Grahn – and had Clara Webster not been a victim of terrible burns, which killed her at the age of twenty-three in 1844, she might have joined the galaxy of Romantic ballerinas. But Perrot's departure for St Petersburg, and the appearance of the Swedish nightingale Jenny Lind to win the London public over to opera, meant that ballet was to go into a decline. It was now to become an art of the music hall. Nevertheless, London continued to enjoy visits from many eminent dancers and ballet masters. From 1865 until 1914 at the Empire and Alhambra theatres in Leicester Square, ballet occupied a not inconsiderable place in entertainments which ranged from light opera to revue and musical comedy.

These entertainments inevitably relied upon brilliant star dancers as a focus for their often foolish components. Luminaries like Rita Sangalli, Pierina Legnani and Emma Palladino were featured in such works as *The Sylph of the Glen*, a fairy musical spectacle called *Rothomago*, and *Monte Cristo* at the Empire Theatre, in which last Adeline Genée (1878–1970) made her acclaimed London debut.

This enchantingly pretty Danish *danseuse* had but to set foot on the London stage to conquer it. Her dancing career, which began in Stettin in 1893, was supervised by her uncle, the ballet master Alexander Genée, and it brought her an unvarying round of triumphs won by her technical brilliance, her delicate charm and the irreproachable respectability of her life. At a time when dancing as a career was unthinkable for any young lady, Genée typified her fellow Dane Bournonville's belief that it was a career which deserved no opprobrium. Until her official retirement in 1914, Genée's triumphant world tours always brought her back to her adoring London public. When she left the stage after her marriage (to an Englishman, Frank Isitt), Genée devoted herself to the cause of dance teaching in Britain. At the invitation of Philip Richardson, founder-editor of *The Dancing Times*, who had been goaded into action by the ballet master Edouard Espinosa, a distinguished group of dancers representing the best of the various national schools of dancing was brought together to establish the first official teaching body in Britain. This was the Association of Operatic Dancing of Great Britain, founded in 1920 with Genée as its President, which in 1936 – largely thanks to Genée's longstanding friendship with Queen Mary – became the Royal Academy of Dancing.

Thus from the disparate activities of the commercial theatre there came at last an attempt to supervise and improve the standards of dance teaching at all levels in Britain. This came as a direct result of the impact of the Diaghilev Ballet in Britain. It was not until 1911, and the Coronation season for King George V and Queen Mary, that the Diaghilev Ballet Russe had visited London. Thereafter Britain was to become an important date in the touring year of the Ballet Russe. Equally significant is the fact that English dancers were to be engaged by Diaghilev. Like Anna Pavlova, whose company was reliant upon English girls, Diaghilev appreciated the qualities of English dancers and among his most valued artists were Lydia Sokolova (Hilda Munnings), Ninette de Valois (Edris Stannus), Alicia Markova (Marks), Anton Dolin (Patrick Healey Kaye), Ursula Moreton, Vera Savina (Clark). These were artists able to perpetuate Ballet Russe ideals after Diaghilev's death.

Another significant factor at this time was that Enrico Cecchetti, then in the last decade of his life, opened a school in London. To it flocked all the Diaghilev dancers when the company was in London, and also English dancers and teachers who recognized the exceptional merit of his teaching system. It was the English critic and ballet historian Cyril W. Beaumont who had the idea of codifying and preserving Cecchetti's

Adeline Genée as Swanilda in Coppélia *at the Empire Theatre, London, in 1906. The endearing prettiness that made Genée loved by a world-wide audience is self-evident. She was the first President of the Association of Operatic Dancing of Great Britain, which was formed in 1920 – forerunner of today's Royal Academy of Dancing.*

teaching method and to this end, with the assistance of Stanislas Idzikowski, a series of textbooks was produced and the Cecchetti Society was formed to preserve and perpetuate the Maestro's precepts. This association was incorporated into the Imperial Society of Teachers of Dancing in 1924. (The 'Imperial' had been founded twenty years previously but until this time had been primarily concerned with social dancing.) Today, both the Imperial and the Royal Academy of Dancing (RAD) perform an invaluable service in watching over standards of teaching, and their work is carried on and respected throughout the world.

The impetus towards the formation of a national ballet in Britain can be found during the 1920s for it was at this time that two women associated with Diaghilev were putting down creative roots in London. Marie Rambert was born in Poland in 1888. Inspired by Isadora Duncan she had started to work with Emile Jaques-Dalcroze, and from his school was engaged by Diaghilev to assist Nijinsky in the preparation of *Le Sacre du printemps*. Following her marriage to the English playwright Ashley Dukes in 1918, Rambert settled in London and it was there she

opened her school. Before long an essential quality was to emerge: Rambert was able to inspire creativity among her pupils. By the mid-1920s she was urging her students into both performing and choreographing: in 1926 her pupil Frederick Ashton made his first ballet. Occasional student performances led on to the formation in 1930 of a small permanent troupe which gave Sunday night performances at the Mercury Theatre in Notting Hill Gate. Rambert's students both made the ballets and performed in them. It would be impossible to over-stress the extraordinary achievement that this represented. On a shoe-string budget and a pocket-handkerchief stage, works were produced which remain to this day in various repertories, and are beacons in the history of British ballet.

Before an audience of regular devotees, who included the cream of British intellectual society at the time, the Ballet Club at the Mercury Theatre presented the early works of Frederick Ashton, Antony Tudor, Andrée Howard, Walter Gore; casts included Alicia Markova, Pearl Argyle, Maude Lloyd, Agnes de Mille, Peggy van Praagh, Hugh Laing and Harold Turner as well as Ashton, Tudor and Gore.

Maude Lloyd and Hugh Laing in Antony Tudor's Jardin aux lilas, *first produced by the Ballet Rambert at the Mercury Theatre, London, in 1936.* Jardin *is one of the seminal works of modern choreography: an intense psychological study – expressed in dancing of the greatest emotional control. Caroline, on the eve of an arranged marriage, tries to take a last farewell of the young man she loves at an evening party in a garden drenched with the scent of lilac. Maude Lloyd was one of the finest of Rambert artists and the ideal interpreter of Tudor's choreography. Hugh Laing was to be the poetic hero for many Tudor ballets in both Britain and America.*

At the same time that Marie Rambert was laying down her foundations another remarkable woman was making comparable preparations for the future of British ballet. This was Ninette de Valois. Born in County Wicklow in 1898, Edris Stannus made her stage debut at the Lyceum Theatre, London in 1914 under the stage name of Ninette de Valois. Her career thereafter found her as principal dancer with various companies and in 1923 she joined the Diaghilev Ballet. This was a deliberate move on her part to learn as much as possible about the working of a first-class ballet company, since her long term view encompassed the establishing of a native ballet tradition. To this end in 1926 she founded her own school in London. Her next move was to bring her into association with Lilian Baylis. One of the most extraordinary women in the whole history of the English theatre, Lilian Baylis (1874–1937) had by that time established the Old Vic Theatre in the Waterloo Road as 'the home of Shakespeare' and had also laid the foundations of an English National Opera. She was sympathetic to de Valois' aspirations for a comparable English national ballet and engaged her to work on small dance assignments in plays and operas and to use her dancers in short curtain-raising ballets.

The eventual aim was that when Baylis rebuilt and reopened Sadler's Wells Theatre in Islington, North London, a home would be provided for de Valois' school and for her small company of dancers. Thus in 1931 Ninette de Valois took up residence at the Wells. Albeit the company numbered but six dancers, with de Valois herself as director, choreographer and principal dancer, they had the unique good fortune of permanent contracts at a time when the commercial theatre could provide only run-of-the-show employment. This permanence, implicit in the school and in a home theatre offering continual work, lies at the heart of the Vic-Wells Ballet's future success.

A contributory factor to the recognition of these pioneer enterprises by Rambert and de Valois was the fact that the appalling void left by the demise of the Diaghilev company in 1929 had to be filled.

A group of ballet enthusiasts led by Philip Richardson, Arnold Haskell and the music critic and associate of Diaghilev, Edwin Evans, had formed The Camargo Society in 1930 with the aim of encouraging British dancers by giving occasional West End performances to demonstrate that Britain did possess not only dancers but choreographers. Between 1930 and 1933 sixteen native-made ballets were presented, in addition to classical revivals. (These last were illuminated by the presence of Olga Spessivtseva, Lydia Lopokova, Alicia Markova and Anton Dolin.) By the end of 1933 both the Rambert and de Valois companies were firmly established and were to inherit the works commissioned by the Camargo Society, which included such enduring and important pieces as Ashton's *Façade* and de Valois' *Job*.

The early years of the Vic-Wells Ballet, a name which derived from the fact that in the very first seasons the company danced both at the Old Vic and Sadler's Wells, marked a serious decision by de Valois to place her company in the mainstream of the classic academic dance. She acquired authentic stagings of several of the greatest repertory works of the Imperial Russian Ballet. Their production was made possible by de Valois' initiative in seeking out Nikolai Sergeyev (1876–1951) and inviting him to re-stage from his Stepanov notation *Coppélia* in 1933, and in 1934 *Giselle, Casse noisette (The Nutcracker)* and *Swan Lake*. The production of these ballets was also made possible because in Alicia Markova the company had acquired an authentic ballerina trained in the greatest traditions of the academic dance. It is worth recording that in these earliest years of British ballet the prestige of Markova's presence and her incomparable technique and artistry were vital both to the Rambert and de Valois enterprises. In 1935 Markova and Anton Dolin were invited to form a company, the Markova–Dolin Ballet, which for two years toured Britain with a classical and a modern repertory, thus building up a public enthusiasm for ballet which was to be important in developing popular taste for dance. In 1938 both artists returned to their Ballet Russe roots by joining the cosmopolitan Russian troupes who were the heirs to Diaghilev.

The other really important fact of the early Vic-Wells years was the arrival as permanent choreographer to the company in 1935 of Frederick Ashton (b. 1904). Between 1926 and 1935 Ashton had created no fewer than twenty dance works for Rambert. At the same time he had been

June Brae as Black Queen, Harold Turner as Red Knight, in Ninette de Valois' Checkmate, first produced by the Vic-Wells in 1937, an enduring work which reveals de Valois' fine theatrical gifts as a choreographer. The ballet was enhanced by outstanding music and design. The score was commissioned from Arthur Bliss, designs from E. McKnight Kauffer. A parable about the triumph of totalitarianism told in terms of a game of chess, it still offers challenges to today's dancers. No-one has yet rivalled Harold Turner in the arduous role of the Red Knight. Photograph by de Valois' brother, Gordon Anthony, the foremost ballet photographer of the 1930s.

choreographing for the Vic-Wells – *Les Rendez-vous*, made for Markova and Idzikowski, dates from 1933 – for the Camargo Society, and for the commercial theatre. In 1935 de Valois could offer him a classical company of already proven quality. Ashton's association with the Vic-Wells company thereafter was to be crucial in providing a repertory and in shaping a native classical dance style. De Valois continued to create ballets: her *Job*, *The Rake's Progress*, and *Checkmate* were cornerstones of the repertory and testimony to a vivid theatrical talent which demanded from her dancers a dramatic ability rooted in the traditions of the English theatre.

By the mid-thirties the identity of the Vic-Wells company had also benefited from the arrival of an Australian dancer, Robert Helpmann. Joining the company in 1933, he immediately made his presence felt as an exceptional theatrical personality.

Never a virtuoso dancer – a function fulfilled by the brilliant Harold Turner – Helpmann had a virtuoso stage presence equally at home in romantic and noble roles and in comedy, for which he had a unique and hilarious talent. When in 1935 Alicia Markova ended her association with the Vic-Wells it might have been thought

that the loss of this ballerina would prove irreplaceable. Certainly her absence was regretted by the Wells public, of whom she was the darling, but de Valois reapportioned her roles among the other dancers and selected one very young girl, Margot Fonteyn, to inherit some of her classical repertory.

With the season of 1935–36 future developments could be seen. De Valois had Frederick Ashton as her choreographer plus her own undoubted gifts as a ballet-master; she had a school from which to feed her fledgling company; an embryonic ballerina in Fonteyn (b. 1919), with Helpmann (b. 1909) as a vitally important partner; her company had a sound classical basis and Constant Lambert (1905–1951) was musical director and artistic conscience.

Lambert had made a precocious beginning in British music, when at only twenty years old he was commissioned by Diaghilev to produce a score for *Roméo et Juliette*. With hindsight, this seemed to be a decisive factor in Lambert's life. A composer of rare gifts and a conductor no less richly endowed, Lambert sacrificed much of his own career in the service of British ballet. His association with the Vic-Wells enterprises until his death gave the company the inestimable advantage of the highest musical standards and the benefit of Lambert's wide ranging cultural understanding. No other ballet company has enjoyed from its beginnings an advisor with so acute a musical intelligence or one so aware of the essential needs of ballet in regard to music. In a tribute to Lambert, Ninette de Valois wrote 'I do not believe that any ballet company can have roots or a policy of lasting value, or hold the prolonged interest of the public, if it lacks first class musical leadership.' It is these qualities which Lambert so generously gave to the Wells.

Today the musicality associated with English dancers is as much a tribute to Lambert's influence as the notable list of scores which he composed, arranged or selected for Britain's national company. His untimely death was the greatest loss the company had suffered.

In 1939 a culmination of eight years' work came with the staging of *The Sleeping Princess*, which offered an authentic choreographic text revived by Sergeyev, hideous sets and costumes by Nadia Benois, immaculate musical performance under Lambert, and Fonteyn and Helpmann leading a young company in performances which enraptured audiences.

The Sleeping Princess marked the end of an era. The quiet years in Islington were to cease by the autumn when war was declared. For the next six years British ballet took to the roads, to the canteens and the factories, as the Sadler's Wells Ballet. It nearly became a prisoner of war in May 1940 while on a British Council tour in Holland when the Germans invaded. The company had to flee, leaving behind scenery, costumes and scores. Both the Sadler's Wells and the Rambert companies put themselves on a wartime footing

The apotheosis of The Sleeping Beauty *as staged by the Sadler's Wells Ballet at the Royal Opera House, Covent Garden, in 1946 with designs by Oliver Messel. Margot Fonteyn and Robert Helpmann are seen as Aurora and her Prince. This image, more than any other, typifies the emergence of the Sadler's Wells Ballet as a great national and international company.*

and various other new companies were initiated to satisfy an exceptional public demand for dance. At a time of bombings, 'black out', rationing and call-up, the public sought escape in the magical world of ballet and a nation-wide public enthusiasm was built up which was to become an enduring factor of British popular taste.

By 1946 both Rambert and the Sadler's Wells Ballets were to find new opportunities. After several successful London seasons, which featured the choreography of Andrée Howard and Walter Gore and showed the strength of the company that included Sally Gilmour, Joyce Graeme and Walter Gore (all of whom shone in an epoch-making production of *Giselle*), the Ballet Rambert set out for Australia. Instead of the scheduled six-week visit the tour lasted a triumphant eighteen months. But on the company's return to London the loss of dancers and an absence of future engagements were to mark a bleak period throughout the 1950s. The departure of Walter Gore and his wife Paula Hinton, an outstanding dramatic ballerina, and the need to offer the provincial audiences a classical repertory very unlike the sophisticated and stylish productions that were so traditionally Rambert, resulted in financial and artistic crises. These were in part alleviated by the presentation of a charming *La Sylphide* in 1960, which revealed Lucette Aldous as the first and most delightful native sylph, and the emergence of Norman Morrice as a new and essentially Rambertian choreographer.

But whatever the aspirations and the illustrious credentials of the company, the financial problems that beset British ballet during the 1960s were to take their toll. In 1966 the company seemed

threatened with extinction. At this moment Norman Morrice made the bold decision to re-form the company and with Marie Rambert he engineered a totally new image for the troupe. Inspired partly by Nederlands Dans Theater's success as a modern ensemble dedicated to a high rate of creativity, Morrice fined down the company to twenty dancers and made the important decision to invite Glen Tetley to help establish the new repertory. Within five years the new Ballet Rambert had regained much lost prestige and had returned to its first essential image as a highly creative group of dancers. In Christopher Bruce it had found a star performer who was also a gifted choreographer. When Morrice finally gave up direction of the company in 1974 another member of the ensemble, John Chesworth, took over the reins of leadership, with Bruce as his associate.

The end of the war was also to mark the end of a phase in the existence of the Sadler's Wells Ballet. Ninette de Valois was astonished to receive an invitation to reopen the Royal Opera House, Covent Garden, as a theatre after its wartime service as a dance hall. Apparently nothing daunted, she arranged for *The Sleeping Princess* to be re-dressed (and renamed *The Sleeping Beauty*) and on the night of 20 February 1946 at seven o'clock the curtains of the Royal Opera House parted to reveal Oliver Messel's beautifully imaginative designs and an enlarged company led by Fonteyn and Helpmann; the irreplaceable Constant Lambert was in charge of the Tchaikovsky score. For a month thereafter *The Beauty* played to packed houses and it is a tribute to de Valois' resources that she could provide no fewer

Le Corsaire with Margot
Fonteyn and Rudolf
Nureyev (1962). *In this*
pas de deux, *which
survives from a famous
nineteenth-century ballet
of the same name,
Nureyev found a
wonderful vehicle for his
tigerish energy and grace.
In this, as in everything
else she danced with
Nureyev, Fonteyn
responded to a challenge
which led to an
extraordinary
prolongation of her
already illustrious career.*
Le Corsaire *was first
performed in 1837; Petipa
interpolated this* Pas
d'Esclave *in 1858.*

than four Auroras and many changes of cast.
Thereafter the company's own repertory was
brought into performance. Of two new ballets
staged, *Adam Zero* was choreographed by Robert
Helpmann who had sustained the company both
as a dancer and choreographer throughout the
wartime years; the other was *Symphonic Variations* by Ashton, which has been recognized as
the summation of the English style of classic
dance at this time.

Although translated into glory at the Royal
Opera House, de Valois did not desert Sadler's

Wells. In April 1946 a new young company
comprising students, recruits from the then Empire
and a few senior artists came into being as the
Sadler's Wells Theatre Ballet. It was to serve as a
nursery for talent both choreographic and interpretative and over the next decades it produced
many of the influential figures who transferred to
the senior company at the Opera House. Nursed
by Ursula Moreton and Peggy van Praagh,
choreographers like John Cranko and Kenneth
MacMillan, dancers like Nadia Nerina, David
Blair, Svetlana Beriosova and Maryon Lane were

Robert Helpmann and Frederick Ashton as the Ugly Sisters in Ashton's staging of Cinderella, *to the Prokofiev score, first produced by the Sadler's Wells Ballet, Covent Garden, in 1948.*
In making his version of the ballet, Ashton turned to the English pantomime tradition for some of the characters, notably by having the Ugly Sisters played as travesty roles. Helpmann was cast as the bossier sister, eager to grab every good thing in sight; Ashton was the more timorous, sympathetic of the two. Over the years these interpretations were embroidered and embellished to marvellous effect by these two masters of comedy.

to win their early laurels in seasons at the Wells and on tour. In 1955 the company became exclusively a touring group under the directorate of John Field, developing its own stars in Doreen Wells, David Wall, Elizabeth Anderton and Brenda Last, and a year later the Sadler's Wells Ballet was awarded royal status by Royal Charter. Various indecisions about the company's identity resulted from the gradual decline in touring conditions during the 1960s and early 1970s. With a reaffirmed link with its home theatre in 1977 and under the direction of Peter Wright the Sadler's Wells Royal Ballet has performed a valuable service as a touring branch of the Royal Ballet.

The post-war years at Covent Garden found the Sadler's Wells Ballet putting down its roots in its new home and developing and extending its repertory to suit its new responsibilities. The late 1940s were marked by two important events: the creation of Ashton's *Cinderella* in 1948 and the company's first visit to the United States in 1949. With *Cinderella*, Ashton accepted the need to continue the company's classic traditions with a native crop of big ballets. The British public had now come to accept the idea of the full-length ballet as being basic to the tradition of classic dancing. Under this banner, International Ballet, a company directed by Mona Inglesby, toured extensively from 1941 until 1953, satisfying the popular appetite for Tchaikovsky ballets. London Festival Ballet, originally founded as a showcase to present the great stars Markova and Dolin in 1950, continued this classic policy, together with sensitive re-stagings of the Fokine ballets. But as the Royal Ballet realized, the creation of a native

tradition of full evening works was inevitable, and after the success of *Cinderella* Ashton was to produce *Sylvia* in 1952 and *Ondine* in 1958, all of which celebrated his long-term artistic collaboration with Margot Fonteyn, and in 1960 and 1961 two two-act ballets, *La Fille mal gardée* and *Les Deux pigeons*, showed him responding to the talents of the next generation of Royal Ballet dancers – Nadia Nerina and David Blair, Lynn Seymour and Christopher Gable.

Cinderella was one of the contributory factors to the triumph of the Sadler's Wells Ballet during its first season at the old Metropolitan Opera House, New York in 1949. The English company opened on 9 October with *The Sleeping Beauty* and New York was at its feet. Uncompromisingly, de Valois had insisted on her company being seen as an ensemble without guests, and by the second interval she had been proved right. When Constant Lambert entered the orchestra pit he received a hero's welcome; Beryl Grey's Lilac Fairy was cheered to the echo; but the revelation was Fonteyn. Suddenly America was aware that the Sadler's Wells Ballet was a magnificent classical troupe headed by a great ballerina and backed by other ballerinas – Pamela May, Moira Shearer, Violetta Elvin, Beryl Grey – who could sustain the traditional masterpieces of the repertory. Thereafter the company was taken to the heart of the American nation. So long as touring from coast to coast was financially viable, the company continued touring.

The financial importance of this success was of considerable value to the Royal Opera House and for several years the transcontinental tours of the Sadler's Wells Ballet became a vital source of dollars as well as of national prestige in the difficult post-war years.

Thus the company grew up and was of recognized international stature. The school continued to feed the company with soundly trained dancers and became a magnet for dancers from the Commonwealth. It is important to stress the contribution made by dancers from South Africa, Rhodesia, Australia, New Zealand and Canada. John Cranko, Nadia Nerina, David Poole, Alexander Grant, Rowena Jackson, Elaine Fifield, Merle Park, Monica Mason and many more, have been of inestimable value to the Royal Ballet in both its companies – the continuation of this link despite the emergence of fine companies in these Commonwealth lands seems to us an essential part of the Royal Ballet's traditions.

It was during the late 1940s and the 1950s that the repertory was enhanced by not only Ashton's creativity, but with the emergence of another generation of 'Royal' choreography from John Cranko and Kenneth MacMillan, and with major revivals from the twentieth-century repertory – *The Firebird*, *Petrushka*, and works by Massine and Balanchine. John Cranko was to show himself an immensely gifted creator, and his work at this time culminated in his first three-act ballet *The Prince of the Pagodas* in 1957, for which

Benjamin Britten provided his only ballet score. But at the end of the decade Cranko decided to seek the larger opportunities of running his own company, and his arrival in Stuttgart in 1961, and the twelve years he spent there before his untimely death, were to bring the Stuttgart Ballet to international renown.

In the mid 1950s Kenneth MacMillan made his choreographic debuts with the Sadler's Wells Theatre Ballet. With Cranko and MacMillan the company proved itself a nursery of choreographic ability, and both men were to learn there a craft which was to serve them later on in the grander surroundings of Covent Garden.

The emergence of these two remarkable talents owed everything to the encouragement and guidance of Ninette de Valois. De Valois had seen the culmination of her efforts in the recognition offered the company by Queen Elizabeth in 1956 when the national importance of the troupe had been recognized by the title The Royal Ballet. Four years later de Valois could, with a certain daring, lead her company to perform in Leningrad and Moscow, taking back to that citadel of the classic dance this young and healthy offshoot of Russian tradition. That the company's triumph there was so overwhelming must have been a wonderful

Christopher Gable as The Boy and Lynn Seymour as The Girl in The Invitation *(above) choreographed by Kenneth MacMillan for the Royal Ballet's touring section in 1960. This tragic and intense ballet brought the first real recognition of Lynn Seymour's gifts. Gable, a most gifted young dancer, left the ballet stage in 1967 to become a successful actor.*

Monica Mason as the Chosen Virgin in the Rite of Spring *as staged by Kenneth MacMillan for the Royal Ballet in 1962. With outstanding designs by Sydney Nolan, this version turned* The Rite *into a compelling, timeless tribal ceremony. In the central role, Monica Mason gave a performance of greatness. (For a view of the first version to Stravinsky's score,* Le Sacre du printemps, *see page 171.)*

accolade for everything that de Valois and her associates had achieved. With characteristic discretion and modesty, de Valois announced her retirement as director in 1963. At that moment she could see not only the Royal Ballet and its junior company flourishing, but also the influence of her enterprise throughout the world. In Canada, a National Ballet had sprung up, directly inspired by the Sadler's Wells visit to Toronto in 1949 and guided thereafter very much in the Royal Ballet's image by a former member of the company, Celia Franca. In Australia another classic national company had been started from the embers of a previous Russian-inspired troupe, the Borovansky Ballet, which was to be directed by Peggy van Praagh (also an associate of de Valois) and by Robert Helpmann (for many years a mainstay of the Sadler's Wells company). Elsewhere throughout the world the influence of the Royal Ballet and its school could be seen. Many of the one-time Commonwealth members of the company returned to their homelands to initiate companies and schools – in Australia and New Zealand, in South Africa and Rhodesia.

The obvious and proper successor to Ninette de Valois was Frederick Ashton, for his massive contribution to the repertory, his vital part in shaping the English style of classic dancing in its precision, lyricism and musicality, had helped bring the Royal Ballet to the pinnacle on which it stood. For the most part external influences had been avoided. There had been occasional illustrious guests – Léonide Massine, Alexandra Danilova and Frederic Franklin from the world of the Ballet Russe; Alicia Markova and Anton Dolin returning to the company whose early years they had so greatly helped. Yvette Chauviré and Erik Bruhn were also among these honoured guests – but the visit of the Bolshoy Ballet to Covent Garden in 1956 and the revelation of the Kirov in 1961 were inevitably to indicate broader horizons in dance. It was the Kirov which indirectly was to influence the early 1960s with the Royal Ballet when Rudolf Nureyev, having left the Kirov Ballet, found a home and a partner in the Royal Ballet and Margot Fonteyn. Nureyev brought with him a new image of male dancing which disturbed and eventually benefited the younger dancers with whom he came in contact. Notably, too, he was to give the Royal Ballet a staging of the Kingdom of Shades scene from *La Bayadère* in which the *corps de ballet* gradually learned to emulate Kirov unity of style and breadth of movement. Nureyev's presence also was to give Margot Fonteyn a new challenge, in a partnership which extended her dancing life and was to become a most acclaimed popular partnership in ballet.

The Royal Ballet, though, was still relying upon its first generation, and it was during the 1960s that there most clearly emerged the new flowering of talent in such dancers as Antoinette Sibley, Merle Park, Lynn Seymour, Doreen Wells, Anthony Dowell and David Wall. These young artists and their colleagues became the darlings of audiences in London and, in the case of Wells and Wall, adored figures throughout the country.

At the same time Kenneth MacMillan emerged very strongly as a choreographer, with Lynn Seymour as his Muse. With *Le Baiser de la fée* in 1960 and *The Invitation* in 1961 (for the touring company) – in both of which Seymour was confirmed as a great dancer – MacMillan entered upon an extraordinary period of creativity. It culminated in 1965 with his staging of Prokofiev's *Romeo and Juliet* at Covent Garden, inspired by Lynn Seymour and Christopher Gable. In *Das Lied von der Erde*, mounted for the Stuttgart Ballet in the same year, MacMillan confirmed his eminence as a choreographer. In the following year, with a desire to try his wings as a director, he accepted an invitation to run the ballet of the Deutsche Oper in West Berlin, a position he was to hold for three years until recalled to London.

Directorial responsibilities curtailed Ashton's output of new ballets, but he took the momentous decision to invite Bronislava Nijinska, with whom he had worked at the beginning of his career and whom he revered, to stage for the Royal Ballet her two early masterpieces, *Les Biches* and *Les Noces*. In 1970 a complete change was to be observed in the Royal Ballet and at the Royal Opera House,

Peter Schaufuss (right) in Etudes (1952) by Harald Lander, as staged by London Festival Ballet in 1960. This is an exuberant display piece which brings to the stage some of the ardours of dancers' daily class. Schaufuss, like several other Danish stars, has made his career largely away from the Royal Danish Ballet in Copenhagen. He is an outstanding danseur, and has produced a much-acclaimed version of Bournonville's La Sylphide for Festival Ballet in 1979.

Alicia Markova (left) in the second act of Giselle *(first performed in 1841). One of the central figures in Western ballet, Markova was not only a great ballerina but a pioneer whose work on both sides of the Atlantic has done much to further the cause of ballet.*
She was a vital contributor to the early days of British ballet, as ballerina at the Ballet Club, with the Vic-Wells Ballet and then the Markova–Dolin Ballet, establishing the highest standards of artistry in the classical and modern repertory. For ten years she worked in Europe and America, with the Ballet Russe de Monte Carlo and with American Ballet Theatre. In 1950 she and Anton Dolin founded Festival Ballet.
Since her retirement in 1962, Markova has lectured, taught and produced throughout the world. Her three Masterclasses on BBC *Television in 1980 proved highly popular.*

Covent Garden. Sir David Webster who had guided the rebirth of the Royal Opera House so successfully from 1946 onwards retired, to be succeeded by his assistant John Tooley, and Frederick Ashton retired and was succeeded by Kenneth MacMillan. The Royal Ballet's touring company was disbanded and the man who had so successfully guided its progress, John Field, became a joint director of the Royal Ballet before resigning to direct the ballet at La Scala, Milan and later to become, first, Director of the Royal Academy of Dancing, and then of the London Festival Ballet.

The touring company was initially re-formed as a small ensemble dedicated to the production of new works and to the presentation of the Royal Ballet's own repertory. But the exigencies of the regional public soon forced the company into reverting to a more conventional repertory. Under the direction of Peter Wright, such works as *Giselle* and *Coppélia* were restored to the repertory but a creative identity was also maintained.

MacMillan directed the Covent Garden company for seven years. During that time he produced two more full-length works, *Anastasia* and *Manon*, and a considerable output of shorter pieces. He also invited contributions from such choreographers as Balanchine, Robbins, Tetley, van Manen and John Neumeier. Natalia Makarova and Mikhail Baryshnikov began a happy association with the company, but the demands of directing proved inhibiting to MacMillan's prime role as creator. In 1977 he decided to resign as director and was succeeded by Norman Morrice. MacMillan remained as chief choreographer and

in 1978 presented the company with the sensationally successful *Mayerling* in which David Wall was to be admired in the most taxing male role ever created, that of Crown Prince Rudolf.

The British public's – the world public's – insatiable appetite for the classics of the repertory has done much to sustain London Festival Ballet. In its first years under Dr Julian Braunsweg the company had revived some of the Ballet Russe material in which Anton Dolin and Alicia Markova had so delighted the world. As artistic director, Dolin invited such stars of the Ballet Russe as Danilova, Toumanova, Slavenska, Riabouchinska and Massine as examples for his young company. During the 1950s and 1960s, with no subsidy, and relying upon the ingenuities of Braunsweg as a financial juggler and the heartwarming response that the public gave to the company, Festival Ballet travelled extensively and maintained a faithful following with a middle-brow audience. The company benefited immensely from the dancing of John Gilpin, a stellar figure, and whatever the uncertainties of the times the company never let its public down. But financial problems which also affected the Ballet Rambert brought the company to its knees. Under new management it was rescued in 1966 and in 1968 Beryl Grey became artistic director of the company for eleven years. During this period the company continued its constant travels but has also preserved its faithful London following through regular seasons on the South Bank and in the West End.

Because ballet depends upon Government financial support in Britain as elsewhere in Europe it must reflect, however slightly, policy decisions about the need to encourage regionalism. In France, André Malraux's great plan for the decentralization of the arts has brought into being a chain of Maisons de la Culture across the country. In Britain, with Arts Council encouragement, two regional companies have been brought into existence: Scottish Ballet and Northern Ballet Theatre. The concept of regional ballet was entirely due to the vision and persistence of Elizabeth West who, from 1957 until her tragic death in an accident in 1962, battled to establish a local company in Bristol in the west of England. Western Theatre Ballet grew from her determination and that of her co-director and choreographer (and subsequent successor as artistic director of the company), Peter Darrell. It was Darrell who from the first gave the company its artistic identity as a troupe concerned with contemporary themes. For twelve years the company endured much hardship before it established itself with its public. During this time Darrell encouraged a diversification of the repertory, and public affection brought its reward in 1969 when the company was transferred by the Arts Council to Glasgow and transformed into the Scottish Ballet. During the next decade Darrell skilfully deployed the resources of this comparatively small company, taking ballet to every corner of Scotland and also continuing a policy of offering both standard classics and new and adventurous creations. The company has admirable Bournonville stagings as well as full-length works made by Darrell himself.

As already observed, influence of one-time members of the Royal Ballet working in former or present Commonwealth countries has been strong. The large classical companies which have grown up in Canada, Australia and South Africa reflect variously the image of the Royal Ballet itself, in their belief in the full-length classical repertory and in a continuing traditional link with what must seem the parent organization. Despite the excellent work done by the Royal Winnipeg Ballet and Les Grands Ballets Canadiens it must seem that the National Ballet of Canada and its school are the most significant examples of the de Valois ideal.

Similarly, the Australian Ballet and its school have successfully transplanted the de Valois method. Here, as in Canada and South Africa, the seed has developed into a different plant but essentially true to its original stock.

FRANCE

The Third Republic which emerged from the disasters of the Franco-Prussian War and the Commune was to mark a period of decadence in French ballet. French dancing was to feel the influence of the Italian school with the arrival of such exceptional figures as Rita Sangalli, and Rosita Mauri – who was to star at the Opéra for twenty years and then become a professor – and supremely, Carlotta Zambelli who from 1898 until her retirement in 1930 was principal ballerina, and thereafter a teacher until 1955. This Italian influence was in part to obliterate the French style of dancing, replacing its gentler manner with something more brilliant. And although ballet was maintained at the Opéra it was hardly an art of much authority or distinction, albeit such works as *Sylvia* (1876), *La Korrigane* (1880), *Les Deux pigeons* (1886), and *La Maladetta* (1893) were successful with the Paris public.

It was the arrival of the Ballet Russe in 1909 which was to show Paris how dated and stale were the conventional affectations of the dance in the Opéra. During the Diaghilev period the director Jacques Rouché engaged Olga Spessivt-seva to appear in *Giselle* and such French dancers as Suzanne Lorcia, Camille Bos and Serge Peretti were to win distinction. But it was the engagement of Serge Lifar as principal dancer and choreographer in 1929 following the death of Diaghilev that was eventually to bring the Opéra back to life and into the mainstream of European ballet. Lifar's talent as a dancer, his personal beauty and magnetism, and his strong views on choreography, were for a period of more than a quarter of a century to bring fame to the Opéra and, more importantly, to bring back an enthusiastic and fashionable audience. In a long sequence

of ballets which used distinguished composers and designers, Lifar repeated the Diaghilev formula in his own choreographic manner. During the war years it was Lifar who managed to maintain performances at the Opéra even during the darkest days of the Occupation. For a brief period public ingratitude banished him at the war's end, but he returned in triumph in 1948 and for a further ten years Lifar was to remain an essential figure in the ballet.

During the whole Lifar period, standards of dancing at the Opéra were raised. Lifar invited great dancers to appear – notably Olga Spessivt-seva – and he showed off a native tradition of fine schooling with such exceptional *danseuses* as Solange Schwartz, Yvette Chauviré, Lycette Darsonval, Nina Vyroubova, Michel Renault, Alexandre Kalioujny and Youly Algaroff. During the Lifar regime the school at the Paris Opéra, already two centuries old, developed the traditions of French dance through the classes of the Italian ballerinas like Zambelli and such professors as Albert Aveline and Gustav Ricaux. It was from the classes of these exceptional teachers and their successors that the generations of fine artists who have shone at the Opéra and throughout the world during the past decades were to emerge.

With the final departure of Lifar in 1958 it

Serge Lifar in his own Les Créatures de Prométhée *(above), the first ballet which he staged at the start of his nearly thirty-year reign at the Paris Opéra. Lifar's great physical beauty and the allure of his presence is everywhere apparent in this photograph, taken at the time of the ballet's première in 1929.*

must seem that the ballet at the Paris Opéra entered upon a period of indecision. Without a strong native choreographer the various directors who have assumed responsibility for the company have invited many celebrated creators as guests – from Balanchine to Grigorovich, from Cunningham to Béjart – but although there have been good evenings the company itself lacks the sharpness and strength of identity which it knew during the Lifar years. There are ranks of vastly talented dancers; there is a wide-ranging and often interesting repertory. What has been missing is a sense of definite purpose and progress for this oldest and most illustrious of Europe's ballet companies.

The generation of dancers who emerged from the school of the Paris Opéra at the end of the war inevitably reflected something of the aspirations and sense of freedom of a France liberated after the years of Occupation. With Roland Petit as their figurehead and principal choreographer, the young dancers gave recitals in 1944 which attracted much favourable attention, and led in due time to the formation of Les Ballets des Champs Elysées in October 1945. Boris Kochno, Cocteau and Bérard were most eminent patrons and advisers, and the young company during its short life achieved productions nearer than anything else to the Diaghilev ideal. *Les Forains,* with its design by Bérard and haunting score by Sauguet, will for ever be associated with the identity of this adorable company. Other works like *Les Amours de Jupiter, Le Rendez-vous, Le Jeune homme et la mort,* remain for those people who saw them unforgettable, magical and beautiful experiences.

Roland Petit himself, and his wife Renée (Zizi) Jeanmaire, the phenomenal Jean Babilée (in whom technique and dramatic skill marvellously combined) and his wife Natalie Philippart, Janine Charrat as dancer and choreographer, Irène Skorik and Serge Perrault, Nina Vyroubova, were but some of the artists who made their names in this *ambiance.* Petit left in January 1948 to form his own Ballets de Paris and his career thereafter has shown him as the most inventive as well as the best-known figure in French ballet. In the cinema and in music hall as well as on the ballet stage, Petit's wonderful sense of theatre and his impeccable feeling for style have been a recurrent source of excitement. Since 1972 Petit has been a director of the Ballet de Marseille, which company he has made an international success. He has throughout his career always collaborated with the finest and most fashionable designers – Max Ernst, Carzou, Bernard Buffet, Christian Dior, Paul Delvaux, Yves St Laurent, Ezio Frigerio among them – and his creativity has ranged from new and delightful versions of *Coppélia* and *Casse noisette* to full-length ballets like *Cyrano de Bergerac* and *Notre Dame de Paris.*

He also remains an extraordinary theatrical personality in performance. His Dr Coppélius is a great and stylish portrayal.

At the time the Ballets des Champs Elysées started at the war's end another much larger and international troupe emerged. This was Le Grand Ballet du Marquis de Cuevas, which combined forces from an American enterprise, Ballet International, and the short-lived Nouveau Ballet de Monte Carlo which Lifar had set up on his dismissal from the Paris Opéra in 1945.

The resultant troupe was that rare phenomenon, an entirely personal company, reflecting the tastes and aspirations of the Chilean-born Marquis and the financial support offered by his wife, a grand-daughter of John D. Rockefeller. Until 1962 the company toured internationally with a repertory which encompassed classical stagings and interesting creations from such choreographers as Nijinska, Lichine, Massine, Taras, Dollar, Ricarda, and Skibine. Its principal ballerina was Rosella Hightower, and among its other stars were Vyroubova, Marjorie Tallchief and George Skibine, Serge Golovine, André Eglevsky, Toumanova, and Skouratoff. The de Cuevas ballet reflected very much, despite its international air, an essentially French manner, and

Renée – (known and adored as Zizi) Jeanmaire (above) in La Croqueuse de diamants *(The Diamond-Cruncher – 1950), a ballet by her husband, Roland Petit, in which she danced and sang. She is a true theatrical star, at home in music hall, revue, and in films, and a dance actress of thrilling presence.*

Nathalie Phillipart as Death, Jean Babilée as The Young Man (left) in Roland Petit's Le Jeune homme et la mort, *first performed by the Ballets des Champs Elysées in 1946. Based on an idea by Jean Cocteau, it created a sensation when first performed. Danced to a Bach passacaglia, it featured an astounding and magisterial performance by Babilée, a dancer of unquestioned greatness.*

The Triumphs of
Petrarch *was first staged
by Maurice Béjart for his
Ballet du XXème Siècle
to perform in the Boboli
Gardens in Florence in
1974.*
*Inspired by the themes of
Petrarch's poetic* Trionfi,
*the ballet showed Béjart
creating for large
spaces and large audiences
on large themes – which
seems his favoured
creative procedure.*

after the death of the Marquis in 1961 the company
was maintained for a year by his nephew
Raimundo de Larrain, whose decoration of the
stagings of *The Sleeping Beauty* and *Cinderella*
was lavishly attuned to French decorators' taste.

An entirely different aspect of French taste can
be seen in the decade of the Ballet-Théâtre Contemporain. Originated in the Maison de la
Culture at Amiens in 1968, it was directed by Jean
Albert Cartier. Cartier insisted on new creations
for this small but adventurous group and his taste
in design resulted from his years as a distinguished
art critic. Every ballet presented by the company
was illuminated by the collaboration of fine
painters as well as designers. Alexander Calder,
Sonia Delaunay and Jesus Raphael Soto were but
three of an exceptional galaxy of decorators.

For ten years the company toured the world, a
travelling exhibition – like Diaghilev's Ballet
Russe – of notable design. In 1978 the company
was reformed as the Ballet Théâtre Français de
Nancy, finding a new home in that city where,
again under Cartier, the troupe sought to include
masterworks of twentieth-century choreography
in addition to its own creations.

Elsewhere in France the traditional network of
opera houses across the country supports dance
companies who take a rather lesser part in the
annual scheme of lyric performances. Among the
more important are the Ballet de l'Opéra de Lyon
and Ballet de l'Opéra du Rhin, while other smaller
troupes throughout France provide both classic
and modern offerings.

BELGIUM

A dominant figure in French ballet is paradoxically
to be found in Brussels. Maurice Béjart (b. 1927)
began his career as a soloist with various classical
companies. During the 1950s he directed his own
company, but it was not until 1959 when he staged
his version of *The Rite of Spring* at the Théâtre
Royale de la Monnaie in Brussels that he found
the ideal base for his operations. He was invited
to direct a company based in Brussels which took
the title of Le Ballet du XXème Siècle. Inspired by
a total dedication to the creative ideals of their
choreographer, the dancers of the Ballet du
XXème Siècle form a remarkable expressive
instrument for the ideas, philosophies and creative
urge of Béjart. He speaks supremely to the young;
in a series of massive spectacles, total theatre
pieces in which dance predominates and which
he presents in opera-house surroundings, but more
readily in sports stadia, tents, large halls or giant
open-air arenas throughout the world, Béjart has
provided a kind of philosophy of the dance which
is very attractive to a youthful audience intolerant
of the supposed stuffiness and bourgeois respectability associated with the traditional opera house
company. No score, no theme is too ambitious or
too sacred for Béjart to attempt. He has produced
realizations of Beethoven's *Ninth Symphony* and
Berlioz' *Damnation of Faust*; he has created full-
evening works about Nijinsky and reworkings of
Diaghilev ballets (among them his early *Rite of*

Spring and later *The Firebird*); he has turned his attentions to Petrarch and Molière, Baudelaire and Heliogabalus. In everything the dedication of Béjart's artists is exemplary. Public response ranges from the immense enthusiasm with which he is greeted everywhere in Continental Europe to the sniping of critics in London and New York. What is inescapable is that Béjart is a phenomenon, and impossible to ignore. At a time when ballet had alienated many of the younger generation in Europe, Béjart provided them with a diet of pseudo-philosophical works and the excitements of a lively if undisciplined theatrical intelligence which have won him a devoted following. No small part of his success is due to the prowess of his company, whose male contingent in particular has ever been a trump card in evenings of Béjart choreography.

Two other companies serve Belgium. The northern Flemish section has the Royal Ballet of Flanders while Charleroi supports the Royal Ballet de Wallonie. With sound schools they provide an international repertory of classics and modern works.

HOLLAND

Ballet in Holland today is dominated by two companies, the Nederlands Dans Theater and Het National Ballet (the Dutch National Ballet). The senior of these two, the Dutch National Ballet, emerged in 1961 from the amalgamation of two earlier companies and was directed from its inception by Sonia Gaskell. The company depended upon the standard international repertory for some time, but Gaskell's encouragement of native choreographic talent produced several interesting young creators, among whom the most notable has been Rudi van Dantzig. The Nederlands Dans Theater had been created as a breakaway in 1959 from the then Het National Ballet and it was a company dedicated from its inception to prodigious creativity (producing at one time ten new ballets every year) and a dance language which combined classical and modern disciplines. It also provided an outlet for American choreographers – its first leader was Benjamin Harkarvy who was soon joined by the Dutch choreographer Hans van Manen. A vital contribution was to come early on from Glen Tetley, and with the participation of Tetley and van Manen the adventurous identity of the company emerged very clearly during the 1960s.

The influence of van Manen and of a designer–dancer Toer van Schayk was also to leave its mark on the Dutch National Ballet in the 1960s. By 1973 van Manen and van Schayk had joined van Dantzig in running this latter company. At this time The Nederlands Dans Theater knew some awkward years when it seemed over-eager to show the works of American *avant-garde* choreographers like Louis Falco and Jennifer

Muller. With the arrival of the Czech dancer and choreographer Jiří Kylián from Stuttgart in 1975, the Nederlands Dans Theater returned to its earlier image. Both Dutch companies are markedly productive. In addition to sustaining an extensive touring schedule which takes them round the world, they continue creating modern works of undoubted relevance to contemporary themes.

GERMANY

Like ballet in Holland, the ballet scene in Germany is essentially a post-war creation. In the early years of this century Germany had been the home of a modern dance idiom typified by the works of Mary Wigman and Harald Kreutzberg. It reflected the unease of German society in the years following the First World War. The best-known choreographer in this style was Kurt Jooss whose efforts in Essen and later in England and America (where he took refuge from Nazi persecution of the Jews) produced a series of modern dance works which were influential in their time. The survival of *The Green Table,* created in 1932, bears testimony to his gift for capturing the spirit of the age.

After the war there was a conscious attempt to implant classical ballet in Germany. The presence of such choreographers as Walter Gore, Alan Carter, Nicholas Beriozoff and Tatiana Gsovsky was to encourage the German audience in accepting ballet in the various opera houses of each of the German states. It was, however, the success of John Cranko in Stuttgart, where he became director of ballet in 1961, that marks the true renaissance of ballet in West Germany. Cranko built up his company very much on the lines of the Royal Ballet.

He was enormously helped by the emergence of a group of exceptional dancers whom he encouraged and whose talents he developed. With Marcia Haydée as his ballerina, with Ray Barra, Richard Cragun and Egon Madsen, and with the excellent school he instituted, which was in its time to produce yet more exceptional dancers – notably Birgit Keil – Cranko achieved the seemingly impossible by creating a strong and healthy company and school within a decade. It was an extraordinary success. Cranko's own dedication to his company and the love he inspired among his artists were to result in an ensemble which early won international acclaim. In classic stagings, in his own prolific output of full-length and one-act ballets, Cranko gave the Stuttgart Ballet foundations and a sense of purpose which survived the appalling shock of his premature death. After a short period in which Glen Tetley directed the company, Marcia Haydée contrived to fulfil the dual role of director and star ballerina – thanks to a sound organization and the unwavering loyalty of her dancers and her public to the ideals of the Stuttgart Ballet as an entity. Much new creativity has been encouraged through 'choreographic evenings' and perhaps the unique distinction of the company is its sense of collective effort dedicated to the single end of a corporate identity.

The company has also been most successful in presenting ballets by Cranko's friend and contemporary, Kenneth MacMillan. Stuttgart's belief in MacMillan when other companies seemed timorous in the face of his choice of music gave them the distinction of creating *Song of the Earth* in 1965 and *Requiem* in 1976 to music by Mahler and Fauré respectively.

One of Stuttgart's great merits lies in its continuity of direction. Many other German ballet companies seem to take part in a game of general post with dancers and directors shuttling annually from one house to another in a complex shifting of forces. The outstanding figure outside Stuttgart is in fact a product of Stuttgart, John Neumeier. A choreographer of alert intellectual response to any theme, Neumeier danced in Stuttgart until 1969, when he become director of the Frankfurt Ballet for four years. In 1973 he became director of the ballet at the Hamburg State Opera for which he produced a series of innovative and psychologically complex re-workings of the traditional repertory: *Illusions – like Swan Lake*, *The Sleeping Beauty*, and an ingenious staging of *Casse noisette*. He has also created a series of major works which include two to Mahler symphonies (numbers three and four), and *Romeo and Juliet*, *Meyerbeer/Schumann* and *Don Juan*. His works are to be seen in the repertories of the Stuttgart Ballet, the Canadian National Ballet, the Royal Danish Ballet and American Ballet Theatre and his Hamburg troupe has been noted for the devotion it has won from its own audience and from the whole German public.

As in France, there are also ballet companies associated with opera houses in most major cities. They range from tiny groups dancing mostly in operettas, to such important troupes as those in Munich and West Berlin, and the *avant-garde* and deeply earnest ensemble guided by Pina Bausch in Wuppertal.

AUSTRIA

Despite its long history, ballet in Vienna has rarely freed itself from the domination of opera. After the days of Angiolini, Hilferding and Gluck and the golden years of the Viganòs and the Romantic Ballet, Vienna has not known any particular balletic distinction. With the exception of a few interesting stagings the Vienna Ballet, richly endowed and magnificently housed, has made little impact upon the world of the dance. In Vienna itself, however, the ballet in recent years has benefited from the participation of Rudolf Nureyev, whose stellar presence has won a new public.

ITALY

In Italy the operatic domination is all too apparent in the great houses in Milan and Rome. Attempts have been made across the years to bring back the glories of Salvatore Viganò's years in Milan, and the great tradition of Carlo Blasis and his school. But these have been abortive, and the efforts of such figures as Vera Volkova, John Field and André Prokovsky have variously been defeated by the operatic system. The most lasting achievements were probably those of Aurel von Milloss working in both Rome and Milan, presenting stagings which during three decades were marked by very distinguished design.

Italian audiences have shown an insatiable appetite for stars – encouraged by such festivals as those at Nervi and Spoleto – and the presence of Carla Fracci, Italy's darling, has done much to satisfy this taste.

EASTERN EUROPE

Many of the People's Republics in Eastern Europe have long ballet traditions which antedate the massive political changes which came with the re-shaping of Europe after the First World War. But it is the Soviet influence after 1945 which has placed so firm an imprint upon the identity of companies and their schools in Poland, Hungary and Czechoslovakia. The post-war years in Poland were spent first in rebuilding the physical premises after the appalling depredations of war. The history of ballet over the past two hundred

Richard Cragun (leaping) and Marcia Haydée (in bridal dress) in John Cranko's Taming of the Shrew *(1969) for the Stuttgart Ballet. Cranko's uproariously comic* Shrew *was one of the several full-length ballets he made in Stuttgart which celebrated the partnership of Marcia Haydée and Richard Cragun – her lyric intensity excellently matched by his bravura dancing and fine dramatic skill.*

years has been marked by the participation of great Polish dancers, from the Kshessinski dynasty to such stars of the Ballet Russe as Idzikowski, Woizikowski and Shabelevski. Today there are eight ballet companies to be found in state opera houses which are fed by five ballet schools. The most important company is that in the Teatr Wielki in Warsaw.

In Czechoslovakia the relationship with Russian ballet is very close and schools and companies reflect this fact very clearly. Czech ballet however has a particularly good record for stage design, and the work of Josef Svoboda has gained international renown.

The more independent Yugoslavia maintains large companies in Belgrade and Zagreb and smaller companies in such cities as Ljubljana, Split and Sarajevo. Many Yugoslav dancers have worked in the West – Milko Sparamblek, Vassili Sulich and Veronica Mlakar among them. Yugoslav ballet itself has moved away from a dependence upon Soviet instruction and under such choreographers as Dimitri Parlić has produced works which reflect a strong national identity.

Strongest of all these Eastern European companies is the Budapest Ballet. Since the war it has acquired stagings by the Russians Vainonen, Zakharov and Leonid Lavrovsky but it also has Ashton's *La Fille mal gardée*. Outstanding among native choreographers have been Gyula Harangozo and Ferenc Nadasi and most recently Laszlo Zeregi whose *Spartacus* has been acquired by the Australian Ballet. The Budapest Ballet has toured widely and Hungarian dancers have become well known in the West.

BALLET IN THE UNITED STATES

The first native American to win widespread recognition as a dancer was John Durang (1768–1822). Born in York, Lancaster County, Pennsylvania, the son of immigrant parents, he achieved fame especially in pantomime (it is recorded that he could 'dance a Hornpipe on thirteen eggs blindfolded, without breaking one'). He was the founder of a well known dynasty of American dancers, but the impetus towards some kind of American tradition of ballet came with the repeal in 1789 of the Anti-Theatre Law. Thereafter, a series of European dancers arrived from the Old World to make such fortunes as they could. There are records of various French performers appearing, and in 1839 members of the Petipa family, including Marius and his father Jean, joined Madame Lecomte in a disastrous season in America. But the great ambassador of the Romantic Ballet was Fanny Elssler. She arrived in America in 1840 with the English dancer James Silvain (né Sullivan) as her partner. Her progress through the United States for two years was a triumph. In Washington President Martin van Buren made much of her; the House of Representatives was not able to muster a quorum on certain evenings when she danced. Her journeyings did something to stimulate native American talent and the ballerinas Mary Ann Lee, Julia Turnbull and Augusta Maywood, and the *danseur* George Washington Smith, must be counted among the first distinguished American dancers. The career of Augusta Maywood (1825–1876) was largely spent in Europe. Born in New York, she trained in Philadelphia – an important centre of dance at this time – but in 1838 left for Paris where she worked with Coralli and Mazilier. Her debut at the Paris Opéra in 1839 was the beginning of an exalted career which took her to most of the important European centres of ballet. She was much loved in France, visited Lisbon and Vienna, and for ten years was the darling of Italy, which she toured with her own company, and a repertory that included a balletic version of *La Dame aux camélias* and *Uncle Tom's Cabin*.

Mary Ann Lee (1823–1899) also worked in Paris, where she learned much of the Romantic repertory. But in 1845, as she noted in a letter to a newspaper, 'Notwithstanding the charms and pleasures which are to be met with in Paris, I much prefer my own dear country.' Thus she returned to the United States with a polished technique and an understanding of the current French repertory which she staged (and in which her partner was George Washington Smith). She made her farewells in 1847 at the early age of twenty-four. Thereafter she made one brief return to the stage, and in 1860 opened a school in Philadelphia.

George Washington Smith (1820–1899) continued his career partnering various *danseuses* – from Lola Montez to the distinguished Giuseppina Morlacchi – and on his retirement he opened a school for both classical and social dancing. (Smith's son Joseph was not only an excellent classical dancer but also invented the *turkey trot* and introduced the *apache* dance to America.)

By the middle of the nineteenth century, American ballet had reduced itself to that extraordinary enterprise *The Black Crook*. This was an extravaganza, first seen at Niblo's Gardens in New York in 1866, which featured dance as one of the more scandalous components in a spectacle that combined elements of musical comedy and vaudeville. A complicated plot was the excuse for every sort of display, and under various guises and revivals it lasted amazingly until 1903. In its time it offered a setting for notable European ballerinas, but something of the attraction of the piece was the presumed lubricious nature of the ballet, whose supposed immodesty meant that ladies visiting the theatre to see it were often heavily veiled.

As an emulation of the money-spinning *The Black Crook*, Niblo's Gardens also sheltered *The White Fawn*, which again relied for appeal on extravagant spectacle and a ballet. The *New York Times*, reviewing *The White Fawn*, noted: 'No spectator is likely . . . to make any strenuous

Norah Kaye and Antony Tudor in Tudor's Pillar of Fire *(1942) for American Ballet Theatre. Based on Schönberg's tone-poem* Transfigured Night, *the ballet tells of a frustrated woman who gives herself heedlessly to a stranger, but eventually finds emotional repose in the arms of the man who loves her. The ballet established Norah Kaye as a notable dramatic ballerina.*

endeavour to follow out the plot of *The White Fawn*. It is but a pretext for the dancers, who are all in all, and whose reign is likely to be long in the land (and broad too) . . .'

Yet it would be unrealistic to say that ballet in the United States was to be anything but an imported novelty for many years to come. The European star, Adeline Genée, ravished the American public in 1908. After the success of her appearances in New York she was given a heart-shaped locket of gold set with seed pearls, inscribed 'Merely a symbol of your conquest of the heart of New York and that of your Yankee managers'.

The great revival of interest in the art in Europe following the first Diaghilev season in Paris in 1909 inevitably had its repercussions in America. Although the Metropolitan Opera House, New York, maintained a ballet troupe chiefly for the dance scenes in operas, it was the cosmopolitan taste and experience of the newly wealthy Americans which encouraged the development of a somewhat spurious Russian tradition in the United States. Anna Pavlova, that apostle of the classic dance, visited New York with Mikhail Mordkin in the spring of 1910 and dazzled the public to such an extent that she returned later in the year for an extended tour.

For the rest of her career Pavlova was to pay regular visits to the United States. But in this early dawn of the Russian Ballet fever other enterprises capitalized on the need for a 'Russian' image to ballet. At the Metropolitan Opera House an Italian couple, Victorina Galemberti and Giovanni Molassi, announced 'classical Russian dances', and the music hall dancer Gertrude Hoffman assembled a troupe with some Russian representatives, including Lydia Lopokova, Theodore Kosloff and Alexis Bulgakov, and presented bastardized versions of the Diaghilev repertory.

The Moscow ballerina Ekaterina Geltzer, with Mordkin and Volinin, appeared in *Swan Lake* and *Coppélia* at the Metropolitan Opera House, and Mordkin was eventually to return to the United States in the 1920s where his work was influential until his death in 1944.

The Diaghilev company came to America only as a temporary refuge from wartime Europe and its seasons in 1916 and 1917 can hardly be described as successes, although a few influential Americans recognized the merits of the company and its achievement even during the difficulties of the second Nijinsky-directed season.

At the same time Anna Pavlova had undertaken a very extraordinary enterprise: an abridged version of *The Sleeping Beauty* which was to form a forty-eight-minute section of a Broadway show, with designs by Léon Bakst (which were later to provide the basis for his work on the Diaghilev *Sleeping Princess* of 1921). This production failed to appeal to the New York audience and it was gradually reduced in length and finally replaced by a collection of divertissements.

Probably the most important figure to find a home in America at this time was Mikhail Fokine. In 1919 he was invited by the impresario Morris Gest to create the dances in a Broadway spectacle based on Pierre Louÿs' *Aphrodite*. Thereafter America was to prove the base for Fokine, but it was in many ways infertile ground for his work. The great choreographer travelled extensively in Europe and in South America, creating and reviving his ballets; in America he performed with his wife Vera Fokina, and gave occasional seasons with a company made up of his students, but America did not benefit as it should from his presence. His work was scattered and disjointed because America itself could not provide the working conditions and the single permanent company he needed. Not until the end of his life was he to find in America a company – Ballet Theater – for whom he could work in harmony, and pass on something of the illustrious traditions of his art.

The beginning of a renaissance of ballet in America was to come in the 1930s when two separate events occurred. The first was Lincoln Kirstein's invitation to George Balanchine to take up residence in the United States and to form a school and a company. The second was the arrival in December 1933 of the newly-formed Ballet Russe de Monte Carlo, then directed by Colonel de Basil, which was to have an enormous success. The company visited the United States regularly thereafter, touring coast to coast, but in 1938 the internecine warfare that created such extraordinary shifts of power within the world of the Ballet Russe brought about the creation of a new company under the guidance of Léonide Massine and Sergei Denham (also called the Ballet Russe de Monte Carlo) which was to dominate the American touring scene, thanks to the patronage of the impresario Sol Hurok. When the declaration of war in 1939 precluded any further European tours, they toured throughout the United States and the Americas, led by such artists as Massine, Danilova and Markova. This company answered the tremendous public call for the glamour and excitement of ballet, and its valuable missionary work was to be vitally important in stimulating America's taste for good ballet. The Russian image was still essential. Hurok patronized the Monte Carlo company, then arranged for the return of de Basil's Original Ballet Russe troupe to the United States, and even billed a third major company – the Ballet Theater (which Fokine joined) – as 'the greatest in Russian Ballet' to satisfy the public image of a 'Russian' art. The de Basil company expired in Europe just after the war – this type of 'Russian' ballet was no longer acceptable. The Monte Carlo troupe, with Danilova and Frederic Franklin marvellously at its head, existed for another decade but eventually it, too, fell a victim to economic stringencies. Ballet Theater alone was able to maintain the traditional 'glamorous' ballet image.

Ballet Theater had been founded in 1939 by Lucia Chase and Richard Pleasant with the

declared aim of presenting 'the best that is traditional, the best that is contemporary and, inevitably, the best that is controversial'. It had its origins in the Mordkin Ballet in which Lucia Chase had performed as a dancer. Miss Chase had studied with Fokine, Nijinska and Mordkin. With the inception of Ballet Theatre, a company which she directed until 1980 (the spelling of 'Theater' was changed to 'Theatre' after its great success in London after the war and it was re-named American Ballet Theatre in 1957), she devoted much of her personal fortune to the preservation of the troupe. Ballet Theatre started off with an international repertory, and from that time it has maintained its image, illuminating its works with the presence of its own stars, such as Nora Kaye, and a roster of invited guest artists which has included Markova, Baronova, Anton Dolin, Toumanova, and more recently Erik Bruhn, Mikhail Baryshnikov and Natalia Makarova. Many other distinguished foreign stars have made shorter stays. Cornerstones of the repertory have been ballets created for it by Antony Tudor (*Pillar of Fire*, *Romeo and Juliet*, *The Leaves are Fading*), Agnes de Mille and Jerome Robbins, as well as the traditional classical repertory, and the Fokine ballets which that great master staged for the company during the last two years of his life. Although the company has suffered from a changing repertory, and from changes of personnel, it has never lost a public following eager to see its stars and also to savour such pieces of Americana as Robbins' *Fancy Free* and de Mille's *Fall River Legend*.

The authentically American classic dancing has a much more serious image. The true foundation of classical dancing as an American art dates back to 1933 and the beginning of the Kirstein–

Balanchine enterprise. Within six months of Balanchine's arrival and the opening of a school, a student performance was given which included the first staging of his *Serenade*.

Within two years a professional group, The American Ballet, had emerged. It presented such Balanchine–Stravinsky works as *The Card Party* and *Le Baiser de la fée*, and a presentation of Gluck's *Orpheus* at the Metropolitan Opera House, New York – celebrated for the blank incomprehension of the opera audience faced with the poetic imagery devised by Balanchine and his designer Pavel Tchelitchev.

Balanchine was also involved in the staging of Broadway shows, and later he worked in Hollywood; Kirstein, with Lew and Harald Christensen (two fine American dancers), worked with Ballet Caravan, a small touring organization which specialized in ballets based on American themes – such as Eugene Loring's *Billy the Kid*, *Filling Station* and *The Great American Goof*. These activities, and a tour of South America which saw the creation of Balanchine's *Concerto Barocco* and *Ballet Imperial*, were a prelude to the post-war years which found Balanchine and Kirstein first concerned with Ballet Society in New York and then with the company which evolved from this, the New York City Ballet (NYCB). This company gave its first performance in October

George Balanchine (left) rehearsing with members of his New York City Ballet. This photograph was taken in 1950 when the company was just establishing itself in New York.

Mikhail Baryshnikov and Natalia Makarova (below). These two stars formerly of the Leningrad Kirov Ballet and then with American Ballet Theatre, are seen rehearsing the Other Dances which Jerome Robbins made as a portrait of their glorious talents in 1976.

1948 at the New York City Center which was to be the company's home. It was in this theatre that the image of NYCB as the instrument for the greatest classical choreographer of this century was realised. With the constant support and inspired proselytizing of Lincoln Kirstein, Balanchine was able to implant the classic dance – as he had learned it in Imperial St Petersburg – into American soil.

Stripped of its old-world nostalgia, extended and developed by a choreographer of genius, the classic academic dance has been made American thanks to Balanchine. In the massive output of ballets which he has produced since 1946, and with the support of the School of American Ballet which trains its dancers in a style which is a logical and beautiful extension of the nineteenth-century *danse d'école* (as impressive in its way as Vaganova's achievement in Leningrad) Balanchine has shown classic ballet at its truest and also most modern. The range of his creativity is amazing, from the sparseness of certain of his Stravinsky realizations – the Balanchine–Stravinsky partnership has begotten marvels – to the exuberance of *Union Jack*. In everything he does Balanchine's supreme musicality informs his choreography.

Recognition of the importance of NYCB and its school came in 1963 with a Ford Foundation grant of seven million dollars. In the following year the company moved into its present home at the State

cated to the choreography of its founder. Eliot Feld began his career as a dancer and choreographer with American Ballet Theatre though he also had experience of modern dance companies, and this double influence is noted in his choreography. His company repertory includes work by Herbert Ross and Glen Tetley.

One of the most significant developments in metropolitan American dance came in 1968 when the black dancer Arthur Mitchell, a leading artist with New York City Ballet, was shocked by the assassination of Martin Luther King into deciding to create opportunities for black ballet dancers in America. From a school in Harlem which was open to any interested passer-by, there evolved a company, Dance Theatre of Harlem, distinctive in the public's affection for the enthusiasm of its performers. In a repertory which includes such demanding works as Balanchine's *Agon*, and in quasi-ethnic works by Talley Beatty and Geoffrey Holder, the company has danced throughout America and in Europe to great public acclaim.

Inevitably New York has claimed pre-eminence in the American ballet scene but under the heading of Regional Ballet it is possible to group a great number of enterprises, both professional and semi-professional, which have done much to bring ballet to the nation. It is significant that now that widespread touring by large ballet companies has been made impossible because of spiralling costs,

Something of the range of New York City Ballet: (far left) final scene in Union Jack (1976), Balanchine's spectacular tribute to Britain; (bottom left) the Balanchine–Gluck Chaconne (1976), a wonderfully serene work with Suzanne Farrell and Peter Martins as its superlative central couple; (left) Merrill Ashley in Balanchine's Ballo della regina (1978), a work which displays the exceptional brilliance, speed and musicality of this lovely dancer.

Lydia Abarca, with Paul Russell and Homer Bryant of the Dance Theatre of Harlem (below) in John Taras' Designs with Strings. This ballet was first produced by the Metropolitan Ballet in 1948 and subsequently revived by many companies.

Theater, part of the new arts complex of Lincoln Center – the first theatre built specifically to suit the needs of a ballet company. (The School of American Ballet which has also won government recognition is housed in the nearby Juilliard School of Music.)

By the 1970s it was obvious that ballet and dance were boom industries throughout the United States. This is to be accounted for by the extensive touring undertaken in previous years, by the support offered to dance in many American colleges. and by one of those mysterious switches in public taste wherein an art seems to satisfy a psychological need. In response to this insatiable demand, a variety of ballet companies have gained public favour, most notably the Joffrey Ballet which has been in existence for nearly two decades.

Despite certain vicissitudes in the 1960s, the Joffrey Ballet has flourished and earned an audience both for its own topical works, largely created by Gerald Arpino, and for a policy of revivals initiated by the company's director Robert Joffrey. His eclectic taste has brought in such diverse works as Jooss' *The Green Table*, Bournonville's *The Conservatory* and important acquisitions from Massine and Ashton. The company also took the enterprising step of inviting the modern dance choreographer Twyla Tharp to create her first work for a ballet company. This was *Deuce Coupe* (1973) which involved her own dancers as well as Joffrey artists.

Among smaller companies based in New York the Eliot Feld Ballet is an ensemble largely dedi-

Fernando Bujones (left), a young star of American Ballet Theatre, in their Don Quixote in 1978. A product of the School of American Ballet and a gold medallist at the 1974 Varna International Ballet Competition in Bulgaria, Bujones is one of the most brilliant virtuoso dancers of today. In ballets which extend his dramatic abilities he is also revealed as a fine dance actor.

Natalia Makarova (right) as Kitri in the American Ballet Theatre's Don Quixote. Makarova is the only one of the three major stars who left the Kirov Ballet (Nureyev in 1961, Makarova in 1970 and Baryshnikov in 1974) to have come to the West as a mature artist. Since then her performances have set standards of artistry and aristocracy of dance which mark her as the finest ballerina of her generation in the West. Her range is wide, encompassing not only the classics in which she is unrivalled today, but also such works as Kenneth MacMillan's Romeo and Juliet and Manon.

the burden of satisfying regional demand has to be met by local companies. (It should be noted, however, that American television has done much, particularly through public service broadcasting, to educate the public with fine programmes of ballet and modern dance.)

From the days in the mid 1930s when Catherine Littlefield founded her Philadelphia Ballet and toured with it successfully for several years, and Ruth Page started her crusade to implant ballet and the best of modern design in Chicago, various pioneers have laboured long and hard. Among the earliest of American regional companies was the San Francisco Ballet, which was founded in 1938 by Willam Christensen, which continues operating today.

The vastness of America explains the emergence over the past couple of decades of a regional ballet movement which has sought to fill the gap in the dance life of the nation caused by the lack of major metropolitan and cosmopolitan touring ballet companies. The word 'regional' could imply any ballet outside New York. In fact it is properly to be understood as the companies, professional and semi-professional, which have united under the National Association for Regional Ballet (NARB). The late Anatole Chujoy, founder–editor of Dance News, recognized the importance of the work being done in Atlanta, Georgia, by Dorothy Alexander, to promote the idea of festivals which would enable companies from different parts of the same region to perform together and exchange ideas. Today the NARB has a membership of one hundred and thirty companies of all levels of ability. But dominating the regional scene are those resident professional companies in Philadelphia, Boston, Cincinnati, San Francisco, Salt Lake City and Houston.

CHAPTER NINE

MODERN DANCE

Whereas Loïe Fuller used fabrics for their own sake to reflect the play of light, Martha Graham (left) made them an integral part of her early dances. Lamentation (1930) was a dance of grief, performed entirely by a seated dancer sheathed in jersey cloth, with only her hands, her bare feet and the central part of her face visible. The anguished movements were emphasized by the stretch and pull of the fabric's lines. This striking photograph was taken in 1935.

Loïe Fuller (right) in one of her movement studies, with yards of silken draperies swirling and billowing around her in suitably art nouveau style. Even her contemporary, Isadora Duncan, was 'dazzled and carried away' by her performances.

'Modern dance is not an exact term. It was invented as a name for "serious-theatrical-dance-that-is-not-ballet" . . . American modern dance meant "serious-theatrical dance-that-is-neither-ballet-nor-German-modern-dance".'[1]

MODERN DANCE can be said to have resulted from the debasement of ballet. As already indicated, ballet was a moribund art everywhere save in Copenhagen and St Petersburg in the latter part of the nineteenth century, and it was at this time that the first shoots of a different form of dancing made their appearance. It was right that this should happen in the New World. America at this time was a country in a massive state of change. The opening up of the country itself, the influx of immigrants, the speedy development of industrial power which was to make the nation a giant in the twentieth century, can be perceived in the emergence of this art form. It is not without significance that it should be an art whose first practitioners were women, and its founding figures are those two dissimilar creatures Loïe Fuller and Isadora Duncan.

Ironically both their reputations were made in Europe, although the repercussions of their work, especially that of Duncan, were to be felt most strongly in America.

Loïe Fuller (1862–1928) was less a dancer than a magician of light. By a happy accident, early in her career as an actress she came upon effects that could be achieved with a light and a piece of gauzy cheesecloth. She discovered that by the manipulation of cloth and of a billowing skirt she could produce exceptional effects when moving in a beam of light. There came from this an elaborate technique of lighting effects, which disguised her feeble basic dance technique, and enhanced it by the play of colour and draperies. In such solos as *The Fire Dance* and *The Serpentine*

Dance she produced imagery that reflected in a mysteriously apt way the sinuous convolutions that were to be found in the fashionable *art nouveau* decoration of her time.

Born in Illinois, Loïe Fuller made her first experiments in the United States, but by 1893 she was creating a sensation in Paris at her debut at the Folies-Bergère, where her appearance seemed to epitomize the mysterious femininity so admired by the symbolist poets. For the Paris Exhibition of 1900 she had her own theatre, in which her performances were described as 'an orgy of colour'. She manipulated costumes comprising yards of silk gauze with long poles held in her arms, producing a form of undulating movement

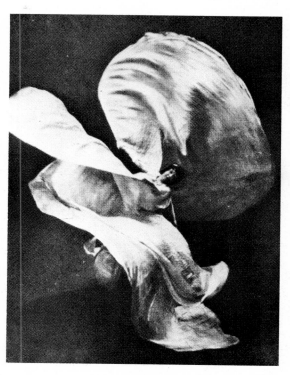

which was transformed by a most complex system of lighting. With coloured beams playing above, below and around her, she was hailed as a sculptor of light, producing poetic images that were entirely attuned to the aesthetic of the time. Not in any strict sense a choreographer, she yet freed dance by suggesting a different sphere of activity, and by disclosing new vistas for decoration itself. It is not unjust to see some parallel between the work of Loïe Fuller and that of Alwin Nikolais today.

With a troupe of dancers, she evolved a form of theatrical presentation which offered an interpretation of music through light and colour rather than through choreography. She was, in effect, a technologist more than a choreographer, her experiments being concerned with the effect of light rather than of movement. Her importance lies in her ability to understand the potential of the theatrical machinery of her time, despite the limitations of the still novel stage-lighting. Yet her influence was to be felt by two greater successors: by Isadora Duncan whose career she helped to launch, and by Ruth St Denis who saw her work in Paris in 1900 and was impressed by her 'inventive genius' rather than her dancing.

The following quotation gives an idea of the effect created by Isadora Duncan on one of her admirers, the distinguished photographer, Arnold Genthe:

'As a creative genius she was both artist and liberator, releasing by her courage and heavenly grace, not the dance alone, but womankind, from the fetters of puritanism. Where her work was concerned she had integrity and patience, knowing no compromise with what she felt to be the truth about beauty. In her personal life she had charm and a naïve wit. Of tact or self control she had very little, not did she wish to have. She was the complete and winning tool of her impulses.

'. . . The curious thing about Isadora was that her body was not exactly beautiful from a classical point of view but when she danced, the nobility of her gestures could make it into something of superb perfection and divine loveliness. This was true even during her last years and after disaster had come upon her.'[2]

Of herself, Isadora Duncan wrote:

'The woman I am is the artist I am. There is no difference . . . I am inspired by the movement of the trees, the waves, the snows, by the connection between passion and the storm, between the breeze and gentleness . . . I always put into my movements a little of that divine continuity which gives to all of Nature its beauty and life.'[3]

In the above quotation you can feel the authentic wind of Duncan's aspirations. She was a most

remarkable woman – and can be considered as the earth mother of modern dance.

Born in San Francisco in 1878, she died in Nice in 1927, strangled by her own scarf when it caught in the wheels of a car. Over fifty years after her death she is still totally fascinating. Misrepresented in a film, the subject of a flood of books still continuing, her dances re-created by pupils and their descendants – or more touchingly and poetically remembered by a great choreographer (Ashton) for a great dancer (Lynn Seymour) – Duncan remains one of the most challenging figures in the whole history of dancing. She is a mass of inconsistencies and contradictions. Her technique, less inspirational than most people thought, was intimately linked to her own thrilling ability to move. Her life was a tragicomedy which contrasted wild and impossible dreams with improvidence and sheer folly, and yet Duncan *did* achieve and her life was authentically tragic. The Irishness of her character, which so impressed her greatest love, Gordon Craig, was allied to a typical Victorian idealism, which thought of Art and Life in capital letters. The unbridled nature of her passions was reflected in the uncorseted nature of her dress, and neither spirit nor body was to be tamed by the conventions of her time. Despite all the follies, the half-built temple, the hapless band of 'Isadorables' (her child students) and the short-lived schools, the preposterous marriage to Esenin, and the drunkenness of her later years, she was beautiful and great.

To her is owed the real impetus behind modern dance. Duncan it was who persuaded the world that her dance, in its freedom and in the profound emotional effect which she herself could have upon an audience, was truth and not artifice.

Dance protagonists such as Judith Jamison and Twyla Tharp carry on the traditions pioneered by Isadora Duncan and Martha Graham – Jamison with her 'statuesque presence and passionate intensity', Tharp (who studied with Graham, Nikolais and Cunningham) with her 're-invention of the contemporary body' and innovations of style. Dancers of the Twyla Tharp company (above) in Baker's Dozen *(1979), an evocation of the 1920s through the dance music and dance steps of the time, to jazz pieces by Willie 'The Lion' Smith. The title stems from its being one of the few pieces using the entire company – twelve dancers and the pianist. Judith Jamison (left) in the solo* Cry, *made for her by Alvin Ailey in 1971 to jazz, modern blues and soul music, and dedicated to 'all black women everywhere – especially our mothers.'*

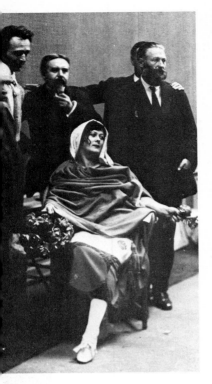

Isadora Duncan in characteristically extrovert pose in her French studio, with some of her devoted admirers (above). She is said to be one of the most portrayed women in the world and amongst the artists who idolized – and portrayed – her and were welcomed in the first quarter of the century to her studio were the sculptor Bourdelle, and Maurice Denis, who featured her in reliefs and murals in the Théâtre des Champs Elysées, and the Fauvist painter Kees van Dongen. (For Gordon Craig's view, see page 4.)

This famous portrait of Isadora Duncan at the portal of the Parthenon in 1921 (far right) says everything about the grand inspiration behind her dancing – which she drew from antique Greece – and about her own grand poses. From the Acropolis series of photographs taken by the painter Edward Steichen, one of her many admirers. (Collection of Museum of Modern Art, New York; gift of Edward Steichen)

Craig who captured her style in many beautiful drawings and woodcuts, said:

'She was speaking her own language . . . and if she is speaking, what is it that she is saying? No-one would ever be able to report truly, yet no-one present had a moment's doubt. Only this can we say – that she was telling to the air the very things we longed to hear and until she came we never dreamed we should hear; and now we heard them, and this sent us all into an unusual state of joy . . .'[4]

Duncan had made her debuts in Chicago in 1889, already having rejected conventional dance in favour of flowing movement in flowing draperies, but it was in Paris, where she established herself in 1900, that her career took wing. Thereafter the beautiful young American dancer was to have a profound influence upon the artistic circles in Paris. She toured briefly with Loïe Fuller, and then moved from city to city (and probably from lover to lover) during the years which took her round Central Europe, and to St Petersburg in 1904. By then the supposedly 'Greek' aspect of her art was manifest. She had been inspired by the ideals of freedom and high seriousness which she perceived in classic Greek art. But her response to it was intuitive and emotional rather than academic, and in this there is a fundamental truth about her teaching as well as her own dancing. Isadora hoped and believed that she might inspire the myriad children she gathered around her, and sought to teach, with the same impulse towards beauty that fired her own dance. The schools which she set up attempted to do this with varying degrees of success: the Moscow Duncan School did not cease operating until 1946, and in the United States a form of 'Duncanism' persisted for many years which, according to the personal testimony of our acquaintances, was profoundly stimulating to young children who experienced it.

Uniquely for her time, Duncan was concerned with dancing to 'serious' music. Beethoven – entire symphonies – Wagner, Gluck, Brahms, were all used as partners in her dancing. No score seems to have been too prodigious for Duncan to dare, but nowhere is there a reproach that she trivialized or debased her scores. Indeed, the massive nature of Duncan's art, an art which deepened and darkened as the years went by, was probably appreciated best when it was accompanied by music of comparable dignity.

In her early years as an artist, when she was the darling of the artistic world and still a young woman whose lissom beauty could inspire her public, Duncan's dances seem in the main to have been light in texture. Gradually, as can be observed in the multitude of drawings and photographs which celebrate her attraction, the figure becomes more monumental, the life-style more desperate. She bore two children, one to Gordon Craig, the other to Paris Singer, an heir of the Singer sewing machine millionaire who bought

her a Paris hotel to use as a studio. In 1913 the children were drowned when the car in which they were travelling slid into the Seine. The shock to Duncan was profound; she retired from performance and devoted herself to teaching, and it took the cataclysm of the First World War to bring her back to the theatre. Her art then acquired the dark and massive qualities to which it was probably best suited. As a gesture of faith to her adopted country, she danced the *Marseillaise*:

'. . . In a robe the colour of blood, she stands enfolded; she sees the enemy advance; she feels the enemy as it grasps her by the throat; she kisses the flag; she tastes blood; she is all but crushed under the weight of the attack; and then she rises, triumphant, with the terrible cry, *Aux armes, citoyens*! Part of her effect is gained by gesture, part by the massing of her body, but the greater part by facial expression. In the anguished appeal she does not make a sound, beyond that made by the orchestra, but the hideous din of a hundred raucous voices seems to ring in our ears. . .

'Finally we see the superb calm, the majestic flowing strength of the Victory of Samothrace. . . At times, legs, arms, or a leg or an arm, the throat or the exposed breast, assume an importance above that of the rest of the mass, suggesting the unfinished sculpture of Michelangelo . . .'[5]

With the war's end there followed the most improbable but most characteristic of Duncan's enterprises. She had been an ardent admirer of the idea of the Russian Revolution; here was the new society whose children – all of them – she might teach to dance in celebration of their new liberty, freeing their bodies as their nation itself had been freed. Her appeals to the commissars had at first seemed in vain, but in 1921 she found herself in Moscow, and by dint of every conceivable artifice she managed to get a school established. It was here, too, that she embarked upon the most ill-fated of her amorous intrigues, when she married for the first time, choosing as her husband a poet considerably younger than herself, the boorish, drunken and consistently unfaithful – but undoubtedly talented – Sergei Esenin. She took him to America for a tour which was marked entirely by the abuse to which she was subjected and the scandal which she aroused. 'The Bolshevik hussy doesn't wear enough clothes to pad a crutch' was the comment of Billy Sunday, an evangelical rabble-rouser.

In 1924 she left Russia and parted with Esenin. Her return to Europe was shadowed by financial disasters, abortive attempts to start a school, and despair when faced with a world with which she could no longer cope. She found a kind of retreat in France, in her studio near Nice. There were occasional performances and constant attempts to raise money – not least through the writing of a thoroughly dubious book of memoirs. The most touching account of these last years has been given by a young English author, Sewell Stokes, who knew her in 1927. His record of part of this last year of her life shows both the undiminished beauty of Duncan as a spirit, and the tragedy of Duncan as a woman who had outlived her fame. Stokes portrays the Duncan of 1927 as:

'The most revolutionary, and adored dancer of her generation, she created for herself an enormous following. Finally she faded from the public's interest as a dancer, becoming instead the object of that sensational curiosity which most of us feel about a celebrity who has dared the conventions.'[6]

Nevertheless, whatever the sorrows of her later years, Duncan is immortal. Her art and her example seem today as beautiful and as inspiring as at any time during the years since her death. No dancer has ever inspired so many fine artists, from Bakst and Bourdelle to Rodin (who said of her 'not talent but genius . . . art supreme and complete'), from Gordon Craig to Cocteau and Walkowitz. In their representations is seen the life of Duncan's art, its grandeur and its freedom, and its power to excite. It is this that has provided the impulse behind the entire modern dance movement.

An almost exact contemporary with Isadora Duncan, Ruth St Denis (as simple Ruth Dennis had become) offers a very different example of the path that modern dance took.

'Ruth St Denis is another revolutionary artist who, like Isadora, felt the need for breaking through the limitations of the ballet. She saw the salvation of the dance not so much in the rhythms of classic Greece as in those of the Orient – Japan and India. Knowing that the Western mind could not assimilate the content of these dances of the East, with their gestures and movements that have come down through long generations as symbols of faith or legend, she made no attempt to reproduce them. Her aim was to give a free and beautiful translation that would make clear the enduring and universal truths of which they were the parables. . . From her dancing we have gleaned much more than the enjoyment of exotic charm and colour. We have been brought nearer to an understanding of the spiritual concepts which had their roots in the Orient.'[7]

Duncans' ecstasies were a vivid if untutored response to 'Life' and 'Beauty' and 'Art' hewn out of her own massive temperament. Ruth St Denis, by contrast, evolved a theology from her quest for mystical experience whether it be Christian, Theosophic or Oriental. Born in New Jersey between 1877 and 1880 (the date is imprecise), she started her career as an actress and 'skirt dancer'. Her dissatisfaction with this aspect of commercial theatre – though she never lost her sound commercial instinct with her own company – was brought about by a curious incident when, in 1904, she was inspired by a poster advertising a brand of cigarettes which featured a picture of the goddess Isis. This rather mundane vision instantly fired her with a desire to create an Egyptian ballet. Her progress towards the realization of this dream led her to research into Oriental dancing and then to staging exotic solos for herself, which excited a good deal of public attention – her *Radha* was a remarkable display of sinuous movement by a very beautiful young woman. Hugo von Hofmannsthal saw St Denis

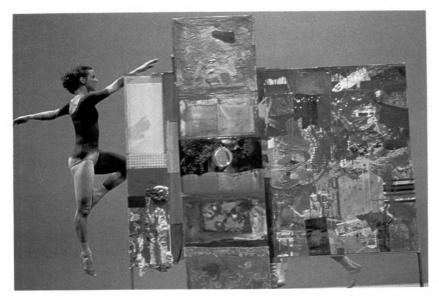

Ellen Cornfield (left) in performance in Merce Cunningham's Minutiae, *which combined painting and photography with dance. The brief to the American painter, Robert Rauschenberg, was to make something 'that could be put in the middle of the stage and around which we could move.' Cunningham, who has danced with both Lester Horton's and Martha Graham's companies, is one of the most influential figures in modern dance today. He produces dances that are austere, sometimes matter of fact, to exist side by side with the multi-media aspect of the subject, decoration and sounds. Alwin Nikolais' The Tribe (right) was first performed in Buenos Aires in 1975. It presents a view of man – his primal and instructive actions', as opposed to the sophisticated and emotional aspects – the psychodrama – so often portrayed in modern dance. By means of projections and skilled lighting effects, Nikolais has become a magician of dance, creating hallucinatory shapes and transforming bodies and costuming into amusing and terrifying entities. Paul Taylor (left) in his own* Book of Beasts *as an anarchic and wildly sequinned being who irrupts throughout the ballet, a humorous bestiary in which celebrated musical gems are sent merrily to perdition, as for example when Taylor (disguised as a moulting bear) becomes involved with Saint-Saëns' Le Cygne – a text once sacred to Pavlova. Taylor has the taste and wit, rare among contemporary dance creators, for making comedy pieces distinguished by a sense of form and richness of imagery that mark them as among the most rewarding of our time.*

on her first European visit in 1906, and wrote about *Radha*:

'The stage was the interior of an Indian temple. Incense rose up, there was the beating of a gong, priests were squatting on the floor, touching the steps of the altar with their foreheads, practising some rites in semi-darkness. The whole light, a strong blue light, fell on the statue of the goddess. Her face was a bluish ivory, her garments of blue-sparkling metal. She sat in the hieratic attitude of the Buddha on the lotus flower: legs crossed, knees wide apart, hands folded in front of her body, the palms pressed together tightly. Nothing in her stirred; her eyes were open, but her eyelashes did not move. Some untold force held together her entire body. This scene lasted fully one minute but one would have wished to go on viewing this motionless figure. It had no resemblance to a statue as imitated by a human being. There was no forced, artificial stiffness in it, but rather an inner spiritual necessity.'

It was this quality which was to remain at the centre of St Denis' dance. She was, however, an astute presenter of her art, and the skill with which she staged her dances and the beauty of her costuming indicated her awareness of its commercial possibilities. During a lengthy European period St Denis could command exceptionally high sums for performances – earning as much as £500 a week at the Coliseum in London. On her return to the United States in 1909 she set out on a tour of vaudeville theatres and succeeded in persuading a management

to stage her long-dreamed-of Egyptian piece, *Egypta*. Thereafter she crossed the continent with dance-dramas – Japanese and Hindu as well as Egyptian – in which expense was not spared to provide an attractive and eye-catching setting for her exotic spectacles. In these, St Denis was bringing dance to the whole of America. The careful merchandising of the commodity – the attractions of 'exoticism', a certain suggestion of Oriental naughtiness which appealed to the public mind, and the very considerable glamour of her stagings – meant that the public took the pill of dance sugared with attractive decoration.

In 1914 she married the dancer Ted Shawn. Born in 1891, Shawn had a proselytizing zeal for dance which reflected an early calling to the Christian ministry. He had seen St Denis dance, he had determined early on to become a dancer, but it was his eventual meeting with her as a prospective dancing partner which was to fuse their two talents, and bring about schools and a company which were the seed-bed of American modern dance.

By 1914 the craze for social dancing in theatricalized form – typified by the immense success of Vernon and Irene Castle – was impelling Ruth St Denis to present just such dances in her programmes. She needed a partner. More by chance than anything else, Shawn became that partner and their marriage a logical extension of their theatrical association. The next development, and the most significant, was the creation of a school, Denishawn, and a company bearing the same name. After wartime service in the army, Shawn returned, and for the next decade the Denishawn school and company was a vital force in the training of hundreds of dancers, and in the giving of thousands of performances throughout America. The Denishawn school syllabus was extraordinarily eclectic, including ballet, Spanish, Oriental forms, and elements from the Delsarte system of gesture.[8] From this curious amalgam there evolved a discipline more important for the reaction against it by such pupils as Martha Graham and Doris Humphrey than for itself. Shawn was the driving force behind the school; both he and St Denis, though, performed their own dances in the extensive tours by the Denishawn company, St Denis continuing her elaborate presentation of Oriental dance, Shawn specializing in Spanish, Mexican and American Indian items.

In addition to extensive tours of the United States, the Denishawn company ventured abroad and a massive Oriental tour, through India to Japan, fed back much local colour and local dance into the repertory.

It is significant that, unlike their breakaway pupils, Shawn and St Denis offered their impressions of various exotic dance forms as portraits: whatever mystical satisfaction an audience might find from St Denis' Oriental poses was merely incidental to their performance, and the psychological depths of Graham and the sociological

The pseudo-Orientalism which lay at the root of the Denishawn enterprise involved Ruth St Denis and Ted Shawn in the kind of 'Eastern dancing', seen here (left) in a 1920s presentation, which was nearer to the world of Kismet *than the Far East. Yet Hugo von Hofmannsthal, the famous poet and playwright, admired St Denis greatly in her earlier – and more disciplined – solo piece, Radha, in 1906. After they performed at Carnegie Hall in 1927, New York newspapers were successfully petitioned to appoint special dance critics, the* Herald Tribune *leading the way, and the* Times *following soon after.*

Doris Humphrey and Charles Weidman (above), in Humphrey's Passacaglia *of 1938, reveal how far dance had progressed within a decade from the attitude of Denishawn.* Passacaglia *set to Bach music, was one of Humphrey's greatest choreographies – a highly serious work.*

concerns of Humphrey were unknown to them. Unknown to Denishawn, too, were the austerities that were to be the result of Graham and Humphrey's lack of commercial success. Denishawn performances were always of eye-catching opulence, and the commercial rewards were great. (Shawn is reported as noting that at one time they had an income of $200,000 a year.)

Part of their income derived from the branch schools which were opened throughout the country; equally successful was their participation in a tour of the *Ziegfeld Follies*. It was this last enterprise which prompted some of the dancers to rebel against what seemed to them an excessive commercialism, which they felt debased the artistic pretensions of Denishawn. When Doris Humphrey reproached Shawn with this he declared, 'Do you mean to say that Jesus Christ was any less great because he addressed the common people?' 'No,' replied Humphrey, 'but you are not Jesus Christ,' to which Shawn's reply was 'But I am the Jesus Christ of dance.' This unanswerable retort was symptomatic of an attitude which prompted Humphrey and her eminent partner Charles Weidman to leave the Denishawn fold in 1928. Dissatisfaction was also felt about the rather superficial attitude evident in the way Denishawn treated a wide range of dance forms, and by 1931 the Denishawn troupe ceased operating as an entity and Shawn and St Denis separated, to pursue for nearly forty years their separate ways. (St Denis died in 1968.)

St Denis concentrated increasingly upon the mystical aspects of dance; Shawn began his propaganda for recognition of the male dancer. His company of male dancers toured internationally for seven years. The remaining years of his life – he died in 1972 – were devoted to running the Jacob's Pillow Dance Festival and summer school at Lee, Massachusetts. By the 1960s both St Denis and Shawn could see the rich harvest of

modern dance which owed so much to their early labours in preparing America to understand and love a form of dance other than classical ballet – a form authentically American and an immensely influential expression of America itself.

The movement of secession which led Martha Graham and then Doris Humphrey to leave Denishawn is one of the continuing and illuminating factors of American modern dance in this century. The amoeba-like splitting, the rejection of one person's disciplines in order to create a more personal idiom by the seceder, continues even to this day. But with Graham and Humphrey you find the major break. Both women had to leave Denishawn because of their desire to deepen dance's response to the world and human nature. The exoticism and showmanship of Denishawn had prepared the ground, but the Denishawn language was neither very precise nor ultimately anything but superficial. As a reaction against the Orientalism of Denishawn there was needed a statement more relevant to America in the darker years of the 1920s and 1930s, a language which would express both the urban tensions and the psychological territory that had been opened up by Freud and Jung.

'So the 1920s started over – from the beginning. For Martha Graham, it began with the act of breath – the start of life itself. Allowing the body to follow the natural ebb and flow of breathing, she watched what happened to the shape of the torso as it contracted in exhalation, expanded in inhalation. The next step was to intensify the dynamics of the act, taking the contraction as a sudden, spasmodic impulse which could send the body into a fall, into a turn, into – as it evolved – any number of motions. It was a primitive use of energy – utterly new as an initiator of dance movement. Dramatically, it provided a basically natural but excitingly theatrical means of portraying the human being in terror, in agony, in ecstasy.

'The approach of Doris Humphrey was equally basic, though totally different. Rather than turning to movement within the body, she viewed the body in relation to space. She saw movement as generated by effort to resist the pull of gravity – gravity as symbolic of all the forces that threaten man's balance, his security. She too discovered a principle of duality: for her it was the contrast of fall and recovery. Where Graham depicted the conflict of man within himself, Humphrey was concerned with the conflict of man with his environment. In both approaches, drama was inherent. But it was a kind of drama the public was unaccustomed to seeing. It was brutally honest; it was not pretty; it was not "nice".'[9]

Doris Humphrey, born in 1895 in Oak Park, Illinois, was a member of the Denishawn company

from 1917 to 1928. In that year she left the company with her partner, the dancer and choreographer Charles Weidman, and founded a school and performing group in New York which continued until 1940.

'Working from a principle of balance and unbalance, fall and recovery, and, later upon an application of gestural material, she created many works of immediate significance and enduring value. Her early efforts included *Colour Harmony, Water Study, Drama of Motion, Life of the Bee, Circular Descent, Pointed Ascent,* and also others in which the titles reflected her immediate concern with the application of her discovery . . .

'In 1936, Humphrey completed her great dance Trilogy, composed of *Theatre Piece, With My Red Fires* and *New Dance,* the first dealing with man's rivalries, competitions and efforts, wasted in oppositions; the second dealing with the tragedy of possessive love; the third concerned with advancement to the ideal human relationship of group harmony co-existent with cherished individuality. In her Trilogy, in some of the earlier dances, in *Passacaglia,* Humphrey made it clear that she had few if any rivals in the field of large scale choreography, in evoking dance from mass groups. With her growing interest in the field of gesture (world-wide, universal gesture as opposed to balletic or codified pantomime), she commenced to

create highly dramatic theatre pieces such as *Inquest, Lament for Ignacio Sánchez Mejías* and *Story of Mankind*, the latter two composed for José Limón and his company. Even in this newer aspect of her work, however, she did not forsake her concern with the problems which beset mankind and behind specific dramatic incidents and specific characters lay dramatic problems and behaviour which pertained to any man, rich or poor, educated or uneducated.'[10]

In 1944 Humphrey was obliged to retire from dancing because of severe arthritis, but within a short space of time she had started to create some of her finest dances for the company directed by José Limón, her protégé. Fatal illness brought her career to an end in 1958 but by then the rigorous intellectual and structural discipline of her works had had a profound influence upon modern dance. Her primer, *The Art of Making Dances*, remains one of the most persuasive and illuminating guides to the principles of choreography – it is characteristic of her art that it should be so – and in their attitudes regarding formal discipline and structural purity American modern dancers owe much to the example of Humphrey. In the Limón company, which survived its founder's death in 1972, are preserved several of Humphrey's dance works, as well as creations by Limón himself which reflect the continued imaginative force of Humphrey's vision.

Martha Graham was born in Allegheny, Pennsylvania, in 1894. Between 1916 and 1923 she studied and danced with Denishawn, but on leaving the company she was quickly to reject its – to her – too pretty manner and by 1930 she had created one of her earliest and most personal dances, *Lamentation*, a study of a grief-stricken woman in which an inspired use of a tube of fabric as the costume contributed to the emotional directness of the dance. By now she was concerned with evolving a technique in which to express her own feelings, a vocabulary of movement concerned not with the external amiabilities but with the tensions and sufferings of the psyche. The Graham technique which resulted is an example of performance feeding language, and that language then being further extended by further performance. Movement which was invented for a dance became a staple of the classroom. In obvious rejection of everything balletic, as well as of much that was Denishawn, Graham turned to the floor as the basis for her class and preparatory exercises – an acceptance of the pull of gravity in direct contrast to the ballet's rejection of this force. Jane Dudley, a long-time associate of Graham, summarizes Graham technique:

'A Graham class always starts with half an hour of floor work. The floor serves the same purpose as the ballet dancer's barre; it eliminates the problem of balance . . . Graham technique is based on two principles: the back is the source of movement with particular emphasis on the lower back and the pelvis; and all movement into space is the result of the subtle off-balancing of the dancer's weight. From the impulse begun in the back, comes the movement of the arms and legs. The "contraction and release" and the "spiral" involve the back as the source of movement.'[11]

With *Primitive Mysteries* in 1931, Graham came to artistic maturity. Based on an amalgam of Spanish Christianity and Indian religious feelings found in the American South West, this dance work offered a ritualistic view of the cult of the Virgin Mary. Stark, grand, it benefited from the collaboration of Louis Horst who was to be for many years musical director and mentor to Graham. Thereafter, Graham concerned herself for some years with carving works out of the American heritage. *Frontier* was notable not only for its portrayal of an American pioneer woman, but also for the fact that it initiated the grand collaboration between Graham and the great Japanese-American sculptor Isamu Noguchi, whose bone-bare settings have done so much to enhance the visual power of the Graham theatre.

Graham's exceptional use of fabric in costuming as an adjunct to dance is worth noting here. The wide arcs made by the voluminous Graham skirt, the possibilities of drapery to mask and yet reveal an emotional state, as in *Clytemnestra*, become part of the dance itself.

During her 'American years' two other notable works were created, in both of which something essential about America was made manifest – *Appalachian Spring*, and from studies of Emily Dickinson *Letter to the World*. After another study, of the novelist Emily Brontë (*Deaths and Entrances*), Graham turned to the antique past where she could find themes of guilt, remorse and self-realization, and here her dance language revealed itself at its richest and most theatrical. In *Clytemnestra*, a full-length work from 1958; in *Cave of the Heart* (1946) which dealt with Medea; and in *Night Journey* (1947) dealing with Jocasta, Graham presented herself as the protagonist viewing the lives of her characters from a still point near death.

But the Graham theatre and the Graham language were not in the later years exclusively centred round Graham the performer. In *Acrobats of God* she was content to act as ring-master to a delightful study about the life of a dancer, and in *Diversion of Angels* she produced a company work of serene lyricism evocative of the visions of the metaphysical writer Thomas Traherne.

For nearly fifty years Graham's influence has been central to the expansion of American modern dance: not merely by the example of her creativity, but because she forged and codified a language of modern dance which was to provide a *lingua franca* for generations who followed her. Though it might be altered by individual temperament, it provided American modern dance with the basic and essential tool which avoided the dissipation of effort through idiosyncratic performance styles. On the solid rock of Graham style the edifice of American modern dance inevitably rests.

In addition to the Graham style, other schools of American dance were also to emerge during the 1920s and 1930s. One, that of Hanya Holm (b. 1898), stemmed from the teaching of the most important and influential European modern dancer, Mary Wigman. Wigman (1886–1973) had been a pupil of Dalcroze and Laban, and by 1920 she had opened her own school in Dresden. It was from this school that the 'Central European' system of movement evolved. From Emile Jaques-Dalcroze (1865–1950) came the ideas of musical analysis through dance rhythm; from Rudolf von Laban (1879–1958) came theories about the codification of physical expression and an appreciation of dynamics. The Wigman style reflected very exactly the underlying tensions and unhappiness of Germany in the inter-war years. Her dances were sombre, dark-hued, heavy in texture and in pulse. Following her American tours in the 1930s, her pupil Hanya Holm opened a branch of the Wigman school in New York. She was to realize, though, that the Wigman style was suited neither to American bodies nor to the ethos of the New World. She renamed the school after herself and developed a style which proved both enriching to her students as a stimulus for their own creativity and also enabled her to work with great success on Broadway. Never a cult figure like Graham, Hanya Holm has had a quiet yet considerable influence upon generations

Martha Graham in her own Letter to the World, *which dates from 1940, in which she was inspired by the life and poetry of Emily Dickinson.*
The importance of costume in Graham's work is very clear in this picture: the movement of fabric, its choreographic 'identity', has always been of prime significance in her dances.

of American dancers, notably upon Alwin Nikolais, Valerie Bettis and Glen Tetley.

Hanya Holm's influence has been aptly summarized by a young American critic of today (at her receiving the Capezio award):

'In the 1930s American modern dance had pioneering vitality. Hanya Holm joined trail blazers like Doris Humphrey, Charles Weidman and Martha Graham in the now legendary summer programmes at Bennington College, Vermont where, as artists in residence, they taught and created seminal new works. *Trend*, one of Miss Holm's major achievements, was prepared for the Bennington Dance Festival of 1937. In the winter of the same year it was given in the capacious auditorium that is now the New York City Center, with the audience seated in the balcony so that the striking patterns of the dance itself could be deployed over the orchestra area as well as the stage . . . As with many modern dance works of the period, *Trend* dealt with broad social themes. (Miss Holm's later *Tragic Exodus* was inspired by the plight of fugitives from Nazi Germany; the Spanish Civil War motivated *They Too are Exiles*.) Still, the most significant element of *Trend* . . . was Miss Holm's ability to manipulate sizeable groups in resonant designs . . . In contrast to Martha Graham's works, which centered on the

charismatic performing power of a brilliant soloist (Graham herself), Hanya Holm's dances tended to be more distanced and objective, reflecting a more logical, less passionate, view of the world. Subsequent concert works also displayed Miss Holm's gift for humour, especially, as in the case of *Metropolitan Daily*, for satire, and her cohesive sense of style.'[12]

Among the other Central European dancer–choreographers of note who owed their first allegiance to Wigman must be accounted Harald Kreutzberg (1902–1968) and his partner Yvonne Georgi (1903–1975). From Laban the most important development has been that of his pupil Kurt Jooss (1901–1979) who worked in Essen from 1927 and who came to international fame in 1932 when his *The Green Table* won first prize in a choreographic competition in Paris. This success encouraged Jooss to form a company which toured in Europe and the Americas. By the 1950s the company had disbanded and Jooss devoted himself to teaching and supervising revivals of his dance works, of which *The Green Table* is still the best known.

Another strand of American dance was to be found on the West Coast of the United States, thanks to the influence of Lester Horton (1906–1953) who, after studies with Adolph Bolm, became involved in research into American Indian culture. From his own performances and

The strength and sincerity of Pearl Primus' dancing are to be sensed in this photograph, taken in 1951, which catches the vivid, expressionistic force of her movement.

productions there emerged a dance theatre in Los Angeles in 1948 and his pupils, who included Alvin Ailey, Bella Lewitzky, Carmen de Lavallade, Joyce Trisler and James Truitte, have provided a strong non-Graham colour to the fabric of American modern dance.

Horton arrived in Los Angeles in 1928 and there undertook to direct a festival of American Indian dance. He decided to stay on in the city to organize and direct his own contemporary dance programme. He admitted some influence from the leading practitioners in the East but it was his abiding interest in American Indian dance which was to dominate many of his early stagings. He lived among the Indians, studied their traditions and learned and performed their dances, and in Los Angeles he began his career as a creator. He believed that this indigenous tradition was fundamental to American modern dance, though he also respected the physical attitudes of other ethnic groups he found on the West Coast. He staged several major pageants and dance displays inspired by Indian legends and in his *Painted Desert* (1934), given at the vast Shrine Auditorium, he presented a cast of one hundred in war dances, fire, rain and rainbow dances and sun rituals all taken from Indian sources.

From Haitian dance he took themes to make his *Voodoo*; other works reflected his interest in Asiatic dance and also his ability to make theatrical capital from costume ideas adapted from national dress. In 1934 he formed the Lester Horton Dance Group – a close collaborator and leading dancer was Bella Lewitzky – and during the next two decades until his death in 1953 he remained the single truly important dance creator working on the West Coast of the United States. Occasional forays to New York in the 1940s were not successful, but with his own company and on his own territory Horton was a creator to contend with. A massive staging of *The Rite of Spring* in the Hollywood Bowl in 1937 was matched in size by his tremendous *Chronicle*, a survey of American history, in the same year; in the following year he created *Conquest* – with Merce Cunningham among the dancers – which dealt with the conquest of Mexico.

Horton's style with its long, well-stretched extensions of the limbs and its insistence upon a linear quality can be savoured in one of his major works which survives, *The Beloved*. Horton's influence can be traced through his best-known pupil, Alvin Ailey (b. 1931). Ailey's work has been crucial in making Horton's manner known to audiences throughout the world.

For some time after Horton's death in 1953, Ailey directed his company but then moved East to work on Broadway where he was to achieve instant success when he appeared in the musical *House of Flowers* (1954) with the Horton-trained Carmen de Lavallade. In 1958 Ailey was able to form his own company, American Dance Theatre, aimed at preserving significant works which chart the emergence of contemporary dance styles – by Horton, Shawn, Katherine Dunham, Geoffrey Holder, John Butler, Pearl Primus and many others. (Bella Lewitzky continues the Horton manner in her school and company in Los Angeles.) It was for American Dance Theatre that Ailey created a work which remains his best-known and best-loved choreography, *Revelations*. Inspired by the religious faith which so vividly shines in Negro spirituals, *Revelations* is full of brilliant imagery which expresses the spiritual vitality of black religious experience in America. Ailey's company made a serious attempt in the 1960s to say something about the traditions of contemporary black dance. To this end Ailey presented works by Katherine Dunham, Pearl Primus, Donald McKayle and Talley Beatty.

Katherine Dunham (b. 1912) studied anthropology and began teaching in Chicago. Following her researches into the dances of the Caribbean, she danced on Broadway (*Cabin in the Sky*, 1940, with choreography by George Balanchine) and in Hollywood. Thereafter she directed and appeared in her own dance revues and in the 1940s and 1950s led a company, with considerable international success, presenting full-scale dance-dramas inspired by her own ethnological researches. In these, and in the way in which the ballets were exotically costumed, Dunham showed how show business skill could combine with authenticity.

Like Dunham, Pearl Primus (b. 1919) made a serious study of anthropology. Her researches in Africa and the Caribbean were to provide themes and attitudes which influenced many of her works, among which was *Fanga* (1949) the first performance being given in Liberia by Primus and local musicians and dancers. Primus had made her first appearances with the New York-based New Dance Group in 1941. (The New Dance Group itself was an influential combine of socially-committed modern dancers, from the Depression onwards, who performed in concerts for nearly two decades; its most important members were Sophie Maslow, Jane Dudley and William Bales.) By 1944 Primus had her own group and for a time directed the Art Centre of Black African Culture in Nigeria. Her choreographies across the years are numerous and some are preserved in the repertory of the Ailey company, notably *Congolese Wedding* (1974). Latterly she has taught at New York's Hunter College.

Of the next generation of black choreographers, Donald McKayle (b. 1930) and a pupil of Graham and Cunningham among others, has been concerned with the social identity of the black community. His *District Storyville* of 1962 treats of the brothel area of New Orleans and the music that sprang from it. A work of undeniably brilliant effect, it also gave a lasting impression of compassion for the way of life it portrayed. *Rainbow Round My Shoulder* (1959) tells of the life of the prison chain gang and the fantasies which allow the convicts to escape from reality.

Its importance as a dance document is recognized by its preservation in the Ailey repertory.

Talley Beatty (b. *c.* 1923) spent his formative years with Katherine Dunham before forming his own company in 1949 which lasted for some two decades. He has choreographed widely for Broadway and films as well as for dance companies. His best-known work today is *The Road of the Phoebe Snow* (1959) a portrait of urban violence in the Mid-West along the sordid railroad tracks below the path of the luxury train, the Phoebe Snow.

Not all the heirs and successors to Graham fully accepted or propagated her manner. In London, Robert Cohan (b. 1925) has implanted Graham technique and teaching to produce an authentically British form of modern dance, which owes allegiance both directly and indirectly to Graham, through classes and through Cohan's own choreographic development. But the most important graduate from the Graham company – in which he danced from 1939 to 1945 – is Merce Cunningham (b. 1919). Cunningham has rejected all the emotional and psychological apparatus of the Graham manner. By temperament and creativity Cunningham is essentially a classicist. Over the decades since his first essays in choreography in 1942, Cunningham has been increasingly concerned with the dance as *dance*. His fundamental interest has been in the function of dance as the expression of a body's actions in time and space. Like Balanchine, he understands this as the truest aspect of choreography. Unlike Balanchine, he has been concerned not with dance's relation to music as a seed-bed for creativity, but with music as a parallel activity coinciding at times with movement but never nurturing or sustaining dance in any continuous or fruitful way. Nevertheless, Cunningham's long-time associate has been the *avant-garde* composer John Cage, and the aleatory composition of music as of dance – chance inspiring form to produce random yet carefully organized structures – has resulted in a new freedom for both arts in performance. Visually, Cunningham's pieces have a very strong identity whether they shock or ravish the eye. Through the collaboration of such artists as Robert Rauschenberg, Jasper Johns, Frank Stella or Andy Warhol, artistic experimentation has been a companion to dance creativity; in several instances the artist has become directly involved with the life of the company as well as with the creation of a specific dance piece.

Despite the supposed choreographic austerity of Cunningham's manner, there is an extraordinary range of emotion to be perceived in his dances, from the serenities of *Summerspace* to the menacing air of *Winterbranch*, the happiness of *How to Pass, Fall, Kick and Run* and the inconsequential delights of *Canfield*. This inconsequentiality is central to Cunningham's method of work. He believes that his dance should reflect the autonomy observed in life, where things exist

side by side and preserve their identity while also offering curious correspondences and inter-relationships. Thus, for Cunningham, the contributory elements to his spectacle – dance, décor, sound – may not meet until the first performance of a work, or the actual components of sound and décor may vary from performance to performance. Nevertheless, their co-existence has been carefully considered and a compatibility, or a deliberate disjunction, is part of the overall concept of the work.

Thus in *Travelogue* (1979) the accompaniment by John Cage will differ in each city in which it is performed since part of the 'score' depends upon calls made to telephone-answering services, and the disparate information which results helps create the feeling that you are indeed watching a report of a journey.

The result of this unpredictability is to heighten an awareness of each of the elements in a Cunningham creation. Even if he succeeds only in making his audiences ask 'why?', he has sharpened their perceptions.

By subverting the accepted procedures in dance, by destroying logic, Cunningham provides entirely new perspectives on the nature of human movement. He can speed it up or slow it down, offer contrasts between solo and group activity, but there is always a guiding respect for the human form itself and, even more important, for the need for great technical ability. Cunningham's dancers are admirably trained; his dances make considerable demands upon them. Unlike certain of the conveniently named 'post modern group' and some dreadful European practitioners to whom technique is an unknown territory, Cunningham's dancers are fully stretched in his work and such artists as Douglas Dunn are supreme examples of the extreme virtuosity called for by the best contemporary choreographers.

It is worth commenting further upon Cunningham's willingness to create dance works for film and television and his desire to explore the possibilities of this medium. *Locale*, for instance, was originally made to be filmed in Cunningham's New York studio in the winter of 1979 and was later transferred to the stage. A newspaper critic noted that both versions of *Locale* had just been shown during Cunningham's season at the New York City Center (March 1980).

'The film contains the most dazzling choreography that has been conceived specifically for the camera since the great movies of Fred Astaire . . . The camera movements and the rhythm of the editing were choreographed, and meticulously rehearsed, together with the dancing, in collaboration with the film maker Charles Atlas . . . Also shown was a documentary *Roamin' I* that hilariously depicts actual filming, with dancers scurrying and crawling out of the camera's way.'[13]

It is some comment upon the distinction of Cunningham's choreography, and upon his uncompromising approach, that from being considered *avant-garde* he is now recognized as an establishment figure in modern dance, and his choreography has been presented at the Paris Opéra – *Un Jour ou deux* with Jasper Johns and John Cage was staged there in 1972.

Cunningham's view is perhaps best caught in his own words:

'You have to love dancing to stick to it. It gives you back nothing, no manuscripts to store away, no paintings to hang on walls or maybe show in museums, no poems to be printed and sold, nothing but that single fleeting moment when you feel alive.'

The emergence of Cunningham from Graham is symptomatic of the creative richness which is encouraged, and has flourished, in American modern dance. The individual style of a choreographer often emerges as the result of a reaction against the parent company. In a survey of modern dance published in New York in 1976, over one hundred contemporary practitioners are listed. Their links with parent companies are indicated, and their lineage back to such seminal troupes as those of Graham, Humphrey, Hanya Holm and Lester Horton is categorized.[14]

Paul Taylor in his own Piece Period, a lively, humorous work which he created in 1962. It is full of incongruities and sharp jokes about 'period' behaviour. The girl deeply involved in a curtsy is Twyla Tharp, at the time a member of Taylor's company.

Typical of this secession is Paul Taylor (b. 1930), one of the dominant figures in the world of dance today. Taylor worked with Graham and Cunningham (and with Balanchine) before his emergence as the director of his own company. Starting off as an unconventional figure, Taylor found his truer identity as a creator of classic distinction and exceptional range. In everything he does the richness of his dance imagination is evident. A plotless piece like his early *Aureole* (1962) is a lyrical response to Handel's music, while *Big Bertha* is a highly dramatic and terrifying short story. In *Orbs*, a full-length piece which dares to use late Beethoven quartets and wins, he produced one of the masterpieces of our time.

Taylor's retirement from dancing in the late 1970s in no way inhibited his creative drive. Indeed, the qualities of his dancing, a noble sensitivity, lightness, and a dazzling sense of humour, seem those which also mark his choreography. Taylor has produced a series of wonderfully funny dance pieces – from the early *Three Epitaphs*, in which three slumping creatures from the Slough of Despond droop and collapse to the sound of primordial jazz, to the ebullient delights of *Book of Beasts* and *Public Domain* – but he has also concerned himself with evoking some of the darkest and unhappiest manifestations of the human spirit. Works like *Dust* and *Churchyard* and *Runes* are night pieces in which the unpredictable, the terrifying and the disquieting are ever present. But Taylor also produces dance that celebrates in a particularly civilized and elegant way the delights of human relationships as, for example, *Guests of May*. Taylor's range can also encompass comments upon the American way of life: *From Sea to Shining Sea* in 1965 satirized much about contemporary life in the United States; *Big Bertha* pin-pointed certain brutalizing aspects of the contemporary scene; *American Genesis* was a complex view of American pioneer life combined with a biblical theme.

Unlike so many of today's contemporary dance creators, Taylor has a taste for good music and his dance works have benefited enormously from the formal support offered by serious and distinguished musical accompaniment. All Taylor's works reflect an almost classical concern with form and structure. They are in the very best sense highly cultivated.

In everything you are aware of an acute sensibility which responds both to drama and dynamics as the matter of dance. If there is a guiding attitude to be seen in the majority of Taylor's dances it may best be described as a courteous respect for the body itself and for the relationships that exist between human beings. Taylor is pre-eminently a craftsman who views his creativity in response to the direct requirements of a forthcoming season: a new work will be devised as a contrast to its predecessor or as a way of featuring a dancer who has been little

used of late. Never coolly analytical, Taylor's dances yet preserve that vitally important distance between inspiration and performance. It is a classicist's view of dancing albeit translated into a contemporary idiom. Even at his darkest and most anguished in *Scudorama* or *Private Domain*, Taylor has kept his cool and thereby maintained the marvellous precision of emotion and dynamics which distinguish his every work. Though now retired as a dancer, Taylor's own performances remain unforgettable. A dancer of splendid physique his movement had an exceptional physical lightness and the most subtle nuance of muscular response to music.

By the 1960s the expansion of modern dance was considerable in America: companies like that of Martha Graham were able to sustain short Broadway seasons. The Graham company, which had first played London to almost empty houses in 1954, returned in 1963 in triumph. As a direct result, the English philanthropist and dance-lover Robin Howard set up a school to provide facilities for the study of authentic Graham technique in London. Graham's principal male dancer, Robert Cohan (b. 1925), assumed direction of the school and under his inspiring leadership a company soon emerged. The London Contemporary Dance Theatre, as it became known, soon proved a hive of creativity. Cohan's own choreographies, and those of the young dancers and choreographers emerging from the company, within ten years had achieved such success and such artistic distinction that the company could appear in the United States and be hailed as an outstanding modern dance ensemble with an English identity. It is to the credit of the London Contemporary Dance Theatre (LCDT) and its school that it has formed not only such choreographers as Siobhan Davies, Richard Alston, Micha Bergese and Robert

Linda Gibbs and Kate Harrison of the London Contemporary Dance Theatre in Class *(1975). This is one of those dance works – like Harald Lander's* Etudes, *Bournonville's* The Conservatory *and Asaf Messerer's* Ballet School for the Moscow Bolshoy Ballet *– which brings the training of dancers to a theatrical form and affords the audience insights into the making of a dancer. Like the classes they honour, these works build to a climax of virtuosity. Cohan's* Class *was his tribute to Graham training from which the London Contemporary Dance Theatre's own dance style evolved.*

Twyla Tharp and two members of her company (below) in Eight Jelly Rolls *(1971), as directed for London Weekend Television by Derek Bailey in 1974 in the programme 'Aquarius'. Tharp much admired the jazz of Jelly Roll Morton, and she created these eight dances to his music. Their style is brilliant, relaxed, free-swinging.*

North, and an outstanding dance ensemble, but also a public throughout Britain which responds with great warmth and understanding to the ideals of modern dance.

It is also to its credit that, in emulation of the American example, the LCDT has gone out to the regions to teach, proselytize and inspire an audience. This has been achieved not only by dancing in theatres throughout Britain but also by moving into colleges of education for 'residencies'. For these the company may divide into two sections, each working in a different location, but giving dance instruction to students in the colleges and to interested teachers. Very significantly, too, members of the company are sent to give classes in schools, thereby bringing a first thrilling awareness of contemporary dance to young people. The pattern of these 'residencies' contains not only instruction but creativity as new works are sometimes prepared in open rehearsals. It is this frankness about the supposedly mysterious art of dancing that has so excited popular response to the company. Furthermore, Cohan and his artists demonstrate an exceptional willingness to 'meet the people' through demonstration programmes and by venturing into unusual performing areas.

The result has been extreme popular affection for the company and an increasing and knowledgeable popular response to contemporary dance. Another result has been a proliferation of small contemporary dance groups labouring with varying ability and success in its wake.

Meanwhile, in the United States the boom in modern dance which began in the 1960s has continued and increased so that today the major companies now find themselves performing regular seasons in theatres far more accessible than the dimmer locations which, in the early years, were both home and performing area. This is not to say that much important work by smaller companies and individual artists does not proliferate in studios and in one of the shrines of modern dance, Judson Church in New York.

This expansion of dance activity is due in no small part to the willingness of many American colleges to welcome dance troupes and to include dance in their curriculum of studies. As early as 1917, Margaret H'Doubler had pioneered dance at the University of Wisconsin; from 1934 onwards Bennington College, Vermont, offered a degree in dance; at Connecticut College, New London, summer festivals featured many of the most outstanding figures of modern dance; at Black Mountain College, Colorado, Merce Cunningham was to be part of an influential radical enterprise. College programmes and summer festivals have meant that students from all over America, and some from Europe, have been able to work with the leading practitioners of modern dance of our time. In conjunction with the many courses in technique, composition and teaching, this has meant that an increasing number of modern dancers are in effect graduates from these university courses.

Today the richness and variety of American modern dance reflects the dominant position of the United States in this field, and is also testimony to the exceptional creative energy of dance in

Douglas Dunn (above), a former Cunningham dancer, in his own Foot Rules *of 1979, with Deborah Riley. Dunn, who has made a number of studies concerning the transference of bodily weight in his dances, emerges as a potent influence not only on the American avant-garde dance scene but also on classical companies. In 1980 he was invited to choreograph a version of* Pulcinella *for the Paris Opéra Ballet.*

America. Dance has now come to encompass almost any style of movement, in any locale, from tightly organized virtuoso movement to minimal activities whose connotation as dance lies more in the mind of the performer than in the eye of the audience. As with much other modern art, the *avant-garde* is too wide-ranging and sometimes too bizarre to be detailed at such close range. Certain themes, though, do seem to have emerged. The demotic of everyday movement has occupied the attentions of performers like Yvonne Rainer, Steve Paxton, Deborah Hay and Lucinda Childs. Meredith Monk's work has involved an audience sometimes moving round the locale for which she has devised specific movement, and her *Juice* was performed in three instalments in different places. The rigorous discipline of such artists as Douglas Dunn offers an intellectually stimulating as well as visually rewarding performance manner. Probably the best known of the generation which came to prominence in the 1970s is Twyla Tharp.

Starting as an uncompromising experimentalist, using all forms of dance as her vocabulary, Twyla Tharp (b. 1942) evolved a highly individual and highly virtuosic style of choreography and dancing which fed from popular social dance forms, tap, ballet, contemporary dance, even baton-twirling. The result, in such dazzling pieces as *Eight Jelly Rolls, The Bix Pieces, Sue's Leg*, has been dancing of a huge and markedly individual brilliance.

Sue's Leg reveals a great deal about Tharp's creative ideals in the late 1970s. She has turned to the jazz dances of the late 1930s and organized them into a theatrical statement. She condenses the experience implicit in them of dance marathons, of showgirls in the movies of the period, of dance hall mannerisms, and from this makes a beautifully succinct choreographic text. A film has been made which preceded and intercut a performance of *Sue's Leg* with newsreels of the 1930s, and the ore from which Tharp refined the gold of that ballet was clearly seen. The result was choreography, as so often with Tharp, of extreme difficulty beneath a glossy free-swinging appearance, dances undanceable save by true virtuosi. It is a dance manner characterized by what looks like controlled anarchy – the closing moments of *Sue's Leg* showed Tharp mauled and thrown by her companions – and it is, paradoxically, very classical in its sense of form, development and dynamic logic. In the internal structure of the work this means that a single movement phrase can be shared between several dancers; the pulse of energy moves not through one body but four, and the result is fast and furious (in the very best sense of the word) but also engagingly fluid and loose-limbed. The dancers' muscular virtuosity lies in making the quicksilver changes of dynamics and direction seem part of a long, easy phrase. It is also, most importantly, very enjoyable to watch. *Sue's Leg*, like so much of Tharp's work of this period, is a homage to the past that is also totally of the present.

A reviewer wrote of Tharp's *Baker's Dozen* (1979) which again feeds happily on the past:

'*Baker's Dozen . . .* is not only representative of the kind of abstract dance to old popular music for which Tharp is now best known, it is one of her most pleasant creations in years. It ever so faintly resembles a party in a garden on some Long Island estate in the affluent 1920s – Santo Loquasto's white sports outfits make everyone seem to have stepped out of the pages of F. Scott Fitzgerald – and the choreography alludes to such dance forms as the tango, Charleston and fox-trot. But these are eccentric, devilishly intricate dances, and they are done with such aplomb that the choreography radiates assurance and well being. This dance of the 1920s, to jazz pieces by Willie 'The Lion' Smith, postpones the Depression indefinitely.'[15]

Tharp is unusual in that she has choreographed for ballet companies as well as for her own group. In 1973 she was invited to produce a work for her own dancers in conjunction with the Robert Joffrey Ballet. *Deuce Coupe* was an enormous success; no less so was *Push Comes to Shove* made for American Ballet Theatre and Mikhail Baryshnikov in 1976.

With Twyla Tharp the two strands of dance in America unite. Ballet and modern dance, which were once sworn enemies, now respect and learn from each other.

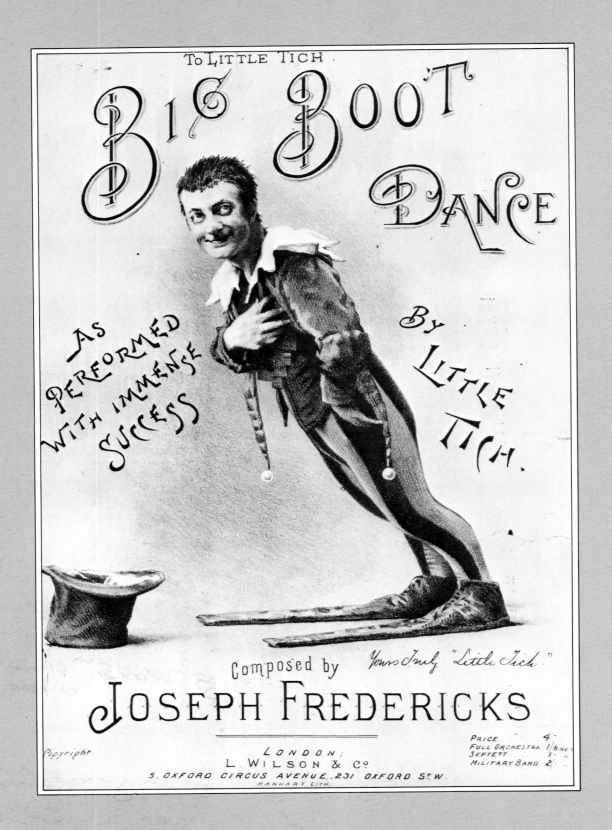

CHAPTER TEN

STAGE & SCREEN

Music cover (left) featuring the great music hall performer Little Tich in his Big Boot Dance which Diaghilev and Nijinsky so admired. Little Tich perfected this dance on an American tour in 1887–89. His boots measured over half his height of four foot six, and wearing them he could lean forward to an angle of forty-five degrees. Jacques Tati, the French comedian, considered the film of this Big Boot Dance to be the 'foundation for everything that has been realized in comedy on the screen'. It is interesting to note that in her first dance in 1965, Twyla Tharp used outsize 'shoes' for keeping her balance in a skiing effect.

Although ballet was reduced to the level of popular entertainment (right) in the Paris of the Belle Epoque, it nevertheless involved dancers of the stature of Carlotta Zambelli, seen on the left in this café-dansant cabaret picture of the 1900s. Zambelli was principal ballerina at the Paris Opéra from the turn of the century until she retired to teach in the early 1930s.

In the popular theatre, far removed from court spectacle or the grandeurs of the opera house, there existed a lively tradition in Europe and America of dancing as part of an entertainment in which there were mingled melodrama and Harlequinades. The traditions of the Italian *commedia dell'arte* permeated the European theatre, surfacing in the performances of Harlequins in London in the eighteenth century, and surviving in the popular theatre of Italy as also in the Danish pantomime theatre still to be seen in Copenhagen to this day. In that extraordinary bastard creation, the English pantomime, the culminating scenes always involved dancing, both academic and grotesque. In France, the popular theatres of the eighteenth century offered dancing as interludes in plays, and by the early nineteenth century there was an established formula in theatres of dance scenes interpolated into dramatic performances.

MUSIC HALLS AND MUSICALS

In Bath in May 1830, the bill at the Theatre Royal included the comedy *Speed the Plough*, a *pas de deux*, a comic song and a 'new dramatic entertainment called *The Somnambulist*'. By the middle of the nineteenth century, dance in popular form could encompass the wild gyrations of the *cancan* in Paris, the song and dance tradition of the English music hall, dance scenes in pantomimes, and in America the use of dancing in the extravaganzas which were to be so popular in the years following the Civil War and which culminated in *The Black Crook* of 1866.

In the music halls of the late nineteenth and early twentieth centuries, dance was a mere

adjunct to the starry antics of the great singers and comedians. A tradition of song and dance entertainers existed, and a few great performers like Lottie Collins, Dan Leno and Little Tich might be said to have incorporated a form of grotesque dancing into their acts – Lottie Collins kicking her heels in *Ta-Ra-Ra-Boom-De-Ay* and Little Tich springing into the air and balancing on the tips of his immense shoes, for which he earned the accolade from Nijinsky 'C'est un grand artiste'. (His impersonation of the Queen of the Fairies in auburn wig and ballet skirt convulsed music halls and pantomime audiences for years.) Dan Leno, who began his career at the age of four dancing outside public houses for pennies (an immemorial tradition in Victorian times), went on to win a championship belt as a clog dancer and even when his youthful energy slackened 'he no longer danced, although he could casually take a stride of six feet or slap the

sole of his shoe on the stage with a report like a pistol shot'.[1]

Such later stars as Lily Morris are an indication of how the traditions of demotic dance, the dance of Londoners, the technique of the 'knees-up', and of urban revels, could be adapted to the stage. In her great song 'Why am I always a Bridesmaid?' Lily Morris danced with wonderful agility, performing those corkscrew gyrations known as *tire-bouchons*. In Nigger Minstrel shows, soft-shoe and eccentric dancing was part of the entertainment and the *cake-walk* in particular was featured both in Europe and America. Probably one of the best known of dance acts in the music halls, which lasted until recently, was the superb comic trio of Wilson, Keppel and Betty whose mock-Egyptian sand dance, performed with utmost seriousness, was one of the joys of the late English music hall.

The music hall, because it was ready to accept every kind of entertainment from performing horses to low comedians, provided a show-place for every kind of dancing. The first Russian dancers seen in the West, Preobrazhenskaya, Karsavina and Pavlova among them, were seen as part of the music hall. Lesser luminaries – such speciality dancers as Maud Allan (1883–1956) with her supposedly scandalous *Vision of Salome*, Napierkowska with her Bee dance (the bee supposedly trapped under her clothing to provide a deliciously naughty nuance for the audience), Kate Vaughan with that epitome of refinement, the skirt dance, Adeline Genée impeccably dainty and respectable – all appeared in theatres and music halls on variety bills. So, too, did Diaghilev's Ballet at the London Coliseum, and Martha Graham in the Ziegfeld Follies and on her first visit to London (when she claims to have been kissed on the shoulder by one of Miss May's

Performing Horses). So, too, did a legion of American and British dancers whose only memorials now are the theatrical postcards which captured their activities, from *cake-walk* to thoroughly dubious Spanish dance, from adagio act to insecure teeterings on pointe. Something of the range of dance which flourished in the music hall and on the vaudeville stage is indicated here. It would be possible to cite examples of every form of dance in this milieu.

The logical extension of all this diverse activity was the tradition of spectacular theatrical extravaganzas which were to be seen on the stages of Europe and America during the later years of the nineteenth century. In America the supreme example was *The Black Crook* at Niblo's Garden (already described in the section on ballet in the United States). Its ballet troupe was led by such ballerinas as Maria Bonfanti and Rita Sangalli, with thirty other *danseuses* and 'fifty auxiliary ladies'. Inevitably it had imitators and successors, and it has been suggested that it was the forerunner of the musical comedy of the twentieth century. Preposterous in every way, and with a generous complement of slightly naughty ladies, it was the most successful theatrical enterprise in America until the long-running musicals of recent years.

In France the music hall tradition flourished. It appeared in small *cafés-concerts* and in much larger centres like the Moulin Rouge, where La Goulue and Valentin-le-Désossé led the *cancan*, the Folies-Bergère where Cléo de Mérode and Loïe Fuller shone, at the Eldorado, and the Palais de Glace where the Tiller Girls (a group of precision dancers from London) appeared in Paris in 1900. Of La Goulue one critic wrote in the *New Yorker* in 1929:

'She did the split amid sixty yards of lace trimming her stylish long skirt, and starred in the quadrilles in the arms of her famous partners: Valentine-le-Désossé (the Boneless Wonder) . . .[2]

In Paris this music hall tradition has never died. Given the passage of the years and the change in public taste, the style of the entertainments has remained very much the same, with the emphasis on beautiful girls, scantily clad if clad at all, and much bedecked with feathers. Among the great stars of the twentieth century, Josephine Baker (1906–1975) occupies a unique place. Arriving in Paris in 1925 in *La Revue nègre* at the Champs Elysées, she stunned Paris by her beauty and the speed and ebullience of her dancing, and remained its darling thereafter for many years. Most recently another fine dancer, Zizi Jeanmaire, has renewed the vitality of the dance in theatrical spectaculars, in shows devised by her husband Roland Petit, her art transcending the barriers between the ballet and the music hall with consummate ease.

In Paris, too, a new theatre opened in 1883, the Eden Theatre, which was to provide a home

Josephine Baker's vivacity, her ravishing 'bronze' figure and her joie de vivre *(below) made her the darling of Paris for nearly half a century. She danced at the Cotton Club in Harlem before conquering Paris in* La Revue nègre *in 1925.*

for ballet and circus spectaculars. 'Paris was accustomed to enjoying its ballet in association with the opera, while in London ballet had taken root in the music hall. The management of the Eden offered a new permutation – Italian ballet and the circus.'[3] In addition to the Italian Virginia Zucchi, such dancers as Cornalba, Palladino and an American dancer from New Orleans, Albertina Flindt, were to be seen in the vastly complex entertainments at the Eden.

In London, Leicester Square provided a centre for the popular forms of dance for here were situated two of the great theatres of the town, the Alhambra and the Empire. The Alhambra offered every possible delight for the mashers of the period from cheap oysters and the staple chops and steaks of the Victorian era to such splendid tipples as potions named 'the stone fence' and 'the locomotive'. The entertainments included every form of popular songster and comedian but the Alhambra was particularly associated with spectacle, from trapeze artists to a ballet company which numbered over four hundred members (and few of them male). The ballets in which these forces were deployed relied upon amazing effects and the naughtiness implicit in any such entertainment. Among the ballerinas, the most celebrated of the 1860s was probably the Italian Emma Pitteri, much fêted in her heyday but destined to die while appearing in a dance hall in the Marseille dockside. Troupes of *cancan* dancers were brought over from Paris and among the most famous exponents of that dance was a skinny English girl, Sarah Wright, popularly known as Sarah the Kicker or Wiry Sal,

whose unbridled gyrations deprived the Alhambra of its magistrate's licence for a time. In the 1870s the Alhambra changed its identity, becoming a theatre and offering a long series of operettas with an attendant *corps de ballet*.

A decade and a fire later, a new Alhambra became the home for the grandest music hall with dancing from the ballets of the period forming an essential part of its programmes. The ladies of the *corps* dressed as soldiers – the combination of busby and silk tights was irresistibly funny – and stars like La Belle Otéro were brought over. From this time the Alhambra was to become, in effect, a ballet house of some distinction, and prior to the arrival of the Diaghilev Ballet with the great *Sleeping Princess* production in 1921 it had also shown to the public a long series of ballets featuring such stars as Pierina Legnani in the 1890s and Ekaterina Geltzer and Vasily Tikhomirov in Gorsky's spectacular *The Dance Dream* in 1911.

It is worth recording that in this year the following dancers were to be found appearing in London: Maud Allan, Lydia Kyasht and a full company in *Sylvia* at the Empire Theatre; Anna Pavlova and Mikhail Mordkin on the bill at the Palace Theatre: Geltzer and Tikhomirov, as mentioned, in the *Dance Dream*; Adeline Genée and Bekeffi at the Coliseum; and the Imperial Russian Ballet (that is, the Diaghilev troupe) at Covent Garden. (No London season today can offer such variety.)

Across Leicester Square at the Empire Theatre a no less vigorous tradition of dance performances was maintained between 1884 and 1914. It was here that *Coppélia* and *Giselle* were given and Katti Lanner became ballet mistress for many years. But the greatest name associated with the Empire was that of Adeline Genée, who made her first appearance in 1897 and reigned there for the next decade. Her roles varied from appearance in pure dance works to participation in such divertissements as *The Pretty Prentice* and the work in which she conquered New York, *The Soul Kiss*.

Genée's American triumph inevitably invited comparisons between her and the darling of the American dance stage, Bessie Clayton. Originally a pupil of George Washington Smith, Clayton had taken to the stage as a child prodigy in vaudeville but had developed her technique to encompass academic dance as well as the more popular forms of ballroom dancing and skirt dancing. She was hailed as America's foremost dancer and as being 'to America what Genée has been to Europe' and her career, which took her to Europe as well as to stardom on Broadway, suggests something of the way in which dancing was to become an integral part of the musical stage. Appearing in such thrilling examples of dramatic art as *Kickette de lingerie* and in Ziegfeld shows, she held her own with stars like Eva Tanguay and Lillian Russell. Her importance can be gauged from the fact that in 1912 when she

Florenz Ziegfeld made his show girls the most elegant and attractive on Broadway. Like the Gaiety Girls of George Edwardes' theatres in London, they were beauties first, clothes-horses second, and dancers – possibly – third. Ziegfeld used to star artists such as Fanny Brice and W. C. Fields in his Follies *in New York, and on one of the Follies tours in 1927 Denishawn – Ruth St Denis and Ted Shawn – performed solos to great effect.*

danced at the Alhambra in London in *The Mad Pierrot* her act required no fewer than two hundred and fifty people, three sets and an orchestra of fifty-five musicians. It lasted thirty-five minutes and cost over £30,000.[4]

It is with the turn of the century that the form of musical comedy emerges, in all its inane charm, from its ancestry in the operettas of the nineteenth century. Musical comedy differed from revue or music hall in that it had a basic plot, no matter how farcical, upon which the dances, production extravaganzas and popular songs were festooned. It was essentially a product of the Edwardian era in England, although exchange of shows with New York had begun as early as 1899 when *The Belle of New York* crossed the Atlantic. The early years of English musical comedy are celebrated in the stagings of George Edwardes and the opulent shows for ever associated with his Gaiety Theatre and his Gaiety Girls – who did so much not only to brighten the English stage but also the British peerage. As a combination of tuneful music, lavish production and cohorts of very pretty girls exquisitely dressed, and with such stars as Lily Elsie, the musical comedy featured dancing as an unimportant background for its stars. In the 1920s there was a notable improvement in the standard of dancing in these shows.

Certain artists who emerged from the British musical comedy tradition were hailed for their excellence as dancers. All musical comedy stars were expected to be 'song and dance' artists and during the 1920s and 1930s – the heyday of British musical comedy – Jessie Matthews, with her ravishing legs and her thistledown lightness, and the superbly stylish partnership of Elsie Randolph and Jack Buchanan, brought great lustre to the British musical stage.

Dancing featured in such hits of the mid and late 1920s as *No, No, Nanette* (1925) and *Show Boat* which exploded onto Broadway in 1927 and from which can be traced the whole subsequent development of Broadway musicals. Based on the novel by Edna Ferber, *Show Boat* with its marvellous Jerome Kern score and brilliant libretto by Oscar Hammerstein, showed through its admirable blend of music, lyrics and libretto a way forward for the American musical. Looking back to the show boats themselves, those floating theatres of the Mississippi and Ohio rivers, a contemporary described the vaudeville performer's task:

'. . . an actor on a show boat is nothing if not versatile. He must play the cornet in the orchestra . . . when the drama begins he must portray the bearded father . . . he must do a tap dance; play the piano strings with a nail as over a harp . . . and one minute before the final curtain is thrown to his death to the Indians waiting in triumph at the foot of Grand Canyon.'

A parallel strain of musical show which was also to be vital in the presentation of dance in the popular theatre came with the great succession of revues which so delighted the public, in Europe as in New York, during the 1920s and 1930s. Thanks to the vision and acumen of such impresarios as André Charlot, Florenz Ziegfeld and Charles B. Cochran, the revue emerged as a vastly popular entertainment which called upon some of the most distinguished choreographers, dancers and designers of the time. Cochran could employ Balanchine, Massine and Lifar to make ballets, and feature Oliver Messel as a decorator (notably in *Helen* in 1932). The fashion for black performers in these revues was initiated in New York in the early 1920s with *Shuffle Along*, starring Florence Mills, and was to reach its highpoint in the celebrated *Blackbirds* of 1926. In Paris the triumph of Josephine Baker is part of theatrical history. Many of the most illustrious names in ballet were associated with revue and musical comedy during the 1920s and 1930s, finding in this popular form of entertainment a source of income and work not yet available within the framework of established ballet companies. In the emergent British ballet scene, for example, Ashton, Markova, Dolin, Gore and Helpmann also worked in musicals and revue.

But the British output of musical comedy retained a fairly conventional image, pretty and tuneful, seldom venturing outside Ruritania for its subject matter although Noël Coward raised the quality of lyric-writing considerably in his revues – in many of which he too sang and danced. The Ivor Novello brand of lush romanticism was to dominate the stage of the Theatre Royal, Drury Lane, by the end of the 1930s.

It was America, where Jerome Kern was already writing enchanting pieces, which was to make the most vital contribution to the form from the 1920s until the present day. A show such as Gershwin's *The Band Wagon* (1931) offered the theatregoer the chance of seeing the incomparable Fred and Adele Astaire with Tilly Losch, and choreography by the queen of Broadway routines, Albertina Rasch. These were the great days of the precision routine, first popularized by the Tiller Girls, which reached its culmination in the immaculately precise high-kicking of the long line of dancers, the Rockettes of Radio City Music Hall.

Ragtime and the use of the new social dance forms, translated into theatrical form by consummate artists, transformed musical comedy into what is now called 'the musical' and made of it an adult entertainment. The young Noël Coward recognized this infusion in 1921 when he saw Fred and Adele Astaire dancing in *The Love Letter*: 'I hadn't realized before then that such rhythm and taste in dancing were possible.'

The Astaires appeared in many shows in London and New York until Adele's retirement upon marriage in 1932. For them the Gershwins wrote *Lady, Be Good* (1924) and *Funny Face* (1927). The Gershwins, with George Kaufman

Design by Anthony Nellé for the Roxy Music Hall in New York. Nellé, at one time a dancer in Warsaw, came to New York in the 1920s with Pavlova and became a choreographer and designer for opera and cinema. He worked at the Roxy in New York in the 1920s and 1930s.

and Moss Hart, Irving Berlin, Cole Porter, Richard Rodgers with Lorenz Hart and Oscar Hammerstein brought an ever-increasing insistence upon the importance of dance as a vital element in their shows.

Political satire was to be recognized as a biting source material during the Depression years and with the production of the Gershwin/Kaufman *Of Thee I Sing* at the Music Box Theatre, New York, in December 1931, the musical can be said to have grown up. It was the first musical to win a Pulitzer Prize and ran for four hundred and forty-one performances on Broadway but was never seen in London – London's loss.

From 1936 onwards George Balanchine worked regularly on Broadway. For eight years he arranged dances for such shows as *I Married an Angel, The Boys from Syracuse, Cabin in the Sky* (for which he directed the entire production, assisted by Katherine Dunham), and *Song of Norway*. His earliest success was the innovatory *On Your Toes* in 1936.

For this Rodgers and Hart show, Billy Rose the impresario engaged George Balanchine to provide the dances, which linked musical comedy and ballet, and in the celebrated Slaughter on Tenth Avenue scene the ballerina Tamara Gevergeyeva became Tamara Geva and joined forces with the tap dancer Ray Bolger. Balanchine's biographer declared that the ballet scenes, including Slaughter on Tenth Avenue:

'. . . were the first ever seen in a Broadway musical that were not just interludes but functioned as an essential, active aspect of the plot. This paved the way for what was done by Agnes de Mille a few years later in

The Dance in the Gym, from West Side Story *(1957). The theme of this immensely successful and influential musical was that of Romeo and Juliet translated into feuding between the white and Puerto Rican communities on the West Side of New York at that time.*

Oklahoma! Thus Balanchine began a trend in American musical comedy that has helped to make it one of the brightest of this country's current theatrical forms.'[5]

In 1940 came the Rodgers and Hart *Pal Joey*, with choreography by Robert Alton, and Gene Kelly playing the 'anti-hero' master of ceremonies in a night club. It made Kelly a star overnight and Rodgers described it as a musical which 'wore long pants'. Not an outstanding success at the time, *Pal Joey* in fact launched the cascade of American musicals that were to give dance increasing importance and employ choreographers of the greatest distinction over the next four decades.

In *Oklahoma!* (1943) the dances by Agnes de Mille were used positively to develop the narrative, notably in the dance scene Laurie Makes Up Her Mind, in which the heroine considers the claims of her rival suitors and makes her decision. The following year came *On the Town* in which Jerome Robbins and Leonard Bernstein translated the basic plot of their first ballet, *Fancy Free*, into a musical in which once again dance was integral to the plot. The work of choreographers such as Hanya Holm in *Kiss Me Kate* and *My Fair Lady*, and Michael Kidd in *Can Can, Finian's Rainbow* and *Guys and Dolls* continued this trend. With *Damn Yankees* in 1955, and the triumphant performance of Gwen Verdon, Bob Fosse was launched on his career as a prolific dance arranger and director of musicals. But the supreme statement about dance as a motor force in the musical is *West Side Story*, first produced at the Winter Garden, New York, in September 1957. With a score by Leonard

the actual structure of a production. A study of the lives and feelings of the members of a chorus line, it offered a mirror image of itself, the cast being the fabric of the action.

The musical throughout its history has provided a not inexact image of the importance of dance and of its identity in society throughout the twentieth century. It has been fed by the social dances of the time; it has in its turn fed the social dances. This general pattern is evident from the jazz and ragtime infusions through the Charleston craze of the 1920s to the disco dancing in the film *Grease* in the 1970s.

FILMS

It is one of the ironies of history that the cinema, which has recorded every kind of event as well as the ephemera of life since the beginning of this century, has maintained an exasperatingly ambivalent response to dance. It is one of the great tragedies of film that there is no record of Vaslav Nijinsky dancing, and all you can see of him in life is a few seconds of an old gentleman walking away from his hotel in Vienna where he was filmed in 1945. Of the magnificent enterprise of the Diaghilev Ballet not one frame was shot, and this at a time when the cinema was capable of preserving performances clearly and well. Of course the great disadvantage as far as the cinema was concerned was that, until the late 1920s, music – the dance's vital partner – could not be successfully married with dance on film.

Nevertheless, in the matter of recording dances for posterity the cinema's record is very bad: there exist some brief fragments of various kinds of dance shot by such pioneers of the cinema as Georges Méliès, and D. W. Griffith included some dancing in his *Intolerance* of 1914. The cinema was prepared to preserve social dance as part of the fabric of life (which was captured in the dramatic films of the 1920s) but it was the arrival of sound which opened up the possibility of making the musical film, in which area the cinema has done its best to bring dance to the public all round the world.

The 1930s must seem both a dawn and a golden age of dance in films, for this period was dominated by such masters as Busby Berkeley and Fred Astaire. In the work of both there is a brilliant understanding of the prime fact concerning filmed dance, that of involving the camera as an integral part of the action. One of the problems of filming any form of dancing is that the straight filmed record of a dance immediately flattens and denies dance's pre-eminent quality as a spatial exercise. Busby Berkeley choreographed for the camera. In a thrilling series of films, Berkeley created amazing dance effects more through the use of the camera moving round and through the dancers than of dancers moving in front of a camera.

A Chorus Line, directed by Michael Bennet (1976). A view of the London production of this highly successful show (left) which used the auditioning of the cast as the action in a completely original manner, directly relating the dance to the structure of the musical.

Busby Berkeley's famous revolving fountain scene (right) in Warner Brothers' Footlight Parade of 1933. His skill in 'patterned drill' (from First World War army service) resulted in memorable film musicals in the 1920s and 1930s.

Fred Astaire (below) in the RKO film Top Hat (1935). In all his work in the theatre and then the cinema the peerless Astaire evolved a style that moved happily between social dancing and tap – delighting the eye while advancing the narrative.

Bernstein, lyrics by Stephen Sondheim and book by Arthur Laurents, *West Side Story* was directed and choreographed by Jerome Robbins. Never before had dance been the dominant factor as it was in this show.

A decade later the American tribal love rock musical, *Hair*, initiated a new style of Broadway show, one in which the demotic of social dance among the hippy generation was to be part of the fabric of a show: it was authentically of its time in attitudes as in dance. Its successors – such pieces as *Godspell, Jesus Christ Superstar* – cashed in on the enormously successful mixture of rock music and religion. But it was *A Chorus Line*, directed by Michael Bennett in 1976, which suggested how intimately dance should relate to

In such films as his three creations of 1933 – *42nd Street*, *Gold Diggers of 1933* and *Footlight Parade* – Berkeley devised an entirely new visual excitement for his audience as his camera recorded the kaleidoscopic patterns of legions of pretty girls moving like automata, playing pianos, outfitted with illuminated violins, or floating in water.

With Fred Astaire the cinema has preserved and shaped the art of a man often described, and with some justification, as the finest dancer of this century. Astaire's impeccably elegant persona – usually in white tie and tails, but sometimes as a sailor and once, improbably, as a member of a Russian ballet company – was reflected in the incomparable elegance of his dancing. The choreography for his dances, which he usually worked out in collaboration with his dance director Hermes Pan, made use of the social dance of the period – transmuting it into something both fluent and daring, as in his partnership with Ginger Rogers which evoked the glamour and stylishness of Vernon and Irene Castle. He was also extremely resourceful in making use of surrounding properties. Astaire, the consummate tap dancer, an artist with flawless rhythmic response, used such props as a ship's boiler room or drums or a table to spark off routines of dazzling bravura with a kind of careless ease which was the result of immense virtuosity totally at the service of his debonair and charming personality. The cinema has committed innumerable crimes against dancing, but it has redeemed itself by revealing the genius of Astaire.

His films of the 1930s, *The Gay Divorcee* (*The Gay Divorce* in Britain), *Flying Down to Rio*, *Roberta*, *Top Hat*, *Follow the Fleet*, *Swing Time*, *Shall We Dance?*, *Carefree*, *The Story of*

Vernon and Irene Castle – all with Ginger Rogers – are an irresistible record of a period and a unique dance style. The success of the Berkeley and Astaire films is an indication of the cinema's delight in the musical, and in these early years of the talkies a proliferation of films featured dancing as part of musical comedies. The British cinema had one adorable dancing star in Jessie Matthews, a performer of exquisite lightness and the greatest charm, whose magic is preserved in the ever green *Ever Green*.

Other great dancing stars were to feature in Hollywood musicals, among them such famous tappers as 'Bojangles' Robinson, Eleanor Powell and Ray Bolger, while during the time that George Balanchine was married to Vera Zorina he worked in Hollywood, most notably on the *Goldwyn Follies of 1938*, *On Your Toes* (1939) and *I was an Adventuress* (1940).

The other major talent to make his mark in the dance film was Gene Kelly. Moving to Hollywood from Broadway, Kelly made his first success with *Cover Girl* (1943) and then was associated with two of the greatest Hollywood musicals of the next decade, *On the Town* (1949)

Seven Brides for Seven Brothers (MGM, 1954) was one of the first films to use highly skilled dancers and give important place to dance numbers. Seen here is the Goin' Courtin' number with Jane Powell in the centre, surrounded by a distinguished group of male dancers. From left to right: Matt Mattox, Marc Platt (who in his Ballet Russe days was Marc Platoff), Russ Tamblyn, Jacques d'Amboise of New York City Ballet, Tommy Rall of American Ballet Theatre, and Jeff Richards, the actor.

and *Singin' in the Rain* (1952). In these it can be seen how Hollywood had developed the musical into a form wherein the dance was to become a vital part of the actual structure of the film.

The cinema was to make, naturally enough, glossy adaptations of successful Broadway shows – *Oklahoma!*, *Guys and Dolls*, *Pajama Game*, *Kiss Me Kate*, *Sweet Charity*, *Cabaret* – but more important have been those works in which, as in *Seven Brides for Seven Brothers*, the cinema generated its own film dance-language for the screen. Unforgettable in *Seven Brides* is the Hoe-down to celebrate the building of a barn, choreographed by Michael Kidd. Unique in the cinema, as in the theatre, was Jerome Robbins' *West Side Story*, truly a work in which the dance was the structural basis for the entire entertainment. If these major Hollywood productions are cited it is because, with very few exceptions, musicals and dance films elsewhere have trodden feebly along the trail blazed by the imaginative skill, the resources, and technical excellence of the American cinema.

A recent triumph has been the work of the modern choreographer Twyla Tharp in the filmed version of the musical *Hair*. In this, as in every other major Hollywood movie, the willingness of the American cinema to use the best talent available is evident. The cinema has also provided for the social historian the most remarkable record of the dance crazes of the century. From Joan Crawford's Charleston in *Our Dancing Daughters* in 1928 to John Travolta in *Saturday Night Fever* and *Grease* in the late 1970s, vivid testimony is preserved of every dance fashion. It is also worth noting that the cinema has helped to launch dance fashions: the Charleston craze was merely recorded in the movie, but John Travolta certainly initiated the disco craze of the 1970s.

The cinema has had another function in connection with dancing, that of a recording eye.

The early film-makers captured a few wildly imperfect moments of dancing at the turn of the century – there is even a brief record of Pierina Legnani – and the Moscow film-makers could preserve some stars of their ballet before the First World War. In Denmark, there exists a priceless film of Hans Beck and Valborg Borchsenius in some Bournonville fragments which give real insight into the true Bournonville style. Anna Pavlova was tantalizingly captured by Douglas Fairbanks in a few short numbers during a visit to Hollywood in 1924, and there exist other snippets of her dancing, thrilling for what they show, maddening in their brevity. But the cinema has in the main been more than remiss in the first decades of this century.

Although there have been several amateur attempts at recording dance on film, including a most valuable record of Olga Spessivtseva and some extraordinary film of the Ballet Russe companies in Australia during the 1930s, the professional cinema has made only intermittent attempts at presenting ballet or dance to a larger audience. The reasons for this are several: the ballet companies' inability to give time to the necessarily lengthy process of filming; the fact that ballet until recently has been outside the experience of the film industry; the absence of any demand from the general public; and the poor financial rewards available to the dancers, let alone to the film companies. But more radical even than this was the long-time unsuitability of the cinema as a means of preserving ballet other than as the flattest record of performance. Ballet is an art existing in the three dimensions of the stage area. The camera is unable to convey the depth of patterning and the spatial relationships between bodies save in long shots. Sudden cuts away from the general pattern of the choreography to a principal dancer at a moment of high importance in the ballet are exasperating and insensitive. When brought into close-up, how destructive of the choreographer's intention is the concentration upon a single part of the body, a head or a foot, when the whole art of ballet depends upon seeing the body, and that usually in relation to an entire *corps de ballet*. Close-ups, furthermore, stress the sweating athleticism that is a part of dancing – nothing could be more destructive of ballet's essential theatrical illusion than the camera's intrusions upon straining muscle or a face beaded with perspiration. Perhaps even more important in alienating ballet from the cinema is the fact that the cameraman and the director intrude their own personalities and preferences between dancer or choreography and audience. The only successful recording of choreography or of performance must depend upon control of shots and angles being in the hands of a choreographer who knows which parts of a ballet must be stressed by the camera work, or by a director who is also a choreographer. Rare are the occasions when this has happened.

Nevertheless, ballet has a glamour and an attraction to which the cinema has responded – increasingly so over the past few decades when ballet's popularity has reassured film-makers that their records of performances can be financially viable.

Among the earliest ballet films for the general public was *La Mort du cygne* made in 1938, with choreography by Lifar, and featuring Mia Slavenska, Yvette Chauviré and the very young Janine Charrat. Hollywood made an attempt to record something of the Massine repertory by filming *Capriccio espagnol* and *Gaieté parisienne*, but sabotaged the value of the enterprise by preferring a pretty *corps de ballet* girl to the incomparable and beautiful Alexandra Danilova when casting the role of the glove-seller in *Gaieté*. Walt Disney used Riabouchinska and Lichine

briefly in his *Fantasia*; other companies involved the participation of Markova, Baronova and Dolin incidentally in films. But the most popular dance film probably remains the dreadful *Red Shoes* (1948). This purported to be about a Russian ballet company, and trapped in its nonsensical convolutions were Moira Shearer, Robert Helpmann and Léonide Massine among others. Its most valid moment was a ballet especially choreographed for the cinema, making use of cinema techniques, and suggesting the rich but still unexplored possibilities of choreography specifically created to use both camera and dancers. Derided by critics and most of the ballet world, *The Red Shoes* had an immense success, stimulating great public enthusiasm and justifying itself by encouraging young people to consider ballet as a career. It also prepared America (where it had tremendous popularity) for the first visit there of the Sadler's Wells Ballet in 1949.

As a sequel, the producers also compiled an opera–ballet *The Tales of Hoffmann* (1951), memorable today only for its singularly hideous design and by the ludicrous sight of Moira Shearer dancing while also apparently surmounting the coloratura hurdles of the doll song. *Hoffmann* involved Sir Thomas Beecham, Massine and Ashton, whose reputations were sufficiently secure to survive the enterprise.

In Hollywood, Gene Kelly was involved in a series of films which sought to use ballet. These included *An American in Paris* (1951) and *Invitation to the Dance* (1952) and they were interesting for the participation of certain celebrated dancers, among them Tamara Toumanova and Igor Youskevitch, while Roland Petit's *Hans Christian Andersen* of 1951 featured Zizi Jeanmaire and Erik Bruhn.

It is to Russia you have to look for a more direct and conscientious attempt at preserving major ballets and major dancers. Among the great performances secured for posterity are those of Marina Semyonova, Natalia Dudinskaya, Galina Ulanova, Vakhtang Chabukiany, Konstantin Sergeyev, Raissa Struchkova and Maya Plisetskaya. Important ballets have also been preserved: *Romeo and Juliet* with Ulanova; *The Little Humpbacked Horse* with Plisetskaya and Vasiliev; Chabukiany's *Othello*; and several more.

One of the great Bolshoy productions was preserved at the time of the company's first visit to London in 1956. Paul Czinner installed a series of cameras at strategic positions in the Royal Opera House, Covent Garden, and throughout one night Ulanova and the Bolshoy Ballet performed *Giselle*. The eleven differently angled shots from the cameras were then edited to provide a compelling portrait of this great ballerina in her great role. Czinner went on to perform this same valuable service for Margot Fonteyn, preserving her interpretations in *Swan Lake* (Act II), in *The Firebird* and, supremely, in *Ondine* – a record which exactly catches the

Robert Helpmann, Moira Shearer and Léonide Massine in The Red Shoes *(Rank, 1948). The ballet scene shown here was inspired by Hans Christian Andersen's fairy tale. Massine is dangling the eponymous shoes in front of Shearer.*

charm and beauty of her presence in the Royal Ballet's staging of Ashton's ballet. Regrettably, Fonteyn and Nureyev were also filmed in *Romeo and Juliet*. The need for star names outweighed the artistic consideration that they were not suited to their roles, and that the ballet had been created by Kenneth MacMillan to enshrine the young and lustrous talents of Lynn Seymour and Christopher Gable.

It is from this time that ballet was to be recognized as a commercially possible commodity in the cinema and there has been a commendable increase in dance films – a star like Rudolf Nureyev can justify the filming of his own productions of *Don Quixote* (with the Australian Ballet) and *Swan Lake* (with Fonteyn and the Vienna Ballet). Throughout Europe ballet films have been made during the past decade which offer a very fair assessment of dance in our time, and it is important at this moment to stress that the cinema has concerned itself not only with ballet but also with modern dance and every form of ethnic dance.

In 1975 a Festival for Filmatic Dance under the auspices of UNESCO was held in Sweden, and the range of its offerings (which also included television dance) stretched from Japanese Noh plays, Albanian folk dance, and ballet, to some of the greatest names of the contemporary dance scene such as Martha Graham, whose creativity has been very honourably preserved on film, to experimental works which venture into the exciting area of choreography for cameras as well as dancers.

Attempts to create authentic ballet films, in which the dance is the entire justification for the action, are rare, though Frederick Ashton's choreography was used with great skill as the text for *The Tales of Beatrix Potter* (1971). A remarkable impulse for ballet-going came with the Herbert Ross movie *The Turning Point* (1978). A glossy woman's magazine melodrama about a ballet company and the various ambitions and disappointments of the dancer's life, it was justified by presenting Mikhail Baryshnikov in a central role and capturing something of his dancing. It gained much from the fact that its director, Herbert Ross, had been a distinguished choreographer before moving to Hollywood.

TELEVISION

Television's insatiable appetite for all forms of entertainment has been of especial benefit to dance. Good, bad or indifferent, dance is guaranteed some sort of showing on television, though in this respect Britain lags sadly behind the admirable example of both Germany and the United States. In its very earliest days, television made some slight nod to dance: Alicia Markova records having been invited to appear in test transmissions by John Logie Baird; Antony Tudor choreographed a *Fugue for Four Cameras* especially for Maude Lloyd in the early 1930s. Three days after its first public transmission on 2 November 1936 the BBC showed a divertissement by Ballet Rambert dancers and up to the outbreak of war and the cessation of television programmes the BBC made several important programmes about ballet. With the post-war boom in television, dance of all forms was to be welcomed into the studios. In Britain, Margaret Dale did valuable work in adapting ballet to the small screen. Her understanding, gained from her distinguished career as a dancer with the Sadler's Wells Ballet, was immensely useful and her transmissions of *Coppélia, Giselle* and *La Fille mal gardée* were admirable examples of television ballet. She was further helped by the participation of Nadia Nerina, a ballerina willing and eager to adapt to the new medium.

In America such programmes as the 'Bell Telephone Hour' regularly featured star dancers in short dance excerpts. They included *pas de deux* danced by many of the greatest stars of the time: notable was a condensed version of *La Sylphide* made by Erik Bruhn for himself and Carla Fracci.

The advent of colour television in the 1960s was to provide a further impetus for television companies to present dance programmes. In Sweden, the choreographer Birgit Cullberg has made many programmes in which her choreographies have been specially conceived for the medium. Similarly in Denmark, Flemming Flindt, in such works as *The Lesson, The Young Man Must Marry* and *The Triumph of Death* choreographed works initially for television and then transferred them to the ballet stage. In Canada, Norman McLaren has made outstanding experimental works, in which the possibilities of the camera have been integral to the realization of the piece. So successful was his *Pas de Deux* that an entire documentary was later devoted to his work by Margaret Dale in 1969. The work of Alwin Nikolais has also proved itself ideally suited to television realization, and in the United States there has emerged a series, 'Dance in America', which has provided one of the most valuable surveys of the whole field of dance. An American modern dancer who has manifested an extreme interest in the television camera as an integral part of his overall creativity is Merce Cunningham.

Television is not always successful in recording dance – the major enterprise of filming the Balanchine repertory of the New York City Ballet in Germany was exasperating through its wilful and bemusing camera work. But Germany has, nevertheless, a very fine record of presentation of both ballet and modern dance, and in America it has been possible to make direct transmissions from the theatre of important ballet performances: Baryshnikov and Makarova in *Giselle* and Makarova in *Swan Lake* have been transmitted across the continent. Despite intractable union attitudes, which often inhibit transmissions, it has yet been possible to beam live performances by the Royal Ballet across the Atlantic and in 1978 and 1980, the BBC under the admirable guidance of Humphrey Burton was able to present a 'Dance Month' in which a rich variety of programmes was shown.

The largest viewing figures in Britain for a television dance programme were achieved for London Weekend Television's documentary about Kenneth MacMillan's *Mayerling* for the Royal Ballet in which the television director, Derek Bailey, provided a masterly insight into the creation and performance of a major new work. It was the first dance programme to win the Prix Italia, the most prestigious award for television programmes.

Today there is an increasing and welcome tendency for television companies to initiate dance programmes as well as to provide a public service in transmitting already existing works. Valuable documentaries have been made about such great figures as Dame Ninette de Valois and Dame Marie Rambert and in 1968 John Drummond devised two informative programmes about the Diaghilev Ballet in which many former Diaghilev dancers participated. Documentaries about artists like Edward Villella and Anthony Dowell have done much to dispel myths surrounding the male ballet dancer. In this way a new audience for dance is educated and developed.

Various catalogues, illuminating if not complete, exist to show something of the material available and afford some indication of the wealth of dance activity preserved on film.[6]

Lynn Seymour and David Wall as Mary Vetsera and Crown Prince Rudolf in the culminating pas de deux *before their suicide in Kenneth MacMillan's* Mayerling *(1978). The television documentary of the same year, MacMillan's* Mayerling, *which charted the making of this ballet, won the prestigious Prix Italia prize for London Weekend Television who produced the programme.*

APPENDIX

NOTATION

Alternative notations are shown here of the girl's variation from the Bluebird pas de deux from The Sleeping Beauty, *Act III, to Tchaikovsky's score.*

Labanotation (to be read from base to top).
The central staff represents the central line in the body and columns at right and left indicate steps (supports), leg gestures, torso movements, arms, hands etc. The centre line also provides a time line and is marked off into regular beats and bars. The shape of block symbols indicates the direction of movement; black, dot or striped shading indicates the level (low, middle or high); the length indicates time duration of movement (longer means slower, short – fast); placement on the staff indicates which part of body; lesser symbols (pins, hooks etc.) modify the main structure of movement.
Sample excerpt (right) shows slower movements separated by a pause in bars one and two, while in bar three fast steps and faster arm gestures occur.

F ROM THE earliest times the need to devise some method of recording dance can be seen as a manifestation of man's desire to fix his knowledge upon a page but, unlike musical notation, dance notation never achieved a universal and efficient system until the emergence in this century of two precise methods of recording movement – those of Laban and Benesh. However, from the first days of Renaissance dance in the fifteenth century there was an attempt to provide some systematic indication of movement, with abbreviations to identify steps so that R meant *reverencia*, P – *passo* and so on.

In 1463 Guglielmo Ebreo of Pesaro notated *basses danses* by means of words and letters and one of the rarest and earliest of dance manuscripts, the celebrated Golden Manuscript – the *Livre des basses danses* (dating from the middle of the fifteenth century and supposedly belonging to Margaret of Austria) – contains music and notation of court dances for the use of the nobility. A century later, in 1588, there was published at Langres one of the most important dance manuals containing descriptions of dances with their music and also an attempt at indicating the basic patterns of the dance through alphabetical symbols. This was the *Orchésographie* of

Thoinot Arbeau. Despite the obvious limitations of this system it served the essential purpose of helping to make the forms of dances more regular by providing basic terms of reference for the floor patterns of the dance.

Floor patterns were the first criteria in considering the identity and first function of choreography, and the most sophisticated system to emerge towards the end of the next century – at a time when theatrical dance came into the hands of professionals – was that devised by Raoul Feuillet, giving a remarkably exact delineation of the floor pattern covered by the dancer. His *Chorégraphie, ou l'art de décrire la danse* of 1700 provides the first true guide to reconstructing some of the dances of the period. As both theatrical and social dance were becoming increasingly important in the life of society, this method was to place a valuable tool in the hands of ballet masters.

The eighteenth century was to be a period remarkably rich in the use of notation and in notation systems. Feuillet, in the collections of dances which he published, and later masters who emulated him (like John Weaver who produced an English translation of Feuillet's treatise under the title of *Orchesography* in 1706) were able to disseminate dances throughout the whole confraternity of dancing masters. In later years the social cachet of knowing the correct dance that was devised for the Royal Birthnight Ball, for example, was to be acquired from dancing masters who purchased the notated forms of the new dance – just as dance teacher organizations today circulate scripts of new inventive dances.

An indication of eighteenth-century attitudes towards notation can be gained from the lengthy title provided by Kellom Tomlinson, a London dancing master, for his book published in 1735, *The Art of Dancing Explained by Reading and Figures – Whereby the Manner of Performing the Steps is made easy By a New and Familiar Method: Being the Original Work First Design'd in the year 1724, And now Published by Kellom Tomlinson, Dancing-Master. In Two Books.* The work contains not only engraved leaves of diagrams but also a series of superb dance plates which provide exceptional testimony to the postures and stance of the eighteenth-century dance.

Three years after Tomlinson, George Bickham in his *An Easy Introduction to Dancing, or the*

Movements in the Minuet Fully Explained used a simple verbal explanation of the steps, which were printed in the correct convolutions of the floor patterns, with illustrations showing the hand positions. More important was the work of Pierre Rameau, the French dancing master at the court of Spain, who adapted Feuillet and improved the system to provide a more complete method of instruction. Other eighteenth-century systems abound and the great French *Encyclo-pédie* by d'Alembert and Diderot (1751–1772) even devoted a section to choreography in its true sense of the writing down of dance. By the end of the eighteenth century, dance itself had outsoared the confines of the premises of the Feuillet system and new methods of recording it had to be sought.

With the emergence of a codified, though still developing, technique for the academic dance, thanks to the work of such men as Carlo Blasis, the concepts of notating dance differed. The most significant would seem to be the *Sténochoré-graphie* devised by Arthur Saint-Léon, published in 1852, which made use of pin figures on the top line of a musical stave and of a five-line stave below to encompass the positions of the legs and feet. Saint-Léon's system is decipherable today; one point of interest is that he recorded the steps as seen by the audience and the notation is thus a mirror image of the actual dance.

The complex work of Albert Zorn in the *Grammar of the Art of Dancing*[1] of 1887 was widely used – and it is from this that it has been possible to reconstruct Fanny Elssler's celebrated *cachucha*. Probably the most widely used system in the theatre in the nineteenth century was that evolved by Vladimir Stepanov (1866–1896). A dancer with the Imperial Ballet in St Petersburg, he devoted himself to evolving a system using musical notation to show movement. His textbook, The *Alphabet of Movements of the Human Body*,[2] was published in 1891 and his system of notation was included in the curriculum of the Imperial Ballet School. It was the method whereby the *régisseurs* at the Maryinsky Theatre recorded much of their repertory of ballets.

Nikolai Sergeyev, in particular, noted down in either full or short form the entire current repertory of the Imperial Ballet at the turn of the century. From these he maintained the ballets in production during his period of office at the Maryinsky from 1904 to 1917. Following the Revolution he left Russia, taking his notebooks with him, and it is from these priceless documents that he supervised all Western European first stagings of the old Imperial repertory (notably for the Vic-Wells Ballet in the 1930s), thereby providing an authentic text of such works as *Giselle, Swan Lake, Casse noisette, The Sleeping Beauty*, from which later recensions have stemmed and, at their peril, diverged.

Across the years, and more so in the present century, a variety of systems have been devised, tried and found variously wanting. Interesting have been those of Margaret Morris,[3] and of Noa Eshkol with its mathematical basis,[4] but the two systems most used and proven are those of Rudolf von Laban and Rudolf Benesh.

The Hungarian-born dancer, teacher and theorist Rudolf Laban (1879–1958) staged large productions for 'movement choirs' throughout Germany where his best-known pupils were Mary Wigman and Kurt Jooss but his prime importance is his book *Written Dance*,[5] in which he propounded the detailed and innovative system of recording movement with which his name is essentially linked. It is all-embracing in its power to encompass human movement and today the work of Dr Ann Hutchinson Guest has been of exceptional importance in making Laban's work readily available to the world through her masterly and exhaustive textbook on the system, *Labanotation.* [6]

The Benesh system emerged from the fact that Joan Benesh, a dancer with the Sadler's Wells Ballet, discussed with her husband Rudolf the need for a speedy system of notation for immediate practical use within a ballet company. The result was the Benesh system,[7] known as Choreology, which is widely used by ballet companies throughout the world for the recording of their repertories. Like other movement systems, Choreology has also been adapted for use in the field of medicine as a method of studying movement behaviour.

With the electronic developments of the post-war years and the emergence of easily manageable television recording machinery, the use of video-taping in rehearsal and performance has become increasingly important as an alternative or complement to written notation. In the pre-war years Léonide Massine (himself devisor of a system of written notation) made ciné-film records of his ballets for use as *aide-mémoire*. Today, the ease with which dance can be recorded by portable television and video cameras means that many companies use this method as a first step in preserving their repertory.

Benesh Movement Notation.
Lines intersect the body at specific points. The dancer is recorded from behind, the body being imposed on the five-line stave. (See key below)

Hands and feet

| in front of body
— level with body
• behind body

Flexed elbows and knees

╁ in front of body
╀ level with body
✕ behind body

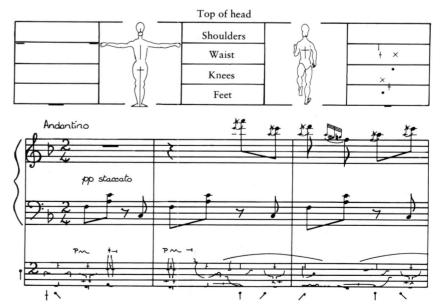

NOTES

INTRODUCTION
1 (p. 6) London *Daily Telegraph* 28 May 1979.

Chapter One
PRIMITIVE AND ANCIENT DANCE
1 (p. 17) Gorer, Geoffrey *Africa Dances* (London, 1949).
2 (p. 17) For superb photographs of these dancers, see Michel Huet's *Dance, Art and Ritual of Africa* (London, 1978).
3 (p. 18) Gorer, op. cit.
4 (p. 20) Information about kangaroo cults from Beth Dean and Victor Carell's *Dust for the Dancers* (Sydney, 1956).
5 (p. 21) See Reginald and Gladys Laubin's *Indian Dances of North America* (University of Oklahoma Press, 1977).
6 (p. 22) Information about the Yuki Tribe from James G. Frazer's *The Golden Bough – a Study in Magic and Religion*, abridged edn. (New York and London, 1957, 1980).
7 (p. 22) See Guillermina Dickins' *Dances of Mexico* (London, 1950).

Chapter Two
RELIGIOUS DANCE
1 (p. 25) Sachs, Curt *Eine Weltgeschichte des Tanzes* (Berlin, 1933) – *World History of the Dance*, trans. Bessie Schönberg (London, 1938).
2 (p. 26) Herodotus *The Histories*, trans. Aubrey de Selincourt (London, 1954).
3 (p. 26) Apuleius *The Golden Ass*, trans. William Adlington (1566); revised by S. Gaselee (Harvard and London, 1915).
4 (p. 27) Homer *The Odyssey, Book* VIII, trans. E. V. Rieu (London, 1946).
5 (p. 27) Webster, T. B. L. *The Greek Chorus* (London, 1970).
6 (p. 27) See Dr. Lillian B. Lawler's *Terpsichore, the Story of the Dance in Ancient Greece* (Wesleyan University Press, Connecticut, and London, 1964).
7 (p. 29) Ibid.
8 (p. 29) Homer, op. cit., *Book* I.
9 (p. 29) Lawler, op. cit.
10 (p. 29) Webster, op. cit.
11 (p. 30) Lucian *The Dance, Book* XV, trans, A. M. Harmon (Harvard and London, 1972).
12 (p. 31) Ibid, *Book* XII.
13 (p. 33) Apuleius, op. cit.
14 (p. 34) Ibid.
15 (p. 35) Oesterley, W. O. E. *The Sacred Dance* (Cambridge, 1923).
16 (p. 35) Ibid.
17 (p. 35) I *Chronicles* 15:29; *Exodus* 32:19; *Psalm* 149:3; *Ezekiel* 6:11.
18 (p. 36) I *Kings* 18:26; *Psalm* 26:6.
19 (p. 36) Oesterley, op. cit.
20 (p. 36) *Exodus* 15:20–21; *Samuel* 18:6.
21 (p. 37) Backman, E. Louis *Religious Dances in the Christian Church and in Popular Medicine* (Stockholm, 1945), trans. E. Classen (London, 1952).
22 (p. 38) *Epist* I *ad Gregor*.
23 (p. 38) de Cahusac, Louis *La Danse ancienne et moderne* (The Hague, 1754).
24 (p. 38) Ibid.
25 (p. 39) Ménestrier, Père, SJ *Des Ballets ancien et modernes selon les règles du théâtre* (Paris, 1657, 1682).
26 (p. 41) For description of ecclesiastical dancing in Spain during the 1920s see Lilla Viles Wyman's account in *The Dancing Times* (London, March 1920).

27 (p. 41) Alford, Violet and Gallop, Rodney *The Dancing Times* (London, February 1934).
28 (p. 43) Yates, George *A Ball or a Glance at Almack's* (London, 1829). (Yates quotes *Evangelical Magazine*, August 1819 and June 1808).
29 (p. 43) Information about the Shaker ritual from *Chronicles of the American Dance*, ed. Paul Magriel (New York, 1948).
30 (p. 43) And, Metin *A Practical History of Turkish Dancing* (Ankara, 1976).

Chapter Three
EUROPEAN FOLK DANCE
1 (p. 47) Alford, Violet and Gallop, Rodney *The Traditional Dance* (London, 1935).
2 (p. 47) See Joan Lawson's *European Folk Dance* (London, 1964).
3 (p. 47) Alford and Gallop, op. cit.
4 (p. 49) von Furstenberg, Florian Daule (pastor at Schellenwalde), *The Dance Devil* pamphlet (Schellenwalde, 1567).
5 (p. 51) See Metin And's *A Practical History of Turkish Dancing* (Ankara, 1976).
6 (p. 52) Galanti, Bianca M. *Dances of Italy* (London, 1950).
7 (p. 58) Armstrong, Lucile, handbooks on Spanish Dancing (London, 1950).

Chapter Four
EASTERN DANCE
1 (p. 67) Gunji, Masakatsu *Buyo* (New York, 1971).
2 (p. 68) See Reginald Massey and Rina Singha's *Indian Dances* (London, 1967).
3 (p. 70) Ram Gopal in *Ballet* (December 1947).
4 (p. 76) Information on these preliminary dances from Faubion Bower's *Theatre in the East* (London, 1956).
5 (p. 78) Winifred Holmes in *Ballet* (October 1952).
6 (p. 81) For invaluable information about dance in Bali, see Beryl de Zoete and Walter Spies' *Dance and Drama in Bali* (London, 1938, 1952).
7 (p. 81) Information on the Chinese sleeve dance from Gloria Strauss in *Dance Perspectives, No 63* (New York, October 1952).
8 (p. 82) Mary Grace Swift in *Thought* (Fordham University, New York, Summer 1973).
9 (p. 85) Gunji, op. cit.

Chapter Five
SOCIAL DANCE
1 (p. 94) Rust, Francis *Dance in Society* (London, 1969).
2 (p. 96) Franks, A. H. *Social Dance: a Short History* (London, 1963).
3 (p. 96) Duke of Bourbon in Shakespeare's *Henry V*, III, v.
4 (p. 98) Gronow, Captain *Reminiscences* (London, 1862).
5 (p. 100) de Cahusac, Louis *La Danse ancienne et moderne* (The Hague, 1754).
6 (p. 101) Quoted in Rust, op. cit.
7 (p. 101) Richardson, Philip J. S. *The Social Dances of the Nineteenth Century in England* (London, 1960).
8 (p. 101) Sachs, Curt *Eine Weltgeschichte des Tanzes* (Berlin, 1933) – *World History of the Dance*, trans. Bessie Schönberg (London, 1938).
9 (p. 101) Nicolson, Harold *The Congress of Vienna: a Study in Allied Unity 1812–22* (London, 1946).
The Belgian-born Prince Charles Joseph de Ligne was Marshal of both Austria and Prussia. Count Auguste de La Garde-Chambonas,

a young Frenchman, published his personal and gossipy *Souvenirs du Congrès de Vienne* in Paris in 1901. Lord Liverpool, then Tory Prime Minister, sent his Foreign Minister, Lord Castlereagh, to represent Britain at the Congress, with Under Secretary Sir Edward Cooke and Private Secretary Joseph Planta. Francis II, Emperor of Austria, danced with Lady Castlereagh and her sister, Lady Matilda. The Arch (Grand) duchess Catherine was sister to the Tsar Alexander I and widow of Prince George of Oldenburg.

10 (p. 102) *The Times*, 22 July 1812.

11 (p. 102) Bournonville, August *A New Year's Gift for Dance Lovers* (Copenhagen, 1829), trans. Inge Biller Kelly (London, 1977).

12 (p. 104) Ivor Guest in *Ballet* (February 1947).

13 (p. 106) Castle, Vernon *The Modern Dance* (New York, 1914).

14 (p. 106) On differing attitudes to dance, see A. H. Franks, op cit.

15 (p. 107) Richardson, op cit.

16 (p. 107) Richardson, Philip J. S. *A history of English Ballroom Dancing* (London, 1948)

17 (p. 111) *The Observer Magazine* (London, 10 December 1978).

18 (p. 111) Richardson, op. cit.

19 (p. 111) Walshe, Gwenethe and The Imperial Society of Teachers of Dancing, 'Teach Yourself Books' (London, 1977).

20 (p. 112) Quoted in Richardson, op. cit.

Chapter Six
BALLET DE COUR

1 (p. 116) See Belinda Quirey, Steve Bradshaw and Ronald Smedley's *May I have the Pleasure* (London 1976).

2 (p. 116) Arbeau, Thoinot *Orchésographie* (Langres, France, 1588) – *The Orchesography*, trans. Mary Stewart Evans (New York, 1948).

3 (p. 120) Guglielmo Ebreo, quoted in Otto Kinkeldey's *A Jewish Dancing Master of the Renaissance: Guglielmo Ebreo* (New York, 1929, 1966).

4 (p. 122) Ibid.

5 (p. 123) The dance steps are explained and analysed most carefully in Ferdinando Reyna's *Des Origines du ballet* (Paris, 1955).

6 (p. 124) Castiglione, Baldassar *Il Cortegiano* (Venice, 1528) – *Book of the Courtier*, trans. Charles S. Singleton (New York, 1975); trans. George Bull (London, 1976).

Chapter Seven
HISTORY OF BALLET

SEVENTEENTH TO NINETEENTH CENTURY

1 (p. 138) Article from *Journal Etranger*, quoted in Deryck Lynham's *The Chevalier Noverre, Father of Modern Ballet* (London, 1950).

2 (p. 139) Noverre, Jean-Georges *Letters on Dancing and Ballets* (1760, 1803), trans. Cyril W. Beaumont (London, 1930).

3 (p. 139) Noverre, Jean-Georges *Lettres sur les arts imitateurs en général et sur la danse en particulier* (Paris and The Hague, 1803, 1807).

4 (p. 147) Quoted by Lillian Moore in *Dance Magazine* (February, 1964).

5 (p. 153) Legat, (Nikolai) Nicolas *The Story of the Russian School* trans. Sir Paul Dukes (London, 1932).

Chapter Eight
HISTORY OF BALLET

TWENTIETH CENTURY

1 (p. 165) Roslavleva, Natalia *Era of the Russian Ballet 1770–1965* (London, 1966).

2 (p. 167) In Arnold L. Haskell's *Ballet Russe* (London, 1968).

3 (p. 167) Benois, Alexander *Reminiscences of the Russian Ballet*, trans. Mary Britnieva (London, 1941).

4 (p. 184) In Mary Grace Swift's *The Art of Dance in the USSR* (University of Notre Dame Press, Indiana, 1968).

5 (p. 185) Roslavleva, op. cit.

Chapter Nine
MODERN DANCE

1 (p. 213) Mazo, Joseph H *Prime Movers* (New York and London, 1977).

2 (p. 215) Genthe, Arnold *As I Remember* (New York, 1936; London, 1937).

3 (p. 215) Duncan, Isadora *The Art of the Dance*, Ed. Sheldon Cheney (New York, 1928, 1969).

4 (p. 216) Steegmuller, Francis, Ed. *Your Isadora: The Love Story of Isadora Duncan and Gordon Craig told through their Letters and Diaries* (New York, 1976).

5 (p. 217) Padgette, P. *Dance Writings of Carl Van Vechten* (New York, 1974).

6 (p. 217) Stokes, Sewell *Isadora – an Intimate Portrait* (New York and London, 1928).

7 (p. 217) Genthe, op. cit.

8 (p. 220) François Delsarte (1811–1871) was a French music teacher who taught control of body movements. He coded human gestures into three categories – eccentric, concentric and normal, and human expressions into three zones – head, torso and limbs. Shawn was one of his followers, and some of the modern dance pioneers have been influenced by his theoretical analyses.

9 (p. 221) Cohen, Selma Jeanne, *Introduction to the Modern Dance: Seven Statements of Belief* (Wesleyan University Press, Connecticut, 1965).

10 (p. 223) Walter Terry in *The Dance Encyclopedia*, Eds. Anatole Chujoy and P. W. Manchester (New York, 1949, 1967).

11 (p. 224) Jane Dudley in *The Encyclopedia of Dance and Ballet*, Ed. Mary Clarke and David Vaughan (London, 1977).

12 (p. 225) Tobi Tobias in *Dance News* (New York, March 1979).

13 (p. 228) David Vaughan in the London *Financial Times* (12 March, 1980).

14 (p. 228) McDonagh, Don *The Complete Guide to Modern Dance* (New York, 1976).

15 (p. 231) Jack Anderson in *The Dancing Times* (London, April 1979).

Chapter Ten
STAGE AND SCREEN

1 (p. 234) Disher, Willson *Winkles and Champagne* (London, 1938).

2 (p. 234) Flanner (Genêt) Janet, © 1925–1929 incl. © 1972 The New Yorker Magazine Inc., reprinted in *Paris Was Yesterday 1925–1939*, Ed. Irving Drutman (New York, 1972; London, 1973).

3 (p. 235) Guest, Ivor *The Divine Virginia: a Biography of Virginia Zucchi* (New York, 1977).

4 (p. 236) Information on Bessie Clayton's career from Camille Hardy in *Dance Chronicle* 2:4 (New York, 1979).

5 (p. 237) Taper, Bernard *Balanchine – a Biography* (New York, 1963, revised edn. 1974; London 1964).

6 (p. 243) See Peter Brinson's *Catalogue of 120 Dance Films* (London, 1954); UNESCO's *Ten Years of Films on Ballet and Classical Dance 1956–65* (1968); John Mueller's *Dance Film Directory* (University of Rochester, New York, 1979); and the *Catalogue of the Dance Collection of the New York Public Library*.

Appendix
NOTATION

1 (p. 245) Zorn, Albert *Grammatik der Tanzkunst* (Leipzig, 1887) – *Grammar of the Art of Dancing* (Boston, 1905).

2 (p. 245) Stepanov, Vladimir *Alphabet des mouvements du corps humain* (Paris, 1892) – *Alphabet of Movements of the Human Body*, trans. R. Lister (Cambridge, 1958).

3 (p. 245) Morris, Margaret *Notation of Movement* (London, 1928).

4 (p. 245) Eshkol, Noa *Movement Notation* (London, 1958).

5 (p. 245) Laban, Rudolf *Schrifttanz – Written Dance* (Vienna-Leipzig, 1928).

6 (p. 245) Hutchinson Guest, Ann *Labanotation: the System of Analysing and Recording Movement* (New York, 1954, 1970).

7 (p. 245) See Rudolf and Joan Benesh's *An Introduction to Benesh Dance Notation* (London, 1956).

BIBLIOGRAPHY

Ajello, Elvira *The Solo Irish Jig* (London, 1932).

Alford, Violet *Pyrenean Festival* (London, 1937). *Dances of France: Pyrenees* (London, 1952).

Alford, Violet and Gallop, Rodney *The Traditional Dance* (London, 1935).

Amberg, George *Ballet in America* (New York 1944).

And, Metin *A Practical History of Turkish Dancing* (Ankara, 1976).

Andral, Marie and Marcel-Dubois, Claudie *Dances of France: Brittany* (London, 1950).

Andrews, Edward *The Gift to be Simple: Dances of the Shakers* (New York, 1940).

Apuleius *The Golden Ass*, trans. W. Adlington (1566), revised by S. Gaselee (Harvard and London, 1915); trans. Robert Graves (London, 1950).

Arbeau, Thoinot *Orchésographie* (Langres, France, 1588) – *Orchesography*, trans. C. W. Beaumont (London, 1925); trans. Mary Stewart Evans (New York, 1948).

Armstrong, Lucile *Dances of Portugal* (London, 1948). *Dances of Spain* Vols I & II (London, 1950).

Atkinson, J. Grahamsley *Scottish National Dances* (Edinburgh, 1900).

Backman, E. Louis *Religious Dances in the Christian Church and in Popular Medicine* (Stockholm, 1945), trans. E. Classen (London, 1952).

Banerji, Projesh *Indian Dancing* (Allahabad, 1947).

Baskerville, Charles *The Elizabethan Jig* (New York, 1965).

Beaumont, Cyril W. *Complete Book of Ballets* (London, 1949).

Benazet, Alexandre *Le Théâtre au Japon* (Paris, 1901).

Bensel, E. van der ven Ten *Dances of the Netherlands* (London, 1949).

Bergquist, Nils W. *Swedish Folk Dances* (London, n.d.).

Binney, Edwin, 3rd *Les Ballets de Théophile Gautier* (Paris, 1965).

Blake, Lois and Karpeles, Maud *Dances of England and Wales* (London, 1950).

Boccaccio, Giovanni *The Decameron* (1353), trans. Richard Aldington (London, 1957).

Bordman, Gerald *American Musical Theatre: a Chronicle* (New York, 1978).

Boulenger, Jacques *De la Walse au tango* (Paris, 1920).

Bournonville, August *A New Year's Gift for Dance Lovers* (Copenhagen, 1829), trans. Inge Biller Kelly (London, 1977). *My Theatre Life* Vols I-III (Copenhagen, 1848–78), trans. Patricia McAndrew (London, 1979).

Bowers, Faubion *Theatre in the East* (London, 1956).

Bradshaw, Steve and Smedley, Ronald – with Quirey, Belinda *May I have the Pleasure?* (London, 1976).

Breuer, Katherine *Dances of Austria* (London, 1948).

Brinson, Peter *Background to European Ballet* (Leiden, 1966).

Brinson, Peter and Crisp, Clement *Ballet for All* (London, 1970).

Brunelleschi, Elsa *Antonio and Spanish Dancing* (London, 1958).

Buckman, Peter *Let's Dance* (New York, 1978).

Buday, George *Dances of Hungary* (London, 1950).

Burchenal, Elizabeth *National Dances of Ireland* (New York, 1924).

Carell, Victor and Dean, Beth *Dust for the Dancers* (Sydney, 1956). *The Many Worlds of Dance* (Sydney, n.d.).

Carner, Mosco *The Waltz* (London, 1948).

Caroso, Fabritio *Il Ballarino* (Venice, 1581), reprinted as *Nobilità di dame* (Milan, 1500) and as *Raccolta di varii balli* (Milan, 1630).

Carroero, Raffaele *La Danza in Italia* (Milan, 1946).

Casanova, Giacomo *Mémoires écrit par lui-même* Vols I-XII (Paris, 1826–38, 1960 – *History of My Life*, trans. Willard R. Trask (New York and London, 1967–1971).

Castil Blaze, F. H. *La Danse et les ballets* (Paris, 1832). *L'Académie imperiale* (Paris, 1855).

Castle, Vernon *The Modern Dance* (New York, 1914).

Cellarius *Fashionable Dancing* (London, 1847).

Christout, Marie Françoise *Le Ballet de cour de Louis XIV* (Paris, 1967).

Chujoy, Anatole and Manchester, P. W., Eds. *The Dance Encyclopedia* (New York, 1949, 1967).

Clarke, Mary *The Sadler's Wells Ballet: a History and an Appreciation* (London, 1955). *Dancers of Mercury* (London, 1962).

Clarke, Mary and Crisp, Clement *Ballet: an Illustrated History* (London, 1973). *Making a Ballet* (London, 1974). *Design for Ballet* (London, 1978).

Clarke, Mary and Vaughan, David, Eds. *The Encyclopedia of Dance and Ballet* (London, 1977).

Crisp, Clement and Brinson, Peter *Ballet for All* (London, 1970).

Crisp, Clement and Clarke, Mary *Ballet: an Illustrated History* (London, 1973).

Dadachanji, Serozh and Gopal, Ram *Indian Dancing* (London, 1951).

Dean, Beth and Carell, Victor *Dust for the Dancers* (Sydney, 1956). *The Many Worlds of Dance* (Sydney, n.d.).

de Cahusac, Louis *La Danse ancienne et moderne* Vols I-III (The Hague, 1754).

de Dash, Comtesse *Mémoires des autres* (Paris, 1840).

de Lajarte, Théodore *Catalogue de la bibliothèque du Théâtre National de l'Opéra* (Paris, 1878).

de Mille, Agnes *The Book of Dance* (New York, 1963; London, 1964).

Denby, Edwin *Looking at the Dance* (New York, 1968).

de Zoete, Beryl *The Other Mind* (London, 1953).

de Zoete, Beryl and Spies, Walter *Dance and Drama in Bali* (London, 1938, 1952).

Dickins, Guillermina *Dances of Mexico* (London, 1950).

Dolmetsch, Mabel *Dances of England and France from 1450–1600* (London, 1949). *Dances of Spain and Italy from 1400–1600* (London, 1954).

Draper, Paul *On Tap Dancing* (New York, 1978).

Duchartre, Pierre *The Italian Comedy* (New York, 1966).

Ellfeldt, Lois *Dance, from Magic to Art* (Iowa, 1976).

Evans, Bess and Evans, May G. *American Indian Dance Steps* (New York, 1931).

Fokine, Mikhail *Memoirs of a Ballet Master* (Boston and London, 1961).

Franks, A. H. *Social Dance: a Short History* (London, 1963).

Frazer, Sir James George *The Golden Bough – a Study in Magic and Religion* (1890–1915); 3rd edn (New York and London, 1907–19); abridged edn (New York and London, 1957, 1980); Vols I-XIII (New York and London, 1980).

Frédéric, Louis *La Danse sacrée de l'Inde* (Paris, 1957).

Gadan, Francis and Maillard, Robert, Eds *A Dictionary of Modern H Ballet* (London, 1959).

Galanti, Bianca M. *Dances of Italy* (London, 1950).

Gallini, John *A Treatise on the Art of Dancing* (London, 1762). *Critical Observations on the Art of Dancing* (London, 1770).

Gallop, Rodney and Alford, Violet *The Traditional Dance* (London, 1935).

Gautier, Théophile *The Romantic Ballet as seen by Théophile Gautier*, trans. C. W. Beaumont (London, 1947).

Ginner, Ruby *The Revived Greek Dance* (London, 1935).

Goldner, Nancy, Ed. *The Stravinsky Festival of the New York City Ballet* (New York, 1973).

Gorer, Geoffrey *Africa Dances* (London, 1949).

Grigoriev, Serge L. *The Diaghilev Ballet 1909–1929* (London, 1953).

Grove, Mrs Lily *Dancing* (London, 1895).

Guest, Ivor *The Romantic Ballet in England* (London, 1954). *Adeline Genée: a Lifetime of Ballet under Six Reigns* (London, 1968). *The Dancer's Heritage* (London, 1960). *The Empire Ballet* (London, 1962). *The Romantic Ballet in Paris* (London, 1966). *Fanny Elssler* (London, 1970). *Two Coppélias* (London, 1970). *The Ballet of the Second Empire* (London, 1974). *Le Ballet de l'Opéra de Paris* (Paris, 1976). *The Divine Virginia: a Biography of Virginia Zucchi* (New York, 1977).

Gunji, Masakatsu *Buyo* (New York, 1971).

Hambly, W. D. *Tribal Dancing and Social Development* (London, 1926).

Harrold, Robert and Wingrave, Helen *Regional Dances of Europe* (Leicester, England, 1970).

Haskell, Arnold L. *Diaghileff – Artistic and Private Life* (New York, 1935; London, 1933). *Ballet Panorama* (London, 1938). *Ballet Russe* (London, 1968).

Havemeyer, Loomis *The Drama of Savage Peoples* (New Haven, 1916).

Herodotus *The Histories*, trans. Aubrey de Selincourt (London, 1954).

Hill, R. *A Guide to the Ballroom* (Lincoln, England, 1822).

Hinckes, Marcelle *The Japanese Dance* (London, 1910).

Huart, Louis *Paris au bal* (Paris, 1845; London, 1847).

Huet, Michel *Dance, Art and Ritual of Africa* (London, 1978).

Humphrey, Doris *The Art of Making Dances*, Ed. Barbara Pollack (New York and London, 1959).

Ishikawa, Yutaka and Umemoto, Rikuhei *Introduction to the Classic Dance of Japan* (Tokyo, 1935).

Ivanova, Anna *The Dancing Spaniards* (London, 1970).

Jacquot, Jean, Ed. *Les Fêtes de la renaissance* (Paris, 1956).

Jamar, Henri and Pinon, Roger *Dances of Belgium* (London, 1953).

Johnston, Mary A. *The Dance in Etruria* (Florence, 1956).

Karpeles, Maud and Blake, Lois *Dances of England and Wales* (London, 1950).

Kennedy, Douglas *England's Dances* (London, 1949).

Kinkeldy, Otto *A Jewish Dancing-Master of the Renaissance: Guglielmo Ebreo* (New York, 1929).

Kirstein, Lincoln *The Book of the Dance* (New York, 1942, 1966; revised edn 1970). *Movement and Metaphor* (New York, 1970). *The New York City Ballet* (New York, 1975).

Klosty, James *Merce Cunningham* (New York, 1975).

Kochno, Boris *Le Ballet* (Paris, 1954). *Diaghilev and the Ballet Russe* (London, 1971).

Koegler, Horst *The Concise Oxford Dictionary of Ballet* (London, 1977).

Kragh-Jacobsen, Svend *The Royal Danish Ballet* (Copenhagen, 1955).

Kraus, Richard *A History of Dance in Art and Education* (New Jersey, 1969).

Laubin, Reginald and Gladys *Indian Dances of North America* (Oklahoma, 1977).

Laver, James *Memorable Balls* (London, 1954).

Lawler, Lillian B. *Terpischore, the Story of the Dance in Ancient Greece* (Wesleyan University Press, Connecticut, and London, 1964).

Lawson, Joan *European Folk Dance* (London, 1964).

Leenhardt, Maurice *Gens de la grande terre* (Paris, 1937).

Legat, Nicolas *The Story of the Russian School* trans. Sir Paul Dukes (London, 1932).

Levinson, André *La Danse au théâtre* (Paris, 1924).

Lexova, Irena *Ancient Egyptian Dances* (Prague, 1935).

Lifar, Serge *Ballet: Traditional to Modern* (London, 1938).

Lloyd, Margaret *The Borzoi Book of Modern Dance* (New York, 1949).

Lubinova, Mila *Dances of Czechoslovakia* (London, 1949).

Lynham, Deryck *The Chevalier Noverre, Father of Modern Ballet* (London and New York, 1950, 1973).

McDonagh, Don *The Rise, Fall and Rise of Modern Dance* (New York, 1970). *The Complete Guide to Modern Dance* (New York, 1976).

Macdonald, Nesta *Diaghilev Observed* (New York, 1975).

Macilwaine, Herbert C. and Sharp, Cecil *The Morris Book* (London, 1909).

Mackenzie, Donald *Illustrated Guide to the National Dances of Scotland* (Glasgow, 1939).

MacLennan, D. G. *Highland and Traditional Scottish Dances* (Edinburgh, 1950).

Magriel, Paul, Ed. *Chronicles of the American Dance* (New York, 1948).

Manchester, P. W. *Vic-Wells: a Ballet Progress* (London, 1942).

Manchester, P. W. and Chujoy, Anatole, Eds *The Encyclopedia of Dance* (New York, 1949, 1967).

Marcel-Dubois, Claudie and Andral, Marie *Dances of France No 1, Vol I* (London, 1950).

Mazo, Joseph H. *Prime Movers* (New York and London, 1977).

Meri, La *Total Education in Ethnic Dance* (New York, 1977).

Moore, Alex *Ballroom Dancing* (London, 1945).

Moore, Lillian *Artists of the Dance* (New York, 1938).

Negri, Cesare *Nuove inventioni di balli* (Milan, 1604).

Nicoll, Allardyce *Masks, Mimes and Miracles* (London, 1931).

Nivelon, F. *Rudiments of Genteel Behaviour* (London, 1737).

Noverre, Jean-Georges *Lettres sur la danse et les ballets* (Lyon and Stuttgart, 1760); revised edn (St Petersburg, 1803) – *Letters on Dancing and Ballets* trans. C. W. Beaumont (London, 1930; New York, 1970).

O'Brien, A. and O'Keeffe, J. G. *A Handbook of Irish Dances* (Dublin, 1921).

Oesterley, W. O. E. *The Sacred Dance* (Cambridge, 1923).

Oppé, A. P. and Sharp, Cecil *The Dance* (London, 1924).

Palmer, Winthrop *Theatrical Dancing in America* (New York, 1945).

Payne, Charles *American Ballet Theatre* (New York and London, 1978).

Pinon, Roger and Jamar, Henri *Dances of Belgium* (London, 1953).

Quirey, Belinda with Bradshaw, Steve and Smedley, Ronald *May I have the Pleasure?* (London, 1976).

Rameau, Pierre *Le Maitre à danser* (Paris, 1725) – *The Dancing Master*, trans. C. W. Beaumont (London, 1931; New York, 1975).

Ranger, T. O. *Dance and Society in Eastern Africa* (London, 1975).

Reeser, Edward *The History of the Waltz* (London, n.d.).

Reyna, Ferdinando *A Concise History of Ballet* (London, 1965).

Rice, Cyril *Dancing in Spain* (London, 1931).

Richardson, Philip J. S. *A History of English Ballroom Dancing* (London, 1948). *The Social Dances of the Nineteenth Century in England* (London, 1960).

Ridgway, William *The Dramas and Dramatic Dances of Non-European Races* (Cambridge, 1915).

Robert, Grace *The Borzoi Book of Ballet* (New York, 1946).

Roslavleva, Natalia *Era of the Russian Ballet 1770–1965* (London, 1966).

Rozier, Victor *Les bals publics à Paris* (Paris, 1860).

Rust, Frances *Dance in Society* (London, 1969).

Sachs Curt *Eine Weltgeschichte des Tanzes* (Berlin, 1933) – *World History of the Dance*, trans. Bessie Schönberg (London, 1938).

Schwenender, Norma and Tibbels, Averil *Legends and Dances of Old Mexico* (New York, 1934).

Sharp, Cecil *The Country Dance Book* Part 1 (London, 1909).

Sharp. Cecil and Macilwaine, Herbert *The Morris Book* (London, 1909).

Sharp, Cecil and Oppé, A. P. *The Dance* (London, 1924).

Shawn, Ted *Gods who Dance* (New York, 1929).

Slonimsky, Yuri *The Soviet Ballet* (New York, 1947).

Smedley, Ronald and Bradshaw, Steve – with Quirey, Belinda *May I have the Pleasure?* (London, 1976).

Sorell, Walter *The Dancer's Image* (New York, 1971).

Spies, Walter and de Zoete, Beryl *Dance and Drama in Bali* (London, 1938, 1952).

Svetlov, Valerien *Le Ballet contemporain* (St Petersburg, 1912).

Swift, Mary Grace *A Loftier Flight* (Connecticut, 1974).

Taper, Bernard *Balanchine – a Biography* (New York, 1963, revised edn 1974; London, 1964).

Tennevin, Nicolette and Texier, Marie *Dances of France* Vol II (London, 1951).

Tibbels, Averil and Schwenender, Norma *Legends and Dances of Old Mexico* (New York, 1934).

Tomlinson, Kellom *The Art of Dancing* (London, 1735).

Tyskiewicz, Alicja *Polish Folk Dances* (London, 1944).

Umemoto, Rikuhei and Ishikawa, Yutaka *Introduction to the Classic Dance of Japan* (Tokyo, 1935).

Urlin, Ethel L. *Dancing Ancient and Modern* (London, n.d.).

Vaillat, Léandre *Histoire de la danse* (Paris, 1942).

Vaughan, David and Clarke, Mary, Eds *The Encyclopedia of Dance and Ballet* (London, 1977).

Viski, Karily *Hungarian Dances* (London, 1937).

Vuillier, Gaston *A History of Dancing* (London, 1898).

Warren, Larry *Lester Horton* (New York, 1977).

Webster, T. B. L. *The Greek Chorus* (London, 1970).

Welsford, Enid *The Court Masque* (Cambridge, 1927).

Wilson, G. B. L. *A Dictionary of Ballet* (London, 1974).

Wilson, Thomas *A Description of the Correct Method of Waltzing* (London, 1816). *A Companion to the Ballroom* (London, 1816). *Analysis of the London Ballroom* (London, 1825).

Wingrave, Helen and Harrold, Robert *Regional Dances of Europe* (Leicester, England, 1970).

Winter, Marian Hannah *The Pre-Romantic Ballet* (London, 1974).

Witzig, Louise *Dances of Switzerland* (London, 1948).

Wood, Melusine *More Historical Dances* (London, 1956).

Wosien, Maria Gabriele *The Sacred Dance* (London, 1974).

Yates, George *A Ball or A Glance at Almack's* (London, 1829).

Yupho, Danit *Classical Siamese Theatre* (Bangkok, 1952).

INDEX

ACKNOWLEDGMENTS

The Publishers would like to thank the photographers Angelo Hornak, Mark Fiennes, and John Freeman Associates for the work they did for this book. They would also like to thank the picture sources listed below who have kindly given permission for their pictures to be reproduced.

The Publishers would, however, like to point out that it has not always been possible to trace the copyright-holder, and apologize for any omission that has unwittingly been made.

Academy Editions (London) 179 left. ©1980 ADAGP (Paris) 183 bottom. Australia Information Service (London) 20. BBC Hulton Picture Library (London) 108 bottom; 109; 110 top; 159; 168; 174–176; 189 right; 196; 198; 205; 226; 232; 239 right. Béjart, Alain (Brussels) 202. © 1955 Benesh Movement Notation Rudolf Benesh (London)/©1980 Benesh Institute of Choreology Limited, The (London) 245. Bettmann Archive Inc. (New York) 9 bottom; 181; 207 top; 233; 235 right; 237–239. Bildarchiv foto (Marburg) 8. Bolt, Anne (London) 9 top. Brown Brothers (Sterling, Pa) 42. CAF (Warsaw) 62. Caravaglia, Tom (New York) 219. Choreology, Institute of (London) 245. Christie Manson & Woods Ltd. (London) 48 bottom. Cooper-Bridgeman Library (London) 41. Crickmay, Anthony (London) 187 bottom; 190; 191; 199; 204; 209 top; 222–223; 228; 229. Dominic, Zoë (London) 186 top; 197; 238. Duncan, Kenn (New York) 210–211. Fine Art Society Ltd (London) 178. Forman, Werner (London) 22; 78; 86. Fotomas (London) 98. Gascoigne, Christina (London) 128; 134. Gosling, Maud (London) 192. Harding Associates, Robert (London): Robin Bath 23; 73. Hirmer Fotoarchiv (Munich) 24. Hoare, Malcolm (London) 2–3. Holford, Michael (London) 28 bottom; 33 top; 143. Humphrey, Mike (London) 188 top. Hutchison, Alan (London) 13; 14–15; 16. IGDA (Milan) 32; 234–235. IGDA (Milan): Bevilacqua 26 top. IGDA (Milan): Nimatallah 28 top: 127. Kobal, John (London) 111; 240; 242. Kochno Collection, Boris (Paris) 213 right. Language of Dance Centre (London) 244. London Weekend Television (London) 230. Mansell Collection (London) 18–19; 31 top; 33 bottom; 53; 64 top; 148; 157. Migdoll, Herbert (New York) 214; 215; 218 bottom. Morgan, Barbara (New York) 212; 220–221; 225. Musées Nationaux (Paris) 74; 77 top; 84. Novosti (London) 184. Peerless, Anne and Bury (Kent) 72. Pictor International (London) 113 top. Picturepoint (London) 82 top. Popperfoto (London) 47; 49 top left and bottom; 57; 61; 63 top; 71. Press Association (London) 110 bottom. Private Collection (London) 52; 75; 82 bottom; 88; 103; 107 left; 122 bottom; 130 top; 133; 136 top left; 140; 141 top; 142; 144 top; 146; 149; 150; 152–153; 155; 158; 160–164; 167; 171 bottom; 172; 177; 185; 186 left; 188 bottom; 194; 200; 201; 220; 227; 241. Ridley, Michael 66. Romanian National Tourist Office (London) 64 bottom. Sakamoto Photo Research Lab. (Tokyo) 87; 89–91. Scala (Florence) 120–121; 123–124. Shuel, Brian and Sally (London) 46 top; 55b. Sotheby Parke Bernet (London) 173; 182 bottom; 183 bottom. Sotheby Parke Bernet (New York) 182 top; 236–237. © 1980 SPADEM (Paris) 173; 178; 179; 182. Spatt, Leslie (London) 195; 243. Sunday Times (London): Eva Sereny 113 bottom. Swope, Martha (New York) 207 bottom; 208; 209 bottom. Sykes, Homer (London) 42–43; 55 top. Tilestone, Nathaniel 231. Vautier, Mireille (Paris) 79 bottom. Wilson, G. B. L. (London) 147; 169. Viollet, Roger (Paris) 100; 122–123. Wood, Roger (London) 58–59. Zefa (London) 15 bottom; 54; 63 bottom; 65; 69; 76; 77 bottom; 79 top; 80; 83; 85.